D1566681

Rational Leadership

Rational Leadership

Developing Iconic Corporations

Paul Brooker and Margaret Hayward

OXFORD
UNIVERSITY PRESS

Great Clarendon Street, Oxford, OX2 6DP,
United Kingdom

Oxford University Press is a department of the University of Oxford.
It furthers the University's objective of excellence in research, scholarship,
and education by publishing worldwide. Oxford is a registered trade mark of
Oxford University Press in the UK and in certain other countries

© Paul Alexander Menzies Brooker and Margaret Jane Hayward 2018

The moral rights of the authors have been asserted

First Edition published in 2018
Impression: 1

All rights reserved. No part of this publication may be reproduced, stored in
a retrieval system, or transmitted, in any form or by any means, without the
prior permission in writing of Oxford University Press, or as expressly permitted
by law, by licence or under terms agreed with the appropriate reprographics
rights organization. Enquiries concerning reproduction outside the scope of the
above should be sent to the Rights Department, Oxford University Press, at the
address above

You must not circulate this work in any other form
and you must impose this same condition on any acquirer

Published in the United States of America by Oxford University Press
198 Madison Avenue, New York, NY 10016, United States of America

British Library Cataloguing in Publication Data
Data available

Library of Congress Control Number: 2017963188

ISBN 978–0–19–882539–5

Printed and bound by
CPI Group (UK) Ltd, Croydon, CR0 4YY

Links to third party websites are provided by Oxford in good faith and
for information only. Oxford disclaims any responsibility for the materials
contained in any third party website referenced in this work.

Preface and Acknowledgements

This book has arisen from two seasoned observers of political and business affairs coming to the conclusion that the prevailing leadership paradigm is outdated and should be replaced with something more relevant. Specifically, it should be replaced by a rationalist paradigm based upon the theory of rational leadership that has been developed by several generations of theorists, such as Weber and Burns, and has reached the stage where it can provide a comprehensive view of leadership. Its theorists have identified and described various forms of rational leadership, such as the transactional and deliberative forms, and now our book will identify and describe a rational type of inspirational leadership that is comparable to the charismatic and transformational types of inspirational leadership. By showing that there is indeed a rational type of inspirational leadership, the book will be showing, too, that the rational theory of leadership has 'all that it takes' to be the basis of a new, more relevant paradigm of leadership.

The obvious way of identifying and describing this rational leadership is to follow the format used by Burns forty years ago in his celebrated treatise *Leadership*. He identified and described transformational and transactional leadership by using numerous examples that were supported or suggested by the writings of many other authors, as was confirmed by the scholarly listing of sources, forty pages in length, with which he ended the book. In following his format our book has made such minor changes as using endnote references and such major changes as drawing its examples from business leadership rather than political leadership. Another major change is focusing attention upon a particularly important or significant version of leadership, namely the corporation-developing version of business leadership. The reasons for these major changes will be explained in Chapter 1 but the changes' implications are apparent to anyone looking at the list of contents or flicking through the book's pages. It has presented its examples in the typical business-studies fashion of presenting a select set of best-practice cases. As the book's subtitle describes, these are classic cases of a rational leader developing—establishing or enhancing—an iconic corporation.

This set of classic examples combines the approaches adopted by three landmark books on business. First, there is the historical and biographical approach of Tedlow in *Giants of Enterprise*, whose seven biographical essays spanned the history of American business from Carnegie's steel-making to Noyce's microprocessors. Second, there is the best-practice approach of Peters and Waterman's *In Search of Excellence*, which presented the lessons to be learnt from more than forty of America's 'best-run companies' and even identified a select group of fourteen 'exemplars' within this elite of best-run companies. Third, there is the developmental approach of Burgelman, McKinney and Meza in their recent *Becoming Hewlett Packard*, which assesses the strategic leadership provided by successive CEOs as Hewlett Packard developed from a 1930s start-up into a high-tech colossus that was split in two in the 2010s. In addition to combining these approaches, our book has spread the net more globally to include not just American but also Japanese, Italian, French, and British examples. Furthermore, all the examples feature the leaders' autobiographical writings, so as to gain a 'leader's eye' view of how these corporations were established or enhanced. The autobiographical material also allows the individual 'voice' of each leader to be heard through the events and over the years or decades. Although these leaders used similar rational methods, they were unique individuals who left behind distinctive corporations as monuments to their life's work as a business leader.

Finally, this book was written to be both an academic monograph and a graduate text and therefore, like any dual-purpose design, has had to make some compromises and adjustments. Hopefully, it will also now appeal to more general readers, even if they skip the first chapter and avoid the appended theory of rational leadership! The book could not have been written, however, without the help of many earlier writers. They have given us the autobiographical, biographical, historical, and theoretical material that we have fashioned into concepts, analyses, and examples. We have also received crucial help and encouragement from family, friends, and colleagues. In particular, Professor Margaret Clark not only read draft chapters but also contributed to the development of the book and deserves to be seen as a co-author. She has long been the authors' mentor, during their academic careers and now in their retirement, and she has always been a source of encouragement and intellectual stimulation. Another reader who gave us crucial help and encouragement was Paul Brooker's father Fred, who is now in his hundredth year and has given us the benefit of his wide reading and his facility with words. Last but not least, there was the professional help given by our OUP editor Adam Swallow and the comments of the three anonymous reviewers. Like most projects, this book has been very much a team effort.

Contents

1. Rational Business Leadership   1
   Developing Corporations Through Rational Leadership   1
   Calculating, Adapting, and Deliberating   3
   Example: Sandberg At Facebook and In Her *Lean In*   10
   Using the Six Methods—Autobiographical Accounts   12

2. GM: Sloan's *My Years With General Motors*   17
   Adaptive Restructuring   19
   Calculated Strategy   25
   Institutionalized Deliberation   28
   Sloanism Versus Fordism   33

3. Toyota: Ohno's *Toyota Production System*   37
   Pioneering Production Innovations   40
   Adapting To Japanese Conditions   47
   Just-In-Time, 'Lean' Production   52
   Toyotaism Versus Fordism   57

4. McDonald's: Kroc's *Grinding It Out*   61
   Adaptively Building a Fast-Food Empire   63
   Calculating Strategy and Revenues   68
   Diverse Deliberation   71
   Globalized Adaptability   75

5. Wal-Mart: Walton's *Made in America*   79
   Adaptively Expanding Wal-Mart   81
   Calculating Numbers and Strategy   86
   Deliberation and Technology   90
   Learning—a Seventh Rational Method   95
   Dassault's *Talisman* Aviation Learning   98

6. Intel: Grove's *Only the Paranoid Survive*   103
   Learning to Adapt Intel   105
   The Three-Stage Adaptive Framework   111
   Experimentation and *The HP Way*   116
   The Steve Jobs Way At Apple   122

Contents

7. eBay: Whitman's *The Power Of Many*   126
   The Internet and eBay   129
   Adapting and Deliberating   132
   Calculating and Learning   135
   Opportunity: eBayism Versus Amazonism   141

8. GA: Armani's *Giorgio Armani*   148
   Adapting Fashion To New Times   150
   Armanian Versus Versacian Adaptations   156
   Adaptive Legacies and Capability   161
   Roddick's *Business As Unusual*   165

Conclusion   170

Appendix: The Theory Of Rational Leadership   175
Notes   187
References   235
Index   243

1

Rational Business Leadership

Developing Corporations Through Rational Leadership

This book highlights and illustrates how various business leaders have developed—either established or enhanced—a corporation in a rational way. They are examples of a rational, modern type of inspirational leader who inspires his or her followers with a modern, rational kind of confidence. Such confidence arises from the fact that the leader is capably using the appropriate rational means of achieving an objective, such as developing a business corporation. The corporation-developing version of this rational leadership is a very specialized but also significant version and the following chapters present a series of classic examples. In these examples, high-level business leaders very capably use the 'appropriate rational means' of developing a business corporation, namely rapid and innovative adaptation, quantitative and strategic calculation, and last but not least, diverse and institutionalized deliberation.

The conceptual foundations of the book are a mixture of the old and the new. In the 1920s–30s Weber and Barnard identified and analysed a rational type of inspirational leadership, as is described in the Appendix. It also describes how their pioneering contributions to the theory of rational leadership have recently been restructured into a more widely applicable analysis of the rational type of inspirational leadership. According to this analysis, the leader's followers are inspired with rational confidence because their leader is capably using the appropriate rational means of achieving the objective, such as developing a business corporation. In a business context, the firm's employees are by definition the followers or 'employee-followers' of the firm's business leader. As their jobs or career prospects depend upon the firm achieving its objectives, employee-followers share a common concern and are most likely to be inspired with confidence—a rational confidence in the firm's success—if their business leader is capably using the appropriate rational means of achieving the objective.

This rational type of inspirational leadership appears not only in business but in all fields of leadership and it appears in many different versions. Each version has its own kind of objective and its own appropriate means of achieving the objective. In the military field, for example, counterinsurgency has a different kind of objective from naval warfare, has different appropriate rational means of achieving the objective, and requires a different version of rational military leadership.

If there are so many versions of the rational type of inspirational leadership, why would a book focus solely on the corporation-developing business version? There are at least three important reasons for focusing on examples of this highly specialized version of rational leadership. First, leading a business organization, large or small, is the most modern and prevalent field of leadership. Second, developing a business corporation, a large public company, is the most economically and socially significant example of business leadership. Back in the 1940s Drucker declared that the business corporation 'has become America's representative social institution' and by the 2010s this was possibly true of not only America but the whole globalized world.[1] Third, developing a corporation is one of the areas of business where individual leaders clearly do 'make a difference'. Any business hall of fame, national or international, would be filled largely by founder developers of corporations, such as Ford, Bezos, and Dassault, and by the most notable post-founder developers of corporations, such as Sloan, Whitman, and Ohno. The proverbial 'man at the top' or his female equivalent plays a crucially important role when it comes to developing a corporation.

So the corporation-developing version of rational leadership will be viewed from a high-level perspective. Development will be viewed as a corporation being either *established* by a founder-CEO or being *enhanced* by a later CEO. Establishing a corporation involves founding a firm and scaling it up into a large public company. Enhancing a corporation may involve taking over the founder's scaling-up role but more often the enhancing leader is adding an important new feature, such as an innovative production system. Whether establishing or enhancing, however, this is high-level leadership provided by a CEO or a leadership team comprising the CEO and one or two other members of the board of directors.

A high-level perspective will also be adopted when examining the rational means that a leader uses to establish or enhance a corporation. Instead of describing them as particular individual strategies, technologies, techniques, or procedures, they will be viewed in higher-level, more general terms and, in fact, as generic rational methods, such as quantitative calculation or strategic calculation. What is more, six of these generic rational methods—two calculative, two adaptive, and two deliberative—form a set of methods that is appropriate for any high-level leader establishing or enhancing any corporation in any circumstances.

The following chapters will provide some classic examples of a high-level leader using these methods to establish or enhance a corporation. In all of these examples, the leader was developing a corporation that became famous and indeed acquired iconic status. So they are 'best-practice case studies' in the sense of leaders inspiring their employee-followers with rational confidence by *very* capably using the appropriate rational methods. Furthermore, the six main examples and most supplementary examples will feature the leader's autobiographical account of how he or she developed the corporation. This autobiographical material provides a 'leader's-eye' view of how the methods were used (corroborated and supplemented by historical and biographical sources).

The examples will cover a wide range of industries and landmark developments in business structure, techniques, and products. The industries range from high-tech to high-fashion, from automobiles to microprocessors, and from fast-food to e-commerce. The landmark developments include General Motors' creation of a decentralized divisional structure in the 1920s, Toyota's pioneering of a just-in-time production system in the 1930s and 1950s, McDonald's use of innovative franchising and joint-venture arrangements in the 1960s–70s and Wal-Mart's introduction of advanced technology into retailing in the 1970s–80s. In addition, the cases studied in the final three chapters cover the key developments of the 1980s–2010s: the introduction of high-tech consumer products, notably computers and mobile phones; the arrival of the Internet's e-commerce opportunities; and, less technologically, the extension of product pyramids in the fashion and luxury industries.

This wide-ranging collection of classic examples will confirm as well as illustrate. They confirm that the set of six generic rational methods—two calculative, two adaptive, and two deliberative—are indeed the appropriate means of developing a corporation. The main examples indicate that a leader tends to use all six methods and that in fact the major variation is in the leaders' choice of favourite or key methods—the one or more methods that they emphasize. As this set of six methods is so important, the next section of the chapter will describe them in some depth and from a theoretical as well as practical perspective.

Calculating, Adapting, and Deliberating

The set of six appropriate corporation-developing methods is a set of *three pairs* of methods: the calculative, adaptive, and deliberative pairs. It is therefore similar in form to the three-pair sets of methods that have been used by political or military leaders to establish new political regimes, as is discussed in the Appendix. Their sets, however, contain very different methods from those used by high-level business leaders to establish or enhance corporations. The business leaders use three pairs of generic rational methods—calculative, adaptive, and deliberative—which form a set of six methods: quantitative and strategic calculation, rapid and innovative adaptation, diverse and institutionalized deliberation.

The two calculative methods, quantitative and strategic calculation, are the most obviously rational and the most clearly associated with developing a business corporation. More than a hundred years ago Weber pointed out that modern business enterprise 'rests primarily on calculation', which even included lawyers' calculating how the enterprise would be affected by 'public administration and the administration of justice'.[2] He singled out the quantitative form of calculation as particularly important, declaring that 'the extent of quantitative calculation or accounting' is the characteristic feature of the modern, rational form of economic activity.[3]

The prevalence of numbers and number-crunching increased markedly during the next hundred years. By the 1960s, Chandler was noting that numbers provide 'a fairly precise and objective criterion' for assessing the performance of not only a firm but also its individual departments and operating divisions.[4] The quantitative assessment of a firm's performance was expanding from the classic profit-and-loss to include such numbers as net income, earnings per share, cash earnings, and EBITDA: earnings before interest, taxes, depreciation, and amortization.[5] Similarly, quantitative assessment of the performance of the firm's divisions and departments has expanded to include even such creative departments as marketing and advertising. For example, in the early 2000s the target of Samsung advertising campaigns was to overtake Sony in the international brand-value rankings, which meant assessing performance in terms of quantitative rankings and billion-dollar brand values.[6]

Of course there are some circumstances in which quantitative calculation does not seem appropriate, such as making decisions under conditions of uncertainty. Back in the 1920s Knight highlighted the distinction between *risk* as any uncertainty that can be 'reduced to an objective, quantitatively determinate probability' and *true uncertainty* as those uncertainties that are 'not susceptible to measurement and hence to elimination'.[7] Many of the crucial decisions made by business leaders are made under conditions of true uncertainty in which relying upon quantitative calculation may be *inappropriate*. For example, Christensen points out that this method is not appropriate—and may even be damaging—when firms are deciding how to respond to disruptive technology:

Companies whose investment processes demand quantification of market sizes and financial returns before they can enter a market get paralyzed or make serious mistakes when faced with disruptive technologies. They demand market data when none exists and make judgments based on financial projections when neither revenues nor costs can, in fact, be known.[8]

In these circumstances the appropriate method is not quantitative calculation but rapid adaptation. The key point, however, is that leaders cannot inspire rational confidence unless they are using a broad enough selection of rational methods and therefore can switch from one method to another when a change in circumstances makes the other method more appropriate.

Furthermore, it may be appropriate to use two rational methods in combination, as often occurs with quantitative and strategic calculation. Although strategic calculation is now clearly associated with developing a business corporation, it originated as the distinctive rational method of high-level military leaders. In the 1830s Carl von Clausewitz's classic treatise *On War* defined strategy in obviously rational terms, namely as furthering the object (ends) of the war through the use (means) of a planned, organized, and coordinated series of engagements with the enemy.[9] In fact he was so rational that he could identify and conceptualize the *limitations* of strategic calculation. Clausewitz's famous concept of 'friction' assumed that whenever some military action is undertaken, the unexpected difficulties 'combine to lower the general level of performance, so that one always falls far short of the intended goal', if only because of 'unique episodes' and effects 'due to chance'.[10] And he pointed out that the interaction between two enemies or competitors adds an element of unpredictability to strategic calculations. When 'calculating' the effect of a measure upon the enemy and what will be the enemy's reactions, a strategist is faced 'with the fact that the very nature of interaction is bound to make it unpredictable'.[11] Clausewitz concluded that a strategist's calculated plan would therefore have to be adjusted continuously to fit war's constantly changing circumstances.[12]

Strategic calculation has similar limitations when it is applied to business activities. Some modern business leaders have been well aware of these similarities and have even adopted a Clausewitzian perspective, as in the case of General Electric's long-time CEO Jack Welch. Early in his 1981–2001 tenure he mentioned the Clausewitzian concept of friction when he espoused an adaptive conception of business strategy, namely 'the evolution of a central idea through continually changing circumstances'.[13] Near the end of his tenure, Welch mentioned Clausewitzian interactive changes when he argued that business strategy should not rely on data-crunched plans (combining the two calculative methods) because business success 'is less a function of grandiose predictions than it is a result of being able to respond rapidly to real changes as they occur'.[14] Clearly some modern business strategists have come to the same conclusion as Clausewitz about having to adapt strategic calculations to fit forever changing, unforeseeable circumstances. In this situation, strategic calculation has to be used in combination or conjunction with another rational method but that method is *rapid adaptation* rather than quantitative calculation.

The other adaptive method, innovative adaptation, is occasionally used in conjunction with a higher level and form of strategic calculation—devising what the military term 'grand' strategy.[15] Grand strategy is concerned with the 'big picture' and 'big issues' that may involve a change in priorities or approaches or even a restructuring of the organization. It has become increasingly prevalent in business and is now an important special case of leaders using strategic calculation to develop a corporation. Indeed, there has recently been an impressively researched study of the role of grand-strategic leadership in the development of an iconic corporation, Hewlett-Packard.[16] And this corporation's founding leaders provide a classic example of using innovative adaptation in conjunction with grand-strategic calculation, as is described in Chapter 6.

The two adaptive methods, rapid and innovative adaptation, were foreshadowed in the writings of Joseph Schumpeter. In any youth he occasionally worked with the much older Weber but Schumpeter was an economist rather than a sociologist and would later become famous for his theories of economic innovation—a recent biography of him was titled *Prophet of Innovation*.[17] In his early writings he viewed innovation and adaptation as separate and indeed contrasting economic processes.[18] He noted that the normal form of economic change is the marginal or incremental, not innovative, adaptive response that a competitive market economy continually forces firms to make, such as making an adjustment to their pricing or production. In contrast, the unusual form of change is the innovative entrepreneurial initiative by an extraordinary individual who is driven by economically *non*-rational motives, such as seeking the pleasure of creating or wanting to prove themselves superior to his rivals. But later, in the 1940s, Schumpeter wrote about the eventual demise of such entrepreneurs. He argued that individuals with entrepreneurial 'personality and will power' and non-rational motivation are less required as societies become accustomed to economic change, and therefore entrepreneurial innovation would eventually become just another form of routine organizational behaviour.[19]

Schumpeter's vision of trends and tendencies was implicitly confirmed in the 1980s by a celebrated theorist of management. Drucker's *Innovation and Entrepreneurship* referred to a form of innovation that was the 'proper and profitable course', was 'systematic innovation' and was the result of a whole business organization developing the habits of entrepreneurship and innovation.[20] Indeed 'in a period of rapid change the best—and perhaps the only—way that a business can hope to prosper, if not to survive, is to innovate': not innovating 'is far more risky'.[21] However, it seems that such innovations are often or typically adaptive responses to changes occurring in this period of rapid change. Successful innovations normally 'exploit change' and in fact systematic innovation involves a 'purposeful and organized search for change' plus a 'systematic analysis of the opportunities such changes might offer'.[22] This routinized innovation will therefore typically be an adaptive innovation or, in other words, an innovative adaptation, which seems to be just routine and indeed what Schumpeter termed a 'forced' adaptive response.

But an innovative adaptation is better viewed as what Schumpeter termed a 'creative' response. In the 1940s he described it as going beyond a merely adaptive response because its creative response to change not only has a significant and lasting effect but also is so innovative that the content of this response could not have been predicted beforehand.[23] However, it is an economically rational response, not an economically non-rational entrepreneurial innovation. So this perspective on innovative adaptation would view it as a rational but not routine innovation that has significant and lasting effects—including the effects it produces as a rational method of developing corporations.

Although it is usually less significant than innovative adaptation, rapid adaptation can be a crucially important method in some situations. Schumpeter raised the issue of rapid adaptation indirectly or obliquely when he was writing about rigidity. He referred to rigidity as 'resistance to adaptation' that slowed or prevented such adaptive responses as a business adjusting its prices to reflect changes in supply or demand.[24] Resisting this merely incremental adaptation was economically irrational and would mean 'loss and reduced output'.[25] Resisting more serious kinds of adaptation will have more serious consequences and may undermine a firm's position or survival. Christensen's disruptive-technology 'innovator's dilemma' epitomizes this situation and is discussed at length in the Appendix. Similarly, Chapter 6 will discuss Grove's inflection-point theory of why leaders must be 'paranoid' about responding rapidly, without delay or resistance, to any kind of adaptive crisis.

But rapid adaptation should not be viewed only from the perspective of rigidity and protecting a firm. In some situations, rapid adaptation will enhance a corporation by giving it a winning advantage over competitors that are slower to adapt. Furthermore, rapid adaptation may even help establish a corporation. For example, part of the disruptive-technology 'innovator's dilemma' is that a firm which adapts too slowly to disruptive technology may well be overtaken by *new* firms which have come from nowhere by exploiting the new market created by this new technology. In some cases the new firms have grown into corporations and so in these situations rapid adaptation has been an appropriate method of not just enhancing but actually *establishing* a corporation.

In these situations, too, the rapid adaptation has been exploiting a new opportunity—the new market created by the disruptive technology. In fact, their leaders have responded in the manner described by a military definition of adapting: 'identifying and taking full advantage of the opportunities offered'.[26] More generally, exploiting an opportunity is often the way in which rapid adaption—and innovative adaptation—have been used to develop a corporation. The two adaptive methods of developing a corporation are the most opportunistic as well as the most creative.

In addition to the adaptive and calculative, there are the two deliberative rational methods of developing a corporation—diverse and institutionalized deliberation. Even some five hundred years ago diverse deliberation was seen as important and as being reduced by reticence. For according to Machiavelli, a prince 'should be very ready to seek information and opinions and to listen patiently to candid views about matters that he raises. Indeed, if he learns that anyone is reticent for any reason, he should be angry'.[27] Modern rulers, too, are plagued by this problem of reticence. For example, an analysis of presidential decision-making in the 1962 Cuban Missile Crisis discovered 'reticence' by the president's advisors and subordinates because they believed that their opinions would alienate him.[28]

Modern leaders also have to deal with a new, modern source of reticence and reduced diversity—bureaucratic politics. Thanks to bureaucratic politicking, policy issues and options 'may not rise to the presidential level, or when they do, they often take the form of concealed compromises that reflect the special interests at lower levels'.[29] But there are ways and means of counteracting this modern form of diversity-reducing reticence. A standard ploy was pioneered by President Franklin Roosevelt and was recounted a generation later by Neustadt, 'the most penetrating analyst of power since Machiavelli'.[30] Neustadt noted how Roosevelt mixed competing jurisdictions with competitive personalities: he would 'keep his organizations overlapping and divide authority among them' and would also tend 'to put men of clashing temperaments, outlooks, ideas, in charge of them'.[31] However, this ploy requires leaders to have a ready supply of diverse people to put in charge of their organizations. And not all modern leaders have favoured diversity to the same degree as Roosevelt or Ray Kroc, the founder of the McDonald's fast-food empire, who declared that 'if two executives think the same, one of them is superfluous'.[32]

The other deliberative method, institutionalized deliberation, was also recognized by Machiavelli. He saw the need for some institutionalization of deliberation, even if only through informal rules of behaviour. He warned that a ruler 'should discourage anyone from giving advice uninvited' and should allow only his chosen advisors to speak frankly to him—and only when he asked for their advice.[33] Some formal institutionalization of deliberation had already evolved by Machiavelli's time, if merely in the form of consultative councils of notables and officials. Even medieval kings' formal policy-making had taken place in their consultative Council, which comprised 'members of the royal family, royal favourites, heads of baronial factions and the chief officers of household and government departments'.[34] The rulers' councils would eventually evolve into parliamentary democracies' ministerial councils or cabinets and their array of specialized committees.

The business equivalent of course is the corporation's board of directors, the board's committees, and the array of specialized committees that was pioneered by Alfred Sloan at General Motors and is discussed in Chapter 2. Other business leaders have used more informal varieties of institutionalized deliberation when enhancing or establishing a corporation. Instead of formal committees and procedural rules, they have used informal rules about how managers should deliberate with their leader, such as when selling the leader a policy proposal.

Such deliberation involves a special form of leadership that has only recently been labelled, defined, and analysed. It is very different from the authoritative form of leadership, which sets a direction by exercising some legitimate authority that followers or subordinates feel obligated to obey. In contrast, deliberative leadership:

> sets a direction not by obedience but by choice and consent; it gives a lead that, if accepted, will have been considered on reflection or after debate to be the best option available.... Deliberative leadership is characteristic of any situation of collective choice or consultation in decision-making, whether by an electorate, assembly, committee or any combination of two or more people.[35]

This politics-oriented definition can be phrased in economic or business terms, too, with a lead being 'sold to a potential customer who has the choice of whether or not to "buy" it or indeed to prefer a different, competing lead from another seller'.[36]

The deliberative rational methods *combine* the deliberative and authoritative forms of leadership and in several different ways or contexts. Perhaps the simplest variant is when an authoritative leader allows one or more followers to 'sell' him or her policy proposals and thereby become deliberative leaders about these issues and options. Even such a hands-on and opinionated leader as Winston Churchill was willing to be sold policy proposals in private deliberations with a trusted individual, as in the case of his wartime naval supremo, Admiral Pound, who 'knew the sure way to get something approved by Churchill was to sell him the idea verbally and then let him draft' it in writing 'as if it were his idea'.[37] Other leaders may prefer to be sold policy proposals in the highly institutionalized context of a committee meeting whose official purpose is to consider and assess policy options.

A more complex combination of deliberative and authoritative leadership is when a leader sells a policy proposal to one or more followers and allows them to choose whether to 'buy' this lead. Wal-Mart's founder Sam Walton claimed that he actually favoured the 'mavericks' who disagreed with him. 'I respected them, and, in the end, I listened to them a lot more closely than the pack who always agree with everything I said.'[38] But this may be more the exception than the rule.

Example: Sandberg At Facebook and In Her *Lean In*

A relatively recent example of a leader using deliberative rational methods is Sheryl Sandberg, who used them to enhance Facebook's business practices and revenue. In 2008 Facebook's youthful founder and CEO, Mark Zuckerberg, recruited the 38-year-old Sandberg from Google to be his firm's chief operating officer (COO) and join him in a dual-leadership team.[39] Such leadership teams will be examined in more detail in the next section of this chapter. The key point here is that the two leaders may well focus on different aspects of their objective. In this case, Sandberg would focus on enhancing the business side of Facebook, making the firm more business-like and transforming its revenue potential by making the firm an online advertising giant. She was obviously better qualified than Facebook's CEO to take on these tasks as she had much more business experience and expertise, including a Harvard MBA. She was also willing and able to use the two deliberative methods— diverse and institutionalized deliberation.

Her use of deliberative methods to set a new, advertising-oriented direction in revenue-earning is recounted in Kirkpatrick's *The Facebook Effect*. Soon after Sandberg arrived at Facebook she 'decided to host a series of meetings to get Facebook's management to focus on the ad opportunity'.[40] With Zuckerberg away on a month's leave, she was clearly in charge of these weekly or twice-weekly meetings.[41] However, she did not take charge of the discussions and clearly lead them in the direction of advertising revenues. She adopted a more subtle approach that encouraged diverse deliberation but also ensured that the discussions were moving down the right track, as when she began the first meeting with the agenda-setting question:

'What business are we in?' These were bull sessions at first, giving everyone a chance to express their views.... Staffers researched various options and brought carefully compiled charts to the next meeting, showing the size of each market, its likely growth rate, the big players, and what Facebook could do uniquely well. After weeks of this, at the final meeting Sandberg went deliberately around the room and asked each person what percentage of Facebook's revenue would ultimately come from each category. Virtually everyone said 70 percent or more would be advertising.[42]

Sandberg's use of diverse and institutionalized deliberation had created the launching pad for an advertising-based take-off in revenues, which would nearly double in the following year and go on to surpass $1.3 billion in 2010.[43] Achieving this revenue take-off would involve other rational methods, such as strategic calculation, but the use of deliberative methods had played an important role. In particular, it had inspired employees with some rational confidence regarding the new revenue-earning direction and the newly arrived member of the dual CEO/COO leadership team.

However, Sandberg's enhancing of the business side of Facebook also involved her making the firm more business-like in its procedures and attitudes—a different task that required a different use of the deliberative methods. Several years later she referred to this task and its complexities in her partly autobiographical *Lean In: Women, Work, and the Will to Lead*.

> When I first joined Facebook, one of my biggest challenges was setting up the necessary business processes without harming the freewheeling culture. The company operated by moving quickly and tolerating mistakes, and lots of people were nervous that I would not just ruin the party, but squash innovation. . . . I faced a dilemma: I needed to bolster the business side of the company while respecting its unconventional culture.[44]

In other words, she had to find a way of making the firm more business-like in its procedures and attitudes without undermining the creative workplace culture that was a crucial factor in the firm's success.

In this context the use of deliberative methods included her informal institutionalization of the anti-authoritarian aspect of diverse deliberation. 'I also let them know that if they hear a bad idea, even one they believe is coming from me or Mark [Zuckerberg], they should either fight it or ignore it.'[45] However, she ran into the reticence problem that has so often hampered leaders' use of diverse deliberation. 'As often as I try to persuade people to share their honest views, it is still a challenge to elicit them.'[46] But it was a challenge worth undertaking, if only because, as she points out, 'reticence causes and perpetuates all kinds of problems'.[47] More immediately, her obvious commitment to diverse deliberation would have again inspired employees with some rational confidence regarding her and the direction in which she was leading them—towards becoming a business-like firm.

Lean In included an example of diverse deliberation that Sandberg experienced and learned from many years before she used such methods at Facebook.

In 1996 she was a new member of Secretary Rubin's Treasury department and attended a policy meeting where Rubin asked for her opinion because 'you're new and not fully up to speed on how we do things. I thought you might see something that we were missing.'[48] He thereby 'sent a powerful message to all of us about the value of soliciting ideas from every corner'.[49] Sandberg, too, has sent a powerful message about the value of deliberative methods but in her case the message was sent through her deeds at Facebook and then her words in *Lean In*.

However, it appears that as late as the 2000s the conventional business wisdom was that leadership is largely about 'charisma' rather than rationality. Khurana's *Searching for a Corporate Savior: The Irrational Quest for Charismatic CEOs* sceptically describes a conventional wisdom that favours charismatic leadership and, for example, believes that CEOs need charisma in order to carry out the key leadership roles of energizing people who are 'lethargic or sceptical' and of 'increasing the self-confidence of employees when the company is collectively anxious'.[50] Yet charismatic leadership is unlikely to inspire rational, discerning employee-followers with commitment and confidence, as is pointed out in the Appendix. And the employees of such twenty-first-century firms as Facebook are very likely to be rational and discerning about the firm's leadership and the direction that he, she, or they are setting.

A similar point can be made about the response to 'strong' leadership. In the 1990s Grove argued that strong leadership is especially needed by a demoralized firm, whose employees have lost confidence in its management and in each other. 'This is exactly when you need to have a strong leader setting a direction', and the direction has to be 'a strong, clear one' because organizations 'are very sensitive to obscure or ambiguous signals from their management'.[51] But rational, discerning followers are also very sensitive to *irrational* signals from the leader; the direction set by the leader must be rational as well as clear if it is to restore these people's confidence in management and in each other. Even more will be needed to inspire them with confidence about achieving such an ambitious objective as developing a corporation: their leader will have to be using the appropriate rational means of achieving this objective.

Using the Six Methods—Autobiographical Accounts

The appropriate rational means of developing a corporation are the set of six generic rational methods delineated in the second section of this chapter. It is worth reviewing that earlier account before going on to discuss how leaders use—select and emphasize—these six methods when establishing or enhancing a corporation. The two adaptive methods, rapid and innovative adaptation, are the opportunistic and creative methods. Their key theorist was Schumpeter, especially in his 1940s writings, but some aspects of these two forms of adaptation have been explored by later theorists, such as Drucker in the 1980s and Grove and Christensen in the 1990s. The two calculative methods, quantitative and strategic calculation, are the obviously rational methods. Their key theorist was Weber in the early 1920s but strategic calculation's founding theorist was the military writer Clausewitz in the 1830s. The two deliberative methods, diverse and institutionalized deliberation, have the longest intellectual heritage. Machiavelli mentioned aspects of both forms of deliberation, if not by name, and many modern writers have discussed or identified these and other aspects, such as deliberative leadership. The two deliberative methods are also the most likely to involve face-to-face relationships between the leader and other individuals.

There are marked variations in how this set of six methods is used to establish or enhance a corporation. The leaders of iconic corporations have tended to use all six methods but other leaders—presumably facing different circumstances—have selected only five, four, or three methods as appropriate means of developing their corporations. Furthermore, leaders usually emphasize at least one of the methods that they are using, because it is a favourite or key method, and there is a marked variation in their selection of which method(s) to emphasize.

This variation in emphasis seems to be due to leaders' personal preferences rather than to differences in their circumstances. For example, Sam Walton's emphasis on quantitative calculation seems to have been due to personal preference rather than because the method was appropriate for the circumstances. He noted that his 'appreciation for numbers' was one of his talents and strengths and that 'my style as an executive has been pretty much dictated by my talents. I've played to my strengths and relied on others to make up for my weaknesses.'[52] Walton did not rely on quantitative calculation, however, when he was making such key decisions as whether to make a major acquisition—he relied instead on a *non-rational* method. 'I try to play a "what if" game with the numbers—but it's generally my gut that makes the final decision. If it feels right, I tend to go for it, and if it doesn't, I back off.'[53]

Was this reliance on gut instinct due to a stronger personal preference or to the appropriateness of non-rational methods in such extraordinary circumstances? Walton went on to say that letting his gut make the decision was by no means a mistake-proof method. 'Sometimes, of course, that leads me into mistakes', as when 'I was mistaken in my vision of the potential the Hypermarket held in this country'.[54] Yet his non-rational methods of vision and gut instinct might be more successful than rational methods in such extraordinary circumstances as the 'true uncertainty' mentioned earlier in the chapter. Of course when leaders use non-rational methods, they are failing—by definition—to provide the rational type of inspirational leadership, even if the non-rational methods are appropriate. In practice, however, the followers may still be inspired with rational confidence if the leader is *rationally selecting* the appropriate method, even if that method is as non-rational as vision or gut instinct.

The issues and insights provided by Walton's remarks also highlight the benefits of using examples that feature autobiographical material. It has similar advantages to interview material and it gives a leader's-eye view that personalizes and humanizes any example of developing a corporation. What is more, autobiographical material allows the distinctive 'voice' of each leader to be heard over the years or decades. It is therefore a constant reminder that although these leaders used the same set of rational methods, they were unique individuals who left behind distinctive corporations as monuments to their life's work.

The classic examples presented in the following chapters will feature autobiographical accounts of how the leaders established or enhanced their corporations. Of course featuring autobiographical material has its problems as well as its advantages. The obvious problem is that the leaders' autobiographical writings may contain biased and even erroneous recollections. However, these distortions can be countered by supplementing and corroborating the autobiographical writings with more objective biographical or historical accounts of what occurred. Another obvious problem is that the leaders often refer to a generic rational method only by implication, not by name or in any conceptual way. Few business leaders use such terms as 'adaptation' and 'deliberation' in their autobiographies! A less obvious but larger problem is that the available autobiographical material is often too limited. The leaders' autobiographical writings often give a too perfunctory account of how they used particular methods and/or describe too few of the methods that they are known to have used, and this is another reason why their writings have to be corroborated and supplemented by biographical and historical sources. The most fundamental problem, however, is that many classic examples have had to be excluded because the corporate-developing leader has not produced an autobiography or any other writings that include relevant autobiographical material.

Nonetheless, the following chapters present a wide range of classic examples of leaders establishing or enhancing an iconic corporation. The times range from the 1920s to the 2000s, the places include Japan, Italy, France, and Britain as well as America, and the industries include automobile assembly, aircraft construction, computer-chip production, discount retailing, high-fashion retailing, e-commerce auctioning, fast-food franchising, and cosmetics franchising. The six main examples are Sloan enhancing General Motors, Ohno enhancing Toyota, Kroc establishing McDonald's, Walton establishing Wal-Mart, Grove enhancing Intel, and Whitman enhancing eBay; the supplementary examples include Dassault establishing Dassault Aviation, Roddick establishing the Body Shop, and Armani establishing his fashion empire.

It is true that this selection of examples contains too many Americans and too few women but there are extenuating circumstances. Tedlow's biographical study of seven American business leaders, *Giants of Enterprise*, noted that 'founding and building new businesses' is 'what Americans do best' and he pointed out that these seven giants were individuals of 'extraordinary inner drive and competitiveness living in a country and culture which encouraged those traits and channelled them into business enterprise'.[55] He also acknowledged that even in America, however, the dice had been loaded against women achieving the same sort of business success. Women 'have not been given the opportunity to lead a large American corporation' and the 'rare, recent exceptions' amounted in the year 2000 to merely three women CEOs among the leaders of the largest five hundred corporations.[56] Presumably the distinctive feature of twenty-first-century business leadership will be the rise of women CEOs throughout the business world and particularly in the role of developing corporations.

Another unrepresentative aspect of the examples is that they include only iconic, extraordinarily successful corporations. This is because such corporations are 'best-practice case studies' in the sense of leaders having inspired followers with rational confidence by *very* capably using the appropriate rational methods. Furthermore, the examples will show that this rational leadership was provided even in the early stages of the corporation's development, well *before* the extraordinary successes that made it iconic and made its leader a celebrated or legendary figure. It is true, though, that these examples differ in various other ways from the more ordinary cases of corporation-developing leadership.[57] For instance, a particularly interesting difference is that the development of iconic corporations has often involved a period of high-level leadership by a *team* of leaders and usually it has been a dual-leadership team.

Such a high-level leadership team combines the CEO with one or two other board members. In the case of corporation-developing teams, however, it is usually dual, two-person leadership and seldom triple, three-person leadership.[58] Like management teams, their teamwork normally involves some division of labour, with each member of the leadership team having particular roles or tasks. If it is a corporation-developing team, it is likely that the whole set of six rational methods will be used but with each member specializing in particular methods or in using the methods in particular circumstances. In fact there are at least three distinct versions of the division of labour between two members of a dual-leadership team that is developing a corporation. The best known version combines a more business-oriented individual with a more creative or technically oriented individual, as in the case of the high-fashion Versace brothers or the high-tech Hewlett and Packard team. Another well-known version combines a semi-retired founder as chairman with a younger-generation executive as the CEO. The third and most complex version combines the CEO with another prominent executive, such as the COO, who is introducing an enhancing innovation. All three versions are to be found among the classic examples of corporation-developing leadership presented in the following chapters and in fact the first two examples include leadership teams introducing an enhancing innovation: a new administrative system at General Motors and a new production system at Toyota.

2

GM: Sloan's *My Years With General Motors*

Alfred Sloan's leadership of the General Motors Corporation in the 1920s is one of the legendary feats in business history. He carried out an administrative rationalization of the corporation that dramatically improved its structure, processes, marketing, and policy-making. This multifaceted enhancement of the corporation would lead to him being 'hailed as the father of the modern corporation, the master of consumer mass marketing and the most effective chief executive officer ever'.[1] For Sloan brilliantly reaped the rewards of his 1920s rationalization during his long tenure as leader of this iconic corporation. He was its president/CEO from 1923 to 1937, then CEO and chairman until 1946 and thereafter its chairman until his retirement ten years later. During this era, General Motors achieved a remarkable series of successes: defeating the legendary Henry Ford to become the leading firm in the automobile industry, trading profitably during the Great Depression, seeing its methods copied by competitors, and becoming the world's largest industrial corporation, with more than half a million employees.

In addition to these feats, Sloan was a pioneering exponent of rational business leadership. His biographer has pointed to the contrast with Machiavelli's view that rulers are either feared or loved; Sloan 'believed that he could run General Motors without fear or love: that reason alone would suffice'.[2] Rationality would inspire his employee-followers with confidence, while neither fear nor love would be needed to inspire them with commitment—this was produced by pay, promotions, and professionalism. His commitment to rationality was reflected in his use of appropriate rational methods of developing a corporation: he used all six of the methods discussed in Chapter 1. This was wholly appropriate in the dire circumstances he was facing in the 1920s when he became leader of the corporation. His wide-ranging administrative rationalization and restructuring was needed to rectify the deficiencies of an earlier era. And his enhancement of the corporation is characterized by the way in which he converted these weaknesses into strengths—through his use of rational methods.

For example, through innovative adaptation he converted an organizational weakness into an impressive new organizational structure, which became a standard type for manufacturing corporations. This type of organizational structure arranges a corporation into a headquarters and several operating divisions: firm-like, virtually self-contained units that are based on particular product lines, such as the Chevrolet or Cadillac car. More importantly, decision-making is largely decentralized to these operating divisions, with most decisions being made at divisional level rather than centrally by the corporation's headquarters. Tedlow considers this 'an organizational innovation of exceptional value' and Sloan noted in the 1960s that it 'not only has worked well for us, but also has become standard practice in a large part of American industry'.[3] Even in the twenty-first century Sloan's organizational structure:

> remains a litmus test for all kinds of organizations today that are struggling to remain agile, efficient, and effective in a world of constant technological change and globalization. Despite the current emphasis on 'flat' and 'matrixed' organizations rather than the 'silos' of the Sloan organization chart, the key elements of Sloan's model are still followed across the globe: indeed, many companies have ended up either returning to it or borrowing from it.[4]

It has been described as 'a machine capable of adapting to any change in its environment' and Sloan noted in his memoirs that there needed to be such forms of organization that 'could adapt to great changes in the market. Any rigidity by an automobile manufacturer, no matter how large or how well established, is severely penalized.'[5]

Sloan's use of rational methods is recounted in his memoirs, which appeared in 1963 and became as legendary as his business success. He began working on *My Years with General Motors* before his retirement and employed a large team of professionals, including an accomplished writer, John McDonald, and an academic researcher, Alfred Chandler, who would later become a celebrated business historian.[6] Of all the autobiographical writings by business leaders, this is the one which is most like a management text rather than a memoir or autobiography. It is also the one that has best stood the test of time. It is still 'in print' in the twenty-first century, over a million copies have been sold, and the front cover displays a testimonial from Bill Gates: 'probably the best book to read if you want to read only one book about business'. Similarly, its 1990 Introduction by Drucker was titled 'Why *My Years with General Motors* is Must Reading' and he declared that it was still 'the best management book'.[7]

Sloan's Introduction to his memoirs expressed his strong commitment to rational management and methods. The book's approach would be 'to deal with business from the logical point of view' and it would be considering 'the logic of management in relation to the events of the automotive industry'.[8] Sloan's biographer suggests that the kind of person who appreciates *My Years with General Motors* is someone 'who wants to understand how to rationally manage men, money, markets, and machines'.[9] The book can also be appreciated, however, by anyone seeking a leader's-eye view of the way Sloan used rational methods to enhance the corporation. He used the whole set of six rational methods and emphasized three—innovative adaptation, strategic calculation, and institutionalized deliberation—largely because of the circumstances rather than any personal preference for these three methods.

The first section of this chapter will focus on his emphasizing of innovative adaptation, which restructured General Motors and produced a new, innovative organizational structure. This section will also assess his use of rapid adaptation and will show how he used quantitative calculation—quantitative controls and assessments—to strengthen his new organizational structure. The second section will describe his emphasizing of strategic calculation and particularly his strategically calculated marketing, which played an important role in reviving the firm's fortunes. The third section will describe his emphasizing of institutionalized deliberation and how his highly institutionalized, committee-based system of deliberation also involved the use of diverse deliberation. The final section will discuss the rivalry between his and Henry Ford's corporations and approaches, which would result in Sloanism's administrative rationality defeating Fordism's focus on efficient production.

Adaptive Restructuring

Sloan's 1920s organizational restructuring of General Motors was an innovative adaptation which influenced many other corporations and became a standard organizational structure. As Chandler noted in his *Strategy and Structure*, the previous corporate standard had been a 'centralized, functionally departmentalized administrative structure' whose several departments each had a specialized function, such as the sales department or purchasing department; Sloan's innovative new structure, though, was a decentralized, multidivisional administrative structure whose several operating divisions each performed 'all the functions involved in the overall process of handling a line of products' in similar fashion to a self-contained, autonomous firm, such as the Chevrolet and Cadillac divisions of General Motors.[10] Even before Sloan's restructuring of the corporation it had a multidivisional structure, because its operating divisions had originally been independent firms acquired by General Motors when it was merely a holding company. Sloan created his innovative new structure by further *centralizing* the too-independent divisions, which had been behaving as if they were still independent firms. But he referred to his new structure, somewhat paradoxically, as a *de*centralized organization. In his memoirs, for example, he describes the new structure as a combination of

19

decentralization with some centralization, and he terms it 'decentralization with co-ordinated control' or being 'co-ordinated in policy and decentralized in administration'.[11] In terms of what he had done to General Motors, however, the accent should have been on *central* control or 'coordination' of what had been a markedly *more* decentralized organization.

Sloan's organizational innovation had originated as his adaptive *conceptual* response to his corporation's organizational failings, which were largely a by-product of the way in which it had developed during the Durant era of 1908–20. William Durant established General Motors as a holding company of largely car-making and parts-making firms but he eventually converted it into an operating company, with the firms becoming operating divisions of the General Motors Corporation. Although Durant had therefore begun the process of centralization, he is depicted by Sloan as 'an extreme decentralizer' whose style of personal management led to a situation of 'almost total decentralization'; he was in fact 'a great man with a great weakness—he could create but not administer'.[12] In the later years of the Durant era, Sloan was an executive vice-president on the board of directors and was in a good position to see that corporate headquarters needed more control over the managers of the operating divisions. 'Without adequate control from the central office, the divisions got out of hand and failed to follow the policies set by the corporation management, to the great detriment of the corporation.'[13]

These organizational failings were highlighted and exacerbated by the corporation's rapid expansion in 1918–20. 'I became convinced that the corporation could not continue to grow and survive unless it was better organized.'[14] In late 1919 he began drafting a systematic plan, the Organization Study, aimed at centralizing and rationalizing the corporation's structure and processes.[15] In that year General Motors had begun a massive expansion programme aimed at doubling production capacity—through the operating divisions acquiring or constructing new factories—and based on the confident assumption that the booming demand for automobiles would continue unabated in the decade ahead.[16] Instead, however, demand began to decline in the summer of 1920 and the economy began an unexpected recession that would lead to 'a new awareness throughout the business world of how complex and unpredictable the economy and the consumer can be'.[17]

General Motors had been hit particularly hard. 'All of the elements of catastrophe abruptly came together: the cost of the 1919 expansion program, the accumulation of huge inventories in anticipation of more demand, the end of cash flow as dealers stopped ordering vehicles, the fall of the stock price, and the lack of an internal structure or mechanism to force the divisions to cut production and costs in a timely or orderly manner.'[18] By November 1920 both the share price and the production of vehicles had fallen to less than a third of what they had been in the spring of that year.[19] Not surprisingly,

November also saw Durant's resignation as president of General Motors and his departure from the board of directors, who appointed their chairman Pierre du Pont to the additional post of president on a temporary, interim basis.

The corporation's directors followed this up with a farsighted response to the crisis. In December the board officially adopted Sloan's Organization Study as the basis for a rationalizing restructuring of the corporation: in his words, the board 'desired a highly rational and objective mode of operation'.[20] As the 44-year-old Sloan was the board's operations expert, the equivalent of a modern chief operating officer (COO), it also relied upon him to *introduce* his planned administrative innovation. In fact an innovation-introducing leadership team was formed between Sloan and Pierre du Pont; the latter would continue to be the corporation's temporary president as well as its chairman. The dual-leadership team of du Pont and Sloan would last until May 1923, when du Pont resigned from his temporary presidential position and Sloan became the new president of the corporation.[21] 'Sloan, at first under the gentlemanly but firm hand of Pierre du Pont, and then as chief executive, would use harsher instruments [than Durant's] to take General Motors from near extinction and lead it upward.'[22]

Sloan would convert his adaptive conceptual response, the Organization Study, into an innovative adaptation—a pioneering organizational restructuring of the corporation. He would be using and indeed emphasizing innovative adaptation as a method of enhancing a corporation. And his emphasizing of this method was not simply due to his personal preferences; it was largely because of the dire circumstances that his corporation was facing. Yet his innovative adaptation was by no means rapid, considering that there was a pre-existing blueprint—the Organization Study plan—which had the support of the chief executive and the board of directors. In fact the new organizational structure was still being developed in the 1930s, with new centralizing features being added or existing features evolving further in a centralizing direction. But much of the organizational restructuring was carried out in the first few years and seems slow only in comparison to his rapid rationalization of marketing strategy. Furthermore, Sloan's restructuring was a major 'political' change that markedly reduced the independence enjoyed by the operating divisions, and so it is not surprising that he took things relatively slowly.

The key to his organizational restructuring was creating a new relationship between central management and the operating divisions. For example, Sloan specified that divisional managers could not be members of the corporation's Executive Committee, because 'the top operating committee should be a policy group detached from the interests of the specific divisions'.[23] In Chandler's words, now central management would be responsible 'for strategic decisions and the divisions for tactical ones'.[24] This strategic/tactical distinction is particularly relevant because Sloan created an organizational structure similar to that of a modern army in the vertical terms of headquarters, corps and divisional units and in the horizontal staff-and-line terms of staff officers advising 'line' officers on how to exercise their hierarchical command authority.

There was nothing new about business firms copying the military's practice of attaching staff units to senior 'line' commanders and headquarters. Large business firms had adopted a similar structure at their company headquarters, with staff units and staff executives providing information or advice about finance, law, and other specialized areas of expertise. General Motors in the Durant era, however, had more impressive staff resources at the divisional level than at corporate headquarters. Indeed even *after* Sloan's centralization, each divisional general manager was 'served by almost as complete a staff as if he were heading an independent business: production manager, chief engineer, sales manager, comptroller, personnel manager, etc.; in other words, each division is organized as an autonomous unit'.[25] But by then Sloan had shifted the balance in favour of the headquarters staff. His Organization Study had called for headquarters to have a much-expanded set of 'advisory staffs, which would be without line authority' and cover a wide range of specialized areas of expertise.[26] His implementation of this plan boosted headquarters staff and gave it new units for research, engineering, personnel, sales, purchasing, and even factory design.[27]

What is more, Sloan gave new, innovative roles to his headquarters staff. In addition to its standard role of providing central policy-makers with information and expert advice, it was given important *divisional* roles that involved monitoring as well assisting the divisions. Staff units were employed 'to keep a check on the divisions, to suggest ways to improve current methods, and to see how various policies were being followed'—eventually staff were even 'coordinating' divisions' activities.[28] In his memoirs Sloan acknowledged that the staff units and executives informally exerted some central authority over the divisions:

> In General Motors we do not follow the textbook definition of line and staff. *Our distinction* is between the central office (which includes staff) and divisions. Broadly speaking, the staff officers—being primarily specialists—do not have line authority, yet in certain matters of established policy, they may *communicate the application* of such policy directly to a division.[29]

In addition to these staff units, headquarters acquired a new type of corporate executive—the *group* vice-president.[30] This Sloan innovation was a follow-up to his Organization Study's plan for the corporation's divisions to be grouped 'according to like activities' while leaving each division as a self-contained unit that handled its own production, engineering, sales, and so forth.[31] The dozens of divisions and smaller units would be organized into four groups: Car, Accessory, Parts, and a residual Miscellaneous that included tractors, refrigerators, and the finance company GMAC.[32] In what was apparently an afterthought, Sloan suggested that an executive should be put in charge of each group, if only to take over the divisional managers' duties of reporting directly to the CEO.[33]

Several other duties, however, were eventually assigned to these group vice-presidents. In particular, they were given the extensive role of supervising, coordinating, and assessing their divisions and 'reflecting' central policies to them.[34] Officially this was still only an advisory role, like that of the staff executives, and officially the group vice-presidents likewise exercised 'only advisory and not line authority'.[35] But by the time of Drucker's 1940s study of General Motors, the group vice-presidents exercised 'informal but very real control' over their group's divisions: they possessed 'a very real power; but it is rarely, if ever, exercised in the form of orders'.[36]

According to Chandler, these group executives and the new headquarters staff 'made possible the transformation of the corporation from a federation into a consolidated enterprise'.[37] He also points out that the newly consolidated enterprise was flourishing under Sloan's centralizing leadership. Its share of the market had grown from less than 19 per cent in 1921 to more than 43 per cent in 1927 and it had taken over the number-one position in the industry: the new 'clearly and rationally defined' organizational structure had 'served General Motors well'.[38] There were other factors, however, involved in the corporation's success, and even the centralization factor had involved new *processes* as well as a new organizational structure.

These new centralizing processes typically involved quantitative calculation and the renowned 'numbers man' Donaldson Brown. Sloan used Brown's expertise to introduce a wide range of quantitative controls and assessments. Some of them were innovative but others were merely standard procedures that had been neglected in the Durant era. For example, Sloan had to enforce limits on divisional capital expenditure and establish a new capital-appropriation process to consider divisional requests for capital investment.[39] They were now considered from a corporation as well as divisional perspective and were evaluated objectively by applying the concept of rate of return on investment—in fact the corporation's financial staff had developed a new equation for calculating the return on investment.

Similarly, rectifying the corporation's lack of uniform accounting procedures also meant strengthening the authority of headquarters' financial staff over their divisional equivalents.[40] This ensured, too, that central management received adequate financial data from the divisions to make accurate assessments of their operations and how they could be improved. The assessments compared divisions with one another, analysed the sources of a division's strengths and weaknesses, and appraised the work of the divisional managers.[41]

These financial assessments of divisional activity were described by Sloan as 'the last necessary key to decentralization with coordinated control'.[42] Headquarters 'could safely leave' divisional operations in the hands of divisional managers because 'we had the means to review and judge the effectiveness of operations'.[43] The divisional managers were therefore left with some opportunity to show their capabilities as leaders and administrators. But although Sloan believed in giving executives such opportunities, he also believed that 'even good corporate men' sometimes forgot that General Motors existed not to make cars but to make money.[44] So it is not surprising that he introduced a range of structural, financial, and even *operating* controls which restricted divisional managers and ensured that they would make money as well as cars for General Motors.

Sloan had initially imposed operating controls as a response to the divisions' disastrously unprofitable tendencies in 1920 to over-produce and to over-stock inventory.[45] Their tendency to acquire overly large inventories of raw and semi-finished materials was countered by enforcing limits on their purchasing of materials and basing the limits on what was required to meet production schedules for a specified period of time.[46] Controlling the divisions' production was a more complicated problem. The new production controls involved more than just approving and enforcing the divisions' production schedules; the new controls also ensured that these scheduled levels of production were based on accurate forecasts of demand and so would not lead to either over-production or unmet demand. Indeed Sloan established a sophisticated system of forecasting consumer demand, monitoring retail sales and adjusting production schedules to meet unpredicted changes in the market.[47]

His various central controls proved of greatest benefit when General Motors had to respond to the economic crisis of the Great Depression. He thanked the corporation's 'financial and operating controls' for the fact that it 'did not approach disaster as it had in the 1920–21 slump. We made an orderly step-by-step retreat.'[48] It was the only car-making firm to operate profitably throughout the Depression, and Sloan claimed that 'the corporation was not demoralized' even in the trough year of 1932, when it operated at less than 30 per cent capacity and made a profit of merely $165,000.[49] He claimed, too, that 'perhaps the greatest payoff' from his strengthening of controls was that 'we had simply learned how to react quickly'.[50] But the rapid adaptation to economic change in the early 1930s was virtually forced upon the corporation by the controls introduced in the 1920s, as these controls were now automatically and quickly reducing production and inventory in an autopilot-like manner.

In fact this was less impressive than the corporation's rapid adaptation in the early 1920s. Sloan and his dual-leadership teammate du Pont had rapidly adapted to the crisis conditions of those years. In particular, they took only months to institute a fundamental rationalization of marketing strategy. What is more, the rapid adaptation produced remarkable results. By the end of the decade there had been a remarkable recovery in the corporation's fortunes. In 1921 it made a *loss* of nearly $39 million on sales of about $300 million and with a workforce of some 80,000; by 1929 it was making a profit of more than $248 million on sales of about $1.5 billion and with a workforce of some 233,000: 'It was the largest turnaround and the most thorough transformation in business history.'[51]

It is, too, a remarkable case of using rapid adaptation as a method of enhancing a corporation. However, the 1920s saw an even more remarkable case of emphasizing the other adaptive method, innovative adaptation. Sloan's emphasizing of this method had underpinned his use of rapid adaptation and had ensured the longer-term success of General Motors. For his innovative adaptation included both a new organizational structure and the innovative strengthening of this structure by quantitative controls and assessments. These were two crucial aspects of his overall administrative rationalization of General Motors, which was in turn the basis of its remarkable recovery. So although Sloan used both the adaptive methods, rapid and innovative, his emphasizing of the more creative form of adaptation had been the key to his enhancing of General Motors.

Calculated Strategy

As was shown in the previous section, Sloan used quantitative calculation very effectively as part of his innovative adaptation and his overall administrative rationalization of General Motors. He also used the other calculative rational method, strategic calculation, and indeed Sloan emphasized this method, most notably in the area of marketing. He calculated marketing strategies that would transform all four of what Tedlow terms the 'basic elements of the marketing mix—product policy, pricing, marketing communications, and distribution'.[52] Sloan's strategically calculated marketing was a very different aspect of his administrative rationalization than his introduction of quantitatively calculated controls and assessments. However, he was again rectifying a lack of rationality and converting a weakness into one of the strengths of his corporation.

Sloan's memoirs describe how he and du Pont quickly began rectifying the major marketing weakness and irrationality—the firm's product policy. In April 1921 a special committee, headed by Sloan, was set up to rationalize a product policy that was allowing the seven car divisions to produce ten different car brands or models, such as Chevrolet and Cadillac, and was allowing each division to make its own 'price and production policies, which landed some cars in identical price positions'.[53] Similarly, the reason why the corporation produced only high-price and middle-price cars was not because of a deliberate policy but simply because 'no one had figured out how to compete with Ford' in the low-price range.[54]

Sloan's committee soon produced a set of recommendations that became the corporation's official policy in June 1921.[55] There were three key recommendations that in combination created a new pricing and product policy.[56] First, General Motors should produce a line of cars and models that catered for each price range or grade, from the lowest price up to the highest grade of quantity-produced car. Second, the price grades or steps should not leave wide gaps nor be too numerous. Third, there should not be any cases of General Motors cars or models competing against each other within the same price range. These policies were the basis of a new strategy that distinguished General Motors from other car manufacturers and would be maintained by Sloan throughout his many years as CEO. As his biographer notes, this idea of 'producing different cars with different qualities along a coherently formulated price spectrum' was a crucial marketing breakthrough; there would be more breakthroughs 'but this rational price spectrum was the paradigmatic first from which the others would spring'.[57]

The immediate implications of the new strategy were a drastic rationalization of car lines and an attempt to compete against Ford in the low-price range.[58] Now there would be only six standard cars/models in the list and there would be only four rather than *eight* cars/models in the middle price ranges. Furthermore, the list would now extend into the low-price range and would compete against Ford's Model T. The 'strategy we devised was to take a bite from the top of his position' by offering a higher-quality product at near enough to the same price to attract buyers from the top of the low-price range.[59]

This strategic move against Ford's Model T was an application of the new strategic principle: 'quality competition against cars below a given price tag, and price competition against cars above that price tag'.[60] Applying such principles would require an almost military-like strategic calculation, as when Sloan was identifying weaknesses in the product range.

> From the strategic standpoint at that time, however, the most dangerous gap in the list was that between the Chevrolet and the Olds...both offensively and defensively; offensively because there was a market demand to be satisfied there, and defensively because competitive cars could come in there and come down on Chevrolet as we planned for Chevrolet to come down on Ford.[61]

His calculations also involved another new strategic principle—variety— which had converted an irrational profusion of cars and models into the strategic principle of offering customers a wide range of variations to suit their budget, their needs, and their personal tastes.

The variety principle was communicated to the public through the new marketing slogan: 'a car for every purse and purpose'. Eventually the variety principle was taken so far that it seemed the objective had become a car for every purse, purpose, and *person*.[62] For by the 1950s the corporation was producing no fewer than 85 different models of its five basic car lines and soon after would boast that its range of optional accessories and variations enabled it theoretically to 'go through a whole year's production without making two cars alike'.[63] What is more, the variety principle was developed in a new direction by constantly *changing* the cars or models and in fact by the 1930s this had become the annual model change described in a later section of the chapter.

Sloan's marketing strategy also included a new concern for the styling of the firm's product. In the mid-1920s he began to highlight the potential of improved styling as a way of improving sales:

> His basis for this judgement was strategic: eye appeal would transform the car market. Consumers would purchase cars not just for utilitarian transportation but for personal pleasure and self-expression. General Motors had the production facilities and organizational know-how to take best advantage of car styling.[64]

He increased that organizational know-how in 1927 by giving headquarters staff an Art and Colour Section, which was later renamed the Styling Section.[65] There was some resistance in the divisions to having their products' design determined by headquarters staff, but soon 'the market made it clear that appearance was selling cars' and that General Motors was enjoying a competitive advantage over other car makers.[66]

Similarly, Sloan was a strong supporter of advertising. Within a year of him becoming its president, General Motors had become the largest buyer of advertising space in magazines.[67] Its 'massive spending' on advertising quickly exploited the corporation's competitive advantage in the styling of cars.[68] Such style-based advertising became controversial but Sloan was not interested in the moral issues raised about this form of advertising; 'He was interested in results'.[69] On the other hand, he was sufficiently concerned about public opinion to create a pioneering public-relations department. 'Sloan personally created the General Motors PR department in the 1930s' and in fact the corporation was 'the first company to have a full-time in-house public relations staff'.[70]

Sloan's focus on marketing strategy is somewhat surprising for an engineer who was known for his operational and organizational expertise. But the circumstances he was facing in the 1920s required him not only to use but to emphasize this marketing form of strategic calculation. It was crucially important to rectify the firm's weakness and lack of rationality in the area of marketing strategy. And Sloan's marketing strategy would play a key role in General Motors' remarkably successful competition against the dominant Ford Motor Company. Yet Sloan's personal preferences may have been an equally important reason for his later emphasis on marketing. After all, when he came to write his memoirs, he devoted five chapters to marketing topics: product policy, styling, the annual model change, the automobile market, and distribution through the retail car dealers. He included, too, a perceptive explanation of why any firm needs a marketing strategy. In 1921 General Motors needed a marketing strategy because 'it was necessary to know what one was *trying* to do, apart from the question of what might be imposed on one by the consumer, the competition, and a combination of technological and economic conditions'.[71]

Institutionalized Deliberation

Sloan's use of the two deliberative methods continued his tendency to emphasize one of each pair of rational methods, which in this case was institutionalized deliberation. Similarly, this section will again focus on the one that he emphasized but in this case because his version of institutionalized deliberation also involved the other deliberative method: diverse deliberation. For Sloan created a highly institutionalized, committee-based system of deliberation that valued rational discussion and was certainly not dominated by the leader; in his committees, policy proposals were 'sold' and assessed without reticence, and policy decisions were made in a collective, collegial manner.

Sloan's creation of this highly institutionalized system was another aspect of his restructuring and administrative rationalization. It was another case, too, of rectifying a Durant-era weakness and administrative irrationality. Sloan's memoirs complained that during Durant's time as leader of General Motors many important corporate decisions 'had to wait until he was free, and were often made impulsively'.[72] Chandler confirms that decision-making processes left much to be desired, with major decisions being made 'by Durant and the heads of the operating divisions in occasional conferences or in individual talks. Sometimes they were made by Durant with no consultation, at other times by the division manager after only the most casual reference or contact with Durant's office.'[73]

In marked contrast to the Durant era, the Sloan era was characterized by institutionalized policy deliberation and decision-making. Sloan's book describes this institutionalized deliberation as safeguarding General Motors 'against [Durant-like] ill-considered decisions' as well as producing policies that were likely to have 'better-than-average results' because they had been successfully defended 'against well-informed and sympathetic criticism' at the policy-deliberation stage.[74] It is true that Sloan's institutionalization went further than was needed to rectify the Durant-era irrationality; his emphasizing of this deliberative method was more a matter of personal preference than of dealing with the circumstances. But a historian of the corporation's early years has suggested that Sloan's most crucial change and legacy was 'the concept of decision making based on facts and open discussion, as opposed to the Durant crew's more mercurial and spontaneous decision-making process'.[75]

Furthermore, Sloan's system of institutionalized deliberation is a revealing case study of a committee-based version of this deliberative method. Institutionalized deliberation occurs in a context created by one or more kinds of institution: (1) informal rules, (2) laws and other formal rules, (3) formal positions or offices, such as president or CEO, (4) formal small-group institutions, such as committees or boards, and (5) formal large-group institutions, such as assemblies or annual general meetings. In Sloan's case, the institutional context was created by formal and informal rules, small-group institutions, and the deliberative aspect of Sloan's position as president/CEO.

The rules were a mixture of informal conventions and formal rules. For example, Sloan was voicing a formal rule when he stated that divisional management 'must "sell" central management on any substantial changes in operating policies'.[76] But he was stating only an *in*formal rule, a convention, when he went on to say that likewise central management 'should in most cases sell its proposals' to divisional management: there was a 'tradition of selling ideas, rather than simply giving orders'. Other informal rules specified that any new policies should be deliberated and decided in formal small-group institutions: the committees. According to Sloan, 'it is doctrine in General Motors that, while policy might originate anywhere, it must be appraised and approved by committees before being administered by individuals'.[77] However, he implied that this informal rule might be difficult or irksome for some executives. For he acknowledged that there was a 'strong temptation for the leading officers to make decisions themselves without the sometimes onerous process of discussion, which involves selling your ideas to others'.[78]

Sloan personally was happy to make decisions through discussion and he publicly highlighted the deliberative aspect of his position as president/CEO. He famously declared in a 1924 interview that 'I never give orders' and explained that it was better 'to appeal to the intelligence of a man than to the military[-like] authority invested in you'.[79] Of course his intelligent subordinates were well aware that Sloan would use the authority invested in him if there was no other way of administering the corporation's policies or if he was facing an emergency that required immediate action.[80] But nonetheless he was presenting a new, more deliberative view of the position of president/CEO of a corporation like General Motors. When he became its president in 1923, he realised that his new position required him to become a public figure, if only to contribute to General Motors' public image, and he wanted to be seen as a professional corporate manager who was more deliberative than authoritative.[81] He depicted himself as 'a facilitator of correct judgements, reached through consensus, achieved after exhaustive consultation with all the relevant members of his corporate enterprise', and as someone who 'was useful because he had the ability to listen to others, to collate their insights and to parcel them together for appraisal and validation by the organization itself'.[82] In this sense he appeared the business equivalent of a British-style prime minister leading a collegial government of cabinet ministers rather than an American-style president heading the executive and administration.[83]

Sloan's strong personal preference for collective deliberation and decision-making best explains his emphasizing of institutionalized deliberation. 'With the pertinent facts before them, Sloan believed, rational men would and could come to agreement on the best available course of action and therefore devote themselves as a team to its implementation.'[84] Such agreement and teamwork was typically achieved in a committee. Sloan was often referred to as 'a committee man' and he agreed that 'in a sense I most certainly am'.[85] His conception of being a committee man included listening to others' opinions or information rather than espousing his own views and in fact he earned the epithet 'Silent Sloan' through 'the relative paucity of his replies' in conversation or discussion.[86]

The corporation's committees were therefore the most important element in Sloan's system of institutionalized deliberation. Legally, the key deliberations were those of the corporation's board of directors, composed of senior executives and outside directors. Yet although Sloan acknowledged that the board was the 'supreme body', he did not describe it as a deliberative and policy-making organ but instead as performing the *auditing* functions of continuously reviewing and appraising 'what is going on throughout the enterprise'.[87] At its monthly meetings, the board was given: (1) audio-visual presentations about the corporation's financial, operating, and competitive position and about forecasted future developments, (2) monthly reports from the board's Finance Committee and Executive Committee, (3) periodic reports from its other standing committees, (4) oral reports from executives (on the board) regarding various areas of the corporation's business, (5) regular reports from staff and group vice-presidents on developments in their areas of responsibility and, last but not least, (6) the opportunity to ask questions and seek explanations.[88]

However, the key deliberative and policy-making discussions occurred in the board's two governing committees: the Finance Committee and Executive Committee. The latter was composed of senior executives who were on the board and 'active in management', but the financial committee was largely composed of outside directors and dealt with the key issues of capital expenditure, raising capital, acquisitions, and setting the annual dividend.[89] These two governing committees' policy recommendations were apparently accepted by the board of directors in similar fashion to a cabinet government or congressional legislature accepting the recommendations of its specialized committees.

Another, lower tier of policy deliberation by committees had been added as part of Sloan's restructuring. In 1922 he began creating a layer of Interdivisional Committees which each dealt with a specialized topic or area, such as purchasing, sales, advertising, and technical/engineering matters.[90] They 'included representatives from the comparable functional departments in each of the five car divisions' and their role was both to coordinate divisional activities and to make policy recommendations not only to the divisions' managers but also to the board's Executive Committee.[91] The Interdivisional Committees were therefore providing a new tier of policy deliberation, which could consider new policies and recommend them to the Executive Committee for consideration and perhaps recommendation to the board of directors. Furthermore, by adding this lower tier of policy deliberation Sloan had increased the *diversity* of deliberation, as the members of these committees were specialized experts who were also representing their particular car division.

In the 1930s, however, the Interdivisional Committees were replaced by the Policy Groups. They, too, were functionally specialized committees, such as those dealing with engineering or personnel, but they were composed solely of headquarters' executives: no divisional representatives were included in the Policy Groups.[92] The change in membership reflected Sloan's principle that policy is made by central management and administered by divisional management, which in practice meant excluding the divisional managers from power at central level.[93] So the demise of the Interdivisional Committees seems to have been simply a logical extension of the centralization that Sloan had begun and largely completed in the 1920s.

But the replacement of Interdivisional Committees by Policy Groups was also reducing the diversity of deliberation. The removal of divisional representatives from this tier of policy deliberations had removed the divisions' close-to-the-coalface viewpoint and their knowledge of local conditions at divisional level. Sloan and his centralizing allies, however, were more concerned about a divisional representative's biases and partiality. They believed that policy-making 'should be dealt with from an impartial understanding of the operating aspect' and that 'it is difficult for the individual to divorce himself from the departmental viewpoint'.[94] Yet they seem to have had no concerns about *central-level* departmentalism affecting the new Policy Groups' deliberations; apparently it was just the divisional, local-level viewpoints that posed a threat to the firm's policy deliberation.

The lack of local-level diversity was not the only weakness of Sloan's definitive version of policy deliberation by committees. The system produced 'a degree of corporate inertia—the many committees through which any one idea must pass did not make for speedy changes. This price Sloan was willing to pay.'[95] There was another price to pay, however, which Sloan acknowledged when describing how his system prevented policy-making by hunches:

> The manager who would like to operate on a hunch will usually find it hard to sell his ideas to others on this basis. But, in general, whatever *sacrifice* might be entailed in ruling out a possibly brilliant hunch is compensated for by the better-than-average results which can be expected from a policy that can be strongly defended against well-informed and sympathetic criticism. In short, General Motors is not the appropriate organization for purely *intuitive* executives, but it provides a favorable environment for capable and *rational* men.[96]

But did his corporation provide a favourable environment for rational and *innovative* executives or was there instead a sacrifice of innovation as well as intuition? It has been claimed that Sloan institutionalized a new, rational corporate culture that also 'fostered creativity, innovation and risk-taking'.[97] Yet the fostering of creativity, innovation and risk-taking does not seem characteristic of General Motors after the 1920s era of change.

For example, the General Motors of the 1950s seems no different from the typical conformist corporation depicted in Whyte's 1950s cultural study *The Organization Man*. Whyte declared that 'corporation man' was the most conspicuous example of the rise of a conformist social ethic—'an organization ethic'—that included 'a belief in the group as the source of creativity' and therefore discouraged an individual from being the first to espouse a new idea.[98] Similarly, a 1955 speech by a senior executive at Ford, Robert McNamara, warned that conformist pressures were discouraging innovation and fresh thinking in society and business corporations. In the latter, there was 'a certain inertia, a tendency to discourage fresh thought and innovation' and it took 'a degree of moral courage to withstand that pressure', particularly 'when you are in competition from half-a-dozen eager beavers who eagerly spout the party line'.[99]

Such conformist pressure has serious implications for the diversity of deliberation. Here is the diversity-reducing reticence that Machiavelli identified long ago and was discussed in Chapter 1. Sloan, too, warned about the 'spirit of venture' being 'lost in the inertia of the mind against change' but he believed that this occurs when success has brought self-satisfaction and has dulled the 'urge for competitive survival'.[100] If he was correct, it must be assumed that in the 1950s Sloan's General Motors was even more likely than McNamara's Ford to experience a conformist lack of diversity and innovation. For ever since the 1920s Sloan's firm had been more successful than Henry Ford's and, more generally, Sloanism had been more successful than Fordism.

Sloanism Versus Fordism

The difference and rivalry between Sloanism and Fordism was recognized by Sloan himself in the opening pages of his book. He pointed to the competition between General Motors and the Ford Motor Company as an example of how firms can compete with one another in their long-term way of doing business and in their type of organization, such as Ford's extreme centralization versus General Motors' decentralization.[101] Here and later in the book he also contrasted General Motors' variety of cars and continual model changes with Ford's belief in producing one static utility model at a constantly lower price—the famous Model T car.[102] He acknowledged that Ford had played the leading role in the industry throughout the 1908–27 lifespan of the Model T, but then what Sloan described as a different 'philosophy' had taken over: in the words of his biographer, 'Sloanism had defeated Fordism'.[103]

The key difference between Sloanism and Fordism was the different approach of Sloan and Henry Ford to the business of producing cars or other manufactured commodities. While Sloan focused on rationalizing his firm's administration, Ford focused on rationalizing *production* through his mechanized assembly-line production system. Fordism's efficient mass production enabled the price of the product to be reduced and the market for the product to be increased. Annual sales of Ford's cheap Model T car would increase from only 20,000 in 1910 to nearly 600,000 in 1916 largely because of price reductions created by the introduction of the assembly-line technique and its technology of 'conveyers, chutes and slides', which reduced the time to assemble a chassis from 12.5 man-hours to 1.5 man-hours.[104] Ford was increasing productivity through new machinery and organization rather than adopting Taylorism's training of individual workers to do their job in a more efficient way: 'why worry about how a man could do a job better if a machine could do it more efficiently than he could?'[105] However, Ford certainly wanted his machines to do their job in an ever more efficient way and he sought continual increases in productivity regardless of how much it cost to replace outmoded machines and systems.[106]

Unlike Sloan, Ford was not interested in administrative rationalization and ran his company in a peculiarly personalist way. Sloan termed it extreme centralization but Tedlow's profile of Ford describes it more accurately as *dictating* company policy.[107] Drucker labelled it 'one-man tyranny' and 'personal misrule' when he presented Ford as a case study of an owner's attempt to run a corporation without sharing the management responsibilities with professional managers—or with managers who were allowed to be professional.[108]

A recent biographer has explained this personal rule as simply Ford's desire 'to run everything by himself'.[109] This preference for hands-on personal control would affect even production technology and product engineering. He frequently interfered in the company's engineering projects, delayed the shift from forged to cast and stamped parts, and even showed a strong commitment to particular types of brakes and springs.[110]

The peculiarities of his personal rule had particularly negative effects on the company's policy deliberations and organizational structure. 'By the late 1910s, Ford found it difficult to deal with men who did not kowtow to him' and any manager 'who risked telling him the truth risked dismissal.'[111] This of course prevented proper deliberation about his company's policy, as even if he had genuinely sought his managers' opinion, they would have been too reticent to provide truthful advice. Furthermore, the company's organizational structure and processes were undermined by his attempts to encourage conflict among his managers. Ford 'early began pitting his lieutenants against one another, giving them overlapping authority to see which turned out to be tougher in defending what he thought was his own territory'.[112] Not surprisingly, his company lacked an organizational chart and this seems symbolic of the difference between him and Sloan, the author of the Organization Study, who had created an organizational structure that Tedlow deems 'far superior' to the level of organization enjoyed by Ford's company.[113]

Ford's personal peculiarities affected several other aspects of administrative rationality. His 'quirky, eccentric management style' included a contempt for accounting, which he viewed as parasitical, and therefore the accounting-like departments were eliminated in his 1919 economy drive.[114] Advertising, too, was not held in high regard by Ford. He spent nothing on advertising in the period from 1917 to 1923 and considered style-based advertising to be a 'trick' that was aimed at 'fooling people into buying what they did not need for reasons that could not stand up to moral scrutiny'.[115]

A similar personal prejudice restricted his company's product development. Ford had come to view the Model T 'not only as a mechanical force but as a moral one. It was exactly as much automobile as people needed, and no more.'[116] So he was reluctant to change the Model T, let alone to consider that it was becoming outmoded. There was some gradual product development, such as replacing wood with sheet steel and adding an electric starter, but the basic shape and engineering was preserved.[117]

These personal prejudices and policies became wholly inappropriate as the times and circumstances changed. By the mid-1920s American consumers were enjoying unprecedented prosperity and the hallmarks of the Model T—cheapness, durability, and utility—were now less important than style, colour, performance, and technical innovations.[118] For example, General Motors was pioneering 'several costly innovations that Ford resisted but which customers were eager to pay for', such as independent front-wheel suspension, electric turn signals, electric windshield wipers, and fully automatic transmissions.[119] As Sloan noted, not only prosperity but also the used-car trade-in and the introduction of instalment financing had encouraged middle-income buyers to demand something more than just basic transportation in their new car.[120] They sought 'comfort, convenience, power, and style. This was the actual trend of American life and those who adapted to it prospered.'[121] Even the low end of the market had been transformed, as the growth of the used-car market meant that low-income buyers now had cheaper and more up-to-date alternatives than a new but outmoded Model T.[122]

Ford's problems also arose, however, from his competitors' success in developing a flexible version of mass production that suited their marketing strategies. For example, Sloan's 1920s product-diversity strategy became less costly when he decided to use many standardized parts in the corporation's different products and annually changing models:

> Sloan's innovative thinking . . . seemed to resolve the conflict between the need for standardization to cut manufacturing costs and the model diversity required by the huge range of consumer demand. He achieved both goals by standardizing many mechanical items, such as pumps and generators, across the company's entire product range and by producing these over many years with dedicated production tools.[123]

His brilliant production engineer William Knudsen also introduced more flexible machine tools to produce the parts that would have to change to fit different cars and models.

> He rejected Ford's reliance on 'single-purpose' machine tools. Instead, he installed 'new heavy type standard machines' that permitted flexible mass production. Knudsen was creating a manufacturing process to regularize consumer-appealing changes—by the mid-1930s annual model changes—in the Chevrolet's appearance and its mechanical components.[124]

Sloan believed that the idea of annual model changes had been implicitly accepted in the 1920s. It had been 'inherent in the policy of creating a bigger and better package each year' and, more generally, in the awareness that the industry had 'entered a new period' that would mean 'continuous, eternal change'.[125]

Not surprisingly, the 1920s were a watershed for Ford's company as well as for the car market and industry. At the beginning of the decade, the company had been the number-one seller, with more than half the market, but in 1927 General Motors took over the number-one position.[126] Ford had attempted to restore the Model T's competitive position by improving its styling and equipment, resuming large-scale advertising, speeding up production, cutting prices, and even reducing production.[127] When these various responses failed the test of the market, he was forced to make the large-scale product adaptation that he had been resisting: in 1927 he ended production of the Model T and replaced it with the newly developed Model A.

With the Model A, Ford seemed to have adapted successfully to the new era in car design and marketing. The new model had up-to-date styling, performance, equipment, interior, and variety—more than a dozen different body styles and a range of colour combinations—plus the significant price advantage created by Ford's still superior production efficiency.[128] The Model A 'offered good looks and impressive mechanical sophistication for almost the same price as its predecessor'.[129] By 1929 it had captured more than a third of the market but the impressive sales figures were partly due to catching up with unmet demand—there had been serious problems in changing production over to the new model—and Sloan argued that Henry Ford never fully adapted to the idea of annual model changes.[130]

What is more, the Great Depression was about to hit the car market. The 1930s Depression decade would reduce Ford's share of the market to less than 19 per cent, compared to General Motors' market share of over 47 per cent, which was nearly a reversal of the firms' market shares some twenty years earlier.[131] Ford responded in 1932 by replacing the Model A with a dramatically new and effective design: an eight-cylinder model known as the V-8. Again Ford had opted 'to reinvent his main product' rather than upgrading it and once again this brought a false dawn, with Ford briefly returning to the number-two position in the market but being relegated to the number-three position in 1936, where it would remain until 1950.[132]

The revival of the firm's fortunes occurred only after Henry Ford retired in 1945 and his grandson, Henry Ford II, instituted a Sloanist rationalization of the company. He not only introduced modern marketing but also hired former General Motors executives to help restructure the company along Sloanist lines.[133] Ford even introduced the Sloan-pioneered quantitative controls and assessments, which were installed for him by a number-crunching newcomer to the industry—Robert McNamara. He rectified the various accounting deficiencies, introduced inventory controls, monitored retail sales to detect changes in demand, and instituted performance targets for divisional managers.[134] Such Sloanism now seemed to be the American and indeed global way of making cars and money.

3

Toyota: Ohno's *Toyota Production System*

The previous chapter showed how Ford and Sloan had created the modern car industry and indeed the modern system of production. Ford had pioneered the assembly-line techniques of mass production and Sloan had given the system sufficient flexibility to meet modern marketing needs for different product lines and frequent changes in product styling or features. By the late 1930s, however, the source of production innovation was no longer America but Japan, thanks to the founding of the Toyota Motor Company and the origins of the famous 'Toyota production system'.

Founding leader Kiichiro Toyoda envisioned a new way of manufacturing automobiles and called it 'just in time' production. But for various reasons, including the outbreak of war, he was unable to introduce this innovative production system. In fact it would not be introduced until some years after he left the Toyota Motor Company in 1950. By then the idea of just-in-time production had been further developed in practice by a second pioneering innovator, Taiichi Ohno, who was adding other innovative features to what would now be called 'the Toyota' production system. His introduction of the new system in the 1950s–60s significantly enhanced Toyota and helped develop the firm into a global automobile giant and an iconic corporation.

Yet Taiichi Ohno was never a CEO-level leader of the corporation. He was part of a dual-leadership team whose other member was the CEO-equivalent president of Toyota. It was the same version of dual leadership—an innovation-introducing team—that Sloan and du Pont created in the early 1920s at General Motors, as was mentioned in Chapter 2. Unlike Sloan, however, Ohno would remain part of a leadership team and would not go on to become the corporation's president and sole leader. When his 1954–61 teammate retired, Ohno formed a new innovation-introducing team with the next president of Toyota. In fact Ohno was still only an executive vice-president when he retired from the corporation in 1978.

Although Ohno never became a CEO-level leader, his production innovations made a notable contribution to the corporation's rapid development in the 1960s. There was a five-fold increase in annual production during the decade, production surpassed a million vehicles a year, and Toyota became the third-largest producer in the world, behind only Ford and the still dominant General Motors.[1] Furthermore, Ohno's production innovations enhanced the global competitiveness of Toyota and indeed the whole Japanese car industry. By the time Ohno retired in 1978 Toyota was exporting half a million cars a year to the United States and soon, only two years later, Japanese vehicle exports reached an annual worldwide total of some six million.[2]

In addition, Ohno had made a significant contribution to global manufacturing. By the time he retired, the 'Toyota production system' was becoming internationally famous and would eventually be imitated in many countries, industries, and organizations. In the 1990s his system received a major boost internationally when it was depicted as the pioneering version of 'lean' production, which uses 'less of everything', in the 1990 Womack, Jones, and Roos bestseller *The Machine That Changed the World: The Story of Lean Production*.[3] In the twenty-first century 'the Toyota Production System has become increasingly a part of how hospitals, governments, universities, banks, mining operations, and retailers are choosing to improve performance and develop their people'.[4]

In 1978 Ohno published a partly autobiographical work about his production system and how it had been developed.[5] An English-language edition of the book appeared several years later under the title *Toyota Production System*. It provides a leader's-eye view of how Ohno used three of the six appropriate corporation-developing rational methods. In addition to using strategic and quantitative calculation, Ohno emphasized innovative adaptation and largely as a matter of personal preference—he was personally determined to develop and introduce an innovative production system. Through a series of innovative adaptations he succeeded in developing this system, the renowned Toyota production system, and introducing it throughout the firm's factories and even throughout its supplier network—the many small firms supplying car parts to Toyota's assembly lines. This series of innovations were largely opportunistic adaptations that took full advantage of the opportunities offered by Japan's distinctive market and factory conditions.

But Ohno's book does not describe him using the other adaptive method, rapid adaptation, nor the two deliberative methods, diverse and institutionalized deliberation. His selection of methods was appropriate, though, for the circumstances he was facing. He was a production expert seeking to develop and introduce a new production system; he was not a business executive seeking to introduce something like Sloan's administrative rationalization of General Motors. The Toyota presidents who formed innovation-introducing leadership teams with Ohno would be much more likely to use the two deliberative methods, and these chief executives may well have used a few other appropriate rational methods. Certainly Ohno and his leadership teammates were using rational methods capably enough to inspire their employee-followers with rational confidence.

The first section of the chapter will outline not only Ohno's production innovations but also the innovation-introducing leadership teams that he formed with two successive Toyota presidents, Ishida and then Nakagawa. They have faded into the background compared to their now world-famous teammate and in fact his main rival for fame is the visionary Kiichiro Toyoda, who was the 1930s pioneer of just-in-time production. Ohno was exposed to the just-in-time idea in 1943 when he joined the Toyota Motor Company as a young production manager.[6] His book describes how impressed he was by Kiichiro Toyoda's idea that in 'automobile manufacturing, the best way to work would be to have all the parts for assembly at the side of the line *just in time* for their use' in the assembly-line process:

> The words 'just-in-time' pronounced by Toyoda Kiichiro were a revelation.... The idea of needed parts arriving at each process on the production line when and in the quantity needed was wonderful. Although it seemed to contain an element of fantasy, something made us think it would be difficult but not impossible to accomplish.[7]

Kiichiro Toyoda had been unable to accomplish just-in-time production but his pioneering was so important that it will be discussed in the first section of the chapter, as a prelude to its account of how Ohno developed and introduced just-in-time production in the 1950s.

The second section goes a step further by showing how he was innovatively adapting to Japan's local conditions. It argues that Ohno was exploiting the opportunities offered by Japan's distinctive factory environment as well as adapting to the requirements of the Japanese car-market environment. Such opportunities enabled him to add continuous-flow production and other features to the innovative production system that he was developing and introducing. The third section explores other features of this just-in-time production system: the Kanban information system, the problems of production levelling, and how parts suppliers were included in the system. Furthermore, the second half of the section shows how Ohno used the calculative rational methods, quantitative and strategic calculation, when developing this 'lean' form of production.

The final section, on Toyotaism versus Fordism, is in a sense a continuation of the final section of Chapter 2. In this case, however, it will be highlighting a rivalry between two different *production* systems. Ohno downplayed this rivalry in his overly generous assessment of Henry Ford but perhaps it was the most appropriate way for him to view his greatest predecessor—as a production innovator and a maker of modern manufacturing.

Pioneering Production Innovations

Toyota has long been an innovative firm and not only in the area of production. For example, its leaders' most obvious innovation has been the Toyoda family's long-term leadership of a corporation that the family does not own. The family founded the Toyota Motor Company in 1937 as a *public* company and soon owned only a minor shareholding but despite this lack of ownership control, it has provided the firm with a series of six presidents. In the eighty years since the firm was founded there have been only two periods when its president was not a member of the Toyoda family: 1950–67 and 1995–2006.[8] So it is not surprising that Togo and Wartman's 1993 history of the corporation was subtitled *The Story of the Toyota Motor Corporation and the Family That Created It.*[9]

The firm's innovative tendencies were evident from its inception in 1937. Japan was then decades behind the West in developing a modern economy but this new automobile firm was founded in a way that would have appeared 'advanced' in any economy of that era. For several years earlier the Toyoda Automatic Loom Works had experimentally diversified into automobiles and was now spinning off this new product department as an independent public company largely in order to fund its move towards mass production of these automobiles.[10] There was even a public competition to design the new company's car logo, which led to the word 'Toyoda' being changed to 'Toyota' when the new company was officially named the Toyota Motor Company.[11] Another innovative or at least unusual feature was that the firm's founding 'leader' was actually a dual-leadership team formed by two brothers: company president Risaburo Toyoda and executive vice-president Kiichiro Toyoda. They were the sons of the parent company's deceased founder, who 'had recognized their potential as a team. Kiichiro was bursting with ideas and spunk, while Risaburo possessed the wisdom to keep him on track.'[12] In fact the leadership team of business-oriented Risaburo and visionary engineer Kiichiro almost became an innovation-introducing version of dual leadership. But they were unable to introduce the innovative way of manufacturing automobiles that Kiichiro had envisioned and labelled 'just in time' production.

Some forty years later Taiichi Ohno described this vision of just-in-time production as the original idea behind Toyota's famous production system. According to his book *Toyota Production System*, 'Toyoda Kiichiro, father of Japanese car manufacturing, originally conceived this [just-in-time] idea which his successors developed into a production system'.[13] Furthermore, the book depicts Toyoda's idea as having been an innovative adaptation to local, Japanese conditions.

In 1933, Toyoda Kiichiro announced the goal to develop domestically produced cars for the general public: 'We shall learn production techniques from the American method of mass production. But we will not copy it as is. We shall use our own research and creativity to develop a production method that suits our own country's situation.' I believe this was the origin of Toyoda Kiichiro's idea of just-in-time.[14]

The idea of just-in-time may well have originated as an adaptation of mass-production techniques to suit Japanese conditions. But the more immediate, short-term conditions prevailing in the 1930s were not conducive to introducing visionary production ideas. Fujimoto's history of Toyota production systems considers Kiichiro's 'vision' of just-in-time production to have been 'unrealistic at that time'.[15] Japan's economy and industrial sector was not sufficiently advanced and the country was facing political and national-security problems that would soon lead to disastrous wars. According to Togo and Wartman, 'Kiichiro knew his master plan would take decades to enact, if it could be done, but in the meantime he carried forward the first parts of it' by keeping inventory warehouses as small as possible and ensuring that no more than one day's supply of components would 'sit idle beside the assembly line'.[16]

However, Kiichiro's opportunity to innovate was being continually reduced by Japan's wartime situation. A recent biography *Courage and Change* shows how he was hampered in the late 1930s by two factors—the supply problem and government pressure—that were intensified by Japan's growing war with China.[17] The government pressured Toyota to prioritize production of trucks and buses rather than cars and to bring the new Koromo plant into production as soon as possible, which meant that 'the move from the experimental production stage to the mass production stage took place more rapidly than Kiichiro had planned for' and obviously left no time for experimenting with a new production system.[18] The expedited move to mass production was also a cause of the quality-control problems that plagued the new plant, but another cause was the increasing supply problem, in terms of both quantity and quality, which in 1939 led Toyota to begin building its own steel mill.[19] The wartime situation became even worse after the 1941 outbreak of war with America and the British empire. The spiralling supply problem led to a manufacturing environment in which 'the availability of materials was determining the flow of production' and so any move towards just-in-time production 'ceased to exist'.[20]

In 1941 Kiichiro Toyoda had succeeded his brother as president of Toyota and therefore presided over the firm's wartime decline into makeshift manufacturing—and making trucks rather than cars.[21] But in these demoralizing circumstances he completed an innovative adaptation that was a landmark in the firm's development and would greatly assist the firm's later innovators. As Togo and Wartman point out, the wartime supply problems offered Toyota an opportunity to develop the supply network that later became a distinctive, crucial aspect of the firm's manufacturing process. 'Toyota was able to develop a more complete and competent network of suppliers. The Japanese automobile parts industry was disorganized and unsophisticated before the war, and Kiichiro had thus put only limited effort into developing suppliers.'[22] Kiichiro's biographers depict the new, wartime effort as a two-way process that included a major organizational effort by the parts suppliers. In 1939 Toyota's suppliers formed a Cooperation Association that developed into the 1943 Cooperation-with-Toyota Association, which was 'still going strong' in the 2000s.[23] Creating these cooperative relationships also required a major contribution from Toyota, including an innovative commitment that 'this company will consider those businesses it has chosen to be its suppliers as *branch factories* of this company, it will make it a general principle not to change to other businesses for no good reason, and it will make all possible efforts to *raise* the achievements of these factories'.[24]

Establishing this network of suppliers was a remarkable example of innovative adaptation. In addition, it was a classic example of identifying and exploiting an opportunity even in disastrous circumstances. But it has been overshadowed by the great 'might have been' of what might have happened if Toyoda had been given the opportunity to develop his idea of just-in-time production. Instead he had seen his car firm sidetracked by 1937–45 wartime conditions into becoming a producer of trucks and finding it difficult to produce even these kinds of automobile.

Kiichiro Toyoda's post-1945 leadership of the firm was plagued by new, post-war problems and he was unable to convert the firm into a producer of primarily cars rather than trucks.[25] In 1950 the firm faced a recession-induced financial crisis that resulted in lay-offs, a lengthy labour-union strike and the resignation of the firm's president.[26] Toyoda had taken personal responsibility for the labour-relations disaster, which psychologically devastated him, and his premature retirement ended two years later with his death at the early age of fifty-seven. In Ohno's words, this 'was indeed a great loss. I believe just-in-time was Toyoda Kiichiro's dying wish.'[27]

The firm's new president, Taizo Ishida, was not a member of the Toyoda family and was not familiar with automobile manufacturing but had been an effective president of Toyoda Automatic Loom Works.[28] He would prove to be a very effective president of the Toyota Motor Company, which would develop into a corporation, a *large* public company, during his 1950–61 tenure. During the Ishida era, however, the most notable achievement was Taiichi Ohno's introduction of a production system that attained Kiichiro Toyoda's vision of just-in-time production. Unlike Toyoda, Ohno was in a favourable situation to make an innovative adaptation to Japan's local conditions. And Ohno's innovative production system significantly enhanced Toyota, perhaps to the same degree as Sloan's 1920s innovative adaptation had enhanced General Motors. In the Toyota case, however, the enhancing innovation was related to production, not administration, and was introduced in a much more piecemeal way. General Motors had been restructured by implementing Sloan's comprehensive and detailed plan, the Organization Study, which he had drawn up years earlier. But Toyota's new production system was based on an idea or vision and was introduced largely by experimentation, trial and error and 'making things up as we go along'.

In other words, Toyota was *developing* as well as introducing a new system. As Fujimoto points out, the 'diffusion' of the new system was therefore 'rather slow, starting as Ohno's informal experiment as opposed to a company-wide movement. Initial experiments were made only where Ohno directly supervised.'[29] Furthermore, this reliance on Taiichi Ohno was typical of a firm that is relying on a brilliant individual or team to develop an innovative new system. 'While Ohno did not reorganize Toyota's system of production by himself, the extension of his techniques corresponded to his movements, between 1948 and the mid-1960s, from one shop or factory to another and up the ladder into top management.'[30] Ohno developed continuous-flow techniques when he was a machine-shop manager in 1948–52, as is discussed later in the chapter. In 1953 he became the plant's manager of manufacturing and began developing techniques inspired by Kiichiro's Toyoda's idea of just-in-time production. But Togo and Wartman point out that 'transforming the vehicle assembly line was far more difficult than transforming a machine shop. Engines and transmissions and other components poured into the assembly building from various locations, and orchestrating everything to arrive just in time was a monumental task.'[31] Ohno's book briefly refers to the long process of trial and error through which he accomplished this task.

> Step by step, I solved the problems related to the system of withdrawal by the later process. There was no manual and we could find out what would happen only by trying. Tension increased daily as we tried and corrected and then tried and corrected again. Repeating this, I expanded the process of pickup by the later process within the company.[32]

His expanding of the process 'within the company' was moving these just-in-time innovations from the development stage to the introduction stage. The continuous-flow innovations he had developed as a machine-shop manager had already reached the introduction stage and by 1955 had been extended, by other managers, to other manufacturing workshops in the plant.[33] But the clearest indication of the shift from development to introduction came at the end of the 1950s. Ohno was appointed general manager of the newly constructed Motomachi plant and now was able to supervise a plant-wide introduction of the new production system.[34] A few years later he returned to the main plant as its general manager, where he completed the company-wide introduction of the system and began extending it to the firm's suppliers.[35]

In the midst of his long pioneering journey, in 1954, the 42-year-old Ohno was made a director of the company.[36] Giving him a seat on the board was both recognizing what he had already achieved and encouraging him to continue with his difficult task, which was at the critical juncture of introducing innovations in the workshops and developing an innovative just-in-time process on the assembly line. Ohno's book mentions how he admires the attitude taken by 'top management' during this period, when there was the inevitable 'psychological resistance' to the innovative just-in-time approach and, he admits, when 'the ideas that I boldly put into practice...might have looked high-handed'.[37] The attitude of top management was made clear to all concerned by not only keeping Ohno on the job but also making him a director of the company. In addition to giving him symbolic support, it was forming an innovation-introducing leadership team that comprised this new member of the board and the president of Toyota, Taizo Ishida.

Ishida's role was particularly important because Ohno was such a junior member of the board and held such a low-ranking managerial position. He was not the equivalent of a chief operating officer (COO), as Sloan had been when he and du Pont formed an innovation-introducing leadership team in the early 1920s. In fact Kiichiro's cousin, Eiji, was the nearest equivalent of a COO and some might say that Eiji Toyoda formed a triple-leadership team with Ishida and Ohno.[38] However, it is simpler to view the team as a case of dual leadership, with Ishida playing the role of 'sponsoring' the innovating member of the team. As well as sponsoring Ohno, Ishida the president had the role of providing Toyota with CEO-level leadership. In doing so, he used rational methods that were also used by Ohno, such as the quantitative and strategic calculation described in the third section of this chapter. But Ishida used these methods in a financial and business context rather than a production and factory-floor context.[39]

More importantly, Ishida used rational methods that apparently were *not* used by Ohno, namely the two deliberative methods. Togo and Wartman provide several examples of Ishida engaging in diverse or institutionalized deliberation, such as allowing a colleague to win a policy argument with him or 'buying' policy proposals that were not such a 'hard sell' as might have been expected.[40] A key example of the latter was his acceptance of Eiji Toyoda's proposal for massive investment in new equipment, specifically 'a five-year plan for modernization of production equipment (1951–1955). The goal was to replace old equipment with new, to introduce conveyors and automation, and to expand production.'[41] Considering Ishida's reputation for prudent expenditure, Toyoda should have had a hard time selling this plan to him. But 'Ishida, who would not let a pencil be wasted, told Eiji he would obtain whatever money he needed for machinery'.[42]

Another key example of Ishida accepting policy proposals occurred near the end of his tenure, when he was in his seventies. This time it enabled Eiji Toyoda and Kiichiro's son Shoichiro Toyoda to introduce an ambitious Total Quality Control programme like the TQC programmes already being introduced by other Japanese firms.[43] During the 1950s Toyota had applied statistical quality-control methods to its production of military trucks; now these methods and other quality-control measures would be applied on a company-wide basis.[44] From June 1961 onwards all worksites sought to reduce 'defects in the processing of materials, claims from customers, and the need for touching-up after painting, welding and other processes'.[45]

Ishida retired from the post of president later in 1961 and became chairman of the corporation. During his time as president he had developed Toyota from a crisis-ridden company into a successful automobile corporation. In particular, Ishida and Ohno (and Eiji Toyoda) had achieved a near ten-fold increase in productivity as well as boosting production from fewer than 15,000 vehicles in 1951 to more than 200,000 in 1961.[46]

The new president of Toyota was Fukio Nakagawa. Like Ishida, he was neither a member of the Toyoda family nor an 'automobile man'. He had been in banking before joining Toyota and had been the executive vice-president for business affairs, not production, in the years before he was appointed president.[47] However, he formed a dual-leadership team with Toyota's production guru, Taiichi Ohno, and sponsored his next innovation-introducing task: extending the new production system to include Toyota's parts suppliers. Ohno's continuing contribution was given some formal recognition in 1964, when he was promoted to a more senior position on the board as now a 'managing' director of the company.[48]

Little has been written about Nakagawa's contribution to the corporation's development.[49] Yet in addition to sponsoring Ohno's supplier innovations, Nakagawa presided over a growth period in which Toyota became a car producer that also made trucks rather than vice versa. During the 1950s more than 70 per cent of its annual production had still been trucks rather than cars but now its new Corona and Corolla car models would lead a surge in car sales and production.[50] For example, in 1965 it expanded its exports to the US by including Corona cars as well as the usual Land Cruiser jeeps and five years later Toyota was second only to Volkswagen for export sales in the US market.[51] In 1966 the corporation at last achieved Kiichiro Toyoda's goal of being primarily a car maker: it produced 316,000 passenger cars versus 271,000 trucks and buses.[52] Furthermore, in the following year the advent of Toyota's popular Corolla car helped stimulate a huge increase in Japanese car-buying, which increased by a third to a total of well over a million passenger cars.[53] Toyota's annual production of passenger cars therefore continued to surge and in 1968 reached 659,000, enabling the corporation to pass the milestone of annually producing more than a million motor vehicles: cars, trucks, and buses.[54]

Nakagawa had not lived to see this milestone, however, as he had died in 1967 and been succeeded by Eiji Toyoda as the new president of Toyota.[55] Although Nakagawa's achievements seem to have been largely overlooked, this may be because they were very much a team effort by the corporation's management. For example, the innovation-introducing team that he had formed with Ohno had made good progress in its difficult task of extending Toyota's new production system to include its network of parts suppliers.

Furthermore, it was the previous innovation-introducing team that had provided the foundation for the achievements of the 1960s. For Ishida and Ohno's innovative production system had given Toyota crucial productivity and therefore pricing/profitability advantages over its competitors. Cusumano's classic *The Japanese Automobile Industry* pointed out twenty years later that in 1965 'each Toyota worker was producing 70 percent more vehicles per year than employees at General Motors, Ford, Chrysler or Nissan [the other major Japanese producer]'.[56] In addition, Toyota's innovative production system was already showing that it could be 'scaled up' to ever higher levels of production without losing its productivity advantages. It had already been applied to levels of production that were far higher than those of the era when it was being developed: in 1954, for example, vehicle production was less than 23,000 and car production less than 5,000.[57] By the mid-1960s it was delivering productivity advantages at levels of production that were twenty times higher. In fact the system would deliver dramatically *greater* productivity advantages as levels of production rose still further in the 1970s, when Toyota was annually producing millions of cars. Cusumano noted that as Toyota's production volumes rose five-fold 'between 1965 and the early 1980s, productivity tripled'.[58] The renowned flexibility of Toyota's production system includes its ability to deliver productivity advantages whether it is producing thousands or *millions* of things each year.

However, its flexibility was best seen when producing large numbers of things in small batches of different varieties. This is why Ohno subtitled his book *Beyond Large-Scale Production*. He was not suggesting that the Toyota system was appropriate for a small level or volume of production; he was pointing to the system's capacity for efficiently producing small-scale batches of different products. Togo and Wartman describe Toyota's production system as having 'the ability to "mass produce" cars by making numerous small lots of different vehicles'—an 'easily adaptable' production process.[59] And the next section shows that this adaptable, flexible system was developed through an 'adaptable' rational method: innovative adaptation, even if the method was by no means 'easily' applied in these circumstances.

Adapting To Japanese Conditions

The Toyota production system was developed through Ohno's innovative adaptations and in fact this may be the most extraordinary case of innovative adaptation in the history of manufacturing or any other kind of business. For example, the system developed into a complex combination that included several distinctive, innovative systems or processes 'in their own right', notably the just-in-time process, the continuous-flow process, and the Kanban information system. Furthermore, Ohno's new production system took decades to develop and to introduce throughout the manufacturing process. So a key factor was Ohno's persistence and his willingness to keep emphasizing innovation as a matter of personal preference, not as something that was forced upon him by the circumstances. 'It took 15 years or more to perfect the process techniques that made O[h]no and Toyota famous. Many engineers might have given up long before.'[60]

The Toyota case is extraordinary, too, because it is a landmark example of adapting to local conditions—in this case, the conditions of Japan's market and factory environment. Kiichiro Toyoda's pioneering production adaptation to Japanese conditions had been virtually foredoomed by the unfavourable economic and political circumstances of the late 1930s. Ohno was in a more favourable situation and made the most of it, even if it took him more than fifteen years to do so!

Ohno's adapting to local conditions is mentioned by Fujimoto in his evolutionary analysis of Toyota's production systems. He notes that Ohno had 'integrated elements of the Ford system in a domestic environment quite different from that of the United States'.[61] In fact Japan's domestic *market* environment was so different that when Toyota and other producers integrated Fordist elements, these had to be adapted to fit the local market environment. Cusumano pointed out that Japanese automobile producers 'had to modify American mass production techniques' as an evolutionary adaptation to a small market with very low volume but an increasing number of variations.

> [T]o a large degree, the changes Toyota made were 'evolutionary' adaptations to the circumstances surrounding the company and the domestic market.... Volume requirements were extremely low in Japan in the 1950s, yet the domestic market called for an increasing number of different car and truck models.[62]

The producers' modification of American Fordist techniques therefore seems to have been a forced adaptive response to Japan's market environment.

Toyota, however, adapted more innovatively than other Japanese producers, thanks to Ohno's ingenuity and perseverance.

In his book Ohno points to the connection between market requirements and the development of Toyota's innovative production system. The 'unsurpassed flexibility' of this production system—which he describes as the source of its strength—had arisen because the system had been 'conceived to produce small quantities of many types for the Japanese [market] environment'.[63] This flexibility may have been a forced adaptive response but it was such an innovative adaptation that it became a source of strength and in fact later gave Toyota a competitive advantage in the American and global car markets. As Fujimoto notes, when the new system 'was implemented in the 1940s and '50s, managers did not regard this emergent system as a way to outperform their Western rivals, but rather as an imperative for surviving in their small and fragmented market'.[64] However, the 'flexibility factors' in the new system 'became a source of its competitive advantage in subsequent years, when the market size and Toyota's productivity both grew rapidly and major automobile markets worldwide began to emphasize product variety'.[65]

Yet Ohno's adaptive response to market requirements was only a part of his innovative adaptation to local conditions. The other, less obvious part was his adaptive response to the domestic *factory* environment. This was an opportunistic rather than forced adaptive response and therefore, as Chapter 1 noted, was exploiting the environment's opportunities rather than meeting its requirements. In Ohno's case he was innovatively exploiting opportunities offered by features—distinctive features—of Japan's factory environment: (1) the work group and its teamwork, (2) the availability (potentially) of multi-skilled workers, (3) the cooperative, company-oriented labour unions, and (4) the firm's enterprise-family solidarity.

Ohno was by no means the only Japanese manager who innovatively exploited these opportunities. For example, some managers in other firms created the famous quality-control 'circles' as an innovative adaptation to the work-group feature of Japan's factory environment. As Cole pointed out, a distinctive feature of Japanese factories was that tasks were assigned:

> to the group, not its individual members, and that the responsibility for performing these tasks is shared by the entire group. . . . Japanese foremen are not only first-line supervisors who regulate job assignments, they are also the senior members of the work group. Members of the work group share a common career ultimately, and this serves to produce a highly integrated and solidary work group.[66]

In the 1950s–60s this feature offered managers the opportunity to develop an innovative method of quality control. Initially, Japanese industry had imported American quality-control concepts and techniques, as in the well-known case of Deming's lectures from 1950 onwards teaching Japanese firms such basic statistical quality-control methods as sampling inspection and control charts.[67] However, some Japanese managers began to develop a new method by requiring foremen and their work groups to learn and implement quality control and indeed to form quality-control study groups.[68] In the early 1960s, the study groups developed into workshop quality-control 'circles' that would be widely adopted in Japanese industry and would be imitated in America and other parts of the world.[69]

Toyota's production system, too, exploited the opportunities offered by the work-group feature of Japan's factory environment. For example, Ohno's book has a section headed 'Teamwork is Everything' and stressing the need for harmony and teamwork in a work group, as 'at work things do not necessarily run smoothly just because areas of responsibility have been assigned. Teamwork is essential'.[70] Similarly, Western exponents of his 'lean' production system included its use of '*teams* of multiskilled workers' as part of their definition of the system.[71]

Another distinctive feature of the factory environment was the fact that these were 'teams of *multiskilled* workers' who epitomized what Western experts term 'job diffuseness'. This is a workplace situation in which job descriptions 'tend to be extremely brief and general', workers are 'less conscious of job changes', and a worker may be carrying out 'a whole range of jobs'.[72] By the 1970s job diffuseness had been identified by Western experts as one of the distinctive and advantageous features of the Japanese factory environment.[73]

Multi-skilled workers and job diffuseness were also a key element of the continuous-flow process that Ohno had developed in the 1940s–50s as part of his new production system. A continuous production flow already existed on Toyota's final-assembly line and Ohno's innovation was to develop a similarly continuous flow in other areas, such as machine-shop production, and eventually create a continuous flow throughout the whole car-manufacturing process. His book's example of continuous flow describes it as 'putting a flow into the manufacturing process. In the past, lathes were located in the lathe area, and milling machines in the milling area. Now, we place a lathe, a milling machine, and a drilling machine in the actual sequence of the manufacturing processing' and so for workers 'this means shifting from being *single-skilled* to becoming *multi-skilled*'.[74] The workers must be multi-skilled because one of the productivity advantages of this continuous flow is that it 'directly reduces the number of workers' by reducing specialization: 'instead of having one worker per machine, one worker oversees many machines or, more accurately, one worker operates many processes'.[75]

But clearly in this case, his first production innovation, Ohno was exploiting the opportunity to *shift* from single-skilled to multi-skilled workers. In other words, a distinctive feature of Japan's factory environment in these pioneering years was that managers could *potentially* use multi-skilled rather than single-skilled workers. Exploiting the opportunity offered by this feature was not easy, though, as Ohno discovered when he tried to introduce the continuous-flow innovation. Furthermore, he succeeded largely because he exploited the opportunities offered by another distinctive feature, namely Japan's company-based labour unions, which was certainly the most significant feature of Japan's factory environment.

Ohno developed his continuous-flow innovation in the late 1940s as an extension of his duties as a machine-shop manager at Toyota's main plant. When he moved from experimental stage to implementation stage, however, he ran into resistance from the machine shop's skilled craftsmen, who had always operated a single lathe or other specialized machine. 'Our craftsmen did not like the new arrangement requiring them to function as multi-skilled operators' overseeing 'many machines in different processes'.[76] His book goes on to describe the situation in positive terms or as a case of all's well that ends well. Apparently, 'the transition from the single- to the multi-skilled operator went relatively smoothly although there was initial resistance from the craftsmen'.[77] But Cusumano presents a rather different picture of events, based partly on his interview with an elderly Ohno:

> The [continuous-flow] reforms in the machine shop were one of the main issues in the 1950 strike. 'Had I faced the Japan National Railways union or an American union,' Ohno mused, 'I might have been murdered.' As it turned out, he was able to control the Toyota union, partly because management threatened to fire dissident workers, which it did in 1950, and partly because he was personally close to the union leaders.[78]

Indeed Ohno 'considered his success in controlling the union to have been the most important advantage Toyota gained over its domestic and foreign competitors' and he claimed that its main domestic competitor, Nissan, had been hindered in its 'attempt to match Toyota in productivity' because the union had 'challenged management policies'.[79]

Ohno's book does not make such sweeping claims but it acknowledges that the labour-union factor was crucial in this case and in the overall development of Toyota's production system. His machine shop's transition to continuous flow had gone relatively smoothly 'because we lacked function-oriented unions like those in Europe and the United States'; in the United States 'this system could not be implemented easily' because 'there is a union for each job function with many unions in each company'.[80]

In contrast, Japan's labour unions were company-oriented, not function-oriented or even industry-oriented. In fact, each labour union was based on the company which employed its members, such as Toyota or Nissan, and included the company's white-collar employees as well as its blue-collar workers.[81] For example, Ohno had served as a full-time union official in 1947 even though he was a production engineer with management experience and had just been promoted to the position of machine-shop manager.[82] Probably no other well-known business leader has ever served as an elected union official! Probably, too, this was why in later years he was personally close to Toyota's union leaders and was so successful in winning the union's cooperation with his production innovations. When Cusumano noted how Japanese unions cooperated with management to increase productivity, he pointed to Toyota as 'the best example of what managers were able to achieve' with such a cooperative work force.[83]

Ohno clearly took full advantage of the opportunities offered by this distinctive feature of Japan's factory environment. But in his book he was careful to say that the cooperativeness of Japanese unions did not mean that they were 'weaker than their American and European counterparts. Much of the difference lies in history and culture.'[84] Certainly there were historical and cultural differences as well as the basic difference in orientation and membership. In the 1920s–30s Japan's emerging labour-union movement had been channelled into an 'enterprise union' mould 'where a union represented the workers of only a single factory or company'.[85] In addition, the unions had been mostly confined to small and medium-sized firms, as the large firms had established new cultural and institutional barriers to unionization.

These large companies had pioneered a version of employer paternalism that incorporated the familial aspects of Japan's traditional culture. The new version was similar to Japan's prevailing paternalist ideal of industrial relations, with its reciprocal obligations of manager-employer's affectionate care and worker-employee's deference and self-sacrifice. Now, however, these reciprocal obligations were based upon the principle that managers and workers were members of the same business-enterprise 'family'. The new ideal of *jigyō ikka* (enterprise family) and 'familial harmony in the firm' was also supported by material benefits, such as free or low-cost nurseries, health clinics, and recreational facilities.[86] The key benefits, however, were the permanent employment (no lay-offs or redundancies) for regular male workers and the *nenkō* (length of service) system for determining individuals' wages and promotions within the enterprise family.[87] These benefits created a compelling institutional context for the enterprise-family culture, which was much more credible and appealing in a context of job and promotion security.

This whole cultural and institutional package was revived by large firms after the Second World War as part of their strategy for dealing with the labour movement. The post-war rebirth of the union movement was so successful that even large firms had to accept unionization but this was channelled into the pre-war mould of company-based unions, thanks largely to the revival of the pre-war package of cultural themes and institutional supports.[88]

The permanent-employment and *nenkō* systems became a standard feature of large firms, who also provided their workers with a variety of other benefits, such as leisure activities and housing assistance.[89] Similarly, there was a revival of familial paternalism and the notion of enterprise-family solidarity. Some of its trappings, such as company songs and badges, were soon recognized internationally as characteristic of Japanese industry.[90] Like other large firms, Toyota had adopted this institutional-cultural package and indeed Cusumano argued that Ohno's impact confirmed that individuals could 'make an enormous contribution even in a large Japanese firm that prided itself on maintaining a "family" atmosphere'.[91]

Ohno made such an enormous contribution, however, because he exploited the opportunities offered by this familial atmosphere—and any other thing that produced a cooperative work force. That was the precondition for developing and introducing an innovative new production system. The pioneering Toyota founder Kiichiro Toyoda had been well aware that changing 'the automobile production process' would require a factory atmosphere 'of mutual trust and cooperation. Without this milieu, the just-in-time production process would never be realized.'[92] When Ohno went on to realize Kiichiro Toyoda's vision of just-in-time production, it was by exploiting the opportunities offered by this atmosphere of cooperation—which was perhaps the most important feature of the local, Japanese conditions.

Just-In-Time, 'Lean' Production

To realize this vision of just-in-time production Ohno also had to develop it into a more comprehensive system of production. He had already created a continuous flow in machine-shop production, but much more would be required in the years ahead. He had to create a new information system and to extend processes 'backward' to include the firm's network of parts suppliers.

More fundamentally, he had to adopt a new perspective on production. His book sums up just-in-time production as having 'the *right* parts needed in assembly reach the assembly line at [just] the *time* they are needed and only in the *amount* needed' and therefore, in conjunction with continuous-flow production, enabling a firm to 'approach zero inventory'.[93] But it also involved a new perspective on production. It meant looking at the production flow 'in *reverse*: a later process goes to an earlier process to pick up only the right part in the quantity needed at the exact time needed'.[94] In fact Ohno's working model of this production flow was the American-style supermarket. 'The later process (customer) goes to the earlier process (supermarket) to acquire the required parts (commodities) at the time and in the quantity needed. The earlier process immediately produces the quantity just taken (restocking the shelves).'[95]

However, Ohno's most obvious innovation was the new information system that he created for just-in-time production. Indeed, his creation became so famous that Toyota's whole production system was often described by outsiders as 'the *kanban* system'.[96] The Kanban (signboard) was a means of communicating information about what parts and production were required to fulfil just-in-time requirements. Each Kanban was simply a rectangular piece of paper in a vinyl envelope that carried information about the pickup, transfer, and production of parts: it specified what part was required, how many were required and when they would be required.[97] The relatively simple individual Kanban were part of a complex system in which, for example, the number of required Kanban was calculated by using an algebraic formula $D(Tw + Tp)(1 + N)$: the D was demand (units per period), Tw the waiting time for Kanban, Tp process time, and N a policy variable.[98] The Kanban system 'pulled' parts and work-in-progress through the assembly line, while comparable computer-controlled systems tended to 'push' them through.[99] Even when improved computer systems became available in the 1970s, Ohno preferred to stick with the Kanban not only because the high-tech alternative was expensive but also because 'the real world doesn't always go according to plan' and the Kanban could more readily adjust to unplanned events.[100]

The Kanban system had been introduced in a similar way to the introduction of just-in-time production processes. In the mid-1950s Ohno had introduced Kanban on particular production lines, in 1959 at the new Motomachi plant, and in 1962 at a company-wide level.[101] The next step would be to extend the Kanban system to Toyota's parts suppliers as part of the wider move to include them within the firm's new production system.

Including its parts suppliers within the new production system was essential because they contributed so much to the firm's manufacturing process. As with any other modern automobile producer, the final-assembly lines that assembled components into automobiles were only a small part of the total manufacturing process. 'The bulk of the process involves engineering and fabricating more than 10,000 discrete parts and assembling these into perhaps 100 major components'—such as engines and suspensions—which are in effect the raw material of the final-assembly lines.[102] Like any other modern automobile producer, Toyota could either produce these components in-house, through divisions or subsidiaries of the company, or have them manufactured by independent supplier firms that specialize in particular parts. The usual approach to parts procurement has been a mixture of in-house and out-sourced manufacturing. For example, Sloan's General Motors made about 70 per cent of its parts in-house and procured the other 30 per cent from independent supplier firms.[103]

Instead of a mixture of in-house and out-sourced, Toyota preferred outsourcing to suppliers who were a mixture of independent firm and Toyota subsidiary. As noted earlier, this approach was adopted at the end of the 1930s as an innovative adaptation to wartime conditions. It was developed further in the 1950s–60s, though, when Toyota integrated its supplier firms into a two-tiered cooperative alliance that avoided both (1) the bureaucratic tendencies of in-house manufacturing and (2) the market problems of out-sourcing to independent suppliers.[104] The first tier of suppliers developed and made major component parts for Toyota automobiles. In addition, it created the second tier of suppliers, which were a multitude of small firms that supplied the first tier with parts for their Toyota components. These second-tier suppliers were organized into cooperative, information-sharing associations. The first-tier supplier firms, however, were integrated with one another and with Toyota through cross-holding of shares as well as through cooperation in technical matters and other areas. Toyota would even lend money or personnel to first-tier suppliers who were installing new machinery or experiencing workload surges.

The strong ties between Toyota and its suppliers reduced the risks involved in being so dependent upon their contribution to the production process. They did much of the value-adding work and employed much of the work force required to manufacture a Toyota automobile. Even when Toyota became the world's third-largest car producer, its assembly plants were responsible for less than a third of the value-adding work and were employing a work force of fewer than forty thousand.[105]

However, this dependence upon parts-supplying firms meant of course that they had to be included within Ohno's just-in-time production process. They would have to deliver their parts 'just in time' so that Toyota's assembly plants experienced neither a build-up of unused parts nor a shortage of the parts needed to keep production flowing. Although Ohno realized that the suppliers would play a big role in the new production system, he waited until after it had been fully developed and introduced company-wide before he began including suppliers within the system's just-in-time processes and Kanban information system.[106]

> Experiments were always carried out at a plant within the company that did not deal with parts ordered from the outside. The idea was to exhaust the new system's problems within the company first. In 1963, we started handling the delivery of the parts ordered from outside. It took nearly 20 years.[107]

One of the reasons why it took so long was simply the suppliers' problems with the new system. For example, Ohno acknowledges that 'the cooperating firms' initially viewed the Kanban system as 'troublesome'.[108] But there were also structural reasons, such as the sheer number of supplier firms. By the end of the twenty-year introduction period there were some 200 firms in the first tier of suppliers and some 5,000 in the second tier.[109] Furthermore, throughout this period Toyota was expanding production at a rapid rate and therefore asking its suppliers to boost production at the same time as they were introducing just-in-time and Kanban. Indeed when Ohno began extending the system to suppliers in the mid-1960s, Toyota was beginning a surge in car production that quadrupled annual production from less than 75,000 in 1962 to more than 316,000 in 1966.[110]

In the midst of this surge in production, suppliers were depending on Toyota to reduce *fluctuations* in its assembly lines' flow of production. As Ohno's book explains, if a final-assembly stage uses parts 'unevenly', its fluctuating requests for parts will force the parts-producing stages to carry 'extra manpower and equipment' to accommodate these fluctuations, and the 'greater the fluctuation in quantity picked up [by final assembly], the more excess capacity is required by the earlier [parts-producing] process'.[111] His book acknowledges, too, that fluctuations in Toyota's production flow affected 'the cooperating firms *outside* Toyota *using kanban*' because their parts production was tied to and synchronized with the corporation's assembly lines.[112] As these suppliers were providing Toyota with the earliest stages in its production system, they fully deserved the effort Ohno made to reduce fluctuations in the assembly plants' flow of production.

Ohno's goal was 'production levelling' that would ideally result in 'zero fluctuation' at the final-assembly stage of production.[113] He levelled out production by such rational means as minimizing the size of each batch-lot. For example, an assembly line producing three different models of a car design might assemble only one car per model batch-lot: 'one sedan, one hardtop, then a sedan, then a wagon, and so on. This way, the lot size and fluctuation in production can be minimized.'[114] However, such small batch lots required a drastic reduction in the time required to change over and set up the machinery required for each particular batch lot. These reductions were accomplished by replacing large stamping presses with smaller, easier-to-change machines, 'using rollers or carts to move dies or other fixtures', adopting simple die-change techniques and of course mobilizing the work force.[115] Ohno's book describes how workers were trained to reduce changeover and set-up times and how their 'desire to achieve the new system intensified' so much that set-up times were reduced to just fifteen minutes in the 1950s and to merely three minutes in the 1960s.[116]

Their achievements had beneficial effects in other areas, too, such as reducing the need to invest in new equipment and plant. Cusumano noted that their rapid changes 'made it economical to produce different models on one assembly line and saved Toyota from having to invest in additional facilities'.[117] This is just one of many examples of the cost-saving that led Womack and others to say that 'lean' production was pioneered by Toyota's production system. He and other exponents of 'leanness' described Toyota's system as lean production because 'it *uses less of everything* compared with mass production', notably its use of 'half the human effort in the factory' and its ability to keep 'far less than half the needed inventory on site'.[118]

When Toyota's system is viewed from a lean-production perspective, it is clear that Ohno used other rational methods in addition to emphasizing innovative adaptation. He used the calculative methods, quantitative and strategic calculation, and even employed a cost-reducing *grand* strategy. Indeed his production innovations can be seen as at least partly an extension of this grand strategy and particularly its aim of eliminating all forms of waste in the production process.

Ohno's cost-reducing strategy focused on production costs and aimed to reduce them by eliminating waste in production processes. According to his book, he was committed to the 'absolute' elimination of waste, which he defined as eliminating anything that only increases cost without adding value, such as 'excess people, inventory, and equipment'.[119] His more complete list of forms of waste included: overproduction, time on hand (waiting), inventory (stock on hand), waste in transportation, waste in processing, waste in movement and, last but not least, making defective products.[120] Cusumano confirms that Ohno 'and his assistants, beginning in 1948, subjected every process, machine, and worker to rigorous analyses to eliminate "waste"— which they defined as anything that did not contribute to "value added"'.[121]

As for *how to* eliminate this waste, Ohno's many production innovations obviously helped eliminate excess inventory and 'excess people'. For instance, the previous section showed how his machine-shop experiment with continuous flow had replaced single-skilled machinists with a smaller number of multi-skilled operators. Ohno had continued to take a calculated approach to labour efficiency, as when his book argues that the term 'using fewer workers' is more accurate than 'labour-saving' because saving the labour of 0.9 of a worker will still leave the labour cost of paying wages to a worker to contribute the remaining 0.1.[122]

Clearly Ohno used quantitative as well as strategic calculation to enhance Toyota. Whether reducing labour costs, levelling production or operating the Kanban system, he was constantly using quantitative calculation. For example, his book contains a humorous anecdote about calculating how many extra workers would be needed to double production of engines for the Corolla car.[123]

As for rapid adaptation, his book does not describe him using this rational method but it advocates adaptive responses that are so rapid that they are analogous to reflexes. They are fine-tuning adaptive responses that are virtually instantaneous and do not involve the firm's leader or managers: firms 'should have reflexes that can respond instantly and smoothly to small changes' and indeed the larger the business, 'the better reflexes it needs'.[124] This seems similar to the autopilot-like controls that Sloan instilled in General

Motors and that were discussed in Chapter 2. But those controls were based on quantitative information, not on human judgement. Ohno describes reflex-like adaptive responses as 'making judgements autonomously' and he advocates that they be decentralized to the lowest possible level.[125]

Toyotaism Versus Fordism

Unlike the Chapter 2 section on Sloanism versus Fordism, this section's contrast of Toyotaism and Fordism is focused on production—on the assembly line and the factory floor. It is a contrast between the greatest *technical* innovation and the greatest innovative *adaptation to local conditions*, specifically to Japanese conditions. As discussed earlier, Toyotaism arose through a series of innovative adaptations to the requirements and opportunities presented by Japanese market and factory conditions. Ohno's book refers to a 'uniquely Japanese production system' and to Toyotaism originating in the 1930s in the thinking of Kiichiro Toyoda.[126] But Toyotaism as a large-scale form of car production did not emerge until the 1950s–60s and has always been an alternative to Fordism, not its opposite or antithesis. 'It is a myth that the Toyota system is a unique antithesis of the Ford system' asserts Fujimoto and he argues instead that Toyota's leaders 'adopted various elements of the Ford system selectively and in unbundled forms and hybridized them with their indigenous system and original ideas'.[127]

This may explain why Ohno's book has such a positive attitude towards Henry Ford and protectively disassociates him from the failings of 'the Ford system' of production. For example, Ford's system apparently was 'never intended to cause workers to work harder and harder, to feel driven by their machines and alienated from their work'.[128] But of course whatever Ford may have intended, he certainly did not abandon or modify his assembly-line system when he discovered how much his workers hated their jobs. His response was instead to offer increased incentives that would reduce the assembly line's high labour turnover—he offered workers in 1914 the unprecedented wage of $5-a-day.[129]

It is true that Ford was ahead of his time in his employment policies, even if for typically Fordist reasons. A recent biographer notes that Ford not only sought a 'clean, light and airy' workplace but also had 'highly enlightened employment policies concerning the handicapped, blacks, ethnic groups, women, and even ex-criminals'.[130] For example, the range of opportunities offered to African-American workers seems a generation ahead of its time. By 1917 Ford had become 'the industry's leading employer of African Americans, many of them on the highly paid assembly lines, and some in supervising positions with the authority—nearly unique in that place and time—to fire white workers'.[131] However, Ford's employment policies were motivated by a rational concern for profit-making productivity. He would characterize them as 'just good business' because through these policies 'he got good, productive, and motivated workers'.[132]

So it is not surprising that Ford did not abandon or modify his productive assembly-line system and its tedious work of 'endless repetition of one single task'.[133] More than fifty years after he created it, Ford's assembly line was still being seen as a symbol of the modern world's combination of efficiency and tedium. According to Beynon, Ford had created 'one of the most powerful images of the twentieth century. An image that combined "efficiency" with "tedium": the twin pillars of modern life.'[134]

In contrast, Toyota's assembly line was both more efficient and *less tedious* than Ford's creation. In particular, Toyota workers were multi-skilled generalists, not specialists confined to a single narrow task, and they were members of small work groups that operated as socially interacting teams. Even Toyota's use of small batch lots, with its rapid change-overs and set-ups, reduced the tedium of working on the assembly line. Cusumano pointed out that as smaller batch lots 'lessened the monotony of assembly work', they also 'improved quality control'.[135] Reciprocally, quality-control roles introduced in the 1960s lessened the monotony by giving workers an additional, less repetitive task and responsibility. In addition to the quality-control circles, there was the rule that any worker had the right and obligation to stop the assembly line if a quality problem emerged. Line-stopping quality control was described by Cole as a policy partly designed 'to encourage workers to believe they drove the conveyor belt, as opposed to being driven by it'.[136] But Ohno described line-stopping in purely quality-control terms, as allowing a quality problem to be investigated at the assembly-line stage, forcing everyone to be aware of the problem and ensuring that countermeasures were taken to prevent the problem recurring.[137]

Similarly, his book's contrast between the large Fordist and small Toyota batch lots does not refer to workers' experiences and instead focuses on the market and economic implications. The Japanese market's demands for many types of cars in small quantities is contrasted with the American market's demand for a few types in large quantities.[138] And Ohno even makes some claim for the superiority of the Toyota system: it 'is better suited to periods of low growth' or, in other words, is better suited than Fordism to the low-growth economies of the 1970s.[139] Yet he then claims that if Henry Ford 'were still alive, he would be headed in the same direction as Toyota,' because 'I believe Ford was a born rationalist'.[140] Presumably Ohno believed that Ford, like any rational business leader, would be adapting to the 1970s low-growth economic environment.

Again, however, Ohno was too generous in his assessment of Henry Ford's motives and actions. For the Ford Motor Company responded to the negative and low growth of the Great Depression by simply reducing the labour costs of its existing system of production. As late as 1938, the company was employing only 11,000 of its work force of nearly 90,000 and was enforcing a notorious speed-up: production quotas were being ratcheted upwards and workers were being closely monitored for 'even the slightest infraction of work rules'.[141]

Furthermore, Ford's lack of adaptability had been a key factor in his 1920s defeat by Sloan's General Motors. Ohno's book acknowledges that Sloanism represented a new era in the American car industry. He refers to *My Years with General Motors*, cites its analysis of the market changes that occurred in the 1920s, and notes that Sloan exploited these changes in the marketplace by offering an increasing number of different models.[142] Yet Ohno has little to say about the more flexible production methods that enabled General Motors to offer a diverse range of five car lines and eighty-five models and to establish the annual model change as another new feature of the American automobile market. In his view the Fordist production system 'was not modified to any great extent' by Sloanism and 'became deeply rooted' in the American automobile industry.[143]

So when Toyota began exporting cars to America, it was entering a market that had been based on Fordism for more than a generation. What is more, Toyotaism had not yet defeated Fordist remnants in its own domestic car market. According to Cusumano, 'not until after the 1973 oil shock did Nissan and other firms in the Japanese automobile industry attempt to match Toyota in lowering inventories' and as late as 1980 'Honda and Isuzu had yet to impose effective controls on inventory and production'.[144] Toyota was therefore still the standard-bearer of just-in-time production when Japanese car producers began to make inroads in the American market in the 1970s.

However, this export aspect of Toyotaism versus Fordism was not discussed in Ohno's 1978 book. This is probably because the expansion of Japanese exports had not involved direct, head-to-head competition between the two systems. Although Japan-to-US vehicle exports grew from some 500,000 to over 2 million in the 1970s, Fujimoto notes that there was still 'a fairly clear division of market territories between U.S. makers, who were producing and selling large American cars, and Japanese makers, who were exporting small cars. The small-car segment grew typically as a second car for American households and partly as a growing preference by young baby boomers for small economical cars.'[145]

The watershed came at the end of the 1970s and was largely due to the international oil crisis. The problems with petrol supplies and prices led to more US consumers buying smaller, more economical cars, which boosted sales by Toyota and other Japanese car exporters.[146] More importantly, the crisis led to US car producers focusing on small and medium-sized cars and therefore beginning direct, head-to-head competition with Japanese imports.

'Many of the new American models had to compete directly with the Japanese small cars' and Fujimoto also points out that 'the Japanese advantages in productivity was first recognized at this time by some American researchers and practitioners'.[147] These productivity advantages would later be seen as not simply 'Japanese' but as specifically Toyotaist advantages developed and introduced by Taiichi Ohno. By the end of the 1980s, Womack and his co-authors were writing their book on Toyota's 'lean' production, which would be described in the book's subtitling as a 'secret weapon in the global auto wars'.

In 1983 Toyotaism finally established a production beachhead in Fordist America. Toyota entered a joint-venture arrangement with General Motors to build Toyota cars at the latter's recently closed plant in Fremont, California.[148] As Togo and Wartman relate, Toyota successfully reorganized its American auto workers into Toyotaist teams:

> Instead of having rigid job classifications, workers would be organized into five- to ten-man teams. Each team member would be trained in every job the team performed and would rotate among them. In addition to installing parts, they would perform their own maintenance, quality inspections, and machine set ups.[149]

Ohno's book had predicted that the Toyota system would be applied successfully in America and would have a competitive advantage over 'the American system' of mass production and quantity sales, which 'generates unnecessary losses in pursuit of quantity and speed'.[150] However, Toyota would not have a complete, parts-to-final-assembly system in place until the 1990s and so there was plenty of time for American competitors to imitate Toyotaism's advantages.[151] In fact by 1989 the Ford Motor Company had imitated them so successfully that American exponents of lean production considered Ford's plants to be 'now practically as lean' as the average Japanese assembly plant in America.[152]

This might be viewed as the ultimate victory of Toyotaism over Fordism, which Ohno lived to see before his death in 1990. Through innovative adaptation to Japanese conditions he had both enhanced the Toyota Motor Corporation and created a Toyotaism whose global influence upon the car industry and many other industries has been comparable to the influence of Fordism and Sloanism. Since then no new 'ism' has been as influential as these three landmark breakthroughs.

4

McDonald's: Kroc's *Grinding It Out*

Ray Kroc's autobiographical *Grinding It Out: The Making of McDonald's* was published in 1977, the year that he became the semi-retired senior, founding chairman of the McDonald's corporation. Unlike Sloan and Ohno, Kroc had *established*, not merely enhanced, a corporation that would become nationally and globally iconic. He had founded the firm more than twenty years earlier and had developed it into the largest and most famous fast-food chain in America. McDonald's was so well known that a year before Kroc's death in 1984 a sociologist used the term McDonaldization to characterize 'the ration-alization process' that was 'sweeping through society'.[1] What is more, Kroc had instituted a global expansion that would make McDonald's a symbol of globalization. For example, in the 1990s a political scientist applied the label McWorld to the cultural effect of globalized commerce and consumer prod-ucts.[2] McDonald's was clearly becoming a globally as well as nationally iconic corporation.

But Kroc's personal fame had declined and would not be restored until the 2010s. The vintage year of the Kroc revival was 2016. Cinematically, there was the film *The Founder*, with Michael Keaton starring as Ray Kroc. Biographically, there was the publication of Napoli's portrait of Ray and his remarkably philanthropic widow Joan: *Ray & Joan: The Man Who Made the McDonald's Fortune and the Woman Who Gave It All Away*.[3] Autobiographically, there was a third, reissued edition of Kroc's *Grinding It Out*. His book, like Sloan's and Ohno's autobiographical writings, is still in print more than thirty years after it was written.[4]

Although Kroc's book is more personally autobiographical than Sloan's or Ohno's, it provides a compelling leader's-eye view of how he established a now globally iconic corporation. Like Sloan, he used all six of the set of appropriate corporation-developing rational methods. And again like Sloan, he emphasized innovative adaptation, strategic (marketing) calculation and a deliberative method, which in this case was diverse rather than institutional-ized deliberation. Kroc emphasized diverse deliberation as a matter of personal preference but his use or emphasizing of the other five methods was due to the circumstances he faced in developing his start-up venture into a business corporation.

He was also facing difficult personal circumstances. Something other than rationality was required for a small-business seller of milk-shake machines to start a fast-food venture late in his business career and not in good health. When the McDonald's venture began in 1954:

> I was a battle-scarred veteran of the business wars, but I was still eager to go into action. I was 52 years old. I had diabetes and incipient arthritis. I had lost my gall bladder and part of my thyroid gland in earlier operations. But I was convinced that the best was ahead of me.[5]

His almost irrational confidence would prove to be justified when his new venture developed into a firm that led and modernized the fast-food industry.

For instance, McDonald's would pioneer the mass production of fast-food items and particularly hamburgers. Watson labelled this a Fordist method of food production, with hamburgers 'produced in assembly-line fashion', and Kroc himself described it in a Fordist or indeed Ohno-like manner: the smoking griddle 'was the vital passage in our assembly line and the product had to flow through it smoothly or the whole plant would falter'.[6] As Watson noted, McDonald's went on to pioneer the automation of fast-food production, as when it installed computers that automatically adjusted cooking time and temperatures.[7]

Kroc's success was largely due, however, to his *administrative* pioneering and in that sense he is a fast-food version of Sloan rather than Ford or Ohno. The franchising system developed by Kroc was a particularly important administrative innovation. Anderson noted in the posthumous second edition of *Grinding It Out* that Kroc's greatest contribution was 'creating the McDonald's franchising system', which 'brought entrepreneurs into a structure that both forced them to conform to high standards of quality and service and freed them to operate as independent business people'.[8]

However, his franchising system was 'selling' a fast-food operation that was *not* a Kroc innovation. As his book acknowledges, the McDonald brothers had developed this innovative operation several years before Kroc began to franchise it. He notes how Mac (Maurice) and Dick (Richard) McDonald had pioneered a new kind of drive-in fast-food operation, which sold only hamburgers, french fries and beverages and, more importantly, prepared them 'on an assembly line basis'.[9] Kroc acquired this innovation through his 1954 licensing agreement with the McDonald brothers, which also included their McDonald's brand name, their golden-arches marketing symbol and their marketing strategy of offering a low-price, 15-cent hamburger.[10] The brothers licensed Kroc to franchise this whole 'package' in return for them receiving a share of the service-fee royalties paid to Kroc's firm by his franchisees. But although he had acquired a brilliant fast-food operation, Kroc still faced the problem of selling the operation to potential franchisees and simply earning enough money to keep his new firm afloat.

His innovative franchising system would be the key to his success and enabled him to develop this start-up venture into a business corporation. The first section of the chapter will show how Kroc created his franchising system by emphasizing innovative adaptation and combining it with rapid adaptation. The second section of the chapter will describe how he emphasized strategic calculation in his marketing and how he used quantitative calculation, especially in relation to the revenue-earning expertise of his 'numbers man Harry Sonneborn'. The third section will describe Kroc's use of often informally institutionalized deliberation and will highlight his distinctive, personally preferred emphasis on diverse deliberation.

The final section of the chapter will explore the international joint-venture system that he pioneered in the last stages of his leadership of McDonald's. This joint-venture system enabled his corporation's formula to be adapted to different cultures and markets around the globe. McDonald's had already expanded into more than twenty countries by the time his book appeared; by the end of the century McDonald's could be found in more than a hundred countries and was a truly global fast-food empire.

Kroc has been called an 'instinctive' leader but he is better described as a rational leader.[11] For he used the appropriate rational methods of developing a corporation and used them capably enough to inspire his employee-followers with rational confidence. It is true, however, that he also used a non-rational method—his visionary imagination. Kroc proudly acknowledged: 'I've been dreaming all my life.'[12] This was not a method that Sloan or Ohno included among their means of enhancing a corporation but it may be one of the appropriate methods of *establishing* an iconic corporation.

Adaptively Building a Fast-Food Empire

Although this section will focus on Kroc's emphasizing of innovative adaptation, he also used the other adaptive method—rapid adaptation. For example, his book mentions the rapid adaptive response to early indications in the 1960s that the market for drive-in eating was declining. His response was 'to experiment with larger buildings and inside seating' and then introduce a sit-down form of McDonald's restaurant.[13] But Kroc's most significant use of rapid adaptation was when he developed his franchising system through a *combination* of rapid and innovative adaptation.

Kroc developed his franchising system by emphasizing innovative adaptation, like Sloan and Ohno, but he *rapidly* as well as innovatively developed this system in the second half of the 1950s. The rapidity of Kroc's adaptation is in marked contrast to Ohno's fifteen years of dogged persistence or to the time that it took for Sloan to implement his preconceived Organization Study plan. Kroc rapidly developed his complex new franchising system through a series of innovative adaptations that were not pre-planned and often followed on from one another or developed in unforeseen ways.

This rapid series of innovations was opportunistically adapting to the fast-food franchising environment of 1950s America. Kroc took full advantage of the opportunities that it offered but, unlike Ohno, he was not adapting to local conditions; he was adapting to a historical interlude in the 1950s that had great potential for developing fast-food franchises. Napoli points out that by then franchising was an idea whose time had come. She notes that the 'franchise model was deployed to distribute all manner of goods and services', from ice cream to motel accommodation, and it had advantages for consumers as well as potential franchisees:

> Franchise ownership was a compelling conceit for the would-be businessman (and it was, more often than not, a man) industrious enough to want more than to punch a clock, but not necessarily confident enough or inventive enough (or wealthy enough) to launch a business entirely from scratch. Consumers were attracted to them for different reasons. As trains, then roads, broke down geographic barriers and allowed for seamless flow from one community to another, the public began to put stock in the cachet of a recognizable brand, trumping the unreliable unknown of a local merchant.[14]

But the franchising of fast-food products was still in its early stages. Kroc notes in his book that 'in the late fifties we didn't have the proliferation of franchise operations and the fierce competition for commercial fringe property that developed in the course of the next twenty years'.[15]

There was room for Kroc to innovate in many different ways and in fact during these years he developed a franchising system with as many innovative aspects as Ohno's production system.[16] For example, he decided not to become a parts supplier (of beef, buns, potatoes, and so forth) to his franchisees but instead would help them deal with suppliers and would help the *suppliers* raise their quality standards, lower their costs, and reduce the prices they charged his franchisees. Another early decision of Kroc's was that his firm would build the restaurants that it franchised: it would offer franchisees not just the rights to a McDonald's operation but also a ready-to-go McDonald's restaurant. Several years later Kroc went a step further by deciding to create a network of company-owned restaurants and indeed eventually almost a third of the McDonald's chain of restaurants were owned and operated by the company rather than franchisees. Kroc could afford to develop these company-owned restaurants because his franchising system also included innovative financial arrangements, the leasing arrangements discussed later in this chapter, which provided his firm with mortgage financing and with much-needed additional franchising revenue.

However, the most well-known aspects of Kroc's franchising system were associated with his early marketing strategy of pioneering a quality-oriented fast-food chain. As Napoli notes, this meant creating 'a consistent dining experience', which was based upon what Kroc viewed as high-quality food:

> We wanted to build a restaurant system that would be known for food of *consistently high quality* and methods of preparation. Our aim, of course, was to ensure repeat business based on *the system's reputation* rather than on the quality of a single store or operator. This would require a continuing program of educating and assisting operators and a constant review of their performance.[17]

It would also require a degree of centralization that had never been seen before in any fast-food franchising system.

For example, the constant review of operators' performance would require the corporation to supervise the franchisees' operation of their restaurants. Love's *McDonald's: Behind the Arches* notes that Kroc 'introduced a level of supervision that was unknown in the fast-food industry'.[18] In the late 1950s McDonald's began to develop a corps of inspectors who would ensure that the restaurants were meeting the chain's quality standards for service and cleanliness as well as for food and methods of preparation. The inspectorate comprised dozens and eventually hundreds of field representatives, the field consultants, each of whom visited a group of twenty or more restaurants several times a year. Although initially intended to be advisors, the field consultants evolved into 'inspectors of system quality' who reviewed franchisees' performance in terms of their compliance with the corporation's operating standards.[19]

There was also a more positive form of reviewing performance—learning from the franchisees' experience. McDonald's sought to document 'all the knowledge that it was gaining from the collective operating experience of its franchisees. While other chains virtually ignored franchisees once their stores were opened, McDonald's studied everything they did, trying to learn what worked and what did not.'[20] This knowledge was then circulated throughout the chain and passed on to new franchisees through the corporation's impressive programme of educating franchisees and helping to train their staff.

Indeed Kroc's education and training programme was yet another innovative aspect of his franchising system. Love points out that no other fast-food chain 'had even thought of opening a full-time training center' until Kroc opened a Hamburger University that awarded a Bachelor of Hamburgerology, with a minor in french fries.[21] Hamburger University started life in 1961 as merely a basement lecture room but even the inaugural class was awarded a B.H. degree, and by the 1970s Kroc could boast that HU had 'a handsome campus with classrooms equipped with the latest teaching aids' and offering an advanced operations course that every new franchisee attended.[22]

In addition, franchisees were provided with an impressive operations manual as a reference work and to help them train their restaurant staff. As early as 1958 there was a 75-page manual and, not long afterwards, a much larger version seemed aimed at converting restaurant operations into a management science.[23] By the post-Kroc era, it had become a 600-page *Operations and Training Manual* that claimed to be the fruit of much experience and research and was up-dated by regular bulletins from the corporation to its franchisees.[24]

Kroc's franchising system therefore involved unprecedented regimentation as well as centralization. Leidner points out that it regimented much more than the restaurants' assembly-line production processes: it 'standardized procedures for bookkeeping, purchasing, dealing with workers and customers, and virtually every other aspect of the business'.[25] It had developed an overall operating system that included administration as well as the production system and was as standardized and uniform as any bureaucracy or assembly line.

But this centralized, uniform operating system was counterbalanced by a decentralization of product development and marketing.

> The rules could provide only a framework, and that alone could not unleash the real potential of any franchising system—the human ingenuity of hundreds of independent businessmen. In essence, the secret to McDonald's success was that its nearly fanatical operations specialists, *led by Kroc himself*, recognized that the chain's operating system—easily the strongest in the fast-food business—was not enough.[26]

Kroc and his operations specialist recognized that an element of decentralization was needed to unleash this 'human ingenuity' and therefore his franchisees were given a limited but important sphere of independence: the equivalent of Sloan allowing his operating divisions to engage in product development and marketing.[27] Kroc's franchisees responded to this 'unleashing' decentralization by duly displaying an impressive amount of ingenuity. He acknowledged their ingenuity when he pointed out that many new items had been added to McDonald's product menu: 'the Filet-O-Fish, the Big Mac, Hot Apple Pie, and Egg McMuffin. The most interesting thing to me about these items is that each evolved from an idea of one of our operators.'[28] In contrast, the corporation's managers and specialists had been unable to come up with a similarly successful product innovation until the 1972 Quarter

Pounder and 1980 Chicken McNuggets. 'All other major new products', Love points out, 'can be traced to the experimentation of local franchisees.'[29]

Marketing was another area in which Kroc's firm had benefited from its franchisees' ingenuity. The most dramatic example is the invention of the clown Ronald McDonald. Love provides a detailed account of how franchisees in Washington had created this clown, named him Ronald McDonald, and featured him in television advertisements as early as 1963, two years before McDonald's included Ronald in its first venture into nationwide television advertising.[30] He was just one of many examples of how 'Kroc's franchisees put McDonald's on the road to becoming the food service industry's most creative marketer'.[31]

Kroc had therefore *de*centralized marketing and product development to nearly the same degree as he had centralized the franchisees' operating system. His book notes that the reason for this decentralization was simply that the corporation depended upon its franchisees for its vitality.[32] This was also a reason for ensuring that a large majority, about 70 per cent, of the McDonald's restaurants were operated by franchisees, not by the extensive network of company-owned restaurants.[33]

However, Kroc recognized that the creativity of his franchisees was almost a forced adaptive response to competition in their local market. Competition had been the 'catalyst' for each of the new items that his franchisees had added to the McDonald's product menu, as when a franchisee 'came up with Filet-O-Fish to help in his battle with the Big Boy chain in the Catholic parishes of Cincinnati'.[34] In other words, this competition had almost forced the franchisee to come up with an innovative adaptation: a fish product for his local market's predominantly Catholic consumers.

Franchisees' marketing innovations, too, were almost forced upon them by local competition, as in the notable case of Ronald MacDonald. His inventors had originally been sponsors of a local television show for children that featured a clown called Bozo. When the show was cancelled, the franchisees tried to preserve the competitive advantage Bozo had given them, but their substitutes for Bozo failed and finally they had to create a new clown, Ronald McDonald, to be the frontman for children-oriented advertising spots on local television—and the rest is history.[35]

Kroc's decentralization had therefore given McDonald's the capacity to make continual innovative adaptations. As Chapter 2 described, Sloan had long ago instilled an adaptive capacity in General Motors. But it was a capacity for automatic autopilot-like *rapid* adaptation and it had been instilled by imposing operating and financial controls. In contrast, Kroc instilled a capacity for *creative* adaptation by giving franchisees the freedom to innovate and by relying on local competition to motivate them to innovate.

Calculating Strategy and Revenues

Kroc's use of the two calculative methods is comparable to Sloan's, as both leaders used quantitative calculation and emphasized strategic calculation in the area of marketing. Another similarity is that both Kroc and Sloan used a 'numbers man', respectively Harry Sonneborn and Donaldson Brown. However, Sonneborn's quantitative calculation was focused on revenue and financial affairs rather than controls and assessments. For his firm's leader was establishing the McDonald's corporation rather than enhancing General Motors through an administrative rationalization. His use of the calculative methods was building for the future, not rectifying the past, especially in the case of his emphasis upon strategic (marketing) calculation.

Two of Kroc's early marketing strategies led to McDonald's pioneering both the quality fast-food market and the family fast-food market. His *quality*-oriented strategy was a central theme of his franchising system, as was noted earlier. His *family*-oriented strategy was less central but was strongly supported by McDonald's operating system. As Napoli notes, 'ensuring that the stores remained as family-friendly as possible continued to be a top priority' in the 1960s and it would continue to be a priority throughout Kroc's time as leader of the corporation.[36] In his book he points out that 'the family image we wanted to create' had been developed in the early years of McDonald's, when it was still a drive-in operation and when other drive-in 'restaurants' were typically, in Love's words, a 'high school hangout' frequented by teenagers.[37] Kroc's strategy therefore seems to have been calculated to distinguish McDonald's from other drive-in chains as well as to exploit the potential 'family' market. The implementation of the strategy required further calculation, such as forbidding McDonald's restaurants to install jukeboxes, cigarette dispensers, and vending machines because they might attract teenagers or detract from the family-oriented image.[38]

In the 1960s Kroc's family-oriented strategy was supported by an increasing amount of television advertising and children-centred marketing.[39] Yet while this proved very successful, it was preventing or hindering the corporation from targeting other, non-family markets. Furthermore, his strategy was likely to be imitated and perhaps surpassed by one or more of his competitors: the increasing number of other fast-food chains.

So it was farsighted strategic calculation by Kroc to strengthen his marketing by reinvigorating the quality-oriented image—which would now highlight McDonald's remarkable operating standards. As Watson notes, 'clean toilets are universally appreciated' and so are high standards of customer service and food preparation.[40] What is more, no competitors would be able to equal, let alone surpass, the operating standards that McDonald's had instilled in its restaurants and had encapsulated in its slogan QSC&V (Quality, Service,

Cleanliness, and Value). According to Love, as early as 1957 the field consultants' assessment of a restaurant's standards included the subject categories of service, quality, and cleanliness, which were abbreviated to SQC, and two years later Kroc 'put quality first in the grading system, and QSC—the universal symbol of performance in the fast-food trade—was born'.[41] Kroc added a Value component to the formula in the mid-1960s, although franchisees were free to choose how they priced products and were not graded on value.[42] The resulting QSC&V formula would later become a performance-based marketing slogan that highlighted his firm's unequalled operating standards.

Kroc viewed QSC&V as more than a marketing slogan and it seems to have been his equivalent of a corporate culture. By the 1960s Hamburger University was sending out a stream of trained franchisees and managers who, in Kroc's words, 'spread the gospel of Quality, Service, Cleanliness and Value'.[43] Leidner, too, refers to the formula in religious terms. She confirms that McDonald's wanted 'both managers and workers to dedicate themselves to the values summed up in its three-letter corporate credo, "QSC". Quality, service and cleanliness' was also the ultimate goal of 'the company's thousands of rules and specifications'.[44]

The corporation's advertising, however, tended to focus on individual components of the QSC&V formula. For example, the cleanliness component was the focus of a television advertisement which featured a song-and-dance routine about staff giving the restaurant its daily clean.[45] In the early years, before the firm could afford such advertising, the quality component of QSC&V was almost inadvertently advertised by media coverage of Hamburger University trainees marching to class in their white uniforms or being presented with their Bachelor of Hamburger diplomas.[46] In later years the firm was paying for an impressive advertising campaign that could make the most of the formula's components and was driving the internal campaign to maintain high operating standards. By the post-Kroc era, 'the strict quality-control standards applied to every aspect of running a McDonald's outlet' were applied mainly 'to help franchise owners keep the promises made in the company's advertising'.[47]

By the 1990s, too, QSC&V was becoming known globally as well as nationally. For instance, when McDonald's restaurants opened in Beijing, the local media publicized 'McDonald's corporate philosophy of QSC & V' in order to reinforce the government's policy of modernizing the city's business environment.[48] McDonald's attention to hygiene was constantly mentioned by the Beijing media and, if Kroc had still been alive, he would probably have been gratified to see his corporation setting the standard for food hygiene even in communist China.[49]

Cleanliness was the component of QSC&V that was the most identified with Kroc. He gave McDonald's its 'passion for cleanliness', such as its operations manual having 'five pages alone on how to clean stainless steel'.[50] The service component of QSC&V was no less important, however, and its accent on friendliness made 'smiling service' an integral part of what Watson calls the 'total experience' of eating at McDonald's.[51] But quality was the first and fundamental component of QSC&V. Kroc's book dwelt upon the high quality of his hamburger patties and, especially, his french fries: 'the quality of our french fries was a large part of McDonald's success'.[52] High-quality french fries may well have been important but no more so than Kroc's distinctive and brilliantly calculated marketing strategies.

Although Kroc did not emphasize the other calculative method, quantitative calculation, he used it in several different contexts. His book mentions how it influenced a crucial pricing decision in 1967. Apparently Kroc decided that an increase in the price of the 15-cent hamburger should be limited to just 3 cents, instead of the proposed 5 cents, partly because his accountant's price/demand graph had predicted the 'diminishing demand for our product for every cent of increase in price'.[53] Furthermore, Napoli mentions that in the mid-1960s Kroc still 'religiously' monitored the sales figures of his restaurants, and even in the 1970s he was monitoring the sales reports from newly established restaurants.[54]

The most important way, however, in which he used quantitative calculation was in relation to the revenue and financing arising from the firm's leasing arrangements. In 1957 Kroc's new 'numbers man', Harry Sonneborn, devised these leasing arrangements to solve the pressing problems of how to finance the development of new restaurants and extract more revenue from their franchised operators.[55] Thanks to his leasing arrangements with owners of sites for new restaurants, the banks were willing to finance the building of these new restaurants by McDonald's development team and its contractors. In addition, he created a new source of revenue by applying a leasing formula to the franchisee-operators of the new restaurants. McDonald's would lease the restaurants to franchisees in return for a percentage of their sales revenue. A franchisee of one or more restaurants would pay a 5 per cent rental, which was calculated on the same sales-percentage basis as the almost 2 per cent service-fee royalties that a franchisee paid Kroc's firm and was shared with the McDonald brothers. The addition of the 5 per cent lease rents to the almost 2 per cent franchising royalties was a huge revenue boost for Kroc's firm and in his book he refers to this as 'the beginning of real income'.[56]

Sonneborn's innovative leasing arrangements were therefore a crucial factor in the development of the corporation. Indeed Love argued that without them, 'McDonald's would never have become a viable competitor in fast food'.[57] But at this early stage in the corporation's development, Sonneborn's position and role were similar to Brown's at General Motors when he devised the quantitative assessments and controls that Sloan introduced in the

1920s.[58] 'Brown and his financial team created the means by which Sloan's goal could be met' and indeed these Brown-led number crunchers were the *human* means through which Sloan met his goal and through which he used quantitative calculation as a rational method of developing the corporation.[59] Similarly, Sonneborn was the human means through which Kroc used quantitative calculation to develop McDonald's. It was not until the end of the 1950s that Sonneborn became something more than Kroc's 'numbers man': he became part of a dual-leadership team with Kroc and in fact several years later began to pursue his own corporate goals, as will be discussed in the next section.

Diverse Deliberation

Kroc seems to have had an ambivalent attitude to using deliberative methods. He distinctively emphasized diverse deliberation but seems to show little interest in the institutionalized form of deliberation, especially the committee-based version epitomized by Sloan's system at General Motors. On closer examination, however, Kroc appears a discerning user of institutionalized deliberation, even if often it was only *informally* institutionalized.

In contrast, Kroc's emphasis on diverse deliberation is very evident and was a well-known feature of his leadership. His public commitment to diverse deliberation was summed up in two remarks: 'if two executives think the same, one of them is superfluous' and 'I like people who level with me and speak their minds'.[60] In other words, he wanted not just diversity in thinking but also the open expression of this thinking, without any reticence. Furthermore, Love confirms that Kroc's desire for diversity was evident in his deeds as well as words. 'From the beginning, his management team consisted of extremely diverse individuals, not the type of managers who typically survive in corporate bureaucracies. These were not organization persons.'[61] They were not the type of corporate managers portrayed by Whyte in *The Organization Man* and discussed in Chapter 2.

For example, Kroc's book describes the remarkable case of McDonald's manager Luigi Salvaneschi. He arrived in America with a PhD in canon law but found himself working in a McDonald's restaurant and, by the mid-1960s, managing the corporation's real estate: 'Luigi was always after me to improve the architecture of our [restaurant] buildings' and 'I would usually wind up getting mad and throwing him out of my office when he started carrying on about aesthetics and Michelangelo'.[62] Yet Kroc recognized that Salvaneschi was right, though financially unrealistic, and eventually the restaurants' architecture was indeed redesigned. Similarly, Kroc mentions that he and his construction manager 'started butting heads' when the latter was still only an area supervisor and 'I have always considered our conflicts creative'.[63]

Although Kroc may have benefited from such diverse 'deliberation' with his managers, his emphasis upon diversity seems to have been a matter of personal preference. He was not facing circumstances that required him to emphasize diverse deliberation as a key method of establishing his corporation. The mere use rather than emphasizing of this method would have been sufficient to provide him with the diversity he needed, such as two key executives he recruited in the 1950s: his 'numbers man' financial expert, Sonneborn, and his operations expert, Fred Turner. Kroc refers to the benefits he gained from this complementary diversity. 'We were different, Harry [Sonneborn] and I, but for a long time we were able to splice our efforts so that the differences made us stronger. Fred Turner added [in 1957] another dimension to the combination.'[64] Turner was more concerned with operational procedures and institution-building, which led to such important contributions as his field-consultants inspectorate and his drafting of a comprehensive operations manual. However, it was Sonneborn who made the crucial revenue-enhancing and financing contributions. In addition to the leasing arrangements discussed earlier, he put together the loans which financed the network of company-operated restaurants and, in 1961, the buy-out of the licensing agreement with the McDonald brothers. Kroc's book describes these two loans in some detail and gives due credit to Sonneborn for his expertise and enterprise.[65]

By the end of the 1950s Kroc had actually formed a dual-leadership team with Sonneborn. In 1959 Kroc gave him the positions of president and CEO: 'I continued as chairman, and we worked substantially as equals.'[66] Such equality is typical of a different version of dual leadership than the innovation-introducing version that arose at General Motors in 1921–2 and Toyota in the 1950s–60s. As Chapter 1 pointed out, there are at least three different versions of a dual-leadership team, and the Kroc–Sonneborn team is an example of not the innovation-introducing version but a more widely known and less complex version. It combines two leaders with different roles but holding similarly high official positions and often similarly high ownership stakes in the firm. The division of labour between the two leaders normally involves one of them performing a more business-oriented role and the other a more creative or technically oriented role. Furthermore, a distinctive feature of the two-role version of dual leadership is its longevity and cohesion.[67] There have been a number of cohesive and enduring two-role leadership teams, such as the remarkable Hewlett and Packard team that will be a focus of Chapter 6. A more recent example is the Larry Page and Sergey Brin pairing that founded Google and was sometimes referred to within Google 'as the single unit LarryandSergey'.[68]

Kroc and Sonneborn, however, were an unusual example of this two-role version of dual leadership. Their division of labour was particularly unusual because it involved two different business and geographical roles. Sonneborn had a finance-administration business role and the geographical role of running the company headquarters in Chicago; Kroc had an operations-suppliers business role and the geographical role of expanding and experimenting in California.[69] More importantly, their dual leadership lacked the typical cohesion and longevity of a two-role leadership team.

By the mid-1960s their differences and conflicts had become irreconcilable. During this period McDonald's was enjoying notable successes: it became a public company, listed on Wall Street, and was on the way to becoming a thousand-restaurant chain. However, the two leaders were now communicating through an intermediary and were even taking their policy disputes to the board of directors.[70] In particular, Kroc and Sonneborn were increasingly disagreeing about the goals of the corporation, not just about ways and means of achieving its goals. Kroc's faith in expansion had 'run headlong into Sonneborn's numbers. Kroc saw the sky as the limit; Sonneborn saw it as the excess' and 'began exercising much stricter financial discipline'.[71]

The situation was resolved by Sonneborn's resignation in 1967 and his replacement by Turner in a new and far more cohesive dual-leadership pairing with Kroc. It lasted beyond the changeover in 1977 that saw Turner shift from being president/CEO to chairman and Kroc shift to the new position of semi-retired senior chairman, which he held until his death in 1984. At Kroc's memorial service, Turner gave a eulogy that referred to their close relationship:

> Ray was the best boss, his best friend—a second father, said Turner. 'He gave us an example—to be generous, to be thoughtful to others, to be fair-minded, to have balance, to do nothing to excess. We loved his sense of humour. And we accepted his shortcomings.'[72]

Among these shortcomings was perhaps Kroc's lack of interest in institutionalized deliberation. But it is easy to underestimate his use of this method if comparisons are made with Sloan's highly structured, committee-based system of centralized deliberation. Kroc's approach to institutionalization is more difficult to discern and analyse than Sloan's formal and systematic approach. The difference in their approaches is reflected in their different deliberative styles. Kroc acknowledged that 'I always say exactly what I think' and that he would 'jump into the fray in administrative sessions and yell and pound on the table'.[73] He differed from Sloan, too, in having a policy of decentralizing decision-making, from headquarters to lower-level managers, and in having a 'less is more' view of management structure: 'for its size, McDonald's today is the most unstructured corporation I know'.[74]

The lack of structure included the absence of a Sloanist committee-based system of deliberation.[75] Some years later Love pointed out that McDonald's was (still) a relatively unstructured corporation and that 'Ideas are never homogenized by committees'.[76] In contrast, Sloan had given General Motors the rule that policy ideas and proposals must be appraised and approved by committees so as to safeguard the corporation against ill-considered decisions or managers following their hunches.[77] This rule would have cramped Kroc's style of policy-making. He acknowledged in his book that he had always been 'willing to take big risks' and therefore was 'bound to blow one once in a while'.[78] More generally, 'the key ingredient in Kroc's management formula is a willingness to risk failure and to admit mistakes'.[79] These risk-taking and trial-and-error aspects of Kroc's policy-making would not have been compatible with Sloanist committees and their protective policy deliberations. So it is hardly surprising that he was not interested in developing or adopting a committee-based system of deliberation.

He used institutionalized deliberation in less obvious ways than Sloan but with similarly beneficial effects on the firm's policy-making. It seems that Kroc's board of directors discussed key policy decisions as well as dealing with policy disputes between Kroc and Sonneborn. For instance, his book mentions that the board resisted management's 1968 plan for a redesign of the restaurants' architecture: he 'had to fight like hell to push it through the board of directors'.[80]

Furthermore, Kroc and his senior managers engaged in some *informally* institutionalized policy deliberations. These were typically one-to-one, off-the-record discussions institutionalized by informal rules. Napoli mentions two instances of such informal policy deliberation.[81] In the early 1960s Kroc persuaded Sonneborn to make the deal through which Ronald McDonald was acquired from his franchisee inventors. Later in the decade Kroc was himself persuaded to back a new way of improving the firm's image but in this case it was through boosting his own public image as a benevolent, philanthropic business tycoon.

What were the informal rules that institutionalized Kroc's informal policy deliberations? Looking again at the Salvaneschi case, it appears that the informal rules allowed a manager to lobby Kroc about policy and to *keep* lobbying him even after having been thrown out of the office. There seem to have been informal rules, too, about the most effective way to lobby Kroc, according to his description of how he was sold the proposal to begin advertising on television. In 1963 he was sold this policy by a manager who presented him with a logical, well-researched, and financially attractive argument: 'the logic of his one page memo was irrefutable. It demonstrated precisely how an ad campaign would repay its cost many times over, while failing to spend the money would cost us much more in the long run.'[82] It has been suggested that Kroc 'had a habit of picking up new ideas from anyone who offered them. What counted was not where the idea came from but whether it worked.'[83] However, when he bought ideas from his managers, the deliberations seem to have been institutionalized by an informal rule that the idea was *likely* to work according to the logic, research, and financial projections of the seller's argument.

Certainly Kroc had made good use of institutionalized deliberation as one of the appropriate rational methods of establishing his corporation. More generally, he had used all six of these appropriate rational methods and had emphasized one of each pair: innovative adaptation, strategic calculation and (from personal preference) diverse deliberation. But Kroc's selection of appropriate methods also included *non*-rational methods, notably the visionary imagination of a dreamer.

His use of this non-rational method is memorably described in a passage near the end of his book. Here Kroc notes that he was looking forward to McDonald's restaurants more than doubling in number, from the present 4,000 to a future 10,000. 'A lot of people would say I'm dreaming. Well they'd be right. I've been dreaming all my life, and I'm as sure as hell not going to stop now.'[84] By the end of the century, the number of McDonald's restaurants had increased to more than 27,000 and, what is more, they could be found in no fewer than 119 countries.[85]

This globalization had been another of Kroc's dreams. 'I'm dreaming about new things for McDonald's International operations' because 'people everywhere—from Japan to Sweden—are welcoming the Golden Arches.'[86] From these people's perspective, the arrival of McDonald's meant a transfer of American business knowhow as well as the opportunity to eat a better hamburger and french fries.[87] From the corporation's perspective, this global expansion meant that by the mid-1990s, McDonald's was earning more than half of its revenue from its international operations.[88]

Globalized Adaptability

The first stage of the global expansion had been achieved under Kroc's leadership. By the time he semi-retired in 1977, McDonald's was already established in twenty-one countries outside the US: its global presence extended from the Americas to Europe, Asia, and Australasia.[89] By then, too, McDonald's had developed a highly successful joint-venture system that took Kroc's franchising system a step further by treating the corporation's foreign subsidiaries as superfranchisees.

According to Love, the model for this approach was the 1971 entry of McDonald's into Japan. It involved a pioneering joint-venture arrangement with a Japanese entrepreneur that gave him the same sort of autonomy and adaptive potential that Kroc franchisees had long been given.[90]

> Japan proved that the key to success in the international market was the same as it was at home: *local control* by local owner/operators. The policy resulted in such a diverse range of local joint-venture partners that McDonald's—now the most international of all retailing organizations—is anything but a typical multi-national corporation. Rather it is a loose *federation* of independent local retailers who happen to market the same thing…but tailor their marketing approach to their country's different cultures.[91]

Watson, too, depicted global McDonald's as resembling a 'federation of semi-autonomous enterprises' and he viewed it as a worldwide system adapted to local circumstances.[92] He attributed McDonald's global success to its 'localization strategy' and its 'multilocal' mode of operation.[93] Furthermore, he pointed out that the foreign joint-venture partners were operating in local environments that differed significantly from the American environment in which McDonald's had evolved. In the Japanese and Hong Kong cases, the joint-venture partners 'are credited with turning what appeared to be impossible tasks ("Selling hamburgers in Tokyo or Hong Kong? You must be joking!") into dramatic success stories'.[94]

The joint-venture partners' adaptations to local conditions therefore often included more than just tailoring their marketing approach to fit their country's culture. Love argued that although they 'made major changes in market-ing to sell the American system', they did not change the American system's menu or restaurant design.[95] But some foreign partners have in fact made changes or additions to the menu. Watson points out that the Israeli oper-ation serves Big Macs without cheese in several outlets, 'thereby permitting the separation of meat and dairy products required by kosher restaurants. McDonald's restaurants in India serve Vegetable McNuggets and a mutton-based Maharaja Mac, innovations that are necessary in a country where Hindus do not eat beef, Muslims do not eat pork, and Jains (among others) do not eat meat of any type.'[96] Other menu innovations have included: cold pasta in Italy; teriyaki burgers in Japan, Taiwan, and Hong Kong; grilled salmon sandwiches in Norway; and chilled yoghurt drinks in Turkey.[97] What is more, there have also been changes to the restaurants' design. For example, British operators distinguished themselves from other fast-food operations by developing large-scale and relatively plush restaurants, with lavish interiors and exteriors.[98]

The two most interesting examples of localization and adaptation are Japan in the 1970s and China in the 1990s. The pioneering Japanese case has been studied by an anthropologist, who points to several innovations carried out by this local joint-venture partner. He added new items to the menu, including Chinese-style fried rice, curried rice with chicken or beef, a shrimp burger, and a teriyaki burger with soy sauce.[99] He innovatively used central-city locations in fashionable shopping areas as the best way for McDonald's to enter a new country, but he also used locations near train stations in order to compete against the stand-up noodle shops that catered for people wanting a quick bowl of noodles before catching a train.[100] Similarly, his marketing promoted McDonald's as an eating place for young people either seeking a fashionable cultural experience of Americana or seeking a practical alternative to traditional fast-food options.[101]

The image of McDonald's as a young people's place had to accommodate a new development introduced by these young customers. They tended to use the McDonald's restaurant as a place to relax and socialize rather than to eat fast-food quickly and then depart. In Japan and other parts of Asia 'McDonald's restaurants are treated as leisure centers, where people can retreat from the stresses of urban life'.[102] In Japan, restaurants in favourable locations spontaneously became meeting places for young people, with high-school and even elementary-school students spending hours relaxing and socializing.[103] This might well be viewed as a revival of the 'high-school hangout' and teenager-oriented approach of the drive-in restaurants that Kroc had competed against so many years earlier—in a different era and society.

In the 1990s McDonald's arrived in communist China. Its arrival in Beijing has been studied by another anthropologist, who mentions several localization and adaptive features that are reminiscent of what occurred earlier in Japan. For example, the McDonald's restaurants successfully attracted 'yuppies' seeking an Americana cultural experience, and the local customers spontaneously used the restaurants as a place to relax and socialize.[104] However, the differences from the Japanese case are just as significant. There were no experiments with local food items and there was no attempt to compete with local forms of fast-food, such as the small boxes of rice sold at street stalls.[105] Furthermore, the young people attracted to McDonald's were from an older age group and used the restaurants for a different purpose. Young couples considered the McDonald's environment to be 'romantic and comfortable', especially for those with limited budgets, and the restaurants responded by creating 'a relatively remote, private service area with tables for two only' that in some restaurants was nicknamed 'the lovers' corner'.[106]

The key difference, however, was that in China 'localization strategies have centered on children as primary customers' and exploited the effect of China's one-child policy upon family life:

> children are the object of attention and affection from up to half a dozen adults: their parents and their paternal and maternal grandparents. The demands of such children are always met by one or all of these relatives, earning them the title of 'Little Emperors' or 'Empresses'. When a Little Emperor says 'I want to eat at McDonald's', this means that the entire family must go along.[107]

This child-based marketing strategy included 'Aunt McDonald' receptionists to support the Ronald McDonald clown figure imported from America and known as 'Uncle McDonald' in China. A restaurant would employ five to ten of these female receptionists to care for children and talk with their parents, to host children's birthday parties, and 'to establish long-term friendships with children and other customers'.[108]

Although this strategy may seem to be re-emphasizing Kroc's children-centred advertising of the 1960s, it was more of an adaptive response—an innovative adaptation—to local Chinese conditions. Like the previous examples described in this section, it shows that the joint-venture system had instilled a capacity for innovative adaptation in *global* McDonald's, just as Kroc's franchising system had instilled a similar adaptive capacity in the American McDonald's of the 1960s–70s. In fact the need to adapt to local conditions and competition was more evident in the case of the international joint-venture system and so it is not surprising that joint-venture partners seem to have been more innovative than Kroc's franchisees in adding to the menu, modifying the design, marketing in different ways, and even developing new markets, such as the teenager-oriented marketing that is reminiscent of Kroc's competitors in the 1950s.

McDonald's had 'come a long way' geographically and commercially since Kroc started up his fast-food venture in 1954. He had taken it from a start-up to a globalized corporation that would soon be part of the global culture. Considering the personal circumstances that he faced, Kroc seems to epitomize the values that he highlighted in the final chapter of his book. 'The only way we can advance is by going forward, individually and collectively, in the spirit of the pioneer' and taking 'the risks involved in our free enterprise system'.[109]

5

Wal-Mart: Walton's *Made In America*

Sam Walton's autobiographical *Made in America: My Story* appeared in the year he died, 1992, at age seventy-four.[1] He was still chairman of the massive retailing corporation Wal-Mart Stores, which he had founded and which had made him the wealthiest man in America.[2] Tedlow's *Giants of Enterprise* describes Walton as arguably 'the most successful retailer in American history. More than that, he was arguably the nation's most successful executive.'[3] Although Walton's book is largely an autobiography, it is less personal than Kroc's and gives a better leader's-eye view of how the appropriate rational methods were used to establish a corporation.

Walton used these methods very capably to establish an iconic corporation that is now almost as internationally famous as McDonald's. Unlike Kroc, Walton did not preside over the early stages of his firm's globalization. In 1992, the year that he died, Wal-Mart was an almost entirely US operation, with nearly two thousand stores and nearly 400,000 employees.[4] Only twelve years later, Wal-Mart (now known as Walmart) was operating in eleven countries and had become the world's largest corporation, with some 5,000 stores and over 1.5 million employees.[5] By 2012 the majority of its stores were located outside America and indeed its international branch Walmart International had become the world's second-largest retailer—second only to the corporation's retail operations in America.[6]

Like Kroc and Sloan, Walton used the whole set of six appropriate corporation-developing methods. More importantly, Walton was also using and indeed emphasizing a *seventh* rational method—learning—that has not been mentioned in earlier chapters. Chapter 1 did not include it among the set of six appropriate corporation-developing methods but the Walton example shows that it must be included as an additional, seventh appropriate method of establishing or enhancing a corporation. Furthermore, like Sloan, Walton seems to epitomize the leader who inspires employee-followers with rational confidence because he or she is very capably using the appropriate rational methods. It is true that Walton also used the non-rational methods of vision and gut instinct but, as was argued in Chapter 1, he seems to have used these non-rational methods only when they were rationally appropriate in the circumstances he was facing. Otherwise he would use one of the appropriate rational methods, as when he was using and indeed emphasizing learning.

Walton's emphasis on learning was not the only way in which he differed from Sloan and Kroc in selecting methods to emphasize. Instead of selecting one adaptive and one deliberative method, he selected *both* calculative methods—quantitative as well as strategic calculation. Unlike Sloan and Kroc, he chose, as a matter of personal preference, to emphasize quantitative calculation: he was his own 'numbers man' and could do without someone like Brown or Sonneborn.

Where Walton was particularly unusual, however, was in the way he 'founded' a corporation. For his Wal-Mart corporation was founded by enhancing an existing firm so successfully that this enhancement, the introduction of 'Wal-Mart' stores, became the driving force behind the firm's development into a corporation and even gave the new corporation its name: Wal-Mart Stores. When he opened his first Wal-Mart store in 1962, the 44-year-old Walton was already the founder and owner of a regional retailing empire in the southwest of the country, primarily in the state of Arkansas. His firm already operated more than fifteen large or sizeable variety stores in a regional chain that Tedlow terms a 'variety store empire':

> By the early 1960s, Walton had achieved an altogether remarkable record: 'That whole period—which scarcely gets any attention from people studying us—was really very successful. In fifteen years' time, we had become the largest independent variety store operator in the United States.' In his early forties, Sam Walton was already a rich man.[7]

His 1962 venture into discount retailing was aimed apparently at protecting his firm from the threat of discount stores challenging his variety stores. Although these challengers had not yet arrived, Walton would pre-empt and perhaps deter them by opening his own discount store, the first Wal-Mart.

The first section of the chapter will describe how he then used rapid and innovative adaptation to develop a superb expansion system, which soon spread these discount stores throughout the region. The second section will describe his emphasizing of both quantitative and strategic calculation and will examine distinctive aspects of his strategic calculation. Unlike Sloan and Kroc, he did not focus on marketing and was instead mainly concerned with an Ohno-like cost-reduction grand strategy and with the more specialized strategies that it drove or influenced, such as his labour-relations and political strategies.

The third section of the chapter will explore his use of diverse and institutionalized deliberation. It will highlight the way in which his use of these methods involved the technocrats and new technology that enabled his firm to expand so rapidly into a retailing empire. The fourth section, however, will explore his use and indeed emphasizing of a method—learning—that has not been mentioned in earlier chapters. Obviously this section has a wider significance than the others and therefore it is followed up by a special, fifth section that presents a supplementary example of another leader, Marcel Dassault, emphasizing learning as a rational method of establishing a corporation—the French aircraft corporation Dassault Aviation.

Adaptively Expanding Wal-Mart

Walton's most significant use of the adaptive methods was when he developed an expansion system for spreading his new Wal-Mart stores throughout the southwest. The expansion system was a major innovation but, as in the cases of Kroc's franchising system and Ohno's production system, it was developed through a series of smaller innovative adaptations, which Walton made during the 1960s. These innovations, the key components of his new expansion system, included (1) a small-town strategy, (2) a policy of rapid-as-possible expansion, (3) a superb distribution system, and (4) a saturation growth strategy. Like Kroc's franchising system, this was also a case of *rapid* adaptation being used in combination with innovative to produce a rapidly developed innovative system. Walton's system was developed largely in the late 1960s, just as Kroc's had been developed largely in the late 1950s, and in both cases the rapidity was crucial because it enabled the system to take advantage of opportunities before they evaporated or were exploited by the firm's competitors.

However, Walton's system was less innovative than Kroc's and Ohno's because it had not been developed by creatively taking full advantage of opportunities. Walton's innovations had instead usually been forced adaptive responses or, in his words, were taking opportunities that had been 'created out of necessity'.[8] The earliest example of this was his small-town strategy, which was also the most obvious component of the expansion system. In a sense it was nothing new but merely the continuation of Walton's existing strategy, as he acknowledges in his book when recounting the 1940s origin of the 'small-town strategy that got Wal-Mart going almost two decades later'.[9]

His small-town strategy had been a feature of how in the 1940s–50s he had created a chain of variety stores located in small towns in the southwest—and with the firm's headquarters located in the small town of Bentonville, Arkansas.[10] When the history of Wal-Mart was written many years later, the historians noted that 'Walton's strategy of using small-town locations would be an undeniable outgrowth of the variety-store years'.[11] They also noted how his variety-store empire was endangered by the rise of discount retailing in the 1950s. Discount retailing was nothing new and was based on high sales volume through rapid turnover produced by low (discount) prices, which were in turn produced by low profit margins, low costs and, particularly, having merchandise supplied not through a wholesaler but directly from the manufacturer. Discounting had evolved in the 1950s, however, into a more sophisticated form of discount store, with a supermarket's self-service techniques and a department store's lay-out and wide range of merchandise.[12] This modern form of discount store could be expected to spread, as had other retailing innovations, even to Arkansas and the small towns in which Walton had established his chain of variety stores. 'Like other merchants before him who had been *forced to adapt* when their businesses had been threatened by new forms of retailing, Sam Walton would be compelled to come to terms with this latest innovation in the history of American retailing.'[13]

Walton's response was to open his own version of a modern discount store. In his book's words, 'I wasn't about to sit there and become a target' and so in 1962 he opened a modern discount store and called it a 'Wal-Mart' store.[14] He was apparently seeking just to pre-empt and perhaps deter a discount-retailing challenge to his small-town variety stores, but his forced adaptive response had 'invented' the innovative retailing strategy of locating modern discount stores in small towns. The first Wal-Mart store was the first of many that would be located in small towns: the first fifty would be located in towns with 'a median population of just under nine thousand people'.[15]

Furthermore, the Wal-Mart stores were soon being opened at a very rapid rate, thanks to the new policy of rapid-as-possible expansion. According to Walton, the small towns were showing much greater demand for discount retailing than he had foreseen, but this also meant it was more likely that other firms would soon copy his strategy of locating discount stores in small towns.[16] 'We figured we'd better [therefore] roll the stores out as quickly as we could' through a new policy of rapid-as-possible expansion.[17] Although it was another forced adaptive response, the new policy was aimed at pre-empting or deterring competition with his new *discount* stores rather than his chain of variety stores. By opening new Wal-Mart stores 'as rapidly as earnings and credit would permit', Walton increased the rate of openings to five stores a year in 1968–9.[18] By converting his firm into a public company in 1970, he was able to finance a more rapid rate of expansion and in fact his Wal-Mart Stores Incorporated added some two hundred new stores during the 1970s by 'stretching our people and our talents to the absolute maximum'.[19]

This rapid rate of expansion was also partly due to another component of his expansion system—the superb distribution system. It, too, was a forced adaptive response but in this case the problem was not potential competitors but the lack of distribution services to supply the firm's small-town discount stores in the rural southwest. Walton notes in his book that being 'out in the sticks with nobody to distribute to our stores', the firm had to supply its Wal-Mart discount stores through its own warehouse distribution centres and in fact was 'forced to be ahead of our time in distribution'.[20] Wal-Mart's historians agree that this forced adaptive response proved very beneficial in the longer term. 'Wal-Mart's rural locations had compelled the firm to invest in its own inventory-replenishing system, which had evolved into an intricate network of distribution centers, an extensive fleet of trucks, and state of the art computer and communications systems that enabled the firm to function with great efficiency.'[21] For example, the new Bentonville distribution centre built in 1969 included one of the first computerized warehouses in the country, and the distribution centre built in Searcy in 1978 had an automated warehouse that pioneered mechanized distribution.[22] According to Ortega, Wal-Mart developed 'perhaps the leanest and fastest distribution system in the country', enabling the firm to supply 'merchandise to its stores faster and at less expense than its rivals'.[23]

In the 1960s, however, the system's limitations forced Wal-Mart to adopt a growth strategy that Ortega terms 'the saturation strategy'.[24] It was markedly different from the growth strategies of Wal-Mart's rivals and it became the fourth component of the expansion system. Although this was another forced adaptive response, Walton made the best of the situation through some innovative strategic calculation. He was adapting to the logistical fact of life that Wal-Mart's distribution system was a hub-and-spoke system that required each new Wal-Mart store to be located within a day's truck drive (spoke) of a distribution centre (hub).[25] Walton's book points out that other, larger discount-retailing firms were expanding 'by sticking stores all over the country' but Wal-Mart 'couldn't support something like that' with its regional hub-and-spoke distribution system.[26] He acknowledges that therefore Wal-Mart's 'growth strategy was born out of necessity, but at least we recognized it as a strategy early on' and devised a new saturation technique: open a store 'as far as we could from a warehouse' and then 'fill in the map of that territory' by opening new stores until the area and market had been saturated.[27]

By the 1970s this growth strategy was being applied in not only Arkansas but also several other states in the surrounding region, such as Missouri and Texas. Later in the decade, new distribution centres were being built some distance from Bentonville. Now Wal-Mart was able 'to overcome the logistical problem that prevented it from expanding beyond the 350-mile [a day's truck drive] ring around Bentonville' and its nation-wide expansion would lead to many more distribution centres 'placed strategically in our trade areas across the country—still mostly within a day's drive, or about 350 miles, of the stores they serve'.[28]

The nation-wide expansion in the 1980s was a remarkable triumph for the expansion system, as is related in Vance and Scott's history of Wal-Mart.[29] By 1981 Wal-Mart was the country's second-largest discount chain, even though these some four hundred stores were confined to a thirteen-state area stretching from Texas in the south to Illinois in the north. By 1985 there were more than seven hundred stores, now in twenty states, and by 1987 there were nearly a *thousand* Wal-Mart stores in America. Only three more states had been added to the empire but it was becoming one of the country's largest retail, not just *discount*-retail, corporations and in 1989 it 'became the nation's third largest retailer, despite the fact that it operated in only half the states'.[30] The remarkable rate of expansion continued into the early 1990s. Wal-Mart now moved into the West Coast and Northeast regions and was operating in two-thirds of the states when it became the nation's *largest* retailer in 1991.[31] This was the ultimate triumph for an expansion system that had originated in Arkansas nearly thirty years earlier and was based on four innovative but forced adaptive responses.

However, Walton's expansion system had abandoned its small-town and saturation strategies when Wal-Mart entered the cities in the 1980s. In his book Walton notes that he had 'never planned on going into the cities. What we did instead was build our stores in a ring around a city—pretty far out—and wait for the growth to come to us'.[32] Ortega described this strategy more clearly as waiting 'for the growth of suburbs to bring out the shoppers. Eventually, Wal-Marts would ring the outskirts of dozens of cities'.[33] But this long-term strategy was superseded or at least supplemented by a more direct approach. For by the 1980s, Wal-Mart was actually going into the cities. Now there would be such combinations as having four stores *in* a city of 150,000 as well as five or more 'within 30 miles'.[34] The urban trend increased during the decade as the corporation expanded into a nation-wide retail empire. Wal-Mart's historians note that this 1980s expansion led to 'a growing interest in more densely populated areas' and the firm 'accelerated its expansion into larger cities'.[35] As Walton acknowledges in his book, 'we've moved into some cities outright'.[36]

In addition to moving into the cities, Wal-Mart had moved into several new regions in the 1980s and into the West Coast and Northeast regions in the early 1990s. So it had to adapt to new *regional* environments as well as the new urban environment of the cities that it was moving into 'outright'. Furthermore, it had to adapt very rapidly during this period of only twelve years. In fact the corporation's most impressive feature in this stage of its development is how rapidly and successfully it adapted to 'local' urban and regional conditions.

Yet Walton's book has little to say, implicitly or explicitly, about rapid adaptation. The only account of Wal-Mart adapting rapidly is the description of how he personally took charge of the firm's response to a competitive challenge in the early 1980s. The challenge came from a new form of discount retailing that was labelled 'sub-discounting' because it undercut discount retailers by (1) selling a wide range of goods at wholesale prices, (2) in warehouse-like stores and (3) to customers who belonged to the stores' sub-discounting 'club' and therefore were entitled to buy these goods at wholesale rather than retail prices.[37] Walton's adaptive response appeared as early as 1983. He created a sub-discounting form of Wal-Mart store, called a Sam's Club store, which supplemented the standard Wal-Mart stores and competed for the newly discovered sub-discounting market. By the end of the 1980s there were nearly a hundred of these warehouse-like Sam's Club stores, and they had taken Wal-Mart further into big-city retailing.[38]

A more important example of rapid adaptation occurred in the 1990s and was foreshadowed in Walton's book. He mentions that Wal-Mart was preparing to 'push on' into the grocery market, 'where we feel the customers are ready for our way of doing business'.[39] The push into the grocery market would be led by a new form of Wal-Mart store—the Supercenter—which had developed out of Walton's failed experiment with 'hypermarkets'.[40] The Supercenter combined a grocery supermarket with a standard Wal-Mart store and therefore gave the corporation a means of competing for the huge grocery market.[41] By 2001 there were more than a thousand Supercentres and they had made Wal-Mart the largest food retailer in America—a remarkably rapid adaptation to this massive market and difficult line of business.[42]

This post-Walton success confirmed that a capacity for rapid adaptation had been instilled in the corporation by Walton in the 1980s. He had instilled it on a much larger scale than Sloan's autopilot-like quantitative controls at General Motors, and Walton seems to have instilled it through a non-rational method—his corporation's culture.[43] In his book he declares that 'I've made it my own personal mission to ensure that constant change is a vital part of the Wal-Mart culture' and, furthermore, he claimed that 'one of the greatest strengths of Wal-Mart's ingrained culture is its ability to drop everything and turn on a dime'.[44] Clearly this was not far from the truth as regards Wal-Mart's capacity for constantly and rapidly adapting to new conditions. And it would be reconfirmed in the 2000s by Wal-Mart's rapid adaptation to being a globalized corporation and operating in global conditions.

Looking back at the corporation's development, the instilled capacity for rapid adaptation therefore seems no less important than the innovative expansion system of the 1960s–70s. This is one reason why the chapter has not suggested that Walton *emphasized* innovative adaptation; the other reason is that the expansion system was obviously not as creative and permanent a contribution as the innovative systems described in the previous two chapters.[45] There are no doubts, however, about his emphasizing of the two calculative methods.

Calculating Numbers and Strategy

This section will examine Walton's use and indeed emphasizing of the two calculative rational methods: quantitative and strategic calculation. Chapter 1 referred to Walton's liking for quantitative calculation as a typical example of a leader emphasizing a particular rational method as a matter of personal preference. In the case of strategic calculation the circumstances were more important than personal preferences. Like Sloan and Kroc, Walton relied on strategic calculation for key elements in his success but in Walton's case it was not his marketing strategy but his cost-reduction strategy that was so important—it gave his firm a crucial advantage over his competitors. As this section will show, cost reduction was a fundamental and wide-ranging 'grand' strategy that influenced Walton's strategic calculation in other areas, such as his distinctive labour-relations strategy.

Quantitative calculation, however, was Walton's personally preferred method of developing a corporation. As Fishman notes, Walton was known as a 'numbers man' who expected his managers, too, to have the numbers at their fingertips and on their mind.[46] It is evident in his book that Walton liked being his own 'numbers man' and emphasizing quantitative calculation. When he described his managerial style as playing to his strengths, the only ones he mentions are an appreciation for numbers and a talent for remembering numbers.[47] An appreciation for numbers had 'kept me close to our operational statements and to all our other information that we have pouring in'.[48] For example, each week Walton checked each and every store's numbers for that week's sales, wage costs and so forth. 'It usually takes about three hours, but when I'm done I have as good a feel for what's going on in the company as anybody here.'[49] This was an incredible feat of analysis and memory, considering that Wal-Mart had hundreds of stores and that Walton would cite their numbers, from memory, in his weekly management meetings. Soderquist quotes a Wal-Mart manager reminiscing about Walton's 'uncanny ability to retain and remember performances. He also expected everyone, from the CFO [chief financial officer] down to the department managers in the stores, to "know your numbers"' and of course to know what they meant.[50]

Walton's appreciation for numbers was focused on interpreting what the numbers meant. He believed that the numbers told him when and where there was mismanagement and also when a concept was 'getting out of control' or where 'the next trouble spot' would appear.[51] This was why he liked the corporation's computerization—'all those numbers'—and its satellite-based communication system: 'I like my numbers as quickly as I can get them'.[52] Such concern with his personal quantitative monitoring of the corporation was one of the most distinctive features of his leadership.

But being his own 'numbers man' was less important to the corporation than his emphasis on *strategic* calculation. Walton was clearly a believer in adapting his calculated strategic plans to fit changing circumstances.

'Dad always said you've got to stay flexible,' reported his son Jim. 'We never went on a family trip nor have we ever heard of a business trip in which the schedule wasn't changed at least once after the trip was under way. Later we all snickered at some writers who viewed Dad as a grand strategist who intuitively developed complex plans and implemented them with precision.'[53]

Walton was a truly 'grand' strategist, however, in the sense of devising a *grand* strategy. Chapter 1 pointed out that grand strategy is concerned with 'the big picture' and 'the big issues' and in Walton's case he devised a cost-reduction grand strategy that was fundamental and wide-ranging, influencing his strategic calculations about many other things, areas, and issues.

What is more, Walton's cost-reduction grand strategy helped produce a revolution in retailing. Lichtenstein's *The Retail Revolution* notes that in the early 1960s it appeared that (1) consumers were paying too much for distribution and retailing, when compared with what they paid for manufacturing, and (2) there was a huge contrast between manufacturers' scrutiny of production costs and the absence of such cost-reduction scrutiny when the products were distributed and retailed.[54] But the times were beginning to change. Soon many retailers would be scrutinizing their costs as closely as any manufacturer scrutinized production costs. One of the reasons for this change was Walton's reorientation of discounting's price-competing formula. He developed a 'frugal' version of discount retailing that reduced his discounted prices still further by frugal cost savings—and a cost-reduction grand strategy.

Walton's book mentions how in the 1960s Wal-Mart stores developed this new, frugal version of discount retailing. 'What we were obsessed with was keeping our prices below everybody else's. Our dedication to that was total. Everybody worked like crazy to keep the expenses down.'[55] This frugality was epitomized at the end of the 1960s by Walton's new headquarters building:

The firm's general headquarters in Bentonville, with its inexpensive décor throughout, was symbolic of Walton's devotion to frugality. Subsequent to its construction, the installation of conveniences such as an elevator and carpeting in some areas provoked complaints from Walton. . . . And he considered the carpeting an outright waste of money.[56]

Achieving a competitive advantage by frugally keeping the expenses down became a well-recognized feature of the Walton way of discounting. Wal-Mart's historians refer to his 'zeal for cost-cutting' and to economy of operation being 'almost a fetish', while Trimble refers to 'frugality in the extreme' being a principal element in Wal-Mart's success.[57] This frugal version of discounting was institutionalized as a cost-reduction grand strategy that Wal-Mart would continue to stress in the 1970s–80s and when it expanded into a global empire in the 1990s.[58]

Walton's grand strategy seems very similar to Ohno's cost-reducing grand strategy. For example, Walton notes in his book that Wal-Mart had 'always operated lean. We have operated with fewer people. We have had our people do more than in other companies.'[59] But Walton was more concerned than Ohno with the competitive aspect of reducing or minimizing costs. Wal-Mart's 'heritage' and 'obsession' was to be 'more productive and more efficient than our competition'.[60] The competitive aspect was also evident when Walton pointed to cost control as one of his rules for running a successful company. 'Control your expenses better than your competition. This is where you can always find the competitive edge.'[61] Furthermore, his book shows that he practised what he preached. It points out that for twenty-five years Wal-Mart 'ranked number one in our industry for the lowest ratio of expenses to sales'.[62] He had increased this competitive edge during the 1980s when the corporation was rapidly expanding into a nation-wide retail empire. Wal-Mart's historians note that its operating expenses as a percentage of sales would decline from about 20 per cent early in the decade to only 15 per cent in 1990.[63] Office expenses were an obvious example of Walton seeking a competitive edge through controlling costs. From the outset he sought to keep office expenses at 2 per cent of sales in an era 'when most companies charged 5 per cent of their sales to run their offices'.[64]

His cost-reduction grand strategy was wide-ranging as well as competitive. Unlike Ohno's, Walton's was not confined to a retailing equivalent of production and indeed it influenced or drove other, more specialized strategies. For example, Walton's reduction of labour costs was supported by an impressively calculated labour-relations strategy. He needed an effective labour-relations strategy to help reduce not only labour costs but also the prospect of unionization or other serious labour 'problems'. In fact his tight control of labour costs was a potentially very problematic part of his cost-reduction grand strategy. Critics indicted him on several counts, notably the heavy reliance on part-time and temporary workers and the reliance on near-minimum-wage workers, who were still being paid 'below the retail industry's average wage' even after Wal-Mart became the country's largest and most successful retail corporation.[65]

His book, not surprisingly, highlights the many positive aspects of his labour-relations strategy, notably the brilliant profit-sharing plan. In 1971 Walton had extended his managers' profit-sharing plan to include store workers who had been employed by Wal-Mart for two years or more.[66] This decision to give store workers 'more equitable treatment in the company, was without a doubt the single smartest move we ever made at Wal-Mart': they would be included in the profit-sharing plan and would be the targets of new share-buying and bonus programmes.[67] The shrinkage and sales bonus programme would also lead to more equitable treatment in the sharing of information. Ortega notes that Wal-Mart employees 'would be told such things as the sales figures at their stores, and the losses from shrinkage, figures that, at other companies, were for management's eyes only'.[68]

Walton's labour-relations strategy was developing in the 1970s into a complex mixture of new features and long-standing policies.[69] The new features included (1) profit-sharing, share-buying, bonuses, and information-sharing, (2) the decision to call workers 'associates' rather than employees, (3) the description of managers as 'servant-leaders' of teams of workers, (4) the 'open-door' policy, which allowed workers to take their problems directly to Walton, and (5) a Wal-Mart company cheer led by Walton himself. The long-standing policies included strongly opposing unionization and, more positively, promoting an egalitarian informality, such as by using first names throughout the corporation—from 'Mr Sam' on down.

His strategic calculations were therefore directed not towards a complex plan of action but towards creating and managing a complex package of interrelated features and policies. This complex, impressively calculated strategy helped prevent unionization and any serious labour problems. But something more was required to deal with the prospect of *political* intervention in the area of labour relations. In 1978 Walton was one of the business leaders who lobbied against proposed new labour legislation, which he believed would favour unionization.[70] Although the proposed legislation did not become law, 'Walton castigated himself for ignoring the political arena too long, until this threat was upon the company, and he warned employees that from now on both he and they would be called upon to address specific issues'.[71]

In fact the prospect of political intervention was a 'wild card' that could threaten the corporation in other ways and in relation to a wide range of issues. The calculating of political strategy therefore often required him to tailor his means to achieve particular ends. For instance, dealing with pro-unionization bills in Congress required different means than defending the corporation against calls to save small-town businesses from having to compete against Wal-Mart. In the latter case, the strategy included a different ideological means to the end. Tedlow points out that Walton's political strategy here was to use the typical 1980s language of 'consumer democracy', which provided a ready justification for small-town stores succumbing to price competition from Wal-Mart.

> He didn't put that Ben Franklin [store] out of business. The customers shut the old store down: 'They voted with their feet.' Walton was a fervent believer in consumer democracy. Consumers have choices in a free country. They 'vote' for us by patronizing our stores.[72]

Furthermore, Wal-Mart did not indulge in predatory or monopolistic pricing. As a 2000s critic acknowledged, it had never engaged in the predatory practice of going into a small town, putting the local merchants out of business with its lower prices and then, some months or a year later, reaping the benefits by increasing its prices: 'Wal-Mart is brutally competitive, but it is not technically predatory. It's not "low prices until the competitors are strangled"—it's *always* low prices.'[73]

These 'brutally competitive' low prices were largely due to Walton's cost-reduction grand strategy. It had played a key role in developing the corporation ever since his 1960s invention of a frugal version of discount retailing. He had long been emphasizing strategic calculation as a key method and in relation to not just his grand strategy but also other, more specialized strategies. Unlike in the case of quantitative calculation, this was not due to his personal preferences but to the requirements of establishing a discount-retailing corporation during a revolutionary era in retailing.

Deliberation and Technology

Walton used both diverse and institutionalized deliberation as methods of establishing his corporation but, unlike Sloan and Kroc, did not emphasize either of them. Yet there were some noteworthy and distinctive features about Walton's use of the deliberative methods. The distinctive structural feature is that he used Kroc-like informally institutionalized deliberation as well as Sloan-like formally institutionalized deliberation by committees and other groups. Another distinctive feature was that technocrats and technology issues played a prominent role in his informally institutionalized deliberations and in his use of diverse deliberation. This was very unusual, indeed unprecedented, for a retailing firm and so, too, was the amount of deliberative time and effort spent discussing when and how to introduce new technology.

The most important aspect of Walton's diverse deliberation was that it provided him with high-tech options and viewpoints. Although Chapter 1 pointed to the liking for 'mavericks' that he displayed in his book, *technocrats* were much more important to him and his policy deliberations. In the 1960s–70s 'Walton had scoured the country for techno-whizzes and experts in distribution, logistics, communication, and any other discipline he felt he knew nothing about'.[74] In his book he acknowledges that this diverse range of technocrats had played an important role in his firm's remarkable growth.[75] In particular, he notes that 'one of the main reasons we've been able to roll this company out nationally was all the pressure put on me by guys like David Glass and earlier,

Jack Shewmaker and Ron Mayer, to invest so heavily in technology. Yes, I argued and resisted, but I eventually signed the checks.'[76]

His technocrats were certainly not reticent in lobbying him about new technology and selling him proposals for specific projects. For example, Glass began 'pushing' for investment in warehouse mechanization as soon as Walton recruited him in 1976, Glass and Shewmaker were also 'pushing hard for heavy investment in more and more, better and better computer systems', and in the 1980s Shewmaker 'worked really hard to get me to invest in bar coding'.[77] He also had to work really hard to get Walton to invest in a satellite-based communication system. According to Ortega, Shewmaker realized this would be 'a tough sell' because the satellite system was not only 'so untried' but also so expensive: possibly the equivalent of a quarter of the corporation's annual capital expenditure at a time when it was rapidly expanding into a nation-wide empire.[78] Although Shewmaker successfully sold the proposal to Walton, the new system ran into technical problems as well as cost overruns and for a time it seemed the project 'might turn into a fiasco'.[79] Yet Walton continued to allow his technocrats to pressure him—successfully—for more investment in new technology.

His technocratic executives participated, too, in deliberations about policies that were not related to technology. Walton has even been described as *goading* his executives to argue about important decisions, though apparently 'there's no shortage of people who can recall Walton, on the short end of some debate or another, shutting it off by booming out "I still own most of the stock in this company, and this is what we're going to do"'.[80]

Walton presumably did not goad his board of directors and shut off their debates in this peremptory manner. But his recruitment of the board's outside directors shows the same concern for diverse expertise that he showed when recruiting his technocratic executives. By the mid-1980s there were 'eight outside directors with particular areas of expertise Walton figured would be useful to his business', such as Charles Lazarus of Toys 'R' Us, who had pioneered the warehouse-size discount retailing of a single category of merchandise.[81] In 1986 Walton markedly increased the deliberative as well as gender diversity of the board by adding a woman lawyer with political expertise, Hillary Clinton, who would push Walton towards more environmentally friendly, 'green' policies in the late 1980s.[82]

His concern for diverse deliberation seems to have increased as his firm grew into a big corporation and a nationwide retail empire. In his book he warns about the stultifying effects of bigness and bureaucratization upon a firm's vitality and enterprise. In this situation 'there's absolutely no room for creativity, no place for the maverick merchant' or for 'the entrepreneur or the promoter' and, not surprisingly, he was 'worried about Wal-Mart becoming that way. I stay on these guys around here all the time about it.'[83] In the

1960s–70s, it had been more appropriate to recruit technocratic executives rather than mavericks, entrepreneurs, or promoters. By the 1980s, however, he was clearly making an effort to counter the effects of stultification.

One of the ways Walton countered stultification was 'his frequent practice of asking his managers to switch jobs'.[84] Both at the time and in his book, he explained this job-swapping as simply a way of ensuring that managers had a wide knowledge of the corporation's various parts and activities.[85] But job-swapping was not just a means of preventing parochial narrow-mindedness; it was also a means of preventing routinized thinking and expectations. Walton apparently had such a 'strong feeling for the necessity of constant change, for keeping people a little off balance,' that he sometimes made a change 'for change's sake alone'.[86]

However, his most dramatic example of job-swapping seems to have been motivated by his need to find a suitable successor. In 1984 president/COO Shewmaker exchanged jobs with CFO Glass in what Walton depicted as just another case of job-swapping.[87] In his book, though, he admits that he wanted to see how Glass would handle the job of president and COO, presumably because Walton viewed him as a potential successor and perhaps even the preferred successor.[88] In 1988 Walton ended the suspense about the succession by passing on his CEO post to Glass but retaining the chairmanship and creating a dual-leadership team with Glass.

The Walton–Glass team was a different version of dual leadership than the two-role and innovation-introducing versions discussed in earlier chapters. Chapter 1 described this version as combining a semi-retired founder as chairman with a younger-generation executive as the CEO. Like the two-role version, it involves each member having their own, particular role to perform. But this is not an equal division of labour, as the older member is semi-retired, and another inequality is that the (in most cases male and elderly) founder-chairman usually retains such a large ownership stake that he has the power to replace his CEO 'teammate'. There is also likely to be a psychologically deferential relationship between the younger-generation CEO and the celebrated or legendary founder-chairman, who will have chosen his younger-generation teammate and may well have mentored or tutored him or her in the earlier stages of their careers. Such a psychologically deferential relationship was particularly apparent in Kroc and Turner's dual leadership of McDonald's and in fact they may have been the model for the 'two-generation' version of dual leadership that Walton adopted in the twilight of his career.

There was no model, though, for his distinctive version of *institutionalized deliberation*. It was a mixture of formally and informally institutionalized deliberation, of Sloan-like and Kroc-like features, but developed into a distinctive combination that included its own unique features. In particular, the Saturday-morning management meetings were an innovative example of institutionalized deliberation and became a widely known feature of Wal-Mart. They were just one of many ways in which Walton used institutionalized deliberation to develop an iconic corporation.

Like both Kroc and Sloan, Walton espoused a deliberative conception of his position as CEO. As noted earlier, he encouraged diverse deliberation and participated in debates, with a deliberative style that seems less like Silent Sloan's and more like the exuberant Kroc's. Walton also used informally institutionalized deliberation in a similar way to Kroc at McDonald's. In both cases the leader allowed senior managers to sell him policy proposals according to informal rules about how, who, and when. Walton's informal rules, like Kroc's, allowed executives to lobby him and to sell him policy proposals and ideas, with the proviso that they were *likely to work* financially, technically, and in any other way.

Considering Walton's focus on his cost-reduction strategy, it is not surprising that he was particularly concerned about costly projects—and particularly if there were doubts about their technical effectiveness. Walton was therefore especially concerned about proposals that involved costly investment in new, untried technology, such as the satellite-based communication system that was mentioned earlier in this section. 'I want them to think hard how they are going to justify the expense before they even come to me with it.'[89] Berg and Roberts point out that he had an ambivalent attitude towards the new technology. While he 'almost certainly' appreciated its potential benefits, 'it is equally certain that he resented the large initial capital outlay on what was then relatively unproven technology'.[90]

So he vigorously enforced the informal rule that any proposed policy should be likely to work as effectively as its seller promised. Walton notes in his book that he 'always questioned everything' because it was important to make a lobbyer or seller think that 'maybe the technology wasn't as good as they thought it was, or that maybe it really wasn't the end-all they promised it would be. It seems to me they try just a little harder and check into things a little bit closer.'[91] Even then, the technology often failed, at least temporarily, to deliver the promised benefits, as in the case of the satellite-based communication system that Shewmaker had sold to Walton. Similarly, there were problems in the 1970s–80s with the introduction of electric cash registers, the mechanization of the Searcy distribution centre, and the introduction of barcode scanning.[92] Without Walton's wariness there would have been even more problems with new technology as well as more difficulty controlling the spending on these expensive items.

Yet he seems well aware that new technology was needed to maintain Wal-Mart's competitiveness as well as its remarkable rate of expansion. Ortega noted that 'Walton's willingness (once convinced) to spring for such technology' gave Wal-Mart an important advantage over its leading competitor, whose tardiness in upgrading its technology contrasts with Walton's pioneering approach, however wary and thrifty.[93] From a broader perspective, the contrast highlights the effectiveness of Walton's use of informally institutionalized deliberation, which enabled an innovative executive to sell a new idea to his or her cautious leader.

However, Walton also used Sloan-like *formally* institutionalized deliberation by committees or other formal groups. To begin at the top, his board of directors was a deliberative as well as auditing institution. For example, a 1980 decision about acquiring Kuhn's Big K stores was debated by the board for over a year before being decided by Walton's tie-breaking vote as chair of the board's Executive Committee.

> Finally, the Executive Committee sat down to vote on it one morning and it came out split right down the middle, fifty-fifty. It was just as well because it gave me the opportunity to take the ultimate responsibility for the decision. The whole thing had been really cloudy all along, with a lot of arguing.[94]

The seven members of the Executive Committee included Walton's brother Bud and son Rob, which reflected the important role played by the Walton family in the corporation's ownership, policy-making, and even management: Rob Walton was company secretary and general counsel, while Bud Walton headed and later supervised the real-estate and construction division.[95] The four non-Walton members of the committee were the COO, CFO, and two other senior executives, which included the CEO after the 1988 shift to Walton–Glass dual leadership.

There were other, lower-level committees and, as mentioned earlier, the unique Saturday-morning management meetings.[96] By the 1980s this weekly meeting was attended by (1) Walton and his senior executives, (2) his regional managers, who were all based in Bentonville, (3) any of his other managers who worked in Bentonville or were visiting headquarters, and (4) often some invited Wal-Mart store workers—which meant that several hundred people might be attending one of these 'management' meetings.[97] Walton presided over the meetings, dominated their agenda, and focused their deliberations on quickly solving relatively low-level problems.[98] 'I like to see a problem come up and then hear suggestions as to how it can be corrected', so that when 'the solution is obvious, we can order changes right then and carry them out over the weekend'.[99] Problems might be raised when the meeting dealt with merchandising issues, discussed competitors' activities, or reviewed 'computer information charting the performance of every store for the week'.[100] These problems and the meeting's solutions were rapidly communicated to all levels of management either by relayed telephone messages or, once the satellite system was operating, by a live television broadcast of the meeting to all the corporation's stores.[101]

Learning—a Seventh Rational Method

The Saturday-morning management meetings were a learning experience as well as a deliberative institution. Those who attended the meeting were sharing and learning about new ideas and information as well as problems and solutions.[102] Walton notes that the Saturday-morning meeting was a focal point 'where we share ideas we've picked up from various places' and therefore even store workers 'who have thought up something' were invited 'to come share those ideas'.[103] Similarly, there was a sharing of new information, such as competitors' activities or merely the stores' weekly performances.

Among the many learners was of course the meeting's and corporation's leader, Chairman/CEO Walton. Ortega argues that learning was actually the distinctive feature of Walton's greatness as a business leader.

> Hailed as the greatest entrepreneur of his age, Walton disclaimed having any genius or unique ability and freely admitted he borrowed ideas from anywhere he could. If he did have a genius, it was in his ability to know what he didn't know, to recognize his own shortcomings as a businessman and to assume, even after his enormous success, that he still could learn something from almost anybody.[104]

Likewise, Tedlow's profile of Walton in *Giants of Enterprise* noted that 'one of the key characteristics of his career was that he kept learning until the day he died' and indeed 'he spent his life in the quest for more knowledge about retailing'.[105]

This entrepreneur's learning fixation highlights the fact that learning is an additional, seventh rational method of developing a corporation. It should be included in the set of methods described in Chapter 1 as the appropriate rational methods of establishing or enhancing a corporation. This set of six methods should be expanded to include learning as a separate and no less appropriate rational method, comparable to any of the other six.[106]

Walton is not the only leader who has used learning as a rational method of establishing or enhancing a corporation.[107] But his use and indeed emphasizing of learning is a classic example of how this rational method is just as appropriate—and can be just as important—as any of the other six corporate-developing methods. Learning is mentioned, explicitly or implicitly, more than fifty times in his book, although in some cases the learning occurred before he founded Wal-Mart and began to use learning as a corporation-developing method. Clearly it was a favourite method, which he would have emphasized as a matter of personal preference, as in the case of quantitative calculation. But it was also a *key* method, which was needed to deal with the circumstances he faced when establishing his corporation. His emphasis on learning was therefore 'doubly determined' and this may explain why it is mentioned so often in his book—in various forms and in various contexts.

There were four particularly important contexts and forms of learning. First, he learnt through reading and research, including what might be termed 'field' research. Walton read 'every retail publication I get my hands on' and became an 'avid student of management theory'.[108] His research into new developments in the retail industry was particularly important in the period leading up to the opening of his first Wal-Mart store. He had spent 'years and years of studying the discount business' by 'visiting every store and company headquarters I could find' and asking questions about pricing and anything else that seemed relevant: 'I learned a lot that way'.[109]

A second form of learning was what he learnt from his mistakes, experience, and experimenting.[110] Even near the end of his career, he was still making mistakes and learning from them, such as the very profitable lesson learnt from his failed venture into 'hypermarkets' in the late 1980s. It 'taught us what our next step should be in combining grocery and general merchandising—a smaller concept called the Supercenter'.[111] The great success of the Supercenter stores is a dramatic example of making the most of mistakes. As Ray Kroc said, 'when you strike out, you should learn as much as you can from it'.[112]

When it comes to learning from more positive experiences, a crucial example was his pre-Wal-Mart experience of establishing a large retail firm. Years before the 1962 opening of his first Wal-Mart store, he had already established a chain of fifteen variety stores, which Tedlow termed a 'variety store empire'.[113] As Tedlow notes, Walton had already 'learned a lot of lessons which were to stand him in good stead in the future'.[114] In particular, he had learnt how to establish a retail empire in this southwest region of the country. In a sense his 1960s–70s creation of a regional Wal-Mart empire was merely applying what he had learnt to a *different type* of retailing—to discount retailing rather than variety-store retailing. It was only when Wal-Mart spread from the southwest to other regions that Walton entered unfamiliar territory in his empire-building.

Walton learnt, too, from experimenting with his pre-Wal-Mart retail empire and small-town strategy. Tedlow points out that he was experimenting with larger-scale variety stores in the same year as he was moving into discount retailing with his first Wal-Mart store. For in 1962 he opened a very large variety store in a very small town and, later in the year, opened another of these Family Center stores in a similarly small town of only two thousand people.[115] According to Walton, he 'learned that by building larger stores, which we called family centers, we could do unheard of amounts of business for variety stores' in small towns.[116] In fact the opening of the first Wal-Mart store may have been a similar experiment, not just a forced adaptive response to the rise of discount retailing.

Certainly the early Wal-Mart stores benefited from Walton's willingness to experiment with large stores in small towns. An early Wal-Mart store was located in a town of six thousand people to find out if customers in such a small town would buy merchandise from this kind of store 'strictly because of price. The answer was yes.'[117] And a larger Wal-Mart store was located in a larger town 'to learn something else: would a really big, nice store work in a larger town?'[118] Once again, the answer was yes and once again Walton had learnt from experimenting.

Perhaps the most memorable example of learning from mistakes, experience, and experimenting was what Walton learnt from an experience on a tourist trip. His book mentions how in 1975 he was visiting Japan and South Korea and came across the idea of a company cheer.[119] He was so impressed that he introduced a similar cheer at Wal-Mart and would lead store workers in this company cheer when he visited their stores. 'During these visits it was Walton's practice, on arrival, to gather his employees around him and lead them in a rousing corporate cheer.'[120]

The company cheer was also an example of a *third* form of learning: what he learnt and copied from other businesses. But this form of learning was largely about copying from his competitors. Walton acknowledged that 'most everything I've done I've copied from somebody else'—who was often one of his competitors.[121] This might be viewed as merely an extension of his research into new developments in the retail industry but Walton was very open about how much he had copied from his competitors and on occasion even described this as stealing ideas.[122] Kmart in particular was a competitor who provided Walton with a lot of ideas in the early years of Wal-Mart. He wandered through their stores 'talking to their people and trying to figure out how they did things'.[123] Trimble refers to him as 'haunting' his competitors' stores, 'on the lookout for methods and means, finesse and fault, the winning and losing tricks of mass merchandisers'.[124]

A fourth form of learning involved visiting his *own* stores, to learn from his store workers. Walton maintained that visiting his stores and listening to store workers was one of the most valuable uses of his time.[125] Ortega describes store-visiting Walton as 'attentive and avuncular, getting hourly workers away from their managers to get their feedback'.[126] They gave him, too, new ideas for marketing and customer-relations improvements. According to Walton, 'our best ideas usually come from our people in the stores' and especially from 'the people who are actually on the firing line, those who deal with the customers'.[127] Furthermore, the store workers provided him with the sort of information about a store that did not show up in its performance figures for sales, payroll, and so forth. Walton learnt much from his computerized monitoring of these figures but he also believed that monitoring store performance by computer could never be 'a substitute for getting out in your stores and learning what's going on'.[128] One of his senior executives later made a similar point in more dramatic fashion. Soderquist suggested that 'nothing will demoralize those who work for you more quickly than when you no longer have an active knowledge of what's going on in the business'.[129]

Dassault's *Talisman* Aviation Learning

The final section will leave Wal-Mart and retailing for a very different industry in a different country: the aviation corporation established in France by Marcel Dassault. For Walton was not the first leader to use learning as an appropriate rational method of developing a corporation: some years earlier, Dassault had used and indeed emphasized learning as a rational method of establishing a corporation. So this section will be confirming, through the Dassault example, that learning is an additional, seventh rational method of developing a corporation and can be just as effective as the adaptive, calculative, and deliberative methods.

In the 1940s–60s Dassault established the iconic aircraft-construction corporation Dassault Aviation.[130] And he became France's wealthiest businessman by developing it into an aviation-based high-tech empire that even in the post-Dassault era was Europe's most successful producer of military and civil aircraft.[131] Furthermore, he provided an autobiographical, leader's-eye view of his use and indeed emphasizing of learning as a method of establishing a corporation.

His autobiography *The Talisman* was first published in France in 1969, with an English edition appearing two years later.[132] However, it dealt very briefly—only about a dozen pages—with his establishing of Dassault Aviation. Many more pages were spent describing his two earlier aircraft-construction firms and his life outside aviation, which included political and media pursuits and being sent to a Nazi concentration camp. When the book does discuss Dassault Aviation, though, it often mentions Dassault's use of learning and in fact this seems to be the only corporation-developing method that is mentioned anywhere in the book. But Dassault, like Walton, emphasized learning as a key method as well as a favourite method: because of his circumstances as well as his personal preferences.

The autobiography's account of even his first aircraft-construction firm displays his emphasis on learning. A chapter titled 'How to be an airplane manufacturer' begins by methodically explaining how he had acquired the expertise which enabled him to establish a successful firm in 1917. He had studied at an aeronautical engineering school, then learnt about design and manufacturing when employed to work on the Caudron G-3 and, finally, learnt about flight testing when in 1916 he became a major supplier of propellers to aircraft manufacturers.[133] They had allowed him to follow the development of their new airplanes and that 'was how I learned the techniques of flight testing and final preparation of a new airplane. Having learned which new models succeeded and which ones failed, I was able to acquire a great deal of experience in deciding what should and should not be done to make a good airplane.'[134] He became confident enough to start up his own aircraft-construction firm, which designed and manufactured a new, two-seater fighter plane.[135] This new learning experience included working with a business partner who was 'a very good engineer, an excellent businessman and a discerning financier. He taught me a lot of things during that period which stood me in good stead in later years.'[136]

When the war ended in 1918, Dassault did not try to keep his firm alive with airplane-related work but instead began a new career as a real-estate developer. The venture was financially successful and taught him many useful business lessons. It 'taught me a great many things which many people who have the luck (or bad luck) to succeed too early and too fast never are able to learn'.[137] And by 1930 he was prepared to start up a new aircraft-construction firm to take advantage of the new opportunities that were emerging.

When Dassault began his second career in aircraft construction, he had much to learn about new technology in this field and industry. As wood-and-fabric construction was becoming outmoded in 1930, he decided that his first aircraft—a postal-courier plane—would be an advanced, all-metal-construction design and therefore he hired several engineers to help him with the design and production.[138] Although the plane failed to win a production order, he used 'the techniques learned' to produce other all-metal-construction aircraft that were more commercially successful.[139]

He went on to become one of France's leading aircraft manufacturers.[140] In addition to building a twin-engine passenger plane for Air France, he built a series of military aircraft—a single-seat fighter, a twin-engine bomber, and a fast reconnaissance plane—as France modernized its air force to meet the threat from Fascist Italy and Nazi Germany. By the end of the 1930s he was building the prototype of a large four-engine transport plane that was impressive enough to be ordered into production by Nazi Germany's armed forces after they conquered France in 1940. Unlike his aircraft, however, Dassault was not well treated and was eventually sent to Buchenwald concentration camp.

After the Second World War this 53-year-old survivor of a concentration camp began his third career in aircraft construction—and once again had to learn about a dramatic change in aviation technology. Now jet propulsion was making propeller-engines outmoded for high-performance aircraft. But Dassault initially focused on simply producing his pre-war design for a large transport plane and developing a new propeller-driven twin-engine transport, which received a three-hundred-plane production order in 1947.[141] By then he had begun developing a jet fighter airplane that would emerge two years later as the Ouragan, followed soon after by the Mystere and the supersonic

Super-Mystere. In 1956 this line of jet fighters culminated in the Mirage prototype, which could fly at twice the speed of sound. All four fighter designs were ordered by the French air force and, furthermore, they won substantial export orders. Dassault Aviation also produced a shipboard fighter for the navy's aircraft carriers, a strategic bomber for the air force, and in the 1960s a business/executive jet—a very successful entry into the civil-aircraft market.

The success of Dassault Aviation was a vindication of the start-up strategy Dassault had learnt from the experience of his previous two careers in aircraft construction. His start-up strategy was noted by the French authors of a book on business heroes, *From Predators to Icons*. They summed up the start of Dassault's third career in aircraft construction by pointing to the similarities with his two previous start-up ventures in this line of business.

> The relaunching of Marcel Dassault's business followed the same pattern as in 1917 [and 1930?]: manufacture of propellers, hiring of engineers, design of an aircraft that was *not* very innovative but responded perfectly to a precise need of the colonial administration, reconstruction of an industrial manufacturing apparatus, and finally the design of a more ambitious and *innovative* airplane: the Ouragan jet fighter in 1949.[142]

Yet his second, 1930s career in aircraft construction had in fact *begun* with an innovative, all-metal-construction design. He had not stuck with the familiar but increasingly outmoded wood-and-fabric construction or, more appropriately, opted for the compromise of metal-and-fabric construction. This compromise was adopted several years later by the British Hawker Hurricane fighter, which was still numerically the RAF's main fighter plane when it defeated the Nazi aerial onslaught on Britain in 1940. The Hurricane has been described by a military historian as a 'derivative' design, in the sense of 'building upon a proven technology', and especially in the case of its braced-frame fuselage of metal frame and fabric covering.[143] It is surprising that Dassault did not choose a similar compromise when he returned to aircraft construction in 1930 and instead had preferred a more advanced, all-metal-construction design.

As the design initially failed to win any orders, he may well have considered in hindsight that this strategy was a mistake—and that he had been taught a lesson for future reference. So his start-up strategy in 1945–47 may well have been based on a lesson he had learnt from the 1930 start-up, namely not to begin too innovatively. Indeed Dassault Aviation's official history notes that as late as 1947 Dassault felt that military jets were an opportunity to be exploited 'on condition that one avoided falling into the trap of trying to produce unduly ambitious aircraft'.[144]

This lesson from the 1930s may even have been the basis of the distinctive Dassault Aviation product-development strategy. It had been evident ever since his military-jet programme began in 1947 and it led to a series of very successful designs. The strategy 'seeks to draw maximal advantage from the technical experience acquired from working on successive aircraft, and to avoid disruptive changes, leading—one step at a time—to progress on new models and to innovations limited to the intended objective, wherever possible using tried and tested solutions at a minimum of risk'.[145]

Dassault's personal contribution to this product development was an area in which his emphasis on learning was very evident. In his autobiography he recounts presiding at Saturday-afternoon deliberative and learning meetings that would 'talk about the final preparation of our planes and new projects to be developed'.[146] Unlike Walton's Saturday-morning meetings, there were not many participants and most were technical specialists, such as his firm's technical director, testing-centre engineers, and test pilots.[147] Dassault's willingness to learn from his test pilots was evident, too, at flight-testing stage and helped him to make improvements during this late stage in the development of his airplanes. 'I analyse the impressions of the test pilots in order to improve the plane's stability and also to make it more responsive to the controls and easier to handle.'[148]

Such willingness to learn about what needs improving was not characteristic of all aircraft manufacturers in this era of aviation. For example, it seems to have been comparatively uncommon in the British aircraft industry during the pioneering 1944–54 decade of the jet age. Waterton's book on test-flying during this decade has argued that British firms tended to be influenced too much by airplane designers, who did not like a test pilot criticizing 'their baby' and, 'like doting parents, blinded themselves to its faults'.[149] The contrast with Dassault Aviation is highlighted by the French firm's test-engineering maxims: (1) the pilot is always right; (2) the engineer can never be too careful; (3) there is no such thing as 'normal'; and (4) optimism is the worst enemy.[150] Waterton claimed that British firms actually ignored test pilots' criticisms and warnings, even though the pilots were representing what customers and potential customers were going to say about the airplane.[151] In contrast, Dassault's autobiography depicts him as keen to learn from his test pilots so that he could improve the plane *before* it was assessed by outsiders and potential customers. His test pilots would therefore never experience the situation which Waterton had in mind when he noted that nothing is 'more infuriating and humiliating than to attempt to put over one's points to someone who just doesn't want to know—especially when he is the person who makes decisions'.[152] At Dassault Aviation, the person who made the decisions certainly did want to know about his airplanes.

Dassault's readiness to learn was evident, too, in his increasingly export-oriented marketing strategy.[153] It involved learning how to deal with foreign governments and companies that were very different from France's but could see the advantages of buying Dassault's excellent aircraft. He notes in his autobiography that the two planes of which he was especially proud had both been great export successes: more than 900 of the Mirage fighters had been sold to foreign air forces and more than 400 Falcon business/executive jets had been sold around the world.[154] The Mirage had become internationally famous as Israel's key fighter plane in its victorious 1967 war with Egypt, Syria, and Jordan. The Falcon had become well known in America, where the majority of Falcons had been sold, but it was not known so much as a Dassault, French product because Pan American Airways had acquired an exclusive agency and set up a Business-Jet Corporation to market the plane.[155]

By the time Dassault was writing about these export successes, he had long since relinquished managerial control of his corporation. In the 1950s he resigned as managing director—though remaining in charge of 'technical and industrial management'—and seems to have formed a dual-leadership team with Vallières, his managing director.[156] Vallières also became company chairman when Dassault Aviation became a public company in 1968 and he would continue as joint-leader until the founder's death in 1986, when Dassault's son Serge took over as chairman and CEO.[157] By then it was a classic example of a leader using learning to establish a corporation in an internationally competitive industry, which had undergone dramatic changes since he first began designing wooden propellers for airplanes that were little different from the Wright brothers' plane.

6

Intel: Grove's *Only the Paranoid Survive*

Some five years after Walton died, Andy Grove became *Time* magazine's 1997 'man of the year' and by then he was 'arguably, the most admired business leader of his era'.[1] He was leader of a brilliantly successful high-tech corporation, Intel, which manufactured silicon semiconductor microchips and specialized in the most sophisticated microchips: the microprocessor CPU (central processing unit) chips which were the heart and brain of desktop personal computers. Intel had been founded by Robert Noyce and Gordon Moore in 1968 but during the early 1970s their dual-leadership team developed into triple leadership, with their key manager, Andy Grove, joining them as the third member of the team. By the end of the 1970s Noyce was taking a less active role in Intel's affairs, leaving CEO Moore and Grove to develop a two-role version of dual leadership.

In 1987 Grove became CEO and the sole leader of the corporation. He held the position until 1998 and then served as Intel's chairman until his retirement in 2005. During his eleven years as CEO, Grove presided over Intel's golden age. Sales increased from nearly $2 billion in 1987 to more than $26 billion in 1998 and there was a spectacular increase in profitability.[2] Intel's ranking on the Fortune 500 list of America's largest corporations rocketed up from 200 to 38, and it became the world's largest manufacturer of semiconductor microchips, with a near monopoly in the production of personal-computer microprocessors.[3]

Another reason, however, why Grove was such an admired business leader is that he had written a highly acclaimed management text *Only the Paranoid Survive*. This partly autobiographical work was published in 1996 and when the paperback edition appeared a few years later, it had several impressive testimonials on its back cover. Reviewers had ranked it with Sloan's *My Years with General Motors* and there was a perceptive testimonial from Steve Jobs: 'This book is about one super-important concept. You must learn about Strategic Inflection Points, because sooner or later you are going to live through one.' The book was indeed largely about inflection-point crises but it also taught the reader how to survive or even exploit these adaptive crises and, furthermore, the lessons were based on what the author had learnt from personal experience.

Grove's book therefore provides a leader's-eye view of learning—the seventh rational method—being used to enhance a corporation. Indeed, Grove emphasized learning as a method of developing his corporation and so this chapter is in a sense extending the previous chapter's account of how Walton and Dassault emphasized learning. Like them, Grove seems to have emphasized learning as both a favourite and a key method: this seems to be due to both personal preference and the circumstances he was facing. Unlike Walton and Dassault, however, he was enhancing rather than establishing a corporation and in fact he enhanced Intel in two different ways. First, through learning from experience Grove enhanced Intel's crisis management in the crucially important area of responding to adaptive crises.[4] Second, by basing a book upon this learning Grove enhanced Intel's reputation in the business world. The corporation was now seen to be led by an executive who was willing and able to teach the whole business world how to deal with these crises.

In addition to these enhancements, Grove was inspiring his employee-followers with rational confidence. He was using and indeed emphasizing an appropriate rational method, learning, and he had very capably learnt (acquiring broad and in-depth knowledge) how to deal with adaptive crises. The evidence was there for all to see in his book's theoretical as well as practical account of these crises. For Grove's book included not just personal experiences but also (1) examples of how other firms and industries had suffered similar adaptive crises, (2) a crisis-management framework for dealing with these crises, and (3) new concepts—'inflection point' and '10×' change—with which to analyse and discuss such extraordinary crises.[5]

What is more, Grove's book and its crisis-management framework showed how to use the appropriate rational methods when dealing with an adaptive crisis. The most important method was rapid adaptation, even if Grove seemed to emphasize it more in theory than practice and as a lesson to be learnt rather than a method that he had used effectively in the past. In fact, the crisis-management framework is best termed the 'adaptive' framework because it is both dealing with adaptive crises and using rapid adaptation as the most important method of dealing with these crises. His framework also mentions, however, all the other rational methods of developing a corporation, even if they are not always mentioned clearly or favourably.

Grove's enhancement of Intel will therefore be viewed through the 'prism' of his book. The first section of the chapter will discuss his book's account of Intel's adaptive crises in 1985 and 1994. The second section will examine the three-stage adaptive framework that he presents as an aid to dealing with adaptive crises. The third section of the chapter will focus on a part of Grove's framework that is especially relevant to high-tech industries and firms: the *pre*-deliberation process of *experimentation*. This process provides alternatives, such as new products, to choose from when senior management is deliberating about how to respond to an adaptive crisis. Furthermore, the process is crucially important even when a firm is not facing an adaptive crisis but instead the more 'ordinary' problem of ensuring that it is producing a constant stream of innovations and even some diversification.

So this third section will look at how Intel encouraged the invention of the microprocessor and then will move on to David Packard's 1995 memoirs *The HP Way: How Bill Hewlett and I Built Our Company*. Packard's book tells how he and the co-founder of Hewlett-Packard (HP) encouraged experimentation and diversification. They even developed an innovative experimentation system that was based upon HP's version of the decentralized organizational structure which Sloan had pioneered at General Motors. However, HP's remarkable experimentation system eventually ran out of steam, and the chapter will end with a section that explores a different approach. This is Steve Jobs's relatively top-down and hands-on approach to experimentation and diversification, which gave Apple a series of brilliantly successful new products in the 2000s: the iPod, iPhone, and iPad.

Learning to Adapt Intel

Grove's book is subtitled *How to Exploit the Crisis Points that Challenge Every Company* and indeed his key concept is the adaptive 'crisis point' that he terms a 'strategic inflection point'. Grove coined this term to describe points in time, in the history of a business or industry, when 'the old strategic picture dissolves and gives way to the new'.[6] The old ways of doing business are giving way to the new and, after the inflection point, business is more like the new ways than the old ways. But these 'full-scale changes in the way business is conducted' are often difficult to identify and understand:

> All businesses operate by some set of unstated rules and sometimes these rules change—often in very significant ways. Yet there is no flashing sign that heralds these rule changes. They creep up on you... You know only that something has changed, something big, something significant, even if it's not entirely clear what that something is.[7]

It is not surprising that 'companies struggle to adapt' to such changes in the rules of business but it is more surprising that Grove wanted 'to share the lessons I've learned' about these adaptive crises—to share the thinking about them that 'has helped our business survive in an increasingly competitive environment'.[8]

His key lesson was the need to emphasize *rapid adaptation* to overcome the tendency towards rigidity—resistance to adaptation—that often occurs in these adaptive crises. The tendency towards rigidity is evident in the two Intel cases that Grove presents as illustrations of a strategic inflection point. The earlier of the two occurred in the mid-1980s, when Intel was led by the dual-leadership team of CEO Moore and Chief Operating Officer (COO) Grove. The origins of the crisis can be traced back to the founding of Intel in 1968 as a manufacturer of memory microchips—the silicon semiconductor chips that were used to store memory in computers and other electronic devices. The new firm was very successful, becoming a public company as early as 1971, and by the 1980s Intel was one of the leading firms in the now greatly expanded memory-chip business. But by then, too, Japanese firms had become increasingly competitive players in the American semiconductor industry. Grove acknowledges that 'the Japanese started beating us in the memory [chip] business in the early eighties'.[9] In fact their mass production of low-priced high-quality memory chips was changing the rules of business in the industry.

Fortunately for Intel, however, its other microchip product—the microprocessor—was becoming increasingly popular and was not so vulnerable to competition. Intel had developed this data-processing, calculating microchip in the 1970s but it seemed to have limited commercial potential until in 1981 IBM included an Intel microprocessor in the design of its first desktop personal computer. Furthermore, Intel's microprocessor was also included in the 'cloned' versions of this IBM PC, which were developed and manufactured by new firms entering the rapidly expanding personal-computer market. This growing microprocessor business could therefore offset the losses produced by the change of rules in the memory-chip business.

But in 1984 the market for microprocessors suffered a cyclical downturn and so Intel's microprocessor sales and profits could no longer offset the losses in the memory-chip business.[10] Intel's forced adaptive response to this crisis was to get out of the memory-chip business and focus its efforts on microprocessor chips and markets. However, it took until mid-1985 to make the adaptive decision and took until 1987 to complete the adaptive change. Jackson's *Inside Intel* argues that the trends which provoked the 1985 decision 'had been at work for at least five years, and possibly more. Had Intel taken steps to respond to them early, it might never have been forced to abandon one of its two core businesses.'[11] What is more, Jackson criticizes the tardy way in which Intel implemented its long-delayed decision to make the appropriate adaptive response. After it was finally decided in mid-1985 to get out of the memory-chip business, 'it took a full further year before Intel had implemented the decision to pull out—and another full year before the company could return to profitability'.[12] So Intel's policy-making and policy-implementing response to the adaptive crisis seems a classic example of rigidity's resistance to adaptation.

Intel's second adaptive crisis occurred in 1994, when Grove was CEO and sole leader of the corporation. Its latest-generation microprocessor, the Pentium microchip, suffered from a slight design flaw that on extremely rare occasions—some once every nine billion times—produced a small error in the chip's long-division calculations. Near the end of 1994, Internet and media reports about the 'Pentium Bug' led to Intel coming under intense public scrutiny and criticism as well as having to handle thousands of inquiries and complaints from users of computers containing the Pentium microprocessor. Initially, Intel's response was to provide only *some* users with an error-free replacement Pentium, namely those who were making a lot of calculations and therefore much more likely to experience the error. It was not until weeks after the crisis began that the corporation changed its response and offered a replacement to *any* user who asked for one. This change in policy ended the crisis but, as in the 1985 case, the correct decision was too-long delayed.

In the Pentium case, however, the delay and rigidity seems to have had both short-term and longer-term aspects. For Jackson argues that the delay of weeks in responding with the appropriate policy was due to a preceding delay of *years* in adopting a more marketing-oriented perspective.

> [Grove] and his colleagues still looked at the world from an engineering rather than a marketing point of view. Branding, image, consumer psychology—all the factors that argued for taking a short-term cost in order to maintain the value of the Intel name in customers' minds were just beginning to appear on the Intel horizon.[13]

If Intel's leadership had adopted a more marketing-oriented perspective in the early 1990s, it would not have been so slow in 1994 to respond in the appropriately apologetic and generous, full-replacement fashion.

Grove explains Intel's rigidity in 1985 and 1994 as largely due to its leaders' failure to perceive that the times or circumstances had changed. In the Pentium case, he acknowledges that the delay was due to his failure to perceive that the rules of business had changed. 'It took a barrage of relentless criticism to make me realize that something had changed' in Intel's marketing environment and that 'we needed to adapt to the new environment'.[14] In hindsight Grove ascribes the change to his firm's early 1990s 'Intel Inside' marketing strategy, because it had led owners of personal computers emblazoned with the 'Intel Inside' label to consider themselves customers of Intel and to view its microprocessor in the same light as any other household goods they had bought—and would want replaced if the product was faulty.[15] But as Grove was not a marketing expert, it is hardly surprising that he had been slow to perceive this change in the marketing environment and had not seen the risks involved in the new marketing strategy when it had been proposed a few years earlier.

In the 1985 crisis, however, the problem and perceptions had been more complex. In this case, there had been a change in the competitive environment, not the marketing environment, and it had been created by the challenge from highly competitive Japanese firms. In this case, too, the resistance to adaptation had involved more than simply a failure of perception; it had also involved intellectual prejudices and an emotional attachment to memory chips—the product on which Intel had been based. 'Intel equalled memories in all our minds. How could we give up our identity?'[16] Grove notes that these are the sorts of situation in which CEOs who have been brought in from outside their firms have the advantage of being 'unencumbered by such emotional involvement and therefore are capable of applying an impersonal logic to the situation'.[17] Such impersonal logic would also be applied by any leader capably using the appropriate rational method—rapid adaptation.

At times it might also be appropriate to use the other adaptive method, innovative adaptation.[18] There seems to have been nothing innovative about Intel's adaptive responses in 1985 and 1994. The latter was merely adopting the standard crisis-management approach of any consumer-oriented corporation; the other was merely a 'strategic exit' downsizing, namely getting out of the memory-chip business. As Grove points out, downsizing is a low-risk as well as unimaginative response: 'after all, how can you go wrong by shuttering factories and laying people off if the benefits of such actions are going to show up in tomorrow's bottom line and will be applauded by the financial community?'[19] In Intel's case, the post-1985 downsizing involved closing factories, cutting more than seven thousand jobs, and laying off more than a quarter of the firm's employment base.[20]

But there may have also been an *innovative* aspect to Intel's adaptive response. For CEO Moore's biographers imply that Intel's innovative shift to sole-source production of its new 386 microprocessor was part of the response to the crisis: it was part of how 'Gordon Moore turned Intel around' and of 'Gordon's plan to reinvigorate Intel'.[21] According to Grove's biographer, becoming 'the sole source for the new microprocessor it introduced in October of 1985' was a 'vital part of Intel's strategy'.[22] By shifting to sole-sourcing, Intel was rejecting the standard practice of providing manufacturer customers with a second source of supply. Such second-sourcing 'was a long established practice in the semiconductor industry' as manufacturers 'demanded that semiconductor suppliers license their technologies to fellow chip companies to guarantee a continuous supply' and of course as protection against sole-source monopolistic pricing and practices.[23]

Intel could now risk, however, disregarding its customers' preferences and shifting to sole-source production of its 386 microprocessor. For its major customers were manufacturing IBM and IBM-clone personal computers that had been designed to use not only Intel microprocessors but also Microsoft software, which was now being designed to run on Intel microprocessors. This monopolistic combination of Microsoft's Windows operating system and Intel's microprocessor—the 'Wintel' combination—gave Intel what Moore judged to be 'enough of a lock' on its computer-manufacturing customers to have them 'buy the processor from us anyhow, even if we were the sole source' and the customers preferred a less monopolistic situation.[24] As IBM/clone personal computers were dominating the growing personal-computer market, Intel's decision to sole-source production led to its microprocessors being included in two-thirds of the nine million personal computers sold in 1987.[25]

This innovative, monopolistic aspect of Intel's adaptive response made a huge contribution to the firm's spectacular revival. 'Monopoly-based profits gave Intel an astounding recovery to revenue of $2 billion and a record $250 million profit' only a year after the corporation had made its first-ever loss.[26] The leadership team's rigidity had been offset and overshadowed by the success and brilliance of its eventual response. Indeed Grove's biographer declares that the 'decision to sole-source the 386 [microprocessor] proved a masterstroke' and was 'among the most important strategic moves in the history of the computer industry'.[27] The lesson to be learnt from this case was that the rapidity of an adaptive response was less important than its *quality* and, furthermore, a high-quality response required some innovation.

When Grove became CEO in 1987, he inherited a crisis-management approach that he and Moore had oriented towards high-quality, innovative adaptations rather than rapid adaptive responses. But Grove significantly reoriented it towards an aspect of adaptation that is normally associated with a non-threatening situation, namely the opportunistic aspect of 'identifying and taking full advantage of the opportunities offered' that was mentioned in Chapters 1 and 3. Taking advantage of an opportunity is mentioned, too, in Grove's book and indeed he points out that an inflection-point change can be an opportunity rather than a threat. 'When the way business is being conducted changes, it creates opportunities for players who are adept at operating in the new way. This can apply to newcomers or to incumbents' who find that the change brings 'an opportunity for a new period of growth'.[28] Grove reoriented Intel's crisis-management approach towards this opportunity-for-growth perspective in the late 1980s and in fact he oriented it towards taking full advantage of this opportunity for growth. During his tenure as CEO, Intel took full advantage of its new position as a monopolistic supplier to the constantly expanding personal-computer market. By 1996, some *seventy* million personal computers were being sold world-wide, more than 80 per cent had an Intel microprocessor inside, and the corporation was enjoying gratifyingly high profit margins on these products: a few years earlier, its more than 25 per cent return on sales had led to Intel being described as the world's most profitable firm of that size.[29]

Taking full advantage of this opportunity had involved Intel's use of the fearsome 'treadmill' strategy. It had been devised by Moore and learnt by Grove in the 1970s and was employed against firms that were manufacturing their own versions of the microprocessor. The treadmill strategy was based on an idea that became known as Moore's Law of semiconductor development: the most famous generalization produced by the high-tech industries.[30] In 1975 Moore had explicitly formulated this 'Law' as a prediction that the capability of semiconductor microchips would continue to double every year for another decade and then would slow to a doubling of capability every *two* years.[31] With microchip capability growing at this rapid and predictable rate, he would aim to put his competitors on the 'treadmill' by continually producing new generations of ever more capable microchips—thereby staying ahead of his competitors and forcing them into perpetually running to catch up. In Moore's words:

> You must keep moving to stay with or ahead of the competition. Anyone who wants to compete has to make a huge investment. If we have 80-plus percent market share and our competitor has 20 percent, we spend fast enough that he has a really tough time keeping up. 'Get 'em on the treadmill'.[32]

His Japanese competitors in the memory-chip business had eventually defeated the treadmill strategy but when it was applied to the microprocessor business, the treadmill would continue to be an effective monopolistic strategy throughout the 1980s–90s.

Grove used the treadmill particularly effectively when Intel was threatened by a surge of competition in the early 1990s. This 'formidable competition' included rival microprocessors, rival technology, and some new competitors, especially a consortium of Apple, IBM, and Motorola that sought 'to break Intel's stranglehold on the personal computer CPU [microprocessor] industry'.[33] In typical treadmill fashion, however, Grove announced in 1993 the arrival of Intel's latest-generation microprocessor, the Pentium, which was *five times* more capable than its predecessor, the 486, and was better than anything the competition could offer.[34]

But the Pentium proved to be a mixed blessing for Grove, as was discussed earlier. The 1994 Pentium-bug adaptive crisis highlighted his failure to perceive an inflection-point change in the marketing environment. This may explain why his book, written the following year, tends to view inflection-point changes as a threat rather than an opportunity. For example, when he examines the causes of these strategic inflection points, his analysis is more concerned with threat than opportunity. He identifies six forces that 'determine the competitive well-being of a business': the power, vigour, and competence of (1) existing competitors, (2) potential competitors, (3) suppliers, (4) customers, (5) complementors, from whom customers buy complementary products, and (6) the 'substitution' factor, which is the 'possibility that your product or service can be built or delivered in a different way'—and is the 'most deadly' of these six forces.[35] A very large change in one of these six forces is called a '10×' change, 'suggesting that the force has become ten times what it was just recently'.[36] Among his examples were two which have been mentioned in earlier chapters. His example of a 10× change in competition was the change experienced by general stores in small towns affected by the arrival of Wal-Mart, and his example of a 10× change in customers was the 1920s change in people's taste in cars, which caused the inflection point that threatened Ford and was an opportunity exploited by Sloan's General Motors.[37]

Grove viewed the Internet as an inflection point that was more of an opportunity than a threat for Intel.[38] Exploiting this opportunity, though, would require Intel to make a major adaptive response to the new environment: 'we won't harness the opportunity by simply letting things happen to us'.[39] Intel was already, however, enjoying an Internet-propelled boom that was in fact simply happening to it without the need for a high-quality, innovative adaptive response. Malone points out that its consumer customers were upgrading their personal computers (and the microprocessors inside) in order to access the new features becoming available on the Internet: 'images, then audio, then video'.[40] Intel's revenue was therefore increasing 'at a pace that seemed almost impossible for a company of its size': from nearly $6 billion in 1992 to $16 billion in 1996 and over $33 billion in 2000.[41] This now iconic corporation was once again taking full advantage of its opportunities and seemed to be a great advertisement for the lessons taught by Grove's book, especially its recommended framework for overcoming adaptive crises.

The Three-Stage Adaptive Framework

Grove's book both described strategic inflection points and sought 'to provide a framework in which to deal with them'.[42] The later chapters of his book explain and explore this three-stage adaptive framework. In addition to adaptation, it involves other rational methods of developing a corporation—the deliberative methods and learning—which in this case are enhancing a corporation or any other firm by reducing the threat and/or exploiting the opportunity created by an adaptive crisis.

In effect Grove provides a framework for using rapid adaptation as a rational method of developing a corporation in these specific circumstances—dealing with an adaptive crisis. However, the adaptive framework is not 'all about' rapid adaptation; there is room for other rational methods to play a role in one or more of its three stages. The first stage is basically about *learning* that an adaptive crisis is coming, the second stage is about *deliberating* how to respond to this inflection point, and the third stage, too, includes a deliberative element because the implementation of the response will involve discussions with employees about why and how the firm is going to implement this new direction.

In the first stage of the framework, learning is crucial because it provides some warning—as early as possible—that a crisis is coming. Learning that a crisis is coming will involve listening to the firm's Cassandra-like 'prophets of doom', because they are 'quick to recognize impending change and cry out an early warning' that the change may well create a crisis.[43] Cassandras are typically middle-management people who have a different perspective from senior management and have a tendency to 'take the warning signs more seriously' because they are serving in the front lines of the firm.[44] Listening to them is 'an investment in learning what goes on at the distant periphery of your business' and of course 'the flow of bad news from the periphery' should never be discouraged by a leader if he or she wants some early warning of an impending inflection-point crisis.[45]

In contrast, Grove is dubious about using quantitative calculation in this first, learning stage. In fact 'when dealing with emerging trends, you may very well have to go against rational extrapolation of data and rely instead on anecdotal observations and your instincts'.[46] Furthermore, relying upon quantitative calculation may cause a delay in moving on to the next stage and making some response to the crisis. 'Timing is everything' but 'that means acting when not everything is known, when the data aren't yet in. Even those who believe in a scientific approach to management will have to rely on instinct and personal judgement.'[47]

It should be noted that Grove was happy to use and indeed emphasize quantitative calculation in *other circumstances*, when dealing with other problems and policy decisions. He 'believed that everything should be measured, quantitatively if at all possible,' and had developed an Intel culture that valued not only quantification but problem-solving based on quantitative data.[48] Yet when the circumstances—an adaptive crisis—demanded it, he downplayed the role of quantitative calculation.

The other calculative method, strategic calculation, has an ambivalent role in his adaptive framework. Grove mentions strategic calculation only by implication—by referring to strategy—and his remarks indicate that not much calculation is required. He expresses a preference for strategic actions rather than plans and for pursuing an 'early-mover' strategy: only through 'such a strategy can you hope to compete for the future' of an industry, even if being early leads to mistakes that require the firm to 'course-correct'.[49] So Grove can hardly be said to advocate using strategic calculation in these inflection-point circumstances, even if in other circumstances he clearly favoured the use of strategic calculation.[50]

Unlike strategic and quantitative calculation, the two deliberative methods play a crucial role in his adaptive framework. In the first stage there may be some deliberation about whether a particular development is indeed an inflection point and then, more importantly, in the second stage there is always deliberation about how to respond to the crisis: a 'powerful adaptive organization' therefore 'tolerates and even encourages debate. These debates are vigorous, devoted to exploring issues, indifferent to rank and include individuals of varied backgrounds.'[51] Such debates are an excellent example of diverse deliberation but Grove does not provide any comparable examples of the institutionalized form of deliberation. In fact his memorable example of this form of deliberation occurs in the following, final stage of the adaptive framework.

The final, third stage is focused on *implementing* the firm's *response* to the inflection-point crisis—implementing the firm's new strategic direction. Grove's account of this stage is largely concerned with how firms' leaders communicate the response, the new direction, to their firms' employees. He stresses that this communication must involve an interactive element, which enables employees to ask the leader for clarification, explanations and solutions.[52] So there will be some discussion about why and how the firm is taking this new direction and the discussion will include some deliberation, even if only about finding solutions to problems that may arise when implementing the new direction.

Furthermore, the interactive communication will involve some *institutionalized* deliberation, such as the leader having workplace discussions with employees. Grove argues that the best method of communicating a new direction to employees is to 'go to their workplaces, get them together and explain over and over what you're trying to achieve' by speaking to them and answering their questions.[53] However, this kind of institutionalized deliberation is not very appropriate in a corporation or any large firm because its leader is 'often distanced from direct contact with many managers and employees'.[54] How can a leader communicate with all a corporation's many employees and still retain an interactive element in the communication?

Email was Grove's solution to the problem of combining interaction with mass communication. He saw email as a way of not only reaching large numbers of employees but also answering their questions: 'the electronic equivalent of answering a question at an employee forum'.[55] Email had begun to be adopted by some firms in the early 1980s and so by the time Grove's book appeared in 1996 email was a well-established way of communicating with employees.[56] However, two shortcomings had already emerged.

Email was an emotionally 'distant' form of communication that lacked the personal, facial, and voice aspect of leaders' workplace visits or even a Walton-like television broadcast.[57] In addition, there was the practical problem that emails from the leader might produce too many replies for personal interaction and discussion to be feasible. For example, there were nearly six thousand replies when General Electric's CEO Jack Welch sent out his first company-wide email.[58]

But there seemed to be no alternative for a corporation as large and global as Intel. Grove argued that in these cases, '"managing by walking around" has to a large extent been supplanted by letting your fingers do the walking on your computer'.[59] Managing by walking around (MBWA) was a Hewlett-Packard invention that Packard described as a technique 'for helping managers and supervisors to know their people and understand the work their people are doing, while at the same time making themselves more visible and accessible to their people'.[60] Now the computer had to provide an electronic equivalent of MBWA and of the workplace employee-forum's questions, answers, and discussion.

Anyway, communicating the new direction was only part of this final, implementation stage in Grove's framework. Implementing the new direction would involve other processes, problems, and perhaps even further stages towards a 'resolution' of the adaptive crisis. Similarly, the second, deliberative stage had both included and been preceded by a process of experimentation. Grove describes this experimentation process as the *pre*-deliberation aspect of the debates about how to respond to the adaptive crisis. He points out that 'in order to explore your alternatives' there have to be alternatives *available*, such as new products that are worth considering.[61] They are products that the firm has been experimenting with and now considers sufficiently credible alternatives to be worth exploring in a debate about how to respond to the adaptive crisis. And it is too late to *begin* experimenting at this stage of the adaptive process. As Grove stresses, 'you can't suddenly start experimenting when you're in trouble' and wondering how to respond:

> It's too late to do it once things have changed in your core business. Ideally you should have experimented with new products, technologies, channels, promotions and new customers all along. . . . Intel experimented with microprocessors for over ten years before the opportunity and the imperative arose to make them the centrepiece of our corporate strategy.[62]

His depiction of the 1985 crisis as 'the opportunity and the imperative' is much more accurate than his remark about Intel having 'experimented' with microprocessors for over ten years beforehand. Intel had been selling this 'new' product for several years and indeed came to depend upon it in the early 1980s as sales of the firm's memory-chip product were increasingly affected by Japanese competition.

In fact, Intel seems to have reduced its experimentation in the ten years before the 1985 crisis. It had publicly announced the invention of the microprocessor as early as 1971 and was producing its third-generation microprocessor by 1975, when co-founder Noyce was Intel's president/CEO, co-founder Moore its executive vice-president and Grove its operations manager.[63] Noyce's biographer suggests that 'the microprocessor would not have happened at Intel if it had not been for Bob' and certainly Noyce seems to have been the leading advocate of the microprocessor's technological and commercial potential.[64] When in 1975 he announced his retirement as president/CEO, he noted that Intel's 'entrepreneurial phase is not entirely over but the emphasis is shifting'.[65] And in the mid-1970s Grove was announcing that Intel would be copying McDonald's standardization of product and production.[66]

Intel's lack of an experimentation process can readily explain the corporation's poor record of diversification in the 1980s–2000s. In 2005 Grove presented a blunt, revealing assessment of his corporation's track record of experimentation and diversification:

> Intel had been 'shitty' at diversifying no matter whether through acquisition or internal venturing [within the firm]. The reason was a combined lack of 'strategic recognition' and 'strategic will.' Whatever Intel tried did not, after a year or two, look as good as the microprocessor. The result was that the company consistently gave up too soon.[67]

If Intel 'gave up too soon' on innovations because they did not 'look as good as the microprocessor', this may have been largely because Grove had reoriented the corporation towards taking full advantage of opportunities—as it had with the microprocessor—instead of coming up with high-quality, innovative adaptations. The post-Grove leadership seems to have been unable to re-reorient and, furthermore, it seems to have been unable to create an effective experimentation process that would supply new products when they were needed.

In the 2000s Intel was in need of new products to consider in its deliberations about how to deal with a new technological change. Mobile high-tech and IT products, especially mobile phones, were becoming more prominent than personal computers, and the change was being exploited not by Intel but by such firms as ARM. Malone notes that this British chip-designing firm had 'spotted the opportunity in mobile early and created superb designs specifically for use in laptop computers, palmtops, and the new generation of cell phones'.[68] As Apple was one of its founding investors, ARM also had 'an inside track to be maker of the processor of choice for the greatest run of innovation in tech history': the iPod, iPhone, and iPad.[69] Although Intel missed out on this run of innovation, its former leader had at least provided an analysis of how to deal with the problem of being an innovative firm and diversifying into new products. His analysis of experimentation and deliberation was arguably his book's most significant and widely applicable lesson, as it applied to not only adaptive crises but also a firm's 'ordinary' problems of innovation and diversification.

Experimentation and *The HP Way*

As Grove described, deliberating about new products and having a pre-deliberative experimentation process are vital aspects of high-tech firms' deliberative and adaptive processes. For example, Intel's successful 1985 adaptation can be traced back to its invention of the microprocessor in the far-off days when the firm still had an effective experimentation process. This invention had been crucially encouraged by Intel's CEO, who at that time was the co-founder Robert Noyce. His biographer relates how Noyce encouraged the microprocessor's inventor when Ted Hoff first broached the idea to him in 1969.

> Noyce, who never would have claimed to know anything about computers, kept pushing Hoff, asking question after question, all of them so basic that Noyce was almost apologizing for his lack of knowledge. 'Um, can you tell me the functions of a computer operating system?'...It was the same Socratic method of forcing people to 'argue ourselves into some smart things,' as Vadasz put it, that had worked so well in the lab. At the end of the conversation, Noyce told Hoff, 'Why don't you go ahead and pursue those ideas?'[70]

This Socratic method was similar to Noyce's style in deliberative policy-making meetings, where he was 'seemingly more interested in understanding his colleagues' ideas than in expressing his own'.[71]

Arguably his encouragement of Hoff was a deliberative meeting, too, even though it was just two people discussing whether and how to develop a new idea. In this case it was deliberation about new products rather than policies but it took the same form of something being 'sold' to the leader: a new product idea that should be selected for more experiments, more development, or even putting into production. Such *product* deliberation was brilliantly institutionalized by another high-tech firm, the iconic Hewlett-Packard.

HP's deliberation about new products is described in David Packard's 1995 memoirs *The HP Way: How Bill Hewlett and I Built Our Company*. His book provides a leader's-eye view of how a two-man firm established in 1939 in a San Francisco garage was developed into one of the world's iconic high-tech corporations. It is included here as only a supplementary example, like the

Dassault example, and in this case to show leaders establishing a corporation partly through the use of both product deliberation and an innovative adaptation—an impressive experimentation system—outlined later in the section. Both factors helped to create the firm's remarkable track record for developing new products, such as hand-held calculators and desktop printers, which in turn explains the firm's development into an iconic corporation. Indeed Packard declares that this 'constant flow of good new products is the life-blood of Hewlett-Packard and essential to our growth'.[72]

The flow of good new products was the result of not just having new ideas but also product deliberation about which ideas to put into production. As Packard points out, 'there is no shortage of ideas. The problem is to select those that are likely to fill a real need in the marketplace' and, furthermore, 'an invention must not only fill a need, it must be an economical and efficient solution to that need'.[73] The problem of selection also involved the problem of turning down creative, innovative ideas while still giving the ideas' inventors some encouragement and helping them 'retain enthusiasm in the face of such disappointment'.[74] He therefore paid special tribute and attention to how Hewlett had brilliantly solved both problems by institutionalizing product deliberation about whether or not to select a new product idea for further development.

Like Packard, Hewlett was an electrical engineer and was the more technically oriented member of their dual-leadership team. When selecting product ideas for further development, he followed a three-stage deliberative process which was based on a series of informal procedural rules. When first approached by the inventor, Hewlett would receive the new idea with enthusiasm. 'He would listen, express excitement where appropriate and appreciation in general, while asking a few gentle and not too pointed questions.'[75] A few days later, there would be an inquisitorial stage. He would go back to the inventor and begin a 'thorough probing of the idea, [with] lots of give-and-take' and 'very pointed questions' but without any final decision.[76] Not long after the inquisitorial stage, there would be a final-decision meeting with the inventor. 'With appropriate logic and sensitivity, judgment was rendered' and even if the decision went against this new idea, the institutionalized deliberative process would have given the inventor some sense of satisfaction: 'a vitally important outcome for engendering continued enthusiasm and creativity'.[77]

This institutionalized deliberation was not the only innovative way in which Hewlett and Packard encouraged the flow of new products. They also developed an experimentation system, involving various parts and levels of the firm, which encouraged the invention and development of new product ideas. It was an institutional and indeed organizational means of ensuring that the inventors and developers were creating a flow of product ideas for the leaders' product deliberations.

Their innovative experimentation system was an adaptive response to a growth crisis that the firm experienced some twenty years after it was founded. By the time HP became a public company in 1957, it was selling over a hundred different products and was adding more each year.[78] These products, however, were specialized high-tech tools and instruments with specialized, narrow markets lacking much growth potential. As Packard's memoirs describe, HP was 'becoming the largest supplier in most of the major segments of the electronic-instrumentation business. But these segments, in total, were growing at only 6 percent per year, whereas we had been growing, out of our profits, at 22 percent. Obviously, that kind of growth could not continue without diversification' into other kinds of high-tech product, perhaps even into new product categories.[79]

So 'the need for diversification was clear' by the late 1950s, when he and Hewlett began to develop their experimentation system by instituting what he terms a 'divisionalizing' restructuring of the firm.[80] HP adopted a version of the organizational structure that had been pioneered by Sloan at General Motors in the 1920s. By introducing Sloanist 'operating divisions', Hewlett and Packard were hoping to encourage the initiative and creativity required for experimentation and diversification. Packard notes that a key goal of this divisionalizing was 'creating an environment that fostered individual motivation, initiative and creativity'.[81] As Malone's biography of Hewlett and Packard argues, their Sloanist restructuring was not motivated by the same concerns as many other firms' move in this direction, which usually 'was done for product line or marketing reasons'.[82] In the HP case, however, the leaders seem to have been mainly concerned with encouraging experimentation and diversification.[83]

This may explain why they took divisionalizing to the level of what Packard termed 'local' decentralization. As he relates, any division which grew to the 'substantial' size of 'producing many different products and employing as many as 1,500 people' was required 'to split off part of the division, giving it responsibility for an established, profitable product line and usually moving it to a new but nearby location'.[84] The key implication of this policy was that each division would produce only a small range of specialized products and therefore would focus on a relatively small, specialized, and 'local' market.

HP's local decentralization produced similar results to McDonald's local-control structure, namely adaptation to the local market. *The HP Phenomenon: Innovation and Business Transformation* notes that HP's small, 'atomized' divisions were able 'to invent their way to success in adaptive fashion, following dictates and whims of markets they had already served'.[85] In addition, the divisions were able to employ treadmill-like strategies against their competitors in these markets and, more importantly, were able to help HP enter or create *new* markets—divisional experimentation with new products would help diversify and transform HP.[86] The firm would be transformed from a maker of scientific instruments into a maker of scientific computers, then business computers and, eventually, desktop printers. Indeed 'HP's experience with product line renewal and company transformation' is 'among the most dramatic and effective of any corporation in history'.[87]

But the small-divisions structure created a major coordination problem. As the firm continued to grow, the number of divisions would also grow and become increasingly anomalous. By the mid-1960s, there were already more than a dozen divisions and during the next thirty years they would spawn more than *fifty* new product-manufacturing divisions.[88] As early as 1968, however, HP dealt with this problem by adopting the Sloan-pioneered measure of organizing divisions into groups headed by group managers. Packard describes HP's shift to a group structure as 'combining, organizationally, divisions with related product lines and markets into a group headed by a group manager with a small staff'.[89] By 1980, there were already ten groups or sub-groups and eventually there would be *thirteen* product groups, each headed by a group vice-president.[90] Unlike Sloan's group managers, they were a separate, intermediate layer of management and leadership which was responsible for the groups' planning, finances, operations, and experimentation.[91]

Another coordinating factor was the influence of the two leaders and their informal rules about experimentation with new products. The most basic rule was the tacit understanding that about 10 per cent of a division's revenues were to be allocated to its research and development department.[92] The key rule relating to coordination was Hewlett's ban on needless duplication. He allowed 'overlaps and cross-divisional competition to flourish, with but one clear rule—if a team had an inferior solution they were expected to abdicate the field'.[93]

The most obvious central contribution to the experimentation system was the assistance provided by headquarters' HP Laboratories. According to Packard, HP Labs was established in 1966 'to help lead the company into new technologies and product diversification'.[94] For example, it transferred new technologies to the divisions through strategy groups that reported to a group vice-president and involved all three levels of the experimentation system, central, group, and divisional, in a combined effort to develop new products.[95] These new products renewed existing product lines and also led to continual diversification into new lines or even a new product category.

Some twenty years later the experimentation system was still 'delivering' such triumphs. For in the 1980s local divisions and the vice-president of the Peripherals Group played important roles in the experimentation stage and development of HP's inkjet desktop printer—perhaps the most lucrative product that the corporation ever developed.[96] The experimentation system had clearly been a very successful as well as innovative adaptation to the growth crisis of the late 1950s.

Furthermore, the system's creation of new product categories had led to diversifications that transformed the corporation not once or twice but several times. Looking back from the early twenty-first century, *The HP Phenomenon* pointed out that by 'changing its leading products each decade', HP 'morphed its main product line six times in six decades—unheard of in American industry at this level'.[97] The first transformation occurred in 1949–59 and was a shift from audio-video to microwave products within the wide category of 'frequency-domain tools'; the second transformation had occurred by 1968, as acquisitions and internal diversification led to the category 'scientific instruments' becoming the leading source of revenue.[98] But by 1976 it had been overtaken by 'scientific computing', thanks to such pioneering new products as a desktop calculator, a hand-held calculator, and a small computer that would be adopted by businesses as well as scientists.[99] Indeed 'business computing' would become the leading product category by 1986—this was HP's fourth transformation—and by then nearly half of the firm's revenue was derived from the two product categories of business computing and scientific computing.[100]

The HP-type of transformation was not created by making a 'strategic exit' from a major product category, as Intel did in 1985. An HP transformation was instead created by a successful expansion into a new product category, which became so successful that the older product categories were soon overshadowed by this latest triumph of HP's experimentation system. It had been the driving force behind decades of consistent expansion into new product categories and, furthermore, expansion into a large and iconic high-tech corporation.

The experimentation system was therefore the greatest product of Hewlett and Packard's dual leadership, which ended in 1978 when Hewlett retired from the post of CEO. By then the corporation had begun its transformation from scientific computing to business computing. Similarly, the rise of the desktop printer—the fifth transformation—was well underway when Packard retired in 1993 from the post of chairman of HP.[101]

But only a few years later the experimentation system was clearly in decline or already defunct. Its decline seems largely due to longer-term tendencies identified in Burgelman, McKinney and Meza's recent history of HP's strategic leadership *Becoming Hewlett-Packard*. These longer-term tendencies can be traced back to the 1980s and to the leadership of Packard and John Young, who became CEO after Hewlett retired. In the 1980s Young focused on developing the new 'business computing' product category and its associated technology, systems, and product lines.[102] He also refashioned HP's organizational structure by integrating and centralizing the various groups and divisions associated with the business-computing product category. However, HP's *other* groups and divisions remained decentralized and continued to contribute to the experimentation system. In fact the long-established system 'delivered' again during these years, as noted earlier, and the 1980s saw the dramatic rise of the desktop-printer product category, specifically the LaserJet and the InkJet printers.

Yet chairman Packard was unhappy and attempted to reduce HP's organizational complexity by restoring the traditional degree of decentralization.[103] The resulting 1990 reorganization, however, saw a new approach to 'decentralization' that weakened central control but was no longer a 'local' decentralization; instead of strengthening the divisions at the periphery, it strengthened the group-level *intermediate* layer of management. Ten years earlier there had been ten groups or sub-groups but now there would be just three huge groups titled 'organizations'.[104] Such powerful and broad intermediate-level entities would prove to be less willing and able than their group predecessors to facilitate divisional-level innovation. And so this inadvertent weakening of the divisions-based experimentation system became the unintended trade-off for Young's success in developing business computing as a new product category.[105]

In 1992 he retired and was replaced as CEO by Lew Platt. Unlike Young, he did not focus on a new product category but instead promoted an existing product category, personal computers, which had been underemphasized by his predecessors. Although he achieved his goal of making HP a leader in the personal-computer industry, he did not develop any new product categories: 'No major new businesses emerged during Platt's time as CEO.'[106] This did not seem to be a problem in his first four years, as annual revenue more than doubled in this period, from $16 billion to $38 billion, and HP was judged by *Forbes* magazine to be the outstanding corporate performer of 1995.[107] However, soon after this triumph HP ran into problems and by the late 1990s the corporation was in a crisis situation. In fact it was a Grove-like adaptive crisis that had been caused largely by the success of Grove's firm, Intel. For HP's business-computing products were threatened by Intel's increasingly powerful microprocessors, by cheaper Intel-based computers, and by 'the rise of Wintel-based industry standards'.[108] HP therefore desperately needed its experimentation system to deliver an innovative new product category like the lucrative desktop printers. But the next transforming diversification would not begin until 2006 and would take the form of 'services' rather than a distinctive and lucrative product category.[109]

The experimentation system failed to deliver in the late 1990s because the longer-term debilitating tendencies had increased during the Platt era.[110] He continued to follow HP's new, intermediate-level approach to decentralization, which strengthened the intermediate level rather than the 'local' or 'grassroots' elements.[111] The 'effect on HP's fabled capacity to innovate' was disabling, as is explained by Burgelman, McKinney and Meza: senior executives 'were not motivated to take on the hard and risky work of activating what we have called the strategic context determination—really discovery processes—necessary to evaluate truly radically new innovative ideas and decide whether to create entirely new businesses based on them'.[112] The authors then point out again that Platt, unlike any previous HP CEO, 'did not launch at least one major new business that generated the profit needed to keep the company outperforming the market'.[113]

This failure of innovation and diversification highlighted the decline of HP's brilliant experimentation system. HP's divisions did not act as the equivalent of start-ups in the late 1990s era of dot.com and e-commerce start-ups, such as Omidyar's eBay, Bezos's Amazon or Page and Brin's Google. Then in the 2000s HP saw the start-up attitude of Steve Jobs produce three HP-type transformational diversifications, including Apple's mobile phone. The next section, however, will show that his HP-type diversifications arose in a very different way from the innovations that had once been produced by HP's decentralized system.

The Steve Jobs Way at Apple

Steve Jobs left no autobiographical writings and so there is no leader's-eye view of his enhancing of Apple in the 2000s. But he has been added to this chapter as a crucial comparison with HP's leadership and legacy in the area of technological innovation and diversification. His biographer describes Jobs as 'the ultimate icon of inventiveness, imagination and sustained innovation'.[114] These qualities were best displayed in the 2000s, when his diversifying innovations transformed Apple into a mobile-tech empire rather than a desktop-computer firm fighting for survival against the dominance of the IBM/clone PCs and their Wintel allies. It was a triumphant vindication or redemption for the co-founder of Apple, who had been ousted from the firm in 1985. Twenty years later in a speech at Stanford University he recalled feeling 'that I had let the previous generation of entrepreneurs down—that I had dropped the baton as it was being passed to me. I met with Dave Packard and Bob Noyce and tried to apologize for screwing up so badly.'[115] But in 1997 Jobs returned to Apple as its new CEO and would carry on from the Packard and Noyce generation by opening up a new field of high-tech entrepreneurship.

Jobs achieved these diversifying innovations with a much more centralized organization than the HP of the 1960s–90s. As his biographer notes, 'Jobs did not organize Apple into semiautonomous divisions; he closely controlled all of his teams and pushed them to work as one cohesive and flexible company, with one profit-and-loss bottom line.'[116] At his regular Monday-morning meetings with senior executives, he instilled 'a sense of shared mission' and discussed Apple's products with them in a 'freewheeling discourse' that focused on the future: 'What should each product do next? What new things should be developed?'[117]

This institutionalized product deliberation clearly included some selection of envisioned products for *top-down* experimentation. In top-down cases, the firm's leadership envisions a product and then asks the firm's researchers to experiment with ways of making that vision a reality. Top-down experimentation therefore typically occurs *after* rather than before the product-deliberation stage of selecting a product for development or production. Jobs's use of top-down experimentation was very evident in Apple's 2001 development of the iPod—the first of his diversifying innovations. According to Young and Simon's account of its development, the iPod began life as Jobs's vision of a pocket-size portable music-player whose music had been downloaded from the Internet by a personal computer and then on-loaded to the portable music-player. 'He saw the new frontier, recognized the market potential, and seized it.'[118] In this case of top-down experimentation, the leader gave his research and development team some exacting specifications about timing as well as design. The envisioned product would have to be not only 'distinctive enough and intuitive enough to use' but also ready 'in time for the Christmas buying season, less than twelve months away'.[119]

What is more, this leader had a hands-on approach to experimentation. He 'stayed close to the project all the way, his brilliance as a marketer and his flawless taste in design shining through in his rigorous-as-ever demands for the highest standards' and in his constant demands for improvements, such as easier use or higher sound volume.[120] The results of his hands-on approach speak for themselves. 'How many companies could tackle a project in a brand-new category, create a groundbreaking widget that looked great and worked better than anyone else's—and do it all in under a year?'[121] Perhaps the nearest recent equivalent of this achievement is Amazon's development of a portable device for reading e-books, the Kindle, which appeared in 2007. And Amazon's Kindle is another example of a leader, in this case Jeff Bezos, adopting a top-down and hands-on approach to experimentation.[122] The Kindle's development was more protracted than the iPod's but of course Jobs and Apple had benefited from their decades of experience designing high-tech widgets—the computers that had made them famous. This high-tech design heritage helped them diversify rapidly and brilliantly into a new category with greater growth potential. By the end of 2002 the iPod was 'vastly outselling' Apple's Macintosh computer and was transforming Apple into a music corporation.[123]

Jobs's other diversifying innovations, the iPhone and iPad, followed the same pattern of top-down, hands-on experimentation, as is described in Isaacson's biography. The 2005 origins of the iPhone can be traced back to Jobs's Grove-influenced paranoia about protecting Apple from a threat, namely the threat that cell phones would pose to the iPod if they were given a music-playing capability.[124] Later in the year, though, he began to see the cell phone as more of an opportunity than a threat, as now it seemed to him that the various cell phones available on the market 'all stank'.[125] He therefore began top-down experimentation with what would become the iPhone. This was also another case of his hands-on experimentation. 'In session after session, with Jobs immersed in every detail, the team members figured out ways to simplify what other phones made complicated.'[126] He made such key decisions as opting for the multi-touch interface, changing from a plastic to a glass screen and demanding a redesign some nine months into the project.[127] The iPhone was eventually unveiled in early 2007 and by the end of 2010 Apple had sold *ninety* million of its new product: 'it reaped more than half of the total profits generated in the global cell phone market'.[128]

The iPad had a more protracted development than the iPhone. As early as 2002, Jobs had envisioned producing a tablet without a stylus or keyboard but the project was put on hold during development of the iPhone and was not 'revved up' until a 'brainstorming' Monday-morning meeting in 2007.[129] Again, this was hands-on as well as top-down experimentation. At 'every step' in the iPad's revived development, 'Jobs pushed to remove and simplify'.[130] The new product was unveiled in early 2010 and within little more than a year Apple had sold fifteen million iPads: this was, by some measures, 'the most successful consumer product launch in history'.[131] Jobs lived long enough to witness his final triumph before dying in 2011 at the age of fifty-six.

During the 2000s, he had pushed through the most successful series of diversifying innovations in high-tech history and perhaps in business history. But his top-down and hands-on approach to experimentation may have been appropriate only for a genius—a special case governed by special rules. Even Sloan's *My Years with General Motors* acknowledged that there were such special cases. 'In some organizations, in order to tap the potentialities of a genius, it is necessary to build around him and tailor the organization to his temperament.'[132]

Genius is in such short supply, however, that most corporations have to rely on some form of organizational substitute. The HP example indicates that a decentralized experimentation system can produce or at least encourage innovation and diversification. A more recent and extreme example of this decentralized approach is Google's 'innovation machine', which was 'designed to create hundreds or thousands of research projects' as part-time and small-scale supplements to the firm's official research projects.[133] Decentralization had been taken down to the level of the individual scientist or engineer by allowing them to spend 20 per cent of their work time—typically one day a week—on their own projects.[134]

Google also decentralized product deliberation down to the level of individual researchers. As Brandt notes, researchers could deliberate in cyberspace about each other's product ideas at the early stages of envisioning or experimentation:

> The [innovation] process goes beyond giving researchers the ability to take time off from their regular jobs. Ideas are shared, discussed, analyzed and criticized. To make that happen, Google has created a database of information about every project every engineer is working on. All the engineers in the company have access to the database and can find out what anyone else is doing.[135]

In addition, there was high-level product deliberation about whether to select a particular project for further development into a commercial product. This deliberation seems to be the equivalent of Hewlett's three-stage deliberative process at HP, as any Google project, official or unofficial, has 'to withstand the scrutiny of Larry [Page] and Sergey [Brin] if they think it has commercial potential. The founders decide where the company will go next. And they are ruthless judges of product designs.'[136]

Google appears to be very like HP in being a high-tech corporation established by a dual-leadership team. But Chapter 7 will suggest that from 2001 until at least 2011 Google was being led by a *triple*-leadership team that included CEO Eric Schmidt as well as the two founders, Larry Page and Sergey Brin. During these years Google's leadership team was therefore less like HP's and more like Intel's in the 1970s, when Noyce, Moore, and Grove formed a brilliant team. The Intel team was based upon a three-role division of labour that was described by Grove in the 1970s. He was referring to a chapter in a favourite management book where:

> Drucker takes on the question of what makes an ideal chief executive officer. He says that such an individual is really a tripartite character or, as Andy read it, applying its message to Intel, *three* people: 'an outside man, a man of thought, and a man of action.' To Andy, who sent copies of this chapter to his two partners, Bob Noyce was Mr. Outside, Gordon Moore was Mr. Thought, and Andy was Mr. Action.[137]

By the 1990s Grove was the sole leader and had to take on all three parts. In doing so, however, he was playing to 'what was his greatest strength: his ability to learn'.[138] Even one of Grove's critics noted that he quickly learnt Noyce's role of Mr Outside. 'Grove was clearly learning, just as he always had. It wouldn't take him too long to pick up the skills needed for his new role' as a 'media star and high-tech visionary'.[139] But it had been his ability to learn Moore's role of Mr Thought—to become a man of thought—that gave him a more lasting fame as the author of *Only the Paranoid Survive*.

7

eBay: Whitman's *The Power Of Many*

Meg Whitman's 2010 autobiographical work, *The Power of Many: Values for Success in Business and in Life*, was written after she had retired as CEO of eBay and was seeking a political career. It provides a leader's-eye view of how she used all seven appropriate rational methods to develop the corporation during her 1998–2008 tenure as CEO. In this sense she is similar to Walton, especially as she, too, emphasized the calculative methods and learning. In fact Whitman and Walton are perhaps the best examples of leaders inspiring rational confidence through their very capable use of the appropriate rational methods.

However, Whitman enhanced rather than established a corporation and she is similar to Grove in the sense of enhancing a high-tech firm that was based on a recent technological revolution. Just as the computer chip was the basis of Grove's Intel, the Internet was the basis of Whitman's eBay and its rapid development from start-up to iconic corporation. As an Internet-based firm it is an example of the most modern type of business—e-commerce—and is a modern-day 'classic' example of how corporation-developing rational methods are used and emphasized by a rational leader.

eBay exemplifies firms that were products of the Internet revolution. Founded in 1995 as a free online-auction site, eBay soon became an e-commerce enterprise and in fact the Internet's standout performer. Cohen's 2003 *The Perfect Store: Inside eBay* described it as the most successful e-commerce firm 'to emerge in the early years of the Internet' and as the one that 'more than any other company, fully harnessed the potential of the Internet'.[1] By the 2010s another early Internet-based firm, Amazon, was overshadowing eBay but the latter was still the leading example of a firm fully harnessing the Internet's potential. Since its inception, eBay has exemplified the advantages of being a 'virtual' goods-trading enterprise that operates in cyberspace and does not need land-based sites and facilities. It was an online-auction site where other people sold their own goods, not eBay's, and paid it fees for the use of its site. So it was an early version of an

Internet 'platform' used by other firms or applications and was pioneering a form of goods trading that is 'completely "virtual": it does not own inventory or warehouses; it does not ship items or take returns. It is an amazingly efficient model', which enabled eBay to expand rapidly and 'to achieve gross profit margins of more than 80 per cent'.[2]

Another example of eBay harnessing the Internet's potential was the late 1990s creation of an online community of eBay-users. The thousands of sellers and buyers who used its auction site were transformed into an online community of eBay-users, serviced by community-building online institutions. Whitman's book points out that this pioneering approach was being widely adopted by the 2010s: 'across the business landscape, more and more companies are talking about the importance of using the Internet to build a community, not just customer base, whether they are selling hybrid automobiles, pharmaceuticals, gardening tools or even diapers'.[3] Through its online user-community eBay also successfully bridged the gap between the Internet's commercial and social spheres, between e-commerce's online selling and e-socializing's online messages, conversations, and social networking. Conversely, by the 2010s Facebook and Twitter had successfully bridged the gap between commercial and social spheres by moving in the opposite direction: from e-socializing to e-commerce and from online meeting place to online marketplace. Van Dijck's history of social media notes that such firms are a *mixture* of 'meeting places (places to make contacts and socialize) and marketplaces (places to exchange, trade or sell goods)'.[4] eBay had pioneered this mixing of social and commercial spheres when, in 1996, its auction marketplace also became a meeting place, thanks to online institutions that allowed and indeed encouraged its growing user-community to engage in e-socializing as well as e-commerce.

Whitman's experience of eBay's impressive user-community inspired her concept of 'the Power of Many' that is highlighted in her book. 'A Power of Many company or organization utilizes the communication and networking powers of modern technology ... not only to save costs and improve efficiencies but also as a way to engage the energy, ideas and goodness of people, their desire to team up with others who share their interests and work together.'[5] The Power of Many company had been pioneered by eBay many years earlier, when it was harnessing the Internet's potential by creating an online user-community as well as a completely virtual goods-trading enterprise.

Whitman had inherited the benefits of eBay's pioneering when she became CEO in 1998 and began her enhancement of the firm. It was a markedly different form of enhancement than (1) Grove's improvement of Intel's crisis management, (2) Sloan's administrative rationalization of General Motors, and (3) Ohno's development of the Toyota production system. Whitman enhanced eBay by *expanding* the firm into a large corporation. When she became CEO, eBay was 'a $4 million company with thirty employees'; when she retired ten years later, it was 'a nearly $8 billion company with 15,000 employees around the world'.[6]

As she points out, expanding or 'scaling up' a company in this fashion is a 'harder act to manage' than it might appear:

> [I]t is not common for an executive who is good at running a $4 million business to be good at running a $400 million business, and then be good at running a $4 billion business, and then an $8 billion one. Each of those steps demands that you focus on different things, withdraw from certain functions while embracing others. Those transitions are hard.... That is the reason why boards tend to recruit individuals from outside a company as it grows, individuals who have experience at that next level.[7]

She, too, had been recruited from outside eBay to be its CEO and in this sense she differs markedly from Grove and from the other two enhancers described in earlier chapters: Sloan at General Motors and Ohno at Toyota. Whitman had been 'headhunted' from not only a different firm but a different industry and business culture in a different region of the country. She was then the manager of the Playskool toy division of Hasbro, located in Massachusetts rather than California. But the forty-year-old Whitman clearly had the expertise to scale up eBay into a major corporation. She was a Princeton economics graduate, with a Harvard MBA and a wide range of practical experience. She had served her post-graduate apprenticeship with Proctor & Gamble and then begun a 1981–89 stint with a large firm of management consultants. This was followed in the 1990s by a series of senior appointments with Disney, Stride Rite, Florist Transworld, and now Hasbro's Playskool. Becoming CEO of eBay in 1998 was a great chance to take her career to new heights and she made the most of the opportunity.

This chapter will show how she used all seven appropriate rational methods of enhancing eBay. The first section of the chapter, however, will look at the early years in eBay's development, before the arrival of Whitman. During its early years, this Internet start-up was developing its distinctive online-auction system and was becoming a Power of Many company as its user-community benefited from its pioneering mixture of e-commerce and e-socializing. The second section of the chapter will describe how Whitman used the two adaptive and two deliberative rational methods in her scaling-up enhancement. The third section will show how she not only used but emphasized the other three methods, namely learning and the two calculative methods: quantitative and strategic calculation. Finally, the fourth section will broaden the chapter's perspective on e-commerce by comparing her scaling-up opportunities with those offered to Amazon's founding leader, Jeff Bezos. It will be seen that Whitman made the most of what was a comparatively short-term opportunity to scale up eBay into one of the iconic corporations of global e-commerce.

The Internet and eBay

In 1994–95 the number of Americans with access to the Internet increased explosively from some 6 million to some 37 million.[8] And in 1995 a young IT expert living in San Francisco, Pierre Omidyar, set up a free online-auction website, Auction Web, linked to the address 'www.eBay.com'. Auction Web soon became a commercial enterprise and thus one of the many examples of a start-up based on the Internet's e-commerce. However, Omidyar's start-up operated in a distinctive field of e-commerce: it was auctioning and, more specifically, hosting other people's auctions; the goods that they auctioned were typically 'used' rather than new; and these sellers were engaged in consumer-to-consumer transactions, not business-to-consumer or business-to-business transactions.[9]

Yet increasingly large numbers of small businesses, new and old, part-time and full-time, would sell goods on Auction Web. Bunnell's *The eBay Phenomenon* noted that by 2000 Omidyar's vision of a consumer-to-consumer channel of exchange had been 'overshadowed by small-business-to-consumer transactions', as some 80 per cent of eBay's revenue was being generated by only 20 per cent of its registered users: 'mostly small businesses that use the site and competing portals as their public storefronts'.[10] By 2005 some half a million people were making most or all their living by selling on the auction website that Omidyar had established ten years earlier.[11]

From the outset, his auction site had let anybody sell anything, from computers to collectibles. This inadvertently gave Auction Web a crucial competitive advantage over more specialized auction sites, not only the existing computer-equipment sites but also the many later sites that auctioned such specialized items as guitars and antique photographs.[12] His auction system was a site-only, single-item, and fixed-duration system. In other words, he did not store or ship the items being sold, each item that a seller listed for sale on the site was individually auctioned, and each auction was of a fixed duration of 'three, five, seven or ten days'—it ended on the final minute or indeed second of that set period, 'even if someone desperately want[ed] to place a higher bid'.[13]

Revenue was derived from the fees that sellers paid Auction Web for using its site. In 1996 Omidyar introduced a small listing fee, charged on a graduated scale, to deter sellers from listing 'junk' on the site, but the main revenue-earner was the 'final sales price' fee that he had introduced earlier in the year.[14] It charged sellers a percentage of the sales price paid to them by buyers who had 'won' the auction by bidding the highest amount: the fee was set at 2.5 per cent for a final sales price of more than $25 but 5 per cent for prices below that amount. Although he was collecting fees from the sellers, his site-only auction system meant that he did not have to deal with the payments between buyers and sellers or with any other aspects of the transactions. As noted earlier, it was a very efficient and profitable model of e-commerce, especially when compared to those e-commerce start-ups that had to sell, ship, and store their goods.

By the end of 1996 Auction Web had more than 40,000 registered users and, furthermore, these users had created their 'own ever-expanding community' that 'took care of itself' through its own online institutions: the Bulletin Board and the Feedback Forum.[15] This greatly reduced the administrative burden on Omidyar and his few employees, enabling his start-up to achieve higher levels of growth and profitability than could otherwise have been expected. However, Whitman's book depicts the user-community as having more than a self-administering, cost-reducing role. 'We trusted our users to figure out the best way to use our services' and 'I have always said that we did not build eBay; our community of users did'.[16] eBay therefore seems to epitomize what she terms a 'Power of Many' company.

The development of a Power of Many company and self-administering user-community began in early 1996 when Omidyar added a Bulletin Board and a Feedback Forum to his website. According to Cohen, these online institutions were 'designed to limit his role and place more of the Auction Web's administration in the hands of the community'.[17] The Feedback Forum was an online public forum where users could post positive and negative feedback—as comments and numerical grades—regarding their dealings with a particular seller or buyer, such as a seller's description or shipping of goods or a buyer's bidding or payment practices. This has been compared to the role that reputation plays in small towns and has also been depicted as self-policing by the user-community.[18] The Bulletin Board was a different type of communal online institution, where users could post their question or problem in the hope that at least one of the users monitoring the Bulletin Board would post a workable answer.

Later in 1996 Auction Web was given another communal online institution: the e-socializing eBay Café. For the Bulletin Board was renamed the Q&A Board and was joined by a new, more social bulletin board that was called 'the eBay Café'.[19] The Café was clearly an e-socializing type of online institution and was described a few years later as the 'chat room', where 'people stop to relax, catch up on news and hearsay, and exchange information. For example, eBay's Café posts a daily mix of remarks, user tips, sociable banter, and even advice for the lovelorn'—an online version of social chatter that 'served the same need for social connectivity'.[20]

Auction Web was here bridging the gap between e-commerce and online social connectivity, between the commercial and social spheres of the Internet. And it was being more successful than attempts to bridge the gap in the opposite direction, from the social sphere to the commercial sphere. Ever since e-socializing appeared in the 1980s, its promoters had been less successful in making a buck than in making social connections through these online messages, conversations, and communities.[21] When 'modern social networking finally began in early 1997' with the launching of sixdegrees.com, this new form of e-socializing gained millions of registered users but so little revenue that the firm went out of business three years later.[22] Internet social networking was revived in the mid-2000s by Myspace and then Facebook but again they were much more successful in attracting users than earning revenue: by the end of 2005 Zuckerberg's Facebook had five million users and revenue of little more than $1 million a month.[23] In 2006 Twitter's 'tweeting' message-sending created a new form of social connectivity and yet again social success did not bring similarly impressive revenues—indeed two years later Twitter was still earning zero revenue.[24] By the 2010s, though, e-socializing was earning billions and in fact Chapter 1 mentioned how Sandberg's arrival at Facebook in 2008 led to its transformation into an online advertising giant. More than a decade earlier, however, Auction Web had bridged the gap between online social connectivity and e-commerce by moving in the opposite direction. Although Auction Web was renamed eBay in 1997, it deserves a permanent place in the history of the Internet.

In addition to being renamed eBay, the site continued to experience huge growth in the number of registered users and of items listed for sale. During 1997 registered users increased to nearly 350,000 and listings to more than 100,000 a day, helping the firm dramatically increase its annual revenue to more than $4 million.[25] The growth in users and listings was partly due to the continued expansion of Internet access and usage, as now more than 50 million Americans were using the Internet, but it was also partly due to eBay's dominance over its competitors, as it now had 'more than 80 per cent of the consumer-to-consumer online auction market'.[26]

Although the firm still had fewer than thirty employees, there was a growing need for more high-powered business expertise. Omidyar had in fact recruited the young Jeff Stoll as co-founder in 1996 to provide his start-up with the business orientation and MBA-graduate training that he lacked.[27] In 1997 the co-founders' recruiting of new staff included three more MBA graduates to help with marketing and business development, but something more was required to transform eBay into a public company and major business corporation:

> Selling shares to the public meant that Omidyar and Skoll had to be more professional about the company's leadership. As Omidyar admitted, 'We were entrepreneurs and

that was good up to a certain stage, but we didn't have the experience to take the company to the next level.' They brought in a headhunter, someone who helped them look for top-quality leaders.[28]

So in early 1998 Whitman arrived at eBay to take on the position and tasks of CEO. The former incumbent, Omidyar, became eBay's chairman, while its former president, Skoll, became vice-president of strategic planning and analysis—the co-founders would soon disengage from the firm and leave Whitman as the sole leader.[29]

Her situation was similar to what Sandberg experienced in 2008 after she was recruited by Zuckerberg to be Facebook's chief operating officer (COO). As Chapter 1 described, Sandberg had the task of professionalizing a typical IT start-up and its free-wheeling business culture. Similarly, Cohen depicts Whitman taking on the task of 'professionalizing a rather unruly start-up' and making professionalization the theme of her first year in the job.[30] However, she was in a stronger leadership position than Sandberg and was joining a firm with impressive profitability and revenue as well as the prospect for continuing rapid growth. Not surprisingly, when eBay became a public company later in the year, its opening share price was just as impressive and gave it a market valuation of more than \$2 billion.[31] It clearly had much potential for the scaling-up enhancement that Whitman had already begun: 'From day one, I could see that eBay had all the ingredients of a great company at a remarkably young age.'[32]

Adapting and Deliberating

Whitman's scaling-up enhancement used all seven rational methods but this section will focus on her use of the two adaptive and two deliberative methods. In the case of the adaptive methods, her book has an almost Grove-like exposition of a 'bias for action'. It included a two-stage conception of rapid adaptation, with the first stage rapidly exploiting opportunities and the second stage fixing the mistakes that had been made during the first. A bias for action 'is about a leader moving an organization quickly to capture opportunities, knowing full well that mistakes will be made but that the organization can adjust and fix mistakes'.[33] The adjusting, mistake-fixing stage also has to be quick and avoid any rigidity:

> In a competitive environment you have to take risks...before you have all the information you might need to make the best possible decision. The trick is to be bold but not stubborn. *Don't put on blinkers or discourage realistic feedback* about what's happening, and if you've made a mistake, *fix it fast*.[34]

This is similar to points that Grove made about rapid adaptation but Whitman has a different perspective on when this method will be used. Unlike Grove, Whitman is not preoccupied with the rare occasions when leaders have to deal with an inflection-point adaptive crisis; she is more concerned with leaders constantly having to make rapid decisions about seizing opportunities.

However, Whitman acknowledges that the leader of a high-tech firm has to be capable of adapting rapidly to crises.[35] And she experienced a technology-related crisis that was similar to the Pentium-chip crisis Grove experienced in 1994. Whitman's crisis began on 9 July 1999 when eBay's website went down. It was by no means the first time its overburdened, unstable system had crashed but this time it seemed that the technical experts might be unable to get the site back up.

> Whitman had to tell her management team she feared the worst—that the engineers might never get the site up. It would, of course, be possible to reconstruct it and relaunch eBay. But if all the data were gone—user registrations, feedback, live auctions that had been underway at the time of the crash—it could be a loss from which eBay would never recover.[36]

She had quickly responded to the crisis by enlisting the aid of firms which supplied hardware or software to the eBay site and by having a plane chartered to bring home eBay's senior systems engineer from his holiday in Venezuela.[37] Thanks to such measures and the technical experts' non-stop efforts, the site was up and running again twenty-two hours after it had crashed.

But this was not the end of the 'outage' crisis. The firm needed to rebuild its relationship with the eBay user-community, especially the thousands of small businesses that depended upon this e-commerce and might be tempted to switch to a more reliable online-auction site. Whitman's response included telephoning 'the thousand or so top sellers' to apologize for the outage, each phone call coming from her personally or from a senior manager.[38]

This response is just one of several examples of innovative Whitman adaptations that are mentioned by her and other writers.[39] Another customer-related innovation was the Voice of the Customer programme, which she introduced in 1999. 'Every few months, a dozen regular customers are flown to company headquarters in San Jose to meet with Meg and eBay managers and express their ideas about what's working and what's not.'[40] This face-to-face interaction with customers was providing a valuable supplement to the feedback given on eBay's message boards and in the thousands of customer emails it received each day. Whitman notes that 'as important as e-mail and message boards were to us, I knew there was a special kind of value to looking real customers in the eye'.[41]

Like the two adaptive methods, the two deliberative methods—diverse and institutionalized deliberation—were used by Whitman and appear in her book. For example, it expresses her liking for diverse deliberation's variety of viewpoints and lack of reticence. 'I can't abide yes-people. I feel energized by other people with new and different perspectives from my own.'[42] And if 'you bite employees' heads off when they don't agree with you, well, you are training them to tell you only good news and conspire to hide problems'.[43] Another writer noted her tendency to elicit colleagues' opinions before giving her own, as when she was chairing a meeting of senior managers and asked each of them, one by one, to rank the options that the meeting was considering.[44] This Sloan-like tendency to elicit other managers' opinions before giving her own 'did not, however, mean that she had any hesitation in making a decision, even if it provoked opposition'.[45]

Furthermore, Whitman mentions two of the policy-making benefits of diverse deliberation. It helps policy-makers to take account of a plan's unintended impact in other areas and to take advantage of 'new opportunities that might emerge in unexpected places'.[46] Cohen described an example that occurred in 1999, when a middle-level manager identified the used-car market as an opportunity for eBay. In a typical case of a subordinate giving deliberative leads to his superiors, he sold them a policy proposal to introduce a used-car category on the eBay site and, later on, he sold them the idea of giving this category its own, separate site: eBay Motors.[47]

This example also illustrates Whitman's use of the other deliberative method, institutionalized deliberation. It seems that she, like Walton and Kroc, used an area of informally institutionalized deliberation, where managers could sell proposals for new policies. More importantly, she combined this with a deliberative conception of her position as CEO and with an almost Sloan-like appreciation for formal small-group deliberation. For example, soon after taking over as CEO 'she instituted weekly management team meetings, each lasting up to four hours'.[48] Even at board level she seems to have viewed the board of directors as another opportunity for group deliberation.[49] Apparently she presented board meetings with a 'parade of horribles'—an agenda of problems to solve—because 'I didn't need my board's input on the happy stuff—I needed their help on the hard stuff.'[50] And when the board was dealing with weighty matters, she would 'go around the table, asking every board member's opinion one by one' and withholding her own opinion until 'every board member had stated his or hers'.[51] This informal rule ensured not only diverse deliberation but also that every board member lived up to his or her responsibilities. It meant that 'we developed a tone of openness and *responsibility* on the board. Every person would be respected for what he or she had to say, but I also made it clear that opinions needed to be heard'.[52]

Years after she retired as CEO of eBay, Whitman herself would provide a prominent example of a board member living up to her responsibilities. She had joined the board of Hewlett-Packard after her unsuccessful attempt in 2010 to be elected Governor of California. And in September 2011 she would meet her board-member responsibilities by accepting the post of CEO and the task of leading HP out of a crisis. The previous incumbent's strategizing had led to a falling share price as well as his early departure and HP was in a similar situation to the late 1990s crisis described in Chapter 6.[53] Whitman's solution was to split Hewlett and Packard's creation into two separate companies. HP Inc would focus on personal computers and printers while Hewlett Packard Enterprise would focus on the business-computing legacy and later further narrowed its focus by spinning off its services operations as part of a new company.[54] So Whitman was associated with a strategy that might be considered 'scaling down' but was calculated to reinvigorate the specialized components of a diversified corporation. In eBay's case, however, she had been using strategic calculation to scale *up* a specialized company and in fact the calculative methods, plus learning, were her three key methods when she was scaling up eBay.

Calculating and Learning

Like Walton, Whitman emphasized quantitative calculation and the 'numbers' or 'metrics'. Her book indicates that it was both personally preferred and required by the circumstances: both a favoured and a key method. She declares, 'I am very focused on what are called key metrics' and she points out that 'the focus on metrics that I believe is *so vital to success*' is particularly relevant in an Internet firm, 'where it is possible to measure many more things than in the land-based world'.[55] As soon as she arrived at eBay, Whitman asked for regular reports about how it was faring in terms of the standard quantitative measures of Internet performance.[56] Her book identifies a few metrics that she watched especially closely, such as the number of new users and listings, but she was also interested in a wide range of other measurements:

> She wanted to know how many people were visiting the site and how many of those then registered to become users. Breaking it down further, she wanted to know how long each user remained per visit and how long the pages on the site took to load ... which days were busiest ... and which days saw a drop-off in sales.[57]

By the mid-2000s the focus on metrics was a well-known feature of Whitman's eBay. She was quoted as saying, 'if it moves, measure it' and 'if you can't measure it, you can't control it', while eBay's managers were depicted as being 'practically obsessed' with measuring the behaviour of its customers.[58] However, Whitman's book warns of the limitations and dangers of number-crunching. She notes that 'when you are metric driven', there is the danger of 'not drawing the right conclusions from your numbers. Numbers alone never tell the whole story.'[59]

Whitman's book has less to say about *strategic* calculation but clearly it was emphasized by her as a key method of scaling up eBay. Whatever her personal preferences, emphasizing strategic calculation was required by the circumstances. And two crucially important instances of strategic calculation are described in her book and by other writers.

The first was in 1998, when she made a key strategic decision about marketing. She calculated that eBay should focus on a relatively narrow market, collectibles, where its online auctions clearly had a competitive advantage. In fact its listings were already 'dominated' by collectibles—such as stamps, coins, magazines, or sports cards—and their collectors seemed to be eBay's most 'ardent' buyers and sellers.[60] 'Instead of spreading our advertising and marketing dollars across huge categories where we would have to compete with established and well-heeled retailers, I argued that we should focus on collectibles, which we could market more effectively and efficiently than anyone else could' and which still had much untapped potential as 'only a fraction of collectors were online'.[61]

Her collectibles-focused strategy was presented in similar terms by Cohen but from a different perspective. He refers to Whitman 'arguing that eBay's success at the moment depend[ed] more on keeping and expanding on the hard-core users than on reaching out to the "periodic buyers" who were stopping by other, more expensive categories'.[62] He also refers to the range of measures taken to implement the new strategy. Advertising was aimed at collectors' magazines and newsletters, such as *Postcard Collector* or *Elvis World*, the marketing department sent representatives to collectors' conventions or trade shows, such as the Doll & Teddy Bear Expo, and some categories of collectors were given their own eBay home pages, discussion boards, and specialized category managers.[63] In these ways eBay encouraged and exploited what was later labelled 'the collectibles boom' of the late 1990s.[64]

Whitman's collectibles-focused strategy therefore succeeded in maintaining eBay's very rapid growth and its dominance over its competitors. In 1999 the number of registered users increased from 2.2 million to more than 10 million, sales figures quadrupled from some $700 million to $2.8 billion, and eBay was hosting more than 90 per cent of the online-auction sales by consumers and small businesses.[65] But a collectibles-focused strategy also had some inherent limitations and disadvantages. Cohen noted that collectibles had low average sales prices, which meant low final-sales fees for eBay, and that the more faddish collectibles, such as Beanie Babies toys, went through hard-to-predict cycles of popularity.[66] Another writer cited a Wall Street analyst's remark that there 'are only so many Beanie Babies and old records you can sell'.[67] In other words, collectibles were sold in vertical markets with limited supply and demand, low prices and final-sales fees, and limited long-term prospects for eBay. It is not surprising therefore that Whitman was soon recalculating her marketing strategy and overall strategic direction; something new and more ambitious would be needed for the next stage in her scaling-up enhancement of eBay.

So as early as 1999 there was another crucial instance of Whitman's emphasis on strategic calculation. There was 'a shift in strategic thinking', which she publicly confirmed in a September speech that declared eBay's intention to 'extend beyond the core business of United States collectibles'.[68] The new strategy included initiatives to diversify what was being sold on eBay, such as the earlier-mentioned move into the used-car market. Cohen describes 'initiatives like eBay Motors' as 'designed to push up the average sales price of items sold and, given eBay's fee structure, to increase revenues'.[69] Other diversifying initiatives would increase revenues by markedly increasing the *volume* of items sold, even if they were relatively low-priced items, such as books and CDs.

But the most important example of diversification was eBay's acquisition of Half.com. This was a strategic move into a new line of e-commerce business, in which a firm's site was a platform for fixed-price selling rather than auctioning. For Half.com was offering sellers and buyers a fixed-price system for selling used items or indeed discount-price new items: the site's name 'Half' was derived from the rule that nothing was to be sold on the site for more than half its retail list price.[70]

Whitman's shift in strategic direction also included a move towards globalization. In 1999 eBay began to move into Britain, Germany, Japan, and Australia; in the early 2000s it would move into many other markets outside the US, including the huge new market emerging in China.[71] Although globalization and the other strategic initiatives were straining eBay's finances, shrewd observers could see the strategic calculation behind Whitman's willingness to squeeze eBay's margins:

> The cause of the big squeeze is clear: aggressive investment in Web infrastructure, sales and marketing, product development and acquisitions.... Like an aggressive army, eBay's strategy is to move quickly to capture territory and key positions in the new world of online auctions before opposing forces can do so, the costs be damned.... Competitors will find eBay deeply entrenched and difficult to dislodge, and margins will return to enviable levels.[72]

Whitman's shift in strategy enabled eBay to achieve the ambitious long-term growth target that she had announced in 1999 along with the new strategy. As a motivating 'stretch goal' she committed eBay to achieving $3 billion in annual revenue by 2005, which would require a 50 per cent growth in annual revenue each year.[73] By 2003 it was well on the way to reaching that goal, with some $2 billion in annual revenue being derived from the $32 billion of business that had been created by eBay customers—who would soon number more than 100 million and be found in some thirty countries around the world.[74] Two years later eBay reached and easily surpassed Whitman's goal, with annual revenue of $4.5 billion, and by then, too, collectibles accounted for less than half of the items sold on eBay.[75]

After the 2005 triumph, however, eBay began to lose momentum, especially when compared to e-commerce's other leading firm. Stone's *The Everything Store: Jeff Bezos and the Age of Amazon* notes that in 2008 Amazon's share-market valuation 'surpassed eBay's for the first time in nearly a decade'.[76] He attributes eBay's loss of momentum to the fact that 'the appeal of online auctions had faded' because customers 'wanted the convenience and certainty of a quickly completed purchase' through a fixed-price system and they were also becoming increasingly 'disgruntled with the challenges of finding items on eBay and dealing with sellers who overcharged for shipping'.[77]

Another explanation, though, is that eBay was reaching the limits of the consumer market for online auctions, just as previously it had reached the limits of the more specialized, collectibles market. As early as 1999, analysts were pointing to the limits of the online-auction consumer market and were predicting that by the mid-2000s 'bargain hunting' shoppers would comprise less than a quarter of the online consumer market in the US.[78] Stone acknowledges that eBay, too, had foreseen the problem and was making an adaptive response, but he argues that its 2004 response was slow and half-hearted:

> It spent two years working on a separate destination for fixed-price retail, called eBay Express, which got no traffic when it debuted in 2006 and was quickly shut down. Only then did eBay finally commit to allowing fixed-price sales to share space alongside auctions on the site and in search results on eBay.com.[79]

But this criticism seems to overlook the fact that Whitman had responded to the fixed-price challenge several years earlier, in 2000, by acquiring the Half.com site that had ventured into what she terms the 'hybrid space between eBay and Amazon'.[80] After a build-or-buy analysis showed that creating an eBay fixed-price system would take too long, she began negotiations to buy Half.com and, furthermore, she gave sellers on eBay the option of offering a fixed-price alternative when they listed an item for auction.[81]

eBay's later moves in the fixed-price direction were riskier, however, because they were bringing it closer to head-on competition with Amazon and other big online retailers. Whitman notes that by about 2006 'we had seen growth in the auction business slow down' and in order to maintain eBay's high growth rate 'we had to embrace fixed-price retailing that involved formidable competitors, such as Amazon'.[82] Moving too far in this direction would have raised the risk and resources issues that she mentioned when explaining how her plan to move into the Japanese market in 1999 had been hobbled by the crisis created by the eBay system's instability. 'The system demanded my full attention and many of the resources we would have needed in Japan. To have moved forward would have put the entire company at risk. That was a failure due to limited resources, not inaction.'[83] Similarly, in the mid-2000s she would have put the corporation at risk by moving forward without the resources that would be needed to compete head-on against such formidable competitors as Amazon. Whitman may in fact have learnt from her 1999 experience that she was right to be cautious about overstretching eBay's resources.

She certainly emphasized learning as a method of developing the corporation. Learning was one of her key methods and especially so when she first joined eBay as its new CEO in 1998. Whitman had to learn about a new firm, a new industry, and even a new business culture: an informal, non-hierarchical culture in which even the most senior executives would not have an office but instead 'would work in a cubicle, even Whitman'.[84]

Learning seems to have been a favourite as well as key method, considering how often it is discussed or mentioned in her book. Often it is mentioned as part of other processes, such as iteration and validation, or in the form of listening to what other people have to say.[85] For example, Whitman declares, 'I am a listener. I do not like to delegate my own education.'[86] Although she therefore seems similar to Silent Sloan, Whitman also makes the Kroc-like remark that she learnt more from the failures in her career than from successes.[87]

She presumably also favoured learning because she had a special aptitude for this rational method, like Walton's special aptitude for quantitative calculation. Whitman had shown an aptitude for learning during her earlier career, before arriving at eBay, and she would show it again in her later career, after leaving eBay. When she became CEO of Hewlett-Packard in 2011, 'Whitman had a reputation as a capable and principled leader, but ... some questioned whether she had the experience necessary to run a $100 billion computer hardware, services, and software company, particularly one facing many strategic challenges'.[88] She soon showed that her aptitude for learning on the job—and learning quickly—outweighed her lack of experience in leading such a huge corporation and dealing with so many strategic challenges.

In the case of eBay, her aptitude for *quickly* learning on the job had been essential. For she was not given as much time as Kroc and Walton to learn how to scale up the company: the e-commerce world was more rapidly evolving than the fast-food world of the 1950s–60s or the discount-retailing world of the 1960s–70s.[89] The rapid evolution of e-commerce was reflected in the rapid development of eBay from start-up to globalizing corporation. Only three years after eBay was founded it had become a public company, with a market valuation in the billions, and only a year later it was shifting its strategy towards diversification and globalization.

Furthermore, eBay was under competitive pressure from other fast-growing Internet firms. As previously noted, its commitment to rapid global expansion was largely because 'eBay wanted to move into key markets before Yahoo, Amazon, or local companies locked them up'.[90] By the time Whitman retired, eBay was even feeling competitive pressure from Google. 'We had seen the rise of Google and its extraordinary search capabilities, which play a larger and larger role in directing consumers to products.'[91]

However, the key competition, comparisons, and contrasts were still provided by eBay's great e-commerce rival, Amazon. The two firms epitomize two different forms of online goods trading that will be termed 'eBayism' and 'Amazonism'. They might have been termed 'Whitmanism' and 'Bezosism' if eBay had experienced the same continuity of leadership that Amazon enjoyed. Bezos launched Amazon in the same year that Omidyar launched eBay's Auction Web, namely 1995, and more than twenty years later this founding leader is still running Amazon. Considering that in 1995 Bezos lacked much business training and experience, he has accomplished a remarkable feat of scaling up and learning on the job.[92] If there were an autobiographical account of his feat, this chapter would have presented an extensive comparison of his and Whitman's use of all seven rational methods in their scaling up of Internet-based firms.[93] Instead, it will end with a section that compares their *opportunities* to use these methods to scale up firms that epitomized two very different forms of Internet-based goods trading.

Whitman highlighted the issue of opportunity when she made a perceptive point near the end of her book. 'I don't think there will be another eBay for me. What we accomplished was so novel, our success so unprecedented, that other business opportunities pale in comparison.'[94] By the time she retired, in 2008, the Internet was not offering US business leaders the same kinds of opportunity that eBay had offered Whitman ten years earlier. But even in that era there had been different kinds of opportunity to use rational methods to develop an Internet-based corporation. For of course many different forms of e-commerce emerged in the 1990s including two markedly different forms of Internet goods trading: eBayism and Amazonism. Each offered a different kind of opportunity for a leader to use rational methods to establish or enhance a corporation.

In the case of Whitman and Bezos, however, there is another factor to take into account when comparing their opportunities to develop an Internet-based corporation. In Bezos's case, he was on the way to *establishing* this corporation, having already founded Amazon.com as an online retailer that specialized, temporarily, in selling books and would 'offer an unprecedented number of books at the cheapest price possible and deliver them quickly'.[95] In Whitman's case, however, she was *enhancing* a start-up, eBay, that had been founded by someone else and whose direction had already been set—as an online-auction platform—before she arrived at the firm.

In addition, eBay and eBayism were already very successful, as was described in the first section of the chapter. So when Whitman took charge in 1998, there was no need for a Sloan-like or Ohno-like enhancement and in fact her options for enhancing eBay may have been limited to scaling up the firm by taking it further in the direction already set by its founders and user-community. Furthermore, her opportunity to carry out this scaling-up enhancement was limited by the form of goods trading that eBay epitomized: eBayism. As the next section's comparison will show, Whitman was more limited, in the longer term, by eBayism than Bezos was by Amazonism.

Opportunity: eBayism Versus Amazonism

This section will look at opportunity from a different perspective than in earlier chapters, where it was viewed as the opportunity to use the adaptive methods, rapid and innovative adaptation, to develop a corporation. In this section, however, opportunity will be viewed in more general terms, as the opportunity to develop a corporation by any or all appropriate rational methods, not just the adaptive methods. In the case of Whitman and Bezos it was the opportunity to scale up an e-commerce firm into a corporation, and the opportunity was provided by two different forms of Internet-based goods trading. eBayism offered an opportunity for rapid and profitable growth that reaches its limits in a decade or so; Amazonism offered a longer-term opportunity for less rapid and profitable growth that continues for a longer period and creates a larger and more diverse corporation.

When Whitman joined eBay in 1998 as its new CEO, she was given an excellent short-term opportunity for a scaling-up enhancement. As her book states, 'eBay proved to be incredibly scalable' and 'at its core is a business model that we scaled up in a remarkably successful fashion, even exporting it to other countries and cultures'.[96] This scalability is highlighted by the contrast with Amazonism's much less 'virtual' form of goods trading, in which an online retailer is selling, shipping, and storing its own goods rather than simply providing a platform for other sellers. Whitman herself made this contrast when she returned from a 1998 visit to Amazon:

> Whitman was not impressed by Amazon's bricks-and-mortar assets. 'They have all these warehouses and inventory they're so proud of,' she told her management team when she returned to Campbell. 'I'm glad that we don't have to deal with any of that.'[97]

But Amazon did have to deal with that and with the problem of expanding these land-based facilities to keep pace with the rapid growth in Amazon's sales and customer numbers. What is more, Amazon therefore had to spend a larger amount of money than eBay to maintain a rapid growth rate and so was under more financial strain, especially as its form of goods trading was inherently less profitable than eBayism. Becoming a public company in 1997 had eased the financial strain, but Amazon's share price reflected its rapid growth and great potential rather than its profitability or in fact *lack* of profits. In the years ahead it would make substantial losses as it acquired new facilities and firms as well as millions of new customers; in late 2001 it finally made a profit, but only after a long efficiency campaign and laying off hundreds of staff.[98]

Amazonism was also more difficult than eBayism to expand on an international scale—to globalize. As Whitman points out, the 'exporting' of eBayism to dozens of other countries is an illustration of its scalability. In contrast, Amazon was operating as an online retailer in only ten countries in the early 2010s, largely because so few countries had both a sizeable enough market and an acceptable 'shipping infrastructure' and 'credit card processing system'.[99] Unlike eBay, Amazon was a seller and shipper of goods and did not have the advantages of being simply a platform that other firms and people used as an online means of selling their goods.

Whitman alludes to these platform advantages when she describes how eBay's scalability was partly due to its user-community and the Power of Many. 'By tapping the Power of Many, we created a virtuous cycle where the better our sellers did and the happier our buyers were, the more successful eBay was as a facilitator of all those transactions.'[100] In contrast, Amazon was a retailer, selling goods to consumers, and so could not rely on other firms and people to make its buyers happier and Amazon more successful. The 'customer obsessed' Amazon devoted much money and effort to making consumers happier with its prices, inventory, shipping, and so forth—to making them not merely satisfied but actually happy customers.[101]

In addition, Amazon introduced an element of eBayism into its goods trading. It would allow other firms to use its online site as a platform, in return for a fee or commission, and would even allow these 'third-party' sellers to compete with Amazon for sales. As early as 1997 it was considering 'how to become a platform and augment the e-commerce efforts of other retailers. Amazon Auctions was the first such attempt, followed by zShops, the service that allowed small retailers to set up their own stores on Amazon.com.'[102] The Auctions initiative made little headway against eBay, but the 1999 zShops initiative was 'very attractive to many small merchants in that it gave them access to Amazon's growing legions of customers, which then numbered 11 million'.[103] These small-business retailers handled their own billing, shipping, and inventory, and paid Amazon both monthly listing fees and a commission on all sales where the customer made a credit-card purchase processed by Amazon. In 2000 its focus shifted from small to *big* retailers, such as Toys 'R' Us, as Amazon began to make online-partnership deals with them.[104] This was the year, too, that it launched the Marketplace initiative, which allowed sellers of used books to compete directly with Amazon.[105] During the 2000s, Marketplace was extended to many other categories of used or new goods and whether or not they were also sold by Amazon.[106]

Despite this move towards eBayism, Amazon continued to be in a less advantageous position than eBay. In fact as late as 2005 this was still the assessment being made on Wall Street. Analysts focused on Amazon's 'slender margins and the superior business models of other Internet companies' but eBay was 'still viewed as a perfect venue for commerce' and had a market capitalization 'three times larger than Amazon's'.[107] Whitman's strategy of diversification and globalization had produced huge increases in scale and revenue in the early 2000s and with markedly better profit margins than Amazon's.

Diversification had been an Amazon strategy, too. This online book store was aiming to become an 'everything' store, which would provide customers with online access to a much wider range and choice of goods than any land-based store could provide. The range of goods available to Amazon customers had been increased by its introduction of platform selling by third-party sellers.[108] And Amazon itself was selling a much wider range of goods. In 1998 it had begun selling CDs and DVDs as well as books; in 1999 it added video games, consumer electronics, and home-improvement products; in 2000, kitchen products, health and beauty aids, and even outdoor furniture.[109] Book-selling still made up more than half of Amazon's business but the title at the top of its website had changed from 'Earth's Largest Bookstore to Books, Music and More, and, soon after, to Earth's Biggest Selection—the everything store'.[110]

However, Amazon lacked two of eBay's advantages, namely 'network effects' and not having to compete with big retailers. Whitman's firm benefited greatly from these advantages, as is evident in her book and other writers' descriptions of eBay. The advantage of not having to compete with big retailers is evident when Whitman relates, as noted earlier, how her strategic calculations in 1998 had included a desire to avoid any form of competition with big retailers. But Amazon, in contrast, *had to* compete with big retailers, as it diversified from books into a wide range of retail items. Indeed it was facing an increasing amount of head-on competition from these giants of retailing, for this was the era in which the big retailers moved into e-commerce and set up Internet versions of their land-based stores. By the end of the 1990s long-established land-based companies were going online in what Bunnell termed at the time: 'the second stage of the Internet revolution'.[111] These e-commerce extensions of land-based companies were increasingly evident in online retailing. Most sold such specialized items as computer equipment but a few of the newcomers sold a much wider range of products. For example, Wal-Mart set up an Internet operation in 1999 and headquartered this e-commerce extension in a town near Silicon Valley rather than in Bentonville, Arkansas.[112] The second stage of the Internet revolution therefore created an increasingly wide area of head-on competition between big retailers and the diversifying Amazon—but *not* between them and eBay's online auctions.

The other advantage enjoyed by eBay, network effects, had helped the firm expand its online user-community and deal with its online competitors. Whitman's book describes network effects largely in terms of the expansion of the user-community and as another example of the Power of Many. Network effects occur when the Internet accelerates growth created by word-of-mouth recruiting: users of a network like eBay's 'actively recruit other users' and 'the more people join the network, the faster even more people join the network'.[113] Whitman points out that the rapid growth of eBay's user-community was an early example of the network effects that would later 'fuel the rapid growth of social sites such as Facebook and Twitter'.[114] Facebook acquired more than five million users in its first two years and Twitter's growth was similarly rapid once Internet users became aware of what this new kind of social site had to offer: in its first six years it acquired some 500 million registered users worldwide.[115] This was much greater expansion than eBay could have achieved in its first six years, having been launched as an e-commerce site and during the first stage of the Internet revolution. But eBay, too, had benefited greatly from network effects, which had rapidly expanded its user-community at so little cost to the firm.

Amazon, however, did not have the advantage of network effects. The rapid expansion of its customer base in its first six years therefore cost the firm a lot of money and effort. Although many customers were attracted by word-of-mouth recommendations, this was the result of Amazon's costly focus on customer happiness—and the firm had spent much money on advertising and other marketing efforts.[116] It did not have the benefit of network effects' cost-free attraction of new users and customers.

Similarly, Amazon did not have the benefit of the *anti-competitive* aspect of network effects. This aspect of network effects was highlighted by Cohen in his description of eBay-like networks and Metcalfe's Law, 'which holds that the utility of a network equals the number of users squared' because 'every new member added to a network like eBay represents not just a single networked relationship, but a relationship with all other eBay users. Those eBay relationships work in both directions: anyone in the network can buy from or sell to the new user.'[117] In contrast, 'one-to-many e-commerce sites' like Amazon add 'only one new relationship' when they add a new user—a new customer for the company's goods or services.[118] However, Cohen was mainly concerned with the contrast between large and small networks and particularly the competitive advantage enjoyed by *larger* networks. He pointed out that 'being the first to build up a large network gives a site a critical edge' over its smaller competitors; from then on, it 'made no sense for users to go to any other site. Buyers who did were less likely to find what they were looking for; sellers were less likely to get a good price.'[119] In fact this competitive edge has been described, in the case of Facebook, as a winner-takes-all effect.[120] The effect is just as strong in an e-commerce network and, in the case of eBay, helped it achieve a monopolistic position as early as 1996.

More importantly, the competitive advantage given by network effects would help eBay maintain its monopolistic position against old and new competitors. This was particularly important because the downside of eBay-ism for eBay was that competitors could so easily set up a new online-auction site to compete with it.[121] The other side of the coin, however, was that competitors found it 'considerably more difficult to build up a *network* that can compete with eBay'.[122]

For example, Amazon's 1999 failed attempt to create an auction enterprise was foredoomed by the network problem. Bunnell's analysis of the failure of Amazon Auctions pointed out that this venture had been well planned and seemed to offer an attractive alternative to eBay. Amazon's auction site was similar to eBay's, provided better customer services and buyer guarantees, and offered sellers a no-fee holiday period.[123] It made a good start and grew impressively for several months but then 'the number of listings stalled out' as eBayism's anti-competitive network effects protected eBay's monopolistic position.[124]

Amazon was in fact being hit with a double whammy. For in addition to suffering from anti-competitive network effects when challenging eBay, Amazon lacked the *benefits* of such effects when its retail operations established a monopolistic or winning position in an online retail market. Without these winner-takes-all and monopoly-protecting benefits, the diversifying Amazon lacked a significant advantage as it dealt with online retail competitors in an increasingly wide range of products.

Nonetheless, by 2007 Amazonism was beginning to overshadow eBayism. Amazon's growth in sales was far higher than 'the growth rate for the rest of e-commerce. That meant Amazon was stealing customers from other Internet players' in retailing and platform selling, for even Amazon's Marketplace 'third-party sellers were reporting a surge of activity on the site and a corresponding decrease on rival platforms like eBay'.[125] What is more, this was the year that Amazon launched its Kindle device for reading e-books. As Chapter 6 noted, the Kindle's development was relatively protracted when compared to the speed with which Apple developed the iPod. But the Kindle was a rapid adaptive response for an online retailer that had never before developed a piece of technology, let alone a portable device using advanced electronic-reading technology.[126] Development had begun in 2004 in response to the threat that Apple or some other high-tech firm might instigate a book-selling version of the iPod music-selling revolution: 'if Amazon was to continue to thrive as a bookseller in a new digital age, it must own the e-book business in the same way that Apple controlled the music business'.[127]

Another impressive Amazon adaptation had occurred as early as 2000, when the firm put its spare computer capacity to work by renting it out over the Internet. Through Amazon Web Services other firms could rent 'basic computer infrastructure like storage, databases, and raw computing power' and in fact would be able to rent exactly as much computing power as they needed through Amazon's Elastic Compute Cloud.[128] Renting these services from Web Services was an attractive proposition and especially for start-up entrepreneurs, who no longer had to invest in their own computing power and could instead 'run their operations over the Internet as if the high-powered servers were sitting in the backs of their own offices'.[129] From Amazon's perspective, too, Web Services was an attractive proposition and it would become an increasingly lucrative area of activity. By 2010 it was earning an estimated $500 million in annual revenue, with much higher profitability than online retailing, and was growing at an extraordinary rate.[130]

Amazonism was therefore harnessing the Internet's potential in an innovative way as well as developing technologically innovative products. The latter included not just the Kindle reader but also the development of a Kindle-based device that would compete against the Apple iPad. By 2010 Amazon was 'preparing to confront Apple in the high stakes tablet market' and would launch the Kindle Fire tablet in the following year.[131]

eBayism, however, had not provided Whitman with similar opportunities for diversification—whether through the Internet or in other areas of technology. When she retired, Whitman felt she 'had reinvented eBay several times in ten years'.[132] But eBayism offered only limited opportunities for reinvention when compared to what Amazonism offered Bezos. Whitman could only play the cards she had been dealt.

This inferiority was part of an overall lack of longer-term opportunity that became evident in the late 2000s as Amazon began to overshadow eBay. By 2008 Amazon was considering what further improvements and initiatives would be required for it to become a $200-billion corporation like Wal-Mart.[133] Although Amazon was still seven years away from reaching even $100 billion in revenue, it was much closer than eBay to ever being comparable to the giant Wal-Mart corporation.[134]

When Whitman became leader of eBay in 1998, eBayism provided a better short-term opportunity than Amazonism for scaling up an Internet-based firm—and she had made the most of that opportunity. But Amazonism provided Bezos with a better longer-term opportunity than Whitman's, so long as he and Amazon could stay the distance and make the most of this opportunity. By the 2010s it was clear that he and his firm had succeeded and had made it big. 'Amazon was spoken of in the same breath as Google and Apple' and indeed it was already paying a political price for its success and fame: 'the rise of Amazon's visibility and market power' led to it facing a 'growing chorus of critics' as it 'now seemed to many like a remote and often arrogant giant'.[135] eBay, too, had suffered from the political factor, as in 2008 Whitman had retired from business in order to pursue a political career. From Whitman's perspective, an advantage of the shorter-term kind of opportunity that she received in 1998 is that it left some room for her as a leader to move on to new things, such as entering the political arena and then returning to the business world as the saviour of an iconic corporation like Hewlett-Packard.

Of course the opportunities offered by e-commerce in the 1990s–2000s included many more options than eBayism and Amazonism. Google, for example, combined the former's advantages with the latter's long-term growth prospects. And it provided the opportunity for a version of scaling up that included recruiting an outside CEO but also saw the founders stay with the firm and eventually take charge again. Google was founded by Larry Page and Sergey Brin in 1998 and it was not until 2001 that they brought in a business expert, the 46-year-old Eric Schmidt, to be CEO and scale up the firm.[136] Unlike eBay's founders, the Google pair did not disengage from the firm. They allowed Schmidt to 'become the public face of Google' but they held the key positions of president of products and president of technology and they remained 'the main arbiters of Google's technology'.[137]

This *triple*-leadership team lasted until at least 2011. In that year 'the company announced that CEO Eric Schmidt was handing the reins back to the founders' and it appeared that there would no longer be 'a three-person team agreeing on major decisions'.[138] But although Schmidt was replaced as CEO by Page, he was given the newly created position of executive chairman. This division of responsibilities continued when Alphabet Inc. was created in 2015 as a holding company that owned not only Google but also the various ventures that were split off from Google so that it could focus on its Internet and advertising activities.[139] The new Alphabet 'corporation' was headed by Page as CEO, Brin as president and Schmidt as executive chairman. Google therefore continued to be developed in a unique way and to be led by a leadership team rather than by a brilliant individual leader like Bezos or Whitman.

8

GA: Armani's *Giorgio Armani*

The earlier chapters have described how leaders used rational methods in highly technological or technical industries. This final chapter, however, will be mainly concerned with a stylistic and indeed artistic industry—the high-fashion line of business. It will show how the fashion designer and business leader Giorgio Armani very capably used rational methods in these unusual business circumstances, where these corporation-developing methods were just as appropriate as in high-tech industries. Even in *artistic* industries like high-fashion a leader's employee-followers will be inspired with rational confidence by his or her capable use of the appropriate rational methods.

A leader's-eye view of Armani's use of rational methods has been provided by his 2015 *Giorgio Armani*. But it is a mainly photographical account of his fashion-designing career and there is only enough textual material to provide a leader's-eye view of him using the two *adaptive* methods: rapid and innovative adaptation. The Armani case will therefore be viewed, like the Dassault case, as one of the supplementary rather than main examples. It shows a leader using a particular pair of rational methods—rapid and innovative adaptation—in the unusual circumstances of the artistic high-fashion business. In fact Armani's designs have been the subject of an art-gallery exhibition.

> I have always said that fashion is not art, and yet I was the first and I think only fashion designer to be exhibited at the Solomon R. Guggenheim Museum in New York. In 2000, that contemporary art institution dedicated itself to a retrospective to my work, analysing it as one would that of a painter, architect or inventor.[1]

But Armani describes his role as a fashion designer as 'closer to that of a sociologist than to that of an artist'.[2] The sociological aspect is apparent in his book's account of how in the 1970s he became an independent fashion designer with his own company. 'I began to perceive the advance of a new kind of femininity' which was linked to the feminism that was 'so explosive in those years when I started'.[3] His stylistic adaptation to the new times resulted in a new high-fashion style and also the establishing of a very successful company that bore his name and derived its iconic status from his prestige—a rare example of a private company becoming as large and famous as an iconic business corporation. The Armani case of rapid and innovative adaptation therefore confirms that these rational methods can be just as appropriate for an artistic, high-fashion firm as for a scientific, high-tech firm like Intel.

The first section of the chapter will show how Armani adapted fashion to the new times—to social change and the accompanying change in fashion preferences. It will also show that Armani, like Kroc and Walton, used the two adaptive rational methods in combination to establish his large and iconic company. For he adapted both rapidly and innovatively in the 1970s when he created a new high-fashion style and then in the 1980s used both adaptive methods when he created a new kind of leading high-fashion firm.

The second section will compare Armani's adaptations with those of another Italian fashion designer of that era, Gianni Versace. The comparison of Armanian and Versacian adaptations will focus largely on the different ways in which they adapted *stylistically* to the opportunity offered by fashion's new times. The two leaders used the same adaptive methods to exploit this opportunity but used them in different ways. While Armani targeted the new market created by fashion's new times, Versace instead targeted what remained of the old market. Although Versace's rapid and innovative adaptation was successful stylistically and commercially, it had a serious flaw that became very evident after his violently premature death in 1997.

The third section will therefore compare the two leaders' adaptive legacies and argue that Versace did not use adaptive rational methods *as capably* as Armani in the 1970s–80s. This difference in capability highlights an aspect of rational leadership that has not been discussed in earlier chapters, which looked for variation in leaders' selection and emphasizing of particular rational methods but ignored the variation in how capably they used these methods. This was largely because there have been no instances of two leaders' times and circumstances being so similar that it is fair to say something about their relative capability in using particular rational methods. In this final chapter, however, capability can be compared in a credible manner because both Armani and Versace used the adaptive rational methods in the same times and circumstances—the 1970s–80s change era in their high-fashion line of business.

But the chapter ends with a section devoted to a classic example of a leader *not* using the adaptive methods or any of the other appropriate rational methods. It is 'an exception that proves the rule' because it shows what occurs when a corporation-developing leader abandons the appropriate rational methods that he or she has used successfully in the past. This case arose in the beauty industry in the 1980s–90s when the British businesswoman Anita

Roddick abandoned the adaptive methods she had used to establish her corporation, The Body Shop, and did not replace them with any other appropriate rational methods. Roddick's move away from rational business methods may have been due to her increasingly prominent charismatic role as a political activist and a publicist for new attitudes towards business and its social responsibilities, as is recounted in her partly autobiographical *Business as Unusual*.[4] However, her increased public profile was no substitute for a decline in business rationality that led to a decline in business success and to her employee-followers losing their jobs or career prospects—and their rational confidence in the future development of the corporation.

Adapting Fashion To New Times

Armani's success was a classic case of adapting to new times. In the 1970s–90s the high-fashion business underwent such a dramatic change that Agins titled her book *The End of Fashion*. She explained the change by pointing to three 'megatrends' in western societies' upper and middle classes: (1) 'women let go of fashion', as they became successful career women, (2) 'people stopped dressing up', as casual wear became more acceptable at the workplace as well as for social occasions, and (3) 'people's values changed with regard to fashion', as they became more concerned with value for money and with finding a bargain.[5] These megatrends brought an end to the traditional high-fashion world, which had been dominated by family firms or 'houses' located in Paris and focused on the *haute couture* (high dressmaking) art of designing and tailoring handcrafted made-to-fit womenswear. But the megatrends also created the opportunity for a previously unknown Italian designer, Giorgio Armani, to gain a huge competitive advantage and establish a very successful firm.

The megatrend that most benefited Armani was the way in which affluent women 'let go of fashion' clothes as their socioeconomic situation changed. Agins refers to this trend as the end of the 'trickle-down' and 'planned obsolescence' fashion system in which 'Paris designers had set the standard' for high-fashion womenswear throughout the western world and had introduced a succession of new styles and modifications through their seasonal fashion shows.[6] This system ran into a new socioeconomic reality as the female members of the upper and middle classes became career women and lost interest in the high-fashion designs being displayed by models on the runways or catwalks of Parisian fashion shows.

> By the 1980s millions of baby-boomer career women were moving up in the workplace and the impact of their professional mobility was monumental. As bank vice-presidents, members of corporate boards, and partners at law firms,

professional women became secure enough to ignore the foolish runway frippery that bore no connection to their lives. Women began to behave more *like men* in adopting *their own uniform*: skirts and blazers and pantsuits that gave them an *authoritative, polished, power look*.[7]

These new fashion preferences therefore both undermined the old fashion system and also offered an opportunity for designers who could meet the new demand: career women's desire for 'their own uniform' of pantsuits, blazers, and skirts that gave them an authoritative and polished look.

Armani responded as early as the mid-*1970s*, when he was starting up his firm. As mentioned earlier, his book refers to him perceiving a new kind of femininity, which 'required a wardrobe that fully complemented the way men dressed' while 'preserving elegance and distinction and the idea that others should notice you for your mind and your self-esteem. I imagined women in new roles,' such as women 'taking their place at the table for a business meeting'.[8] His response was a new fashion style that was an *innovative* as well as rapid adaptation to the new times.

Giorgio Armani SpA was founded in Milan in 1975, soon after Armani's forty-first birthday and more than a decade after he became a full-time fashion designer.[9] Armani's biographer notes that the firm's first womenswear presentation featured his first jackets for women and that his 1976 runway presentation 'introduced tweed women's suits. The jacket had a decidedly mannish cut' and in fact he had 'invented a different kind of women's jacket' that 'conferred an unprecedented authority on the female figure'.[10] A similar point is made by White in her book on the Armani contribution to fashion. His redesign of the jacket offered career women a mixture of 'femininity and power-dressing' in a restrained, not over-exposed fashion, just as 'easy' trouser suits became signature garments of his style, included in each new collection of Armani womenswear.[11]

Armani's rapid adaptation to women's new fashion preferences may have been because he was primarily a *menswear* designer until he started up his own firm in 1975. In fact for the rest of his career he would design men's as well as women's high-fashion clothing and he would become famous for inventing a new style of men's jacket in the mid-1970s. His biographer describes this deconstructed or unstructured style of jacket as a blend of the 'hippie tradition' and the 'bourgeois uniform' but White views the blend in gender terms, as 'bringing the sexes closer together sartorially' and creating a design theme of 'languid androgyny'.[12] Armani, too, refers to his designs taking on 'a more androgynous image' but he also presents the gender issue in terms of his supportive response to social change and 'liberation, both female and male':

I became convinced that those attitudes could be created out of the way people dressed. How was a women rising up the ranks of power going to be credible, in an environment that was still all-male, if she was dressed like a doll or restrained by excessively formal feminine clothing? How was a young, dynamic, and uninhibited man going to contrast with the old modes of thinking if he was constrained inside a suit that denied his individuality and oppressed his energy and physique?[13]

Men as well as women were expressing two of the new fashion preferences discussed by Agins: it was 'people', not just women, who 'stopped dressing up' and whose 'values changed in regard to fashion'. These two changes in fashion preferences therefore suited Armani's menswear as well as womenswear. He was still, however, having to adapt rapidly and innovatively to take full advantage of the opportunities offered by fashion's new times; he was not simply benefiting from the fact that they were moving in the same direction that he had chosen.

The change in values regarding fashion—this new concern with value for money—suited Armani because he was a designer of ready-to-wear rather than handcrafted, individually tailored and therefore very expensive garments. Armani stuck with the ready-to-wear approach that he had learnt as a menswear designer and he out-sourced the production of his designs to womenswear and menswear manufacturers in northern Italy's modern clothing industry.[14] Agins noted that 'setting himself apart from the rest of high fashion, Armani consistently manufactured high-quality tailored garments on an industrial scale. Nobody did it better, retailers agreed.'[15] Any affluent customers who showed the new preference for value for money needed to look no further than Armani's garments.

The other change in men's and women's fashion preferences—the shift to casual wear rather than dressing up—suited Armani in a less obvious, almost indirect way. A 1973 article on fashionable elites' liking for blue-denim jeans pointed to the difference between the elite who had 'turned their backs on the idea of "fashionable" clothes' and the elite who were 'still in revolt against the old sartorial rules but continue to be concerned with the way they dress'.[16] The latter group of elite denim-wearers were therefore receptive to Armani's elegant styling. 'He understood back in the mid-1970s, that although consumers were rejecting formality in favour of more casual clothing, they did not want to give up elegance' and would be receptive to what became known as 'Armani' styling: 'refined yet relaxed modernity in clothing, in muted colours'.[17] Armani's book, too, refers to his pursuit of elegance in his menswear and womenswear designs of the 1970s. He was 'always seeking a sort of elegance that never turned into arrogance' in his menswear designs and he was 'offering women the unusual elegance of pantsuits' that were the elegant equivalent of denim jeans as well as women's equivalent of a business suit.[18]

Armani's rapid adaptive response to fashion's new times brought him early rewards and recognition. His firm had been founded in 1975 with capital of only some $10,000 but had a turnover of some $500,000 in 1976, some $2 million the following year and by 1982 had worldwide sales of some \$140 million.[19] Armani also received dramatic international recognition in 1982 when he appeared on the cover of *Time* magazine. The cover bore the headline 'Giorgio's Gorgeous Style' and inside there was an eight-page story that included 'a confident judgment: Armani is the best'.[20] Buoyed by such recognition, his firm would achieve total worldwide sales of \$300 million by 1985, with North America contributing some 25 per cent of these sales and another 25 per cent coming from parts of Europe outside Italy.[21] In the decade since its founding, Armani's firm had become a big-earning international fashion company that derived its earnings and iconic status from its leader's fashion-designing successes.

The rapid rise of Armani's firm seems similar to the way in which Kroc and Walton rapidly established their corporations. Armani's combination of rapid and innovative adaptation, however, was adapting to the kind of dramatic change that Grove categorized as a '10×' change. As Chapter 6 mentioned, Grove's book listed some examples of the '10×' kind of change and one of them was customers 'drifting away from their former buying habits', such as when Americans' taste in cars changed during the 1920s: 'style and leisure had become important considerations in people's lives'.[22] Clearly this is similar to the change in customers' fashion preferences in the 1970s–80s and just as the car example was exploited by Sloan's General Motors, so the fashion example was exploited by Armani's Giorgio Armani SpA.

But in Armani's case the change was exploited by a *new* firm, not an established corporation like Sloan's General Motors. In this respect it is similar to cases where new firms have exploited the opportunity offered by disruptive technology. As the Appendix describes, Christensen's theory of disruptive technology points out that new firms can win the leading position in an industry by adapting rapidly to disruptive technology and the new market that it creates. Similarly, Armani's new firm won a leading position by adapting rapidly as well as innovatively to the new market created by the change in fashion preferences.

What is more, Armani's new firm became a new *kind* of leading high-fashion firm—adapted to fit the fashion and business world of the 1980s–90s. This new kind of high-fashion firm would have an extensive, diverse range of products and a globalized retail network, with stores in many countries around the world. In fact this was a second case of Armani using innovative and rapid adaptation in combination to develop his firm and in this second case he was similar to Kroc and Walton. Like them, he was creating a new system or organization that would play a crucial role in expanding his firm into a large-scale, very successful operation.

If Armani had not created this new kind of high-fashion firm, he would not have reaped the full business reward for his rapid stylistic adaptation to customers' changing preferences. In particular, he would not have been able to establish a large company that was a modern business corporation in all respects except that it was not a public company. Even after it became an iconic billion-dollar company, Armani did not take this final step—going public—that would have created a high-fashion *corporation*. Nonetheless, developing Giorgio Armani SpA into a new kind of firm was a major achievement by Armani and his partner Sergio Galeotti, whose death in 1985 prematurely ended this two-role leadership team of creative designer and business-oriented partner. Even before his death, however, it was clear that the firm would reap great rewards from having followed up the 1970s adaptation with another rapid and innovative adaptation: the 1980s creation of a new kind of high-fashion firm.

It sold a much more extensive 'pyramid' of products than any previous leading firm in the high-fashion business. Armani's product pyramid extended downwards through several different price levels and extended horizontally across a wide range of clothing, accessories, and related products.[23] In pre-Armani times, the leading French haute couture firms had shown little tendency to diversify beyond crafting womenswear and perfumes and, more recently, selling their designs and licensed brand name to other firms. Then in 1966 Yves Saint Laurent 'changed the fashion paradigm' by supplementing his haute couture collections with a line of *ready-to-wear* clothing that was aimed at a younger market and was much more affordable.[24] 'Now there was a new pyramid model' that set a new standard for any leading firm in the high-fashion business.[25]

The new model was adopted and further developed by Armani in the 1970s–90s. Initially, the distinctive feature of his pyramid of products was that it *lacked* the traditional summit or peak—a haute couture collection of womenswear—and was instead crowned by ready-to-wear lines of womenswear *and* menswear.[26] However, the Armani pyramid became distinctive, too, for how far it extended downwards through different price levels and for how far it extended horizontally across a diverse range of products. By the end of the 1990s the Armani range of products included 'not only the main clothing ranges for men, women and children, but also jeans, skiwear, underwear, shoes, sunglasses, jewellery, hosiery, watches and perfume'.[27]

The vertical extension downwards into lower price levels came largely through the introduction of cheaper lines of clothing. As early as 1978 Armani 'started a more affordable line, which he named Le Collezioni', and a few years later he took the key step: starting Emporio Armani. The Emporio clothes were aimed at 'a younger market at around 60 per cent below the [prices of the] top Borgonuovo (or Black Label) line'.[28] In fact Armani's book observes that initially many experts thought the Emporio Armani level of menswear and womenswear was a marketing mistake:

[They were] casual clothes, most made of denim, all at affordable prices. It was seen as being the wrong move in terms of marketing, an irreparable blow to my image. Was *the* fashion designer of the 'power woman' and the 'new man' really lowering himself to making things for the Average Joe?[29]

On the other hand, Emporio Armani met two of the new fashion preferences—casual wear and value for money—and might well be viewed as an adaptive response to these changes in customers' fashion preferences. Not surprisingly, the 'downmarket' Emporio soon vindicated Armani, proving to be very successful and playing an important role in the firm's expansion. Ten years later he was still moving in the same direction: 'the new A/X (Armani Exchange) line which was launched in the US in response to the economic recession' was 'considerably cheaper than the other clothing labels' sold by Armani.[30]

In 2005 he added the traditional summit to his pyramid of products by launching an Armani haute couture 'house' in Paris—some twenty or even thirty years 'late'.[31] Although this had removed some of his pyramid's distinctiveness, its vertical and horizontal extensiveness made it a still distinctive 'Armani' creation. The clothing lines now descended from the new haute couture Armani Prive to 'Giorgio Armani, then Armani Collezione, then Emperio Armani for the young, and then beneath these the very casual Armani Exchange or Armani Jeans'.[32] Each of these clothing lines and pricing levels also extended horizontally into a set of appropriate accessories, 'leather, shoes, watches' et cetera, and then there were the stand-alone horizontal extensions into 'glasses, cosmetics, perfumes' and the furnishings and interior design of Armani Casa.[33] Although the Armani brand was being widely stretched by these extensions, the brand continued to be imbued with the personal charisma—the personal touch or vision—of the iconic designer. 'From jeans to underwear, from haute couture to handbags and watches, I offer a piece of my vision to everyone, making no distinctions, and always with the same creative rigor.'[34]

In addition to this pyramid of products, Armani's firm developed a globalized retail network, which he and his partner instigated several years after the firm was founded. In the 1970s 'there were virtually no single-brand boutiques, most shops sold an array of French and Italian brands. But that left a designer at the mercy of the boutique owner, who decided how much to buy and how to display the clothes.'[35] In the early 1980s, however, Armani established his Emporio Armani chain of stores, which sold only his brand and indeed was selling a new line of Armani clothes specially designed for these new retail outlets. The first store opened in 1981 and two years later 'there were ninety Emporio Armani shops scattered throughout Italy'.[36] Eventually, each of the Armani clothing lines and its accompanying accessories would be sold exclusively or specifically through its own particular chain of stores.[37] Furthermore, during the 1980s–90s the firm's retail network expanded throughout Europe, Asia, and North America, becoming virtually a global network with stores in more than *thirty* countries. At the end of the century, Armani's 'billion-dollar empire' boasted a retail network that 'included 53 Giorgio Armani stores, 6 Le Collezioni stores, 129 Emporio Armani, 48 A/X Armani Exchange stores, 4 Armani jeans and 2 Armani junior stores in 33 countries'.[38] In the US, for example, there were nine Giorgio Armani boutiques and twelve Emporio Armani shops, plus the new A/X Armani Exchange stores.[39] By creating this far-flung retail network Armani was again, as with his product pyramid, adapting his firm to fit the new times—even if this meant creating a more complex firm that was more difficult to lead in the personal manner of the pre-Armani era.

Another structural complexity was that Gorgio Armani SpA became just one of a group of companies belonging to the Armani Group. However, GA SpA and the Group were still private companies wholly owned and controlled by Armani: the 'sole shareholder, president and managing director'.[40] In fact he had increased his control over the Armani empire through having his firm become more involved in the manufacturing of Armani clothes and accessories.[41] By the mid-2000s he was an industrialist as well as a retailer and designer. 'Gruppo Armani is now one of the largest manufacturing groups in the world of fashion, with forty-nine hundred employees and thirteen plants.'[42] As in many other ways, Armani's firm was now very different from a Parisian fashion house making handcrafted haute couture.

Armanian Versus Versacian Adaptations

Any account of Armani's career, adaptations, and opportunity requires some comparison with those of the other great fashion designer of his time, Gianni Versace. Like Armani, he emerged from the ready-to-wear clothing industry of northern Italy in the 1970s and became an international figure in the 1980s. His career and life came to a violently premature end on 15 July 1997, when the fifty-year-old Versace was murdered by a serial killer in Miami, but in his relatively short career he had made a remarkable impact on the fashion world: in 1999 White's *Versace* referred to the Versace fashion label as perhaps the world's best known.[43]

Furthermore, Versace's style had become famous despite being very different from Armani's and in fact being virtually a *contrasting* style. The contrast between the two styles is most apparent in their high-fashion womenswear collections. Versace's collections became famous for their 'blatantly sexy, body-revealing clothes, brash prints and the ostentatious use of gilt' and indeed 'the overt display of wealth and sexuality' were the two facets that seemed 'to encapsulate the essence of Versace's style'.[44] Versace's style was often analysed in terms of *glamour*, including glamour that was 'intrinsically linked to the creation of sexual fantasy. There has been considerable debate about whether Versace's clothes empower or subjugate women.'[45] If they did in any way empower women, it was not in the way that Armani's suits empowered career women. And the exuberant glamour of Versace's style was clearly very different from the Armani style's understated elegance. So it is hardly surprising that the high-fashion world had divided views about these two famous designers. Armani's biographer dramatically describes this conflict of opinion:

> Skirmishes over the relative merits of the two designers swept the small but prickly world of fashion. Fashion journalists coined unwieldy adjectives such as 'Armanian' and 'Versacian' and used them whenever possible . . . [as] the rivalry between these two designers split the world of fashion into two armed camps.[46]

These terms, Armanian and Versacian, may seem similar to the terms Fordism and Sloanism but the fashion terms refer to differences in artistic style, not to differences in business approach or to the difference between production rationality and administrative rationality.

Yet the Armanian versus Versacian distinction can in fact be viewed from a 'rationalist' as well as stylistic perspective. For the difference in style can be seen as the result of two leaders using the same rational methods to exploit the same opportunity but using them in *two different ways*. Both Armani and Versace were rapidly and innovatively adapting to fashion's new times but their adaptive responses went in two different directions and produced contrasting artistic styles. While Armani targeted the new market, Versace instead targeted what remained of the old market, as the new times had given him the chance to 'catch a jump' on the firms which dominated this market: the French haute couture firms. They were too distracted or too much 'in denial'—thanks to the new fashion preferences, new market, and new styles—to be capable of fending off a modernizing challenge in what remained of their old market.

Versace's adaptive response came soon after his ready-to-wear firm was founded in Milan in 1977. So in a sense it was less rapid than Armani's response of some two years earlier and in a sense Versace's response was also less innovative. For he aimed to conquer the *old* market by *modernizing*, not reversing, the haute couture style; he would change femininity into sexuality, not androgynous jackets, and he would change dressed-up stylishness into extravagant glamour, not the elegant casualness of Armanian style. Furthermore, Versace would keep up-to-date with cultural trends, which in the 1980s became a combination of the sexual freedom of the 1960s and the ostentatious or frivolous display of the 1920s.

From an adaptive perspective therefore the dramatic differences between Versacian and Armanian styles seem to be simply different adaptive responses to fashion's new times. From a business perspective, too, this is simply two different ways in which new firms can replace the leading firms in an industry. Armani's firm replaced them by taking over a new market; Versace's firm replaced them by competing for the remains of the old market while its leading firms were unable to respond effectively. In fact as late as the 1990s the French haute couture firms had still not responded effectively to the Versace challenge, even when he competed head-on by adding a haute couture collection to his pyramid of ready-to-wear lines. Ball's *House of Versace* depicts the 'traditional Parisian couture houses' as relatively 'stodgy' when compared to how Versace projected the latest cultural trends onto his haute couture clothes: the French couturiers 'would struggle to compete with such bracing, exciting designs'.[47]

What is more, Versace developed his modernized haute couture market into such a rewarding niche that he rivalled Armani commercially as well as stylistically. Versace's start-up was no less successful than Armani's and by 1983 the Versace firm had sales of some $150 million.[48] Continuing success took its total sales to some $700 million by 1991 and its total retail sales to the one-billion-dollar mark by 1997.[49] So Versace, like Armani, was eventually the leader of a 'billion-dollar empire' that derived its iconic status from the prestige of its designer-leader. The Versacian adaptation therefore seems comparable to the Armanian not only stylistically but also as a way of establishing a firm with a rewarding niche in the fashion environment of its times.

But this begs the question of how did Versace glean such commercial rewards from the remains of an old market. Part of the explanation is that this was potentially still a sizeable market, which also had potential for growth and development. Gastel's *The Versace Legacy* argues that 'Armani and Versace divided the territory' in the 1980s, as Armani 'created the perfect image for the professional, the career woman' and Versace became 'the great interpreter of the decade's drive for show, for appearances'.[50] As she implies, Versace was not being left with a small patch of territory in a far corner. After all, many affluent women did not have a career and some affluent career women would wear Versace designs, if only in their after-work social life. In Italy, Versace's 'core market was the so-called "Signora", the established woman who is perhaps not in the first flush of youth, but is keen to convey her sexuality and her wealth. Versace was also enviably successful in most other countries': they provided him with ample territory for a flourishing high-fashion firm.[51]

In some countries, too, notably the US, Versace's territory seems to have increased in later years. He had difficulty selling in the US in the early 1980s but by 1995 North America was contributing nearly a fifth of his annual sales.[52] Ball refers to a 'new yen for fun, exuberant clothes' in the 1990s and she suggests that 'women who had flocked to safe designers such as Armani when they first entered the workforce wanted to cut loose'.[53] This new tendency was encouraged by the continuing economic boom, with its 'rampant consumerism', and by the American fashion media, which had adopted a more Versacian attitude.[54]

Another factor, however, was that Versace had moved into Armani's territory. There were now Versacian 'day suits, jackets, pants. His daywear was popular with women who wanted a more feminine uniform than Armani's androgynous suits.'[55] These Versacian uniforms not only were relatively feminine but also were manufactured in realistic sizes. Versace reminded the factories that not all women were runway fashion models.[56]

The new daywear was an example of how Versace extended his market by extending his *pyramid of products*. In the 1980s he added several new ready-to-wear lines, including the expensive Couture daywear and two more affordable lines, Update and Versus.[57] These two were aimed at the younger market and indeed Versus was launched with his 33-year-old sister, Donatella, as its youth-oriented designer.[58] Such lines are not simply lower pricing levels on the pyramid; they are also adjusting the *style* of the clothes to suit younger customers. Similarly, Versace adjusted the style of clothes to suit the many customers who did not want to wear the more outlandish or extreme examples of Versacian style. For Versace was the forerunner of a technique that was described by Agins in *The End of Fashion*:

> Even though the leading designers tart up their runways with outlandish, crowd-pleasing costumes, they are grounded in reality. The bulk of the actual merchandise that hits the sale floor is always palatable enough for millions of consumers around the world, thus generating the bottom line that Wall Street expects.[59]

Versace had been doing something similar when he marketed realistic or palatable versions of the Versacian style displayed on the runway. Ball refers to them as 'more-wearable versions' or 'toned-down variations' and an Italian boutique owner observed that Versace 'could take that striking item and dilute it, dissolve it into ten other versions that would sell like crazy because they had his fashion edge but not the extremism shown on the runway'.[60] This diluted extremism was sold through supplementary lines of clothing that are often termed 'diffusion' lines. In 1997 Turner noted that 'the Versace diffusion lines sell by the bucket load' and she listed no fewer than seven diffusion lines, which were 'a little cheaper' than the 'core lines' but were clearly contributing their fair share to the firm's billion-dollar sales revenue.[61]

The extension of Versace's product pyramid had therefore markedly extended his modernized haute couture market—and made it much more rewarding. In addition, the pyramid was extended horizontally into *non*-clothing products. Turner's figures show that by 1996, the year before Versace's death, his clothing items were earning little more than half of the firm's revenue: $560 million versus $250 million from accessories, $150 million from perfumes and $40 million from homeware.[62] The accessories category included jewellery as well as 'bags, belts, shoes, ties, scarves, gloves, hats, sunglasses and, most recently, cosmetics'.[63] Like Armani's pyramid, each kind of item was sold at various price levels, with each variant linked to particular clothing lines. For example, a handbag linked to the Istante diffusion line would be different in design and less expensive than 'a Versace main line handbag'.[64] Clearly the modernized haute couture market had come a long way and been developed in many directions since Versace started up his firm in the late 1970s!

However, this process was not part of his adaptation to change in the late 1970s but instead was part of a second rapid and innovative adaptation, which began in the early 1980s. As in the Armani case, establishing a high-fashion empire required the adaptive rational methods to be used in combination not once but twice: first stylistically in the 1970s and then organizationally in the 1980s. In Armani's case the organizational adaptation, as described earlier, produced a new kind of leading high-fashion firm that was well adapted to fit the new fashion and business world of the 1980s–90s. In Versace's case, too, the organizational adaptation produced a new kind of high-fashion firm but it was a *modernized haute couture* firm that had been adapted to fit the new fashion and business world.

Versace's new kind of firm was generally similar to Armani's but there were also some marked differences. The similarities included the modernizing of production and marketing, the extension of the product pyramid, the creation of a globalized retail network, and the anomaly of remaining a private company even though going public would have better adapted the firms to fit the new fashion and business world. The differences between the two kinds of firm were sometimes only differences of degree or emphasis, such as Versace's great concern with marketing. His marketing grand strategy included (1) massive magazine advertising, (2) dramatic fashion shows, (3) pioneering the use of celebrity 'supermodels', and (4) adopting the Armani-pioneered strategy of having celebrities wear his designs at media events.[65]

Marketing strategies aside, there were marked differences between the two firms' product pyramids. Perhaps the most obvious and characteristic was the 'dilution' of Versacian stylistic extremism. While Versace's extreme or outlandish designs were realistically toned down in his diffusion clothing lines, Armani's new-market designs were not extreme enough to need such dilution. Another characteristic structural difference was that Versace had added haute couture to his pyramid by 1990, only thirteen years after founding his firm, but Armani waited *thirty* years, until 2005, before adding a haute couture line.[66] A further characteristic difference was that menswear was less prominent in Versace's product pyramid than Armani's, as would be expected of a modernized haute couture firm when compared with a new-market fashion firm.[67]

There were also marked differences between the two firms' globalized retail networks. Both firms began developing these networks in the early 1980s but Versace focused on boutiques selling top-line products, not on downmarket stores like the Emporio Armani stores that were the backbone of Armani's new retail network. Another difference was that Versace's firm adopted a more 'modern' approach, namely franchising, which was so new to Italy that there was no business or legal term for such an arrangement.[68] The network of franchised retailers soon spread beyond Italy and Europe to New York, Los Angeles, and even far-off Sydney in Australia.[69] By the mid-1980s there were more than a hundred Versace boutiques around the world, and the network was further developed and globalized during the 1980s–90s: by 1997 there were 'over 300 boutiques [and] in every major capital in the world'.[70] But by then, too, the company had still not gone public and, as Versace's death revealed, this meant that his firm had no long-term solution to a problem that had originated twenty years earlier and in fact was a side-effect of Versace's 1970s stylistic adaptation to fashion's new times.

Adaptive Legacies and Capability

Gianni Versace's death in 1997 left his family firm in the hands of his sister Donatella and his older brother Santo, who had been its CEO and joint-leader for some twenty years. The two Versace brothers' dual-leadership team, like Armani and Galeotti's, had been a two-role team in which the creative designer was supported and protected by a business-oriented teammate. However, Santo's business expertise was being challenged by a difficult business situation in the late 1990s, and his planned remedy evaporated when Gianni's unexpected death ended their plan to take the company public.[71] But Gianni's death left Donatella with an even worse predicament. She would have to take on his role as the firm's internationally famous designer, who had imbued Versace products with the personal charisma of an iconic designer.

She was also facing the negative consequences, the side-effects, of a crucial difference between Versace's and Armani's stylistic adaptations to fashion's new times. By seeking to modernize haute couture Versace had placed great artistic demands on himself and on his successor as the firm's chief designer. Not only was there a need to dilute stylistic extremism to fit the diffusion lines of clothing but also there was a need to create a succession of *new* designs, seasonal collection after seasonal collection, to maintain the designer's reputation for novelty. For Versace's modernization of haute couture had retained the traditional high-fashion accent on what Agins described as 'planned obsolescence': the seasonal changes in what is fashionable and what is out-of-fashion.[72] His modernized version of this planned obsolescence had become more intensive as he attracted an increasing amount of media attention. Versace noted not long before he died that 'the media exhaust the new quickly' and therefore he would be adding another two more collections to the four he was already presenting each year.[73] Here again, as with his diluted extremism, he was the forerunner of a later tendency. In the 2000s the high-fashion business, 'with its bottomless hunger for something new, had become a treadmill for designers who must churn out frequent flash collections between their semiannual runway shows'.[74]

This treadmill of constantly having to create 'something new' puts great pressure on the designer and the firm. It is much greater than the pressure produced by the microprocessor-manufacturing treadmill discussed in Chapter 6. As Turner noted, are any manufacturing industries 'required to produce a totally new product line, with all its attendant production and marketing problems, every six months'?[75]

In contrast, Armani's stylistic adaptation to new times had been directed towards a new high-fashion market that did not require a dramatically new product line each and every fashion season. Armani could instead adopt the standard manufacturing approach of continually making incremental modifications or marginal variations but only occasionally producing a dramatically *new* product line. Agins described Armani as producing something 'new and original in 1975' and then 'only a few modifications each season' but pointed out that 'variations of his look continued to remain in style for two decades'.[76] More importantly, she explained why he retained his customers despite his lack of novelty. 'Armani epitomized the end of fashion' partly because his customers 'no longer cared if fashion moved forward or backward; they just wanted fashion to provide them with attractive clothes suited for modern living'.[77] In other words, customers' preferences in this new high-fashion market allowed him to avoid the novelty treadmill and its pressure for new products—this was a key advantage of the direction his stylistic adaptation had taken in the mid-1970s.

Another key advantage was that if Armani had died in the 1990s, his firm would have been left a manageable stylistic legacy. For his successor as chief designer would have needed only to continue in the Armanian style and with Armani's approach to stylistic innovation. This approach has been characterized by his biographer as 'triggering a great initial revolution and then introducing many small advances, all clustered around the central core of what constitutes his style'.[78] However, White pointed out that 'Armani's style has in fact seen several revolutions' as he moved from the unconstructed jacket to the power-suit shape, to the roomier 'sack suit' and, in the mid-1990s, to a more feminine, occasionally Versacian style of womenswear.[79] Yet she also acknowledged that Armani was 'not dominated by a need for novelty in every collection'.[80] Armani puts it more colourfully in his book. He describes himself as 'allergic to the fireworks of fake revolutions that fizzle out in the time it takes to see the fashion show' and he is 'not particularly interested in the idea that radical renewal every six months is of value'.[81]

Unlike Armani, Versace *was* seeking radical renewal in each collection—he had climbed on the novelty treadmill. Gartel depicts Armani as an 'extremist' of consistency compared to Versace, who 'took a different route every time', and indeed his 'creative turnover was so fevered that his style never settled into a definite mould'.[82] So if he did create a distinctively Versacian style, he was certainly not a consistently Versacian designer—the pursuit of novelty required him to explore other possibilities. For example, in 1992 his sado-masochistic collection was followed by a collection in an almost hippie-like 'country' style, in 1995 his haute couture collection displayed 'demure women' wearing long skirts and high necklines, and this so-called 'conservative chic glamour' was followed by a relatively Armanian ready-to-wear collection aimed apparently at 'busy women, women who work hard in their careers'.[83] In fact Versace showed amazing artistic creativity in his search for a new theme for each of his collections, as is evident from even a partial analysis of the 1987–97 period. In addition to varying the 'Versacian' style, he also presented at least *thirteen* major changes in style, beginning with a collection showing mini-skirted models wearing 'jackets perfect for high-powered women executives' and ending with a collection inspired by the Ravenna church mosaics and using 'metal mesh fabric woven with Byzantine crosses'.[84]

Without such creativity and novelty, Versace's famous marketing 'sizzle' would have been unable to transform him into an iconic designer. He might still have gained the attention of the fashion and mass media through his marketing efforts but the media attention would have soon led to cynical media comments about too much sizzle and not enough steak. So whatever the Versacian style may have been, the Versace *image* and *charisma* were based on creativity and on mastery of the novelty treadmill.

This was a daunting legacy to leave to Donatella or anyone else who succeeded Versace as the firm's leading designer. Ball notes that Versace 'had dipped into so many different themes and references over twenty years that Donatella was left without a single clear path to follow'.[85] But the crucial point is that Donatella would have to follow her brother onto the treadmill and, like him, dip into many different themes and references. This would also provide the extremist designs that were required, no matter how diluted, by the firm's array of diffusion lines. Only then, too, would the Versace brand retain the charisma that was so important in selling the non-clothing items on the product pyramid.

Furthermore, the late 1990s were a period of intensified competition in high-fashion design. For luxury leatherwear companies had entered the field in order to gain more publicity and prestige for their brand of handbags and other luxury products.[86] They were producing notable high-fashion collections through Gucci's Tom Ford, Prada's Miuccia Prada and the designers associated with Arnault's LVMH (Louis Vuitton). In addition, they were producing increased competition in the *non*-clothing items on the Versace product pyramid at a time when the firm's business problems made it difficult to respond.[87]

Not surprisingly, Versace's firm was unable to meet this huge challenge. For example, Donatella was a talented designer but at this stage in her career, according to Ball, 'she lacked the creativity and ingenuity to conjure up her own ideas from scratch' and so she inevitably fell far short of her brother's mastery of the novelty treadmill.[88] Similarly, she was unable to continue his practice of diluting extremist designs to suit the diffusion lines and in fact 'the various lines took off in different directions'.[89] The challenge also took a huge toll on her psychologically and in 2004 she entered a rehab clinic to deal with her drug problem.[90] She would go on to rebuild her career as a designer and soon achieved international renown. But by then the firm had lost momentum in the highly competitive markets for high-fashion clothes and luxury goods. By 2003 sales had dropped to 'less than half' the level they had been in 1997, the firm 'fell from no. 2 among fashion companies in 1997 to no. 10 in 2004', and its sales were only one-fifth the size of Armani's by 2006.[91] Management consultants and outside CEOs were brought in and there were two rounds of lay-offs that led to hundreds of employees losing their jobs.[92] The firm was eventually put on a sound enough footing to face the 2010s with some confidence but it was no longer in any sense a rival of Armani's increasingly large company.

Versace's firm was going down a path that had been set decades earlier by the direction of his stylistic adaptive response in the late 1970s. And the path had been confirmed by his failure to include a key feature of the modern firm—becoming a public company—in his organizational adaptation in the 1980s. If his company had gone public as early as possible, it could have coped with the risks of Versace's attempt to modernize haute couture. For it would have had the salary and stock options available to hire a world-class designer or strategist to handle the post-Versace era, whether by climbing on the stylistic treadmill or devising a strategy that put the firm on a new path.[93] However, Versace had not used the adaptive rational methods as capably as Armani, who had made a less risky stylistic adaptation in the 1970s and so, unlike Versace, could both keep his firm a private company and also protect his employee-followers' jobs and career prospects.

Roddick's *Business As Unusual*

Like Armani and Versace, Anita Roddick used the two adaptive methods in the 1970s–80s to establish a large and iconic company—which in her case was the British cosmetics corporation, The Body Shop. It was smaller and less iconic than their high-fashion companies but in 1984 it became a public company and therefore, unlike their firms, was truly a corporation. Furthermore, Roddick used the two adaptive methods in a different manner from Armani and Versace; instead of combining them, she used one after the other, with an innovative adaptation being followed by a separate rapid adaptation.

In addition to establishing The Body Shop, Roddick wrote, co-authored, or edited several books before she died in 2007, aged sixty-four, and these writings included the partly autobiographical *Business as Unusual* published in 2000 and the earlier, largely autobiographical *Body and Soul*. This relative abundance of autobiographical material provides a fascinating leader's-eye view but there is a scarcity of biographical or historical material describing how she established The Body Shop corporation.[94] In combination, however, there is sufficient material to cover the key feature of this example of rational leadership, namely the *abandoning* of adaptive rational methods in the latter half of the 1980s.

Roddick's abandoning of adaptive rational methods provides a crucial 'exception that proves the rule' example of what occurs when a leader fails to use the appropriate rational methods. For in this case the corporation lost momentum and was in a crisis situation by the late 1990s, which led to layoffs and to employee-followers losing all rational confidence in the future development of the corporation. In fact, there would have been a major loss of rational confidence years earlier, when it was clear that the corporation had lost momentum and that its leader had abandoned the adaptive rational methods which she had used so successfully in the past.

Roddick began using adaptive methods even before she opened her first Body Shop in 1976 in Brighton. Her decision to open this new kind of store was an innovative adaptation to a drastic change in her personal situation. Her husband had decided to pursue his 'long-term ambition to undertake a horseback expedition from Buenos Aires to New York and while he made plans for that we decided that I would make ends meet [financially support herself and their two young children] with a small shop of some kind'.[95] And she decided that it would be a *new* kind of shop:

> When we started out, we invented a new concept—a shop where you could buy anything for the bath and the body and the hair. Nobody had done that before. The department stores couldn't really compete with us because they had 20,000 other products to sell.[96]

Another advantage was that specialized retail outlets for such items as skin-care or hair-care products could not compete with Roddick's wide range of products for the bath, the hair, the face, and various other parts of the body—her new shop was aptly named The Body Shop. Classifying The Body Shop as a cosmetics store and corporation is therefore a narrow approximation; it might be better described as belonging to the beauty industry, with its wide range of cosmetic and other personal products.[97]

Roddick's success in this industry, however, arose from her use of *rapid* as well as innovative adaptation. For her innovative shop had another competitive advantage—the opportunity to ride a new, 'green' wave in consumer preferences—and she rapidly adapted to these new, greener times. Roddick would later acknowledge that the green market had not been part of her initial adaptive innovation: 'I make no claim to prescience, to any intuition about the rise of the green movement.'[98] But her shop's use of recycling and natural ingredients was both accidentally and ideally suited to meet the green movement's preference for natural and environmentally friendly products.

This happy coincidence was apparently due to several improvizations Roddick had made when she was preparing to open her new kind of shop. Her use of natural ingredients seems to have been largely because of her lack of chemical expertise and lack of laboratory and factory facilities. 'I'm not a cosmetics chemist or a pharmacist' and before opening the shop she had been 'doing a lot of research on do-it-yourself cosmetics in Worthing public library and mixing ingredients in the kitchen'.[99] She had also discovered that mainstream cosmetics manufacturers were not interested in producing the small quantities she needed and were even less interested in using the natural ingredients she wanted, such as cocoa butter and aloe vera.[100] However, she found a herbalist manufacturer who was willing to produce small quantities 'and we drew up a list of twenty-five possible products using those natural ingredients that were readily available'.[101] Another forced improvisation was her environmentally friendly use of packaging and containers.

> The cheapest containers I could find were plastic bottles used by hospitals to collect urine samples, but I couldn't afford to buy enough so I thought I would get round the problem by offering to refill empty containers or fill customers' own bottles. In this way we started recycling and reusing materials long before it became ecologically fashionable. *Every element of our success was really down to the fact that I had no money.*[102]

In fact, the firm's obvious lack of resources was itself one of the things that attracted customers to The Body Shop in the new, greener times of the 1970s–80s. 'It was clearly evident to everyone that the The Body Shop was a hick little cottage industry, and therein, I think, lay a lot of its attraction.'[103]

But it was Roddick's rapid adaptation to the new, greener times that enabled her to scale up a small shop into a famous public company—and as early as

1984. She created a green public profile for her firm and exploited its competitive advantages in the green niche market. The Body Shop is described by Jones as one of the 'iconic "natural" firms of the era' and he also notes that its retail chain had '43 outlets in Britain and 83 abroad' by 1984.[104] This was largely because Roddick had created a sizeable demand for Body Shop franchises as well as products. Franchisees provided the financing for their new shops and 'we provided a license to use the Body Shop name and the products to sell'.[105] The result was comparable to the network of franchised stores established by Versace in these years as he, too, rapidly adapted to his market opportunity. However, Roddick went a step further by going public and providing her firm with the resources and status of a public company. She was therefore well-positioned to go on and create a global empire within the beauty industry.

Instead of taking this step, however, Roddick abandoned the adaptive methods she had used to establish The Body Shop and that she needed to *continue* using if she was going to expand it into a global empire. For this meant expanding into the giant American market and, furthermore, making the move quickly, before US firms adapted to the opportunities offered by the new, greener times. Already 'many mass market firms had joined the "natural" bandwagon. During the late 1970s Clairol captured a large share of the US shampoo market with Herbal Essences, a green shampoo with a high fragrance content based on the essences of sixteen herbs and wildflowers.'[106] And by the late 1980s even Wal-Mart was launching a green campaign that displayed its environmentally friendly practices, as was mentioned in Chapter 5. Yet The Body Shop did not rapidly adapt to the mid-1980s window of 'green' opportunity in the American market—there would be years of delay before it belatedly went for the biggest prize in its industry.

Roddick's abandoning of rapid adaptation in the mid-1980s can be explained by two factors: the influence of her husband Gordon and the diversion into charismatic leadership. After his 2,000-mile ride around South America, Gordon became the 'numbers man' in his wife's start-up and later her teammate in their dual leadership of The Body Shop corporation.[107] According to Roddick's 1991 *Body and Soul*, she and Gordon initially had different views about expansion into the American market. 'Initially, I was much more enthusiastic than Gordon about going into America'; his view was that 'while the United States offered The Body Shop the greatest potential for growth, it also represented the greatest potential for disaster'.[108]

The other likely explanation for the delay is that she was diverted and distracted by her new role as a charismatic leader. It was not charismatic *business* leadership but instead the role of celebrity political activist publicizing new social issues and values. Roddick's activism was often an extension of her and The Body Shop's green public profile, such as their campaigning to save the whales and to support Greenpeace and Friends of the Earth pressure groups.[109] However, her personal political activism eventually covered a wide range of social issues and values: someone writing about Roddick declared that she had 'campaigned about everything, from stopping tests on animals to getting housing for homeless people'.[110] In particular, she campaigned for a new attitude towards business and its social responsibilities, which she sums up in her 2000 *Business as Unusual*:

> Businesses have become hypnotized by the bottom line and have forgotten their moral obligations to civil society. The message I have been repeating *in every speech I've made and every article I've written* on business in the last 15 years is that we must include in our measures of success enough to sustain communities, cultures and families.[111]

As her reference to the 'last 15 years' confirms, Roddick took on this time-consuming charismatic role in the mid-1980s, just when her corporation should have begun to move into the American market.

But instead this move would be delayed until the *late* 1980s. As Roddick acknowledges, 'we had more than two hundred stores in thirty-three countries around the world before the first Body Shop opened in the United States in the summer of 1988'.[112] By then the green movement and attitudes were so well-established that there was no chance of The Body Shop becoming an iconic green corporation as it had in Britain; it was just one of many firms in the American market, including Wal-Mart, which were already or soon would be presenting themselves as green or greenish. Furthermore, The Body Shop would be facing competition from firms selling 'natural' beauty products and from at least one firm that would sell such products in a similar kind of store to her once innovative Body Shop format and range of products. What Jones describes as her 'retail model' was 'later used by other companies selling green brands, such as the [American] clothing retailer Limited Brands, which founded a natural-toiletries store chain called Bath & Body Works in 1988'.[113] So an American equivalent of The Body Shop was founded in the same year that Roddick's corporation arrived in the country. By 1990 The Body Shop had twenty-two stores in the US but the Bath & Body Works (B&BW) chain had opened nearly five times as many stores.[114]

Roddick acknowledges in *Business as Unusual* that she had not anticipated 'how incredibly fast the competition would come in'.[115] She refers to B&BW as 'a copycat of The Body Shop' and seems to view anyone selling natural beauty products as an imitator as well as competitor: 'there were around 30 different lookalikes of The Body Shop' and such competitors as 'H2O Plus, Goodbodies, Origins and Garden Botanika jumped on the natural products bandwagon, developed their own lines of fruity potions and sold them for less'.[116] She also mentions several other features of the retail and business culture that had not been anticipated or that involved a more difficult adjustment than she had anticipated.[117] Furthermore, she explains that initially The Body Shop opened only company-owned stores—waiting until 1990 to begin franchising—in order 'to give us time to adjust to the new market'.[118]

As in the mid-1980s, however, Roddick needed to adapt more rapidly. The alternative was to use innovative adaptation, such as seeking a joint-venture arrangement with an American entrepreneur, like the international joint-ventures that McDonald's had pioneered in the 1970s. This would have markedly increased The Body Shop's chances of becoming an iconic green corporation in America as well as other regions of the world.

Not surprisingly, the failure to use either of the adaptive methods led to the eventual failure of the American expansion. Roddick describes a 'golden age' of growth in the early 1990s as more than a hundred franchised stores were opened, but the growth slowed in 1993 and by the following year was in reverse: The Body Shop actually began to lose customers.[119] This disappointing end to high expectations was reflected in the corporation's share price. 'The share market decided we were no longer their darling and hacked our share price to pieces' to such an extent that at one point the corporation had 'lost more than half its value'.[120] The share price would never return to its early-1990s peak. Looking back at this turning point, Roddick commented that hopefully The Body Shop would 'always be the leader—if not in profits, then in ideas and principles. In those areas, I don't believe anybody can offer us any competition.'[121]

Roddick's move away from rational leadership was confirmed by the lack of rapid or innovative adaptive response to the loss of momentum. For example, there was no business-oriented equivalent of Roddick's innovative social auditing of the corporation's activities.[122] A management consultant was employed in the mid-1990s but his reorganization ended when the firm's leaders realized that they 'had made a mistake trying to fit a business with a distinct social agenda into the straitjacket of the standard disciplines of management, marketing, finance and operations'.[123] Not surprisingly, the adaptive methods had not been replaced by other appropriate rational methods, such as strategic calculation. Eventually a new situation developed and in 1998 an outside CEO was brought in, with Anita and Gordon now becoming co-chairs of the corporation.[124] The new CEO pruned the firm's administration, closed its manufacturing plant, and laid off some three hundred employees.[125] By then, 'Roddick's focus was really more on social causes than on the company itself' and three years later she and Gordon resigned as co-chairs.[126] In 2006 they sold The Body Shop was sold to the French corporation L'Oréal for more than a billion dollars—thirty years after Roddick had opened her first shop.[127]

Conclusion

The preceding chapters have described how various business leaders have developed—established or enhanced—a corporation in a rational way. They are examples of a rational, modern type of inspirational leader who inspires his or her followers with a modern, rational kind of confidence. This confidence arises from the fact that the leader is capably using the appropriate rational means of achieving an objective, such as developing a business corporation. The corporation-developing version of this rational leadership has been explored through seven chapters of classic examples, which have shown how high-level business leaders very capably used the appropriate rational means of developing a business corporation. These 'appropriate rational means' were a set of six generic rational methods: rapid and innovative adaptation, quantitative and strategic calculation, diverse and institutionalized deliberation.

A series of classic examples have shown how leaders used these six methods as means of developing iconic corporations in various industries, times, and places. What is more, the examples provided a 'leader's-eye' view by featuring the leaders' autobiographical accounts of how he or she developed an iconic corporation. The six main examples were Sloan enhancing General Motors, Ohno enhancing Toyota, Kroc establishing McDonald's, Walton establishing Wal-Mart, Grove enhancing Intel, and, finally, Whitman enhancing e-Bay. Five other autobiographical examples were added to illustrate particular methods and issues. Two of these cases also extended the range of industries being covered, with Sandberg enhancing social-media Facebook and Packard establishing a remarkably diversified high-tech corporation. The other three cases broadened the coverage of countries as well as industries by describing Armani's Italian fashion, Roddick's British cosmetics, and Dassault's French aircraft construction. Furthermore, the corporate-developing efforts of a few other renowned leaders—including Steve Jobs of Apple and Jeff Bezos of Amazon—were each compared with one or more of the autobiographical examples of developing a corporation.

The key comparisons, however, involved only the six main examples and focused on the similarities and differences in the leaders' selection and emphasizing of methods. Each example identified which of the six methods were selected by 'its' leader as appropriate to use in this case—and which of these selected methods he or she emphasized.

There was a surprising amount of uniformity in the six leaders' selection of methods. Sloan, Kroc, Walton, and Whitman used the whole set of methods in their establishing or enhancing of General Motors, McDonald's, Wal-Mart, and eBay respectively. The two other leaders, Ohno and Grove, described themselves using only three of the six methods. Ohno's book described him enhancing Toyota through the use of innovative adaptation plus both the calculative methods, while Grove's book espoused an analytical framework which involved rapid adaptation plus both the deliberative methods. But their autobiographical writings were more narrowly focused than those of the other leaders. Grove was focusing on how he handled adaptive crises—strategic inflection points—and did not refer to the methods he used when dealing with other aspects of Intel's development. Similarly, Ohno was focusing on his innovative production system and did not refer to the methods used by his leadership teammates, first Ishida and then Nakagawa, when they performed their roles of CEO-level leader of the corporation. So in reality the Grove and Ohno cases may well have involved a much wider selection of rational methods that was in fact little or no different from the pattern shown by the other four leaders.

There was much less uniformity, however, in the leaders' selection of which methods to *emphasize*. Innovative adaptation was emphasized by Sloan, Ohno, and Kroc, rapid adaptation by Grove, quantitative calculation by Walton and Whitman, strategic calculation by Sloan, Kroc, Walton, and Whitman, diverse deliberation by Kroc, and institutionalized deliberation by Sloan. It had been expected that leaders' selection of methods to emphasize would be largely a matter of personal preferences (and aptitudes) but in fact in these cases it was more often due to the circumstances that the leaders were facing. For example, circumstances required Grove to emphasize rapid adaptation, required Sloan and Kroc to emphasize innovative adaptation, and required four of the six leaders to emphasize strategic calculation, usually in relation to marketing.

The most unexpected feature of the six examples was that three of them used learning as an additional, seventh appropriate method of developing a corporation. From Chapter 5 onwards there were accounts of how Walton, Grove, and Whitman used and indeed emphasized this highly rational method. In all three cases, too, learning was emphasized as both a key and favourite method: both because of personal preferences and because of the circumstances that the leader was facing. Furthermore, the Walton case showed that there were several different forms and contexts of learning, and the Whitman case highlighted the importance of being able to learn quickly.

Another unexpected feature was the prevalence of dual-leadership teams. They appeared in most examples and, furthermore, there were important appearances by all three versions of the dual-leadership team: the two-roles, the two-generations, and the innovation-introducing team. In fact the Toyota case was based upon the innovation-introducing teams of Ohno and Ishida and then Ohno and Nakagawa. The two-role team of Kroc and Sonneborn led McDonald's through a crucial period in its development, even though there were increasing tensions and disagreements between the two leaders in the years before Sonneborn's resignation in 1967. Then the two-generation team of Kroc and Turner led McDonald's into a further period of expansion and the new, globalized era of international joint ventures. Similarly, the two-generation team of Walton and Glass took Wal-Mart in important new directions, including the Supercentre, in the years before Walton's death. However, it is the two-role teams that dominate the final few chapters. Intel is established by Noyce and Moore and then enhanced by Moore and Grove, Hewlett and Packard operate as perhaps the greatest ever dual-leadership team, Armani and then Versace show that the two-role team is effective in high-fashion as well as high-tech industries, and, finally, The Body Shop is led by the Roddicks' two-role wife and husband team.

The dual-leadership team was so prevalent among the examples that it may be a distinctive feature of corporation-developing rational leadership and perhaps even rational business leadership in general. Certainly, dual leadership is not prevalent or important in the political, military, and religious fields. It may in fact be one of the business field's most important contributions to the development of distinctively modern forms of leadership.

This book's contribution has been to the long-established, continually developing theory of rational leadership. As the Appendix describes, several generations of theorists have enhanced the theory by examining various forms and areas of rational leadership. Now it has been further enhanced by examining some classic business, corporation-developing examples of the rational type of inspirational leadership. They have shown that this rational leadership is 'alive and well' in the institution that exemplifies the modern world—past, present, and future. The theory of rational leadership is therefore now comprehensive enough to have 'all that it takes' to be the basis of a new, rationalist paradigm of leadership.

The next order of business is to apply the theory to other fields of leadership, such as military and political leadership. The military field of leadership has some obvious organizational and historical similarities with the business field. Furthermore, the Appendix shows that the rational type of inspirational leadership was favoured by business-like military leaders as early as the 1940s, and Chapter 1 mentioned that there were different versions of this rational military leadership, such as counterinsurgency and naval warfare. Military equivalents of this book could therefore present classic examples of military leaders winning campaigns by very capably using one of these versions' appropriate rational means of achieving the objective.

The political field of leadership, however, is markedly different from the business and military fields. For example, the political chief executive of a contemporary democracy has to inspire not just state employees but also the political elite and the general public. Inspiring this huge and varied 'group of followers' with rational confidence is a difficult task for any leader. But it is far easier than inspiring them with emotional or moral confidence and commitment. The rational type of inspirational leadership is therefore the most that can realistically be expected of political chief executives in the twenty-first century. After all, nothing more is expected of business leaders than their capable use of the appropriate rational means of achieving the objective, such as developing an iconic corporation!

APPENDIX

The Theory Of Rational Leadership

This Appendix examines the theory of rational leadership that originated in the 1920s–30s and has been developed in two different ways by later generations of theorists. Such renowned theorists as Burns and Christensen have enhanced the theory by showing how it can be expanded to incorporate new areas and issues, as will be discussed in the third section of the Appendix. However, the latest generation of theorists, namely the present authors, are enhancing the theory in a different way. They are instead restructuring the original, 1920s–30s contributions into a highly focused but flexible analysis of an early-identified variety of rational leadership—the rational type of inspirational leadership.

This restructuring will be described in the first and second sections of the Appendix, which examine the original contributions made by Weber 'the prophet' and Barnard 'the theorist'. However, first there will be an introductory summary of their contributions and of how these have been restructured into an analysis of the rational type of inspirational leadership. The summary will include, too, some comparisons between this rational leadership and other modern varieties of leadership.

The most well-known varieties are charismatic leadership and the transformational-transactional leadership dimensions identified by Burns. However, modern leadership appears in many different forms, types, and versions.[1] What all these varieties of leadership have in common is that they are setting a direction, giving a lead, in some way or another. In fact there are forms of leadership which do little more than giving a lead, as in the cases of transactional and deliberative leadership. But more is expected of an inspirational form of leadership. In this case a leader is expected to inspire people as well as give a lead or set a direction. For example, the charismatic and transformational types of leadership inspire followers with an emotional or moral confidence and commitment. In contrast, the rational type of inspirational leadership does not inspire followers with commitment, only with confidence, and it inspires them with a confidence that is not emotional or moral but only rational.

Nonetheless, this rational leadership is the most appropriate type of inspirational leadership for the modern times and circumstances of the twenty-first century. As Weber pointed out in the early 1920s, the increasing modernity of societies in the West and then other parts of the globe has been exemplified by the increasing rationality of their institutions, processes, and attitudes. It is true that this rationality has been more a matter of form than content and has not always produced rational behaviour.

But in an increasingly rational world a rational type of leadership becomes increasingly appropriate, if only because people's more rational attitudes have made them more discerning followers, who are less likely to be swayed by tradition or emotion and more likely to be sceptical. Only in unusual circumstances, such as religious revivals or ideological politics, will the rational type of influential leadership be less appropriate than other types.

Furthermore, this tendency towards 'rationalization' affects not only attitudes but also all a society's institutions and processes. So sooner or later, to a lesser or greater degree, the society's *leadership* institutions and processes will be affected by rationalization, as in the political case of a ruling monarchy evolving into a constitutional monarchy or being replaced by a presidential democracy. Likewise, a society's various forms and types of leadership will eventually be 'rationalized' to some degree, as in the case of the charismatic type evolving into a rationalized version of charismatic leadership.

Weber should therefore be viewed as the 'prophet' of rational leadership. But he did not foresee that the tendency to rationalize leadership would actually produce a whole new type of inspirational leadership. This new type was identified in the 1930s by a pioneering analyst of organizations, Chester Barnard. In his book *The Functions of the Executive* he pointed to the 'technical' aspect of the leadership provided by organizations' executives. The technical aspect inspires followers with confidence because their leader (1) has the ability to use technological means to accomplish the organization's objective and (2) has the ability to select the *appropriate* technological means of accomplishing the objective, such as selecting the 'better' method under the conditions that the organization will be facing as it pursues this objective.

Barnard's theory of technical leadership can be restructured into a more focused and more flexible, widely applicable analysis. It becomes more focused when the leader is described as inspiring followers with confidence through the capable use of the appropriate technological means of achieving a particular objective. And the analysis becomes more widely applicable when the technological means are described in broader terms. Barnard employed a peculiarly broad definition of 'technological'— which included technical systems and organizational schemes—but an even broader term is needed to encompass such methods as devising a strategy to achieve a particular objective. Such methods are used at the higher levels of leadership and in many different fields, including political and even religious leadership.

So there is good reason to integrate Barnard's theory of technical leadership into Weber's theory of rationalization, as a new extension or branch covering a key development in the rationalization of leadership. Then Barnard's technical aspect is categorized as a *rational type* of inspirational leadership, which inspires followers with *rational* confidence through the capable use of the appropriate *rational* means of achieving a particular objective. The broad term 'rational means' includes a wide range of technological and other means, even such general, generic-level rational methods as quantitative calculation or rapid adaptation. Furthermore, the term is still sufficiently precise to distinguish the rational leader's means or methods from those used by less rational leaders, as will be described in the fourth, Machiavellian section of the Appendix.

Weber—the Prophet

The rise of rational leadership was prophetically foreshadowed by Max Weber in the early 1920s in his great sociological treatise *Economy and Society*. It identified the historical process of rationalization through which various fields and spheres of social life were being increasingly dominated by what Weber termed 'formally' rational—in the sense of rational in form—processes and institutions, such as quantitative calculation and administrative rules. Now authority was being rationally legitimated by legal rules, now the administration of states and large businesses was being rationally carried out by modern bureaucracies, now politics was being rationally organized by constitutional democracy's rules and numbers, and now economic activities were being rationally directed by modern market capitalism. In fact Weber argued that 'thorough market freedom'—free of business cartels as well as state distortions—was the precondition for 'the highest level of rationality' in accounting and its calculating approach to economic activities.[2]

Weber did not refer to a similar rationalization of *leadership* but his theory implied that leadership would sooner or later succumb to the spread of formal rationality. In fact leader–follower relations were already being affected by the rationalization of cultural attitudes. Weber believed that this change in attitudes was due to rationality becoming a 'revolutionary force' that was felt in two different ways: it 'intellectualizes the individual' and it changes attitudes through 'altering the situations of life and hence its problems'.[3] Intellectualization was a cultural process that had been going on for thousands of years but the most important part of the process was modern scientific progress and the accompanying use of technical means and calculations.[4]

The other way in which attitudes were being rationalized was through a social process—changes in people's life situations and problems. For example, there were the changes that had been instigated by Taylorism's scientific-management approach to organizing the workplace. Weber noted that 'organizational discipline in the factory has a completely rational basis' and that the 'American' scientific-management system also brought about the 'rational conditioning and training of work performances'.[5] This scientific-management system had been invented by the American management theorist Frederick Taylor. He and Taylorism have been described by his biographer as embodying 'the implacable currents of rationalism that swirled through early twentieth century life' and predated Ford's introduction of assembly-line mass production.[6] Taylor's definitive 1911 text *The Principles of Scientific Management* presented a very wide-ranging, comprehensive system for managerially maximizing workers' productivity.[7] It included selecting the best-suited workers, training them in recuperative work habits and efficient work methods, discovering the most efficient work methods through time-and-motion studies, motivating workers through a task-and-bonus approach and, most importantly, increasing management's control over the workplace: 'all of the planning which under the old system was done by the workman, as a result of his personal experience, must of necessity under the new system be done by the management in accordance with the laws of the science'.[8]

Clearly this scientific-management system was rationalizing the attitudes of managers as well as workers. Like workers, managers were experiencing new, rationalized working-life situations and problems. In addition, managers were being culturally intellectualized by a supposedly 'scientific' management system that emphasized technical means and calculations. And this rationalization of both managers' and workers' attitudes would soon affect their leader–follower relations.

Already Weber had noticed how a rationalizing of attitudes was changing *military* leader–follower relationships. Military leaders now 'rationally calculated' how to inspire soldiers to fight: 'everything is rationally calculated, especially those seemingly imponderable and irrational emotional factors'.[9] The military was developing rationally calculated methods of leadership that would inspire soldiers to fight with an emotional commitment and confidence. Soon the civilians, too, would develop what Burns has labelled the 'how to' approach to leadership. He argued that 'how to' manuals on leadership 'may be useful for gaining and exercising leadership in highly predictable and structured situations' but 'the manuals treat persons [followers] as *things*, as tools to be used or objects to be stormed like a castle'.[10]

Indeed Weber's account of military leaders' rationalized attitudes and leadership had highlighted two crucial distinctions. The first is the difference between (1) uncalculated, 'natural' leadership and (2) calculated, 'how to' inspirational leadership, in which leaders use rationally calculated methods of inspiring followers with emotional commitment and confidence. The second distinction is between (1) this partly rational type of inspirational leadership and (2) the *wholly* rational type, in which leaders inspire their followers with rational confidence because the leader is using the appropriate rational means of achieving the organization's objective. Weber had identified only the first of these two distinctions but in doing so he had highlighted the importance of the second distinction, even though he had not foreseen the appearance of a wholly rational type of inspirational leadership.

Some twenty years later, however, military leaders were moving from the partly to the wholly rational type of inspirational leadership—because by then their *followers'* attitudes, too, had been rationalized. This development was noted by a military historian when discussing the military leadership of the British army fighting in North Africa in 1942. The 'tough, deferential, uncomplaining privates who had died like lemmings on the Western Front in an earlier war had not bred their kind to replace them. These men wanted to stay alive, wanted to get home, wanted to know what was happening and why.'[11] These conscript soldiers had such a rational attitude to military service and leadership that they were discerning or even sceptical 'followers' of their commanders. So it is not surprising that the commander of this army, General Montgomery, presented his soldiers with an image of himself as:

> a professional giving reliable reassurances; one who did not promise more than he could perform, and one who was thoroughly, almost insolently on top of his job. There would inevitably be casualties, he indicated, but no more than strictly necessary to achieve the objective.[12]

Montgomery had therefore invented a method of inspiring confidence among soldiers who had a rational, discerning, and possibly sceptical attitude to military service and leadership. He had come close to the wholly rational type of inspirational leadership that had recently been identified in the pioneering theory of rational leadership presented in 1938 by Chester Barnard.

Barnard—the Theorist

Like Montgomery, Barnard had practical experience of high-level leadership of an organization. Since 1927 he had been president of New Jersey Bell Telephone, a company associated with Bell-ATT.[13] However, his 1938 monograph *The Functions of the Executive* was also based on his familiarity with a wide range of academic sources, including major works in philosophy and sociology.[14] He therefore epitomizes the rationalization of managers' attitudes through what Weber termed 'intellectualization'. Furthermore, Barnard's broad intellectual interests may be why he presented his arguments in a theoretical and general way that would be applicable to not just business firms but *all* formal organizations, even churches and armies. In fact his book is widely recognized as a landmark in the theory of organizations—and a very influential landmark. For example, a 1990s collection of articles on organization theory was titled *Organization Theory: From Chester Barnard to the Present and Beyond* and a celebrated institutional economist declared that the 'incipient science of organization' is 'inspired, directly and indirectly, by Chester Barnard's classic book'.[15]

Barnard's work included innovative theories about organizational leadership, such as its role in creating the culture of the organization. In fact Barnard foreshadowed the concept of 'corporate culture' that became prominent in business-management theory several decades later.[16] He stressed the importance of organizational culture, as when he described the 'creation of organization morality' as the thing that 'gives common meaning to common purpose, that creates the incentive that makes other incentives effective, that infuses the subjective aspect of countless decisions with consistency in a changing environment'.[17] And apparently this cultural, moral aspect of the organization is created through the *responsibility* aspect of organizational leadership, as it involves a 'moral creativeness' that encompasses 'the creation of moral codes for others' and also 'securing, creating, inspiring "morale" within the organization'.[18]

This morally creative, responsibility aspect of organizational leadership is very similar to what Weber had called 'charismatic' leadership. For example, creating moral codes for others is a feature and concern of religious leaders with charismatic authority.[19] They and secular charismatic leaders are also capable of 'securing, creating, inspiring' morale, if only through their followers' emotional devotion to the leader and to 'the normative patterns or order revealed or ordained by him'.[20] But Barnard's morally creative, responsibility aspect of leadership was not a typical example of charismatic leadership and in fact it seems more like a calculated, partly rational type of inspirational leadership. For when Barnard discussed—and apparently prescribed—creating moral codes and inspiring morale, he implied that it was premeditated and instrumental: a means to an organizational end. It seems therefore to be a calculated, partly rational version of charismatic leadership and a new example of the partly rational type of inspirational leadership that Weber had identified when he described the changes in military leader–follower relationships.

However, Barnard's study of organizational leadership had also identified a *wholly* rational type of inspirational leadership. He argued that in addition to the morally creative, responsibility aspect of leadership there is also what he termed the 'technical' aspect of leadership. This aspect involves individual superiority in skill, knowledge, perception, imagination, and other personal qualities or abilities.[21] Among them is a superiority in what Barnard described as *technology*, which he viewed in peculiarly broad terms. For example, technology included 'schemes of organization' and 'technical systems, as well as the techniques of the applied sciences where they are pertinent'.[22] But these schemes, systems, and techniques are all formally rational and in this sense the superiority in technology is the 'rational' component of leaders' individual superiority and, furthermore, of the technical aspect of their leadership.

More importantly, this rational component of leadership inspires followers with confidence—it is an inspirational form of leadership. For Barnard noted that confidence is 'engendered' by executives who combine their hierarchical authority with a technical 'authority of leadership' arising from their superior ability, knowledge and understanding.[23] As this superiority will include the technological, rational component of leadership, the executives will at times be inspiring confidence through their superiority in using rational schemes, systems, techniques, and other technology. Their followers will therefore at times be inspired with a rational confidence that is based on the leader's use of rational means to an end. In that case the followers will be showing the kind of rational attitudes to work and leadership that makes them rational, discerning followers—like the conscript soldiers led by General Montgomery. So Barnard is here referring to a wholly rational type of inspirational leadership in which both leader and follower have a rational attitude to their relationship and the follower is inspired with rational confidence by the leader's 'superiority' in using rational means to an end.

Such superiority includes the leader's selection of the *appropriate* rational means to an end. For example, when Barnard described organizational effectiveness, he pointed out that the use of technology—of rational means—includes selecting the appropriate rational means of accomplishing the organization's objective.

> [Effectiveness] relates exclusively to the *appropriateness* of the means selected under the conditions as a whole for the accomplishment of the final objective. This is a matter of *technology* in a very broad sense of the term...At a given time, for a given end, under given conditions, which specific technology is to be selected is the variable factor. We select which is the 'better' method under the conditions.[24]

The technological, rational component of leadership therefore inspires followers with confidence because their leader is *selecting* the appropriate rational means—the 'better' method—as well as *using* it to accomplish the organization's objective. In other words, they are being inspired with confidence because their leader has the ability not only to use rational means but also to select the appropriate rational means of accomplishing an objective at a given time and under given conditions.[25]

In fact Barnard's theorizing about a 'technical' aspect of organizational leadership had explored the key features of a new, wholly rational type of inspirational leadership. It inspired followers with only a rational confidence rather than the emotional—and possibly moral—confidence and commitment that charismatic leaders inspire in their followers. Nonetheless, it was the most effective way of inspiring employees whose rationalized attitudes had made them rational, discerning followers—who might become sceptical and even cynical about leadership. So although this rational type of inspirational leadership emerged long ago, it is still very 'modern' and is the appropriate type for our twenty-first-century world.

As was argued at the beginning of this Appendix, Barnard's theory of technical-rational leadership can be restructured into a highly focused and flexible analysis of the rational type of inspirational leadership. The analysis becomes highly focused when the leader is described as inspiring followers with confidence through the capable use of the appropriate technological means of achieving a particular objective. And the analysis becomes highly flexible, widely applicable, when his theory is combined with Weber's theory of rationalization. For then Barnard's notion of 'technological' means is replaced by the broader Weberian concept of 'rational' means, which covers a wider range of formally rational means—and includes generic rational methods.

This combination of Barnard and Weber is best viewed as a restructuring of their contributions to the theory of rational leadership. Barnard's technical-rational leadership has been integrated into Weber's theory of rationalization as a new extension or branch that applies to a rationalization which Weber did not foresee—the emergence of a wholly rational type of inspirational leadership. More importantly, these 1920s–30s contributions have now been restructured into a new, twenty-first-century analysis of the rational type of inspirational leadership.

Later Theorists: Burns and Christensen

But of course after the 1920s–30s there were other major contributions to the theory of rational leadership. Forty years after Barnard's book, a political scientist presented a more widely applicable equivalent of its dualistic, moral/rational conception of leadership. In his 1978 *Leadership* Burns presented a moral-transformational and rational-transactional dualistic conception of leadership that could be applied to a much wider range of social contexts than just the leadership of organizations. And his conception of rational-transactional leadership had expanded the theory of rational leadership by incorporating a new and very wide area of leader–follower relationships.

On the other hand, Burns had eclipsed the rational type of inspirational leadership by stressing what he referred to as the 'transformational' type. It transforms both leader and followers as 'leaders and followers raise one another to higher levels of motivation and morality'.[26] In fact followers may be inspired with new sources of motivation, if they have a leader who can 'mobilize within them newer motivations and aspirations'.[27] More importantly, the followers are being inspired with a *moral* motivation, whether it is something new or an existing source of motivation being used in a new way. For instance, Gandhi 'aroused and [morally] elevated the hopes and demands of millions of Indians'.[28]

This morally inspirational leadership can be readily contrasted with the form of *rational* leadership—the transactional form—that was identified and described by Burns. Transactional leadership is rational rather than moral and is pragmatic rather than inspirational.

> Such leadership occurs when one person takes the initiative in making contact with others for the purpose of an *exchange* of valued things. The exchange could be economic or political or psychological in nature: a swap of goods or of one good for money; a trading of votes between candidate and citizen or between legislators; hospitality to another person in exchange for willingness to listen to one's troubles. Each party to the *bargain* is conscious of the power, resources and attitudes of the other.[29]

Each party to this pragmatic bargain has presumably calculated the pay-off in a formally rational fashion. Indeed, Burns depicted transactional leadership in the marketplace of public opinion as 'dominated by quick calculations of cost-benefits' by leaders and followers, whom he characterized here as 'sellers' and 'buyers'.[30] These rational leaders and followers also have a relatively tenuous and temporary leader–follower relationship. Unlike transformational leadership, the transactional leadership act 'is not one that binds leader and follower together in a mutual and continuing pursuit of a higher purpose'; they may 'have no enduring purpose that holds them together' and 'may go their separate ways' after the bargaining and exchange.[31]

As Burns acknowledged, there was a marked similarity between his theory of transactional leadership and sociology's exchange theory.[32] Another marked similarity is with psychology's transactional-analysis theory, which was made famous in the 1960s by Berne's *Games People Play* and Harris's best-selling *I'm OK—You're OK*. This theory viewed the transaction as the basic unit of social interaction and defined it as one person acknowledging the presence of another in some way (transactional stimulus) and the other person then saying or doing something that is related to this stimulus (transactional response).[33] Such a broad definition can be applied to a very wide range of social contexts and in fact Harris ended his book by applying transactional analysis to international relations and to the relationship between American voters and public officials.[34]

Similarly, the transactional form of rational leadership occurs in a very wide range of social contexts—much wider than any other variety of rational leadership. From this perspective it seems surprising that Burns's book focused on transactional leadership in political contexts and had so little to say about how it operated in other social contexts, such as within business organizations. A similar political focus or bias was evident when another political scientist, Brooker, identified in 2010 another pragmatic form of rational leadership—the deliberative leadership that is discussed in the second section of Chapter 1.

However, a business theorist made the most important post-Burns contribution to the theory of rational leadership. Christensen's 1997 *The Innovator's Dilemma: When New Technologies Cause Great Firms to Fail* became famous for its contribution to management theory and practice but it should also be celebrated for expanding the theory of rational leadership. For in this book a Barnard-like concern with using the 'better' method—the appropriate rational means—was applied to a new issue or problem that exemplified the technologically driven market economy of the 1980s–2010s.

Christensen's book was 'about the failure of companies to stay atop their industries when they confront certain types of market and technological change'.[35] These changes are caused by what he termed 'disruptive' technologies.[36] They have a very different economic and commercial effect than the 'sustaining' technologies that 'improve the performance of established products'.[37] Disruptive technologies lead to products, such as the desktop personal computer, which have less performance than established products but are 'typically cheaper, simpler, smaller, and, frequently, more convenient to use'.[38] The new products generally 'underperform established products in mainstream markets' but their new features are valued by 'a few fringe (and generally new) customers' who are the basis of a new market and a new marketing challenge.[39]

Firms that fail to adapt rapidly enough to this situation will be overtaken by competitors, often new firms, which have seized the opportunities offered by the new market.[40] Furthermore, Christensen argued that an industry's *leading* firms are especially vulnerable to this challenge. For the highly focused management effort and skills that bring success when dealing with *sustaining* technology also produce a tunnel vision that prevents the firm from seeing the opportunities and threats presented by disruptive technology.[41]

Like Barnard, Christensen emphasized that management methods are appropriate only for given ends, times, and conditions. He pointed out that 'many of what are now widely accepted principles of good management are, in fact, only *situationally appropriate*' and that an alternative set of principles is sometimes appropriate: 'times at which it is right to invest in developing lower-performance products that promise lower margins, and right to aggressively pursue small, rather than substantial, markets'.[42] Executives therefore have to be flexible enough to adopt whichever set of management principles—the widely accepted or the disruptive alternative—are appropriate for the situation they are facing at the time. Fortunately, Christensen gave them some rules for judging when it was appropriate to adopt the alternative set of management principles. He provided rational, research-based rules 'that managers can use to judge when the widely accepted principles of good management should be followed and when alternative principles are appropriate'.[43]

This would be a twenty-first-century version of what Barnard described as selecting the 'better' method under given conditions—and thereby inspiring employee-followers with confidence. Christensen did not explore the confidence-inspiring implications of leaders' selecting the appropriate set of management principles. But by expanding the theory of rational leadership to deal with a very modern business issue, he had very convincingly illustrated why using the *appropriate* rational means is such a crucial element of the rational type of inspirational leadership.

Machiavelli and Rational Leadership

This Appendix will end by looking back some five hundred years to a book that was a pre-modern precursor of the theory of rational leadership. Machiavelli's *The Prince* presented an analysis of princely rule that became more notorious than famous and led to the term Machiavellian being used to characterize devious and deceitful strategies or policies.[44] But his book includes passages that are a pre-modern precursor of both the theory of rational leadership and, more specifically, the analysis of corporation-developing rational leadership presented in Chapter 1. For Machiavelli advised princes (1) to select the *appropriate methods* for the times and circumstances and (2) evaluated these methods in terms of effectiveness and success in *achieving an objective* that was the pre-modern political equivalent of establishing or enhancing a business corporation.

The best modern interpretation of *The Prince* has pointed out that Machiavelli was describing princes who are operating 'in the context of innovation and in the role of innovator'.[45] They are *new* princes, who are establishing a new state or regime through conquest, coup, or rebellion and so lack the legitimacy enjoyed by hereditary, traditional monarchs. The new prince therefore seeks to increase the loyalty of his subjects through innovations that enhance the new state or regime, as it is 'in the world of innovation' that 'the new prince can outshine the hereditary and evoke more loyalty'.[46] These innovations to enhance a newly established state or regime are pre-modern political equivalents of high-level business leaders establishing and enhancing corporations. And the princes' politically innovative leadership is a pre-modern political equivalent of the corporate-developing version of rational leadership discussed in Chapter 1.

Machiavelli even identified the methods that princes used to make these political innovations. He noted that 'men proceed in different ways: one man cautiously, another impetuously; one man forcefully, another cunningly; one man patiently, another impatiently, and each of these different ways of acting can be effective' if it is appropriate for the times and circumstances, because 'we are successful when our ways are suited to the times and circumstances'.[47] In other words, he had identified a three-pair set of six methods (cautiously-impetuously, forcefully-cunningly, and patiently-impatiently) which were potentially appropriate ways of achieving the objective. He also drew the obvious conclusion that princes should be flexible enough to change their methods to fit changes in the times and circumstances, as princes are more successful if their 'methods are appropriate'.[48] A less obvious conclusion was that princes should be ready to alternate quickly between the contrasting methods of fox-like cunning and lion-like forcefulness. A prince 'should imitate both the fox and the lion, for the lion is liable to be trapped, whereas the fox cannot ward off wolves. One needs, then, to be a fox to recognise traps, and a lion to frighten away wolves.'[49]

Machiavelli's set of methods is therefore similar in form but not in content to the three-pair set of rational methods delineated in Chapter 1.[50] His three-pair set does not contain generic rational methods or indeed methods that seem very rational to a modern reader. Furthermore, Machiavelli is well known for preferring the method of 'impetuosity' to the highly generic rational method of 'calculation'. For *The Prince* included the notoriously sexist remark that 'fortune is a woman' and 'is more inclined to yield to men who are impetuous than to those who are calculating'.[51] Whether or not this assessment was ever correct, it would now have to be reversed: success is more likely to be achieved by calculating leaders than by those who are impetuous. Machiavelli's political analysis of the appropriate methods is therefore almost a *pre-rational* precursor of the analysis of corporate-developing leadership presented in Chapter 1.

However, modern political analysts, too, have published three-pair analyses of the methods that are used to establish new political regimes—and these methods would have to be described as at least technically 'rational'. For example, a three-pair set of rational methods appeared in a 2000s analysis of how military leaders established new political regimes.[52] Unlike Machiavelli's set, these three pairs of methods were not pairing opposite or contrasting methods; each pair were contrasting, mutually exclusive forms of the *same* method.[53] In this sense they are similar to the pairs of rational methods delineated in Chapter 1. On the other hand, they are specialized, relatively technical methods, not generic rational methods, and they are applied in a different way, as each of the pairs are *either/or* forms of the same method. A military intervention will therefore always include one method from each pair but never two methods from any pair, and the variation is in which three of the six methods are selected or, more specifically, which method is selected from each of the three pairs.

Chapter 1's three-pair set of methods might well be viewed as a combination of this modern political example and the pre-modern political example provided by Machia-velli. For its three pairs are each two forms of the same rational method—namely, quantitative and strategic calculation, rapid and innovative adaptation, diverse and institutionalized deliberation—but they are not either/or forms. A Machiavelli-like flexibility allows both members of a pair to be used and indeed allows *all six* members of the set to be used by a leader who is establishing or enhancing a corporation. What has been added to this combination is (1) generic-level instead of specialized rational methods and (2) recognition of leaders' tendency to emphasize one or two of the methods that they are using to establish or enhance.

Finally, it should be noted that this book's emphasis on autobiographical sources can be linked to a research methodology that was pioneered by Weber more than a century ago. As evidence that the 'Protestant ethic' and 'capitalist spirit' had existed in the Western world in the 1500s–1700s he cited the writings of 'representatives' of that era who were implicitly describing or prescribing this ethic or spirit.[54] He preferred repre-sentatives who were theological or business experts with some practical experience, such as printing and publishing businessman Benjamin Franklin.[55] Weber quoted extensively from Franklin's *Advice to a Young Tradesman* and *Necessary Hints to Those That Would be Rich*, as a characteristic example of the spirit of capitalism.[56] The best modern equivalents of these Franklin writings are business leaders' autobiographies or partly autobiographical writings about business.

Notes

Chapter 1

1. Drucker 1993: 5, and see also 7, 8, 15.
2. Weber 1978: 152 and 1394, which comes from an article he wrote in 1917.
3. Weber 1978: 85.
4. Chandler 1990: 322.
5. Thorndike 2012: 44, 90–1, 163.
6. Michell 2010: 97, 39, 102. Sony was then ranked at 18th, with an estimated brand value of $16 billion, while Samsung was ranked only 43rd thanks to its brand value of only $5 billion (Michell 2010: 102). But O'Boyle describes how in a corporation suffering from 'the tyranny of numbers' these numbers 'take on a life of their own' and management is expected to accept quantitative assessments even when their conclusions seem to defy logic (1999: 210, 214–15).
7. Knight 2014: 231–2. Similarly, the humorous *How to Lie with Statistics* long ago provided a pithy warning about the unreliability of quantitatively calculated predictions. 'The trend-to-now may be a fact, but the future trend represents no more than an educated guess. Implicit in it is "everything else being equal" and "present trends continuing". And somehow *everything else refuses to remain equal*' (Huff 1954: 140).
8. Christensen 2000: xxii.
9. Clausewitz 1984: 95, 128.
10. Clausewitz 1984: 119–20.
11. Clausewitz 1984: 139.
12. Clausewitz 1984: 177.
13. Welch 2003: 448. In this and the latter case, Welch was referring to post-Clausewitz Prussian military thinkers who were applying and developing Clausewitz's concepts.
14. Welch 2003: 390.
15. In fact Welch's theory of a central idea evolving through continually changing circumstances is referring to what could be a grand strategy. For his example was an idea that he presented at the beginning of the 1980s. He predicted that the decade would see 'slower world-wide growth' and that the winning companies would be 'those who search out and participate in the real growth industries and insist upon being number one or number two in every business they are in' (2003: 449). In practice, this meant what he terms the 'No. 1 or No. 2, "fix, sell or close" strategy' of fixing, selling, or closing down any division, subsidiary, or associated company

that was not the number-one or number-two firm in a growth industry or business (2003: 109). Although he describes it as a strategy, it is more like a grand strategy or indeed an innovative adaptation to the expected low-growth economic environment!

16. Burgelman et al. 2017.
17. McCraw 2007: 44.
18. Schumpeter 1961: 61–7, 81, 92–3; Brooker 2010: 39–41, 210–12.
19. Schumpeter 1974: 132.
20. Drucker 2007: 25, 31, 160.
21. Drucker 2007: xv, 127.
22. Drucker 2007: 25, 31.
23. Schumpeter 1989: 222. He defined the creative response as having three essential features: (1) the content of the response could not have been predicted beforehand, (2) the response has a significant and lasting effect, and (3) the frequency of such creative responses has something to do with the quality of the available personnel and their individual patterns of behaviour (Brooker 2010: 221 n. 27).
24. Schumpeter 1974: 105.
25. Schumpeter 1974: 105. It is true that he seems to be referring to the loss and reduced output suffered by an economy rather than by firms resisting adaptation, but resisting adaptation was likely to have similarly negative effects on a firm.
26. Cohen and Gooch 2006: 161, and see also 139 for an example of failing to take full advantage.
27. Machiavelli 2012: 82.
28. Allison 1971: 179.
29. George 1972: 753.
30. Allison 2007: 138. This may have been because Neustadt, like Machiavelli, had been a 'practical man' in administration and politics before he became a scholar. He had worked for four years in the Bureau of the Budget's legislative division and then for three years in the White House staff of President Truman (Dickinson 2007).
31. Neustadt 1990: 132. Similarly, George's classic article on 'multiple advocacy' among presidential advisers argued for central intervention 'to maintain and make use of internal competitive processes' within the bureaucracy (1972: 760).
32. Kroc 1987: 191–2.
33. Machiavelli 2012: 81–2.
34. Strayer 2005: 74.
35. Brooker 2010: 4–5.
36. Brooker 2010: 4. Similarly, Drucker's classic 1954 text on management noted how the president/CEO of a company has to deal with managers who 'want to "sell" him their ideas' (2006: 168).
37. Marder 2015: 177, citing a member of Pound's personal staff.
38. Walton 1993: 314.
39. According to Zuckerberg, a CEO's basic roles are recruiting a team and setting a vision for the firm (Beahm 2012: 111). He and his board of directors wanted Sandberg for the post of COO because of 'her willingness to be number two' as well as because of 'her role developing Google's ad business, and her experience as a manager' (Kirkpatrick 2011: 254).

40. Kirkpatrick 2011: 256.
41. Kirkpatrick 2011: 256–7. He notes that Zuckerberg was 'on a month-long around-the-world-trip, now that he'd completed his search for his number two' and could entrust her with such a key task as leading the firm in the direction of exploiting its advertising opportunity (2011: 257). Their long-lasting leadership team makes a dramatic contrast with the problems experienced by Twitter, the other social-media phenomenon of the 2000s. The firm was established in 2007, with three official co-founders and with one of them, Jack Dorsey, as CEO, but in 2008 he was replaced by another co-founder, Evan Williams, who was himself replaced in 2010 by the firm's COO, the non-founder Dick Costolo (Bilton 2013: 105, 4).
42. Kirkpatrick 2011: 257–8.
43. Kirkpatrick 2011: 273.
44. Sandberg 2013: 74, 82.
45. Sandberg 2013: 83.
46. Sandberg 2013: 85.
47. Sandberg 2013: 77, but she pointed out that reticence is often caused by people backing away from honesty 'to protect themselves and others'.
48. Sandberg 2013: 81–2.
49. Sandberg 2013: 82.
50. Khurana 2002: 152.
51. Grove 1999: 152.
52. Walton 1993: 147.
53. Walton 1993: 253.
54. Walton 1993: 253–4.
55. Tedlow 2003: 1. The seven individuals were Carnegie, Eastman, Ford, Watson, Revson, Walton, and Noyce.
56. Tedlow 2003: 4.
57. It might even be argued that the more ordinary cases are in a sense more modern. The president of Sony noted in the 2000s that a modernized company 'means a company that stands independent from past glories, and the founders; a company that can be managed [and developed] by ordinary people like myself' (quoted by Chang 2008: 163).
58. Drucker noted in his discussion of management teams that 'if two men [sic] can work together closely, they form an ideal team. But two people like this are rarely found' (2006: 177). However, in the case of *leadership* teams this phenomenon is not as rare as finding *three* people who can work together closely.

Chapter 2

1. Pelfrey 2006: 1.
2. Farber 2004: 198.
3. Tedlow 2003: 171; Sloan 1990: xxi.
4. Pelfrey 2006: 246.
5. Pelfrey 2006: 236; Sloan 1990: 437.

6. McDonald 2003: 41–2. He describes it as a 'remarkable team of professionals—altogether twenty-some persons at one time or another' (2003: 42). McDonald's book about his experiences with the project explains why it was so protracted, beginning in 1954 and finishing in 1959, and why the book's publication was then held up for another four years!
7. Drucker in Sloan 1990: x. Gates's endorsement was originally quoted in the 16 January 1995 issue of *Fortune* magazine, according to McDonald 2003: 189.
8. Sloan 1990: xxiii.
9. Farber 2004: 243.
10. Chandler 1990: 12, 390.
11. Sloan 1990: xxi, 4, 429.
12. Sloan 1990: 4, 46. For example, 'all the units in the General Motors empire were still structured and managed the way they had been before Billy bought them, and the heads of each unit all reported directly to him' (Pelfrey 2006: 215).
13. Sloan 1990: 429–30.
14. Sloan 1990: 48.
15. Sloan 1990: 31. Sloan dated his drafting of the Organization Study to 'after December 5 [1919] and before January 19, 1920' (1990: 45 n. 2).
16. Pelfrey 2006: 13, 221.
17. Pelfrey 2006: 13, 224, 236.
18. Pelfrey 2006: 224.
19. Pelfrey 2006: 228; Sloan 1990: 41, graph on stock prices adjusted for a 10 for 1 split in March.
20. Chandler 1990: 130; Farber 2004: 50; Sloan 1990: 51–2. Chandler described this restructuring in Schumpeterian terms as an innovative 'creative' response rather than a merely adaptive response: it was 'a creative response to new needs and new conditions' (1990: 284).
21. Sloan 1990: 52, 55, 56. Farber 2004: 72, 214, 240 details the various high offices and positions held by Sloan during his years with General Motors.
22. Farber 2004: 51.
23. Sloan 1990: 113. He gave the divisional managers some representation at central level by combining them with the members of the Executive Committee to form the large Operations Committee. However, Sloan acknowledged that it 'was not a policy-making body but a forum for the discussion of policy or the need for policy' (1990: 113).
24. Chandler 1990: 158, 160.
25. Drucker 1993: 42.
26. Sloan 1990: 55. See Snow 2014: 313 on Sloan apparently copying the military model of a headquarters' general staff.
27. Chandler 1990: 138–9.
28. Chandler 1990: 154, 160.
29. Sloan 1990: 431, emphases added.
30. Chandler 1990: 135.
31. Sloan 1990: 54.
32. Chandler 1990: 135–7.

33. Sloan 1990: 52.
34. Chandler 1990: 135.
35. Chandler 1990: 133, 135.
36. Drucker 1993: 52. Drucker also noted that a 'vice-president in charge of a group of divisions acts as a constant liaison on policy and performance between head office and division' (1993: 60).
37. Chandler 1990: 138.
38. Chandler 1990: 158.
39. Sloan 1990: 30, 121, 140–1.
40. Chandler 1990: 147. In 1921 central management moved to 'co-ordinate financial organizations of the divisions and the central Financial Staff' and reaffirmed the principle of dual responsibility for the divisional comptrollers, that is, their responsibility to the corporation comptroller as well as to their divisional managers (Sloan 1990: 143).
41. Chandler 1990: 152. The financial data from the divisions was used to analyse 'the critical revenue and cost factors determining the rate of return on investment', which was the key quantitative calculation 'used to measure the effectiveness of each division's operation' and 'to evaluate divisional performance' (Chandler 1990: 152; Sloan 1990: 141).
42. Sloan 1990: 140.
43. Sloan 1990: 140.
44. Sloan 1990: 429; Farber 2004: 59.
45. Sloan 1990: 30.
46. Sloan 1990: 124–7.
47. Sloan 1990: 138. As Sloan pointed out, the accuracy of the forecasts was less important than 'the sensitivity to actual market changes through prompt reports and adjustment' (1990: 138).
48. Sloan 1990: 176.
49. Sloan 1990: 176–7, 148; Pelfrey 2006: 265 on being the only car-maker to operate profitably throughout. Pelfrey also points out that, apart from 1932, during the Depression 'it showed a profit margin of at least 10 per cent (high by even today's standards), despite slow sales and reduced volume' (2006: 265).
50. Sloan 1990: 199.
51. Pelfrey 2006: 265, and 262 on number of employees.
52. Tedlow 2003: 167. Sloan pointed out that his new marketing strategy had been 'formulated before its time. It took a number of events in the automobile market to give full substance to its principles' (1990: 69–70). It was therefore more of a *pre*adaptation than an adaptation to market conditions or changes (Gould 2002: 1231–2).
53. Sloan 1990: 59, 60, 62.
54. Sloan 1990: 59.
55. Sloan 1990: 62–3.
56. Sloan 1990: 65.
57. Farber 2004: 64.
58. Sloan 1990: 67–9.
59. Sloan 1990: 69, 68.

60. Sloan 1990: 67.
61. Sloan 1990: 155, and 155–60 on the replacement. The founder of modern military thinking pointed out in the 1830s that war could be compared to commerce, 'which is also a conflict of human interests and activities' (Clausewitz 1984: 149).
62. Sloan 1990: 442.
63. Sloan 1990: 441–2.
64. Farber 2004: 101.
65. Sloan 1990: 269, 274.
66. Sloan 1990: 272; Pelfrey 2006: 255.
67. Farber 2004: 103.
68. Farber 2004: 103. In addition to this concern with market communication, he improved the corporation's product distribution by including GM's franchised car retailers in his marketing strategy and overall administrative rationalization. Favouring of course 'a rational approach to the problem of distribution', Sloan established a new approach—enlightened and exemplary—to relations with the franchised car dealers (1990: 284–5). His achievements in this area led Drucker to suggest that GM's principles of inter-business federalism and harmonious resolution of conflicts could provide a model for relations between big business and small business in other branches of the economy (1993: 114).
69. Farber 2004: 103–4.
70. Pelfrey 2006: 40.
71. Sloan 1990: 60.
72. Sloan 1990: 25.
73. Chandler 1990: 125. In 1919 the ever-expanding corporation 'was still largely run and coordinated on a day-to-day basis by Billy [Durant] himself. By the end of the year, he was overseeing more than seventy factories in forty cities' and 'with no fewer than fifty senior operating executives reporting directly to him' (Pelfrey 2006: 223).
74. Sloan 1990: 433.
75. Pelfrey 2006: 271.
76. Sloan 1990: 433.
77. Sloan 1990: xviii.
78. Sloan 1990: 434–5. Managers were still 'allowed and encouraged to offer new ideas on their own, but the concepts would be thoroughly vetted before being acted on' (Pelfrey 2006: 236).
79. Farber 2004: 90.
80. For example, it was in response to the 1924 downturn in the car market that 'I issued one of the few flat orders I ever gave to the division managers', namely 'to curtail production schedules immediately', and his memoirs also declared: 'I never minimized the administrative power of the chief executive officer in principle when I occupied that position. I simply exercised that power with discretion; I got better results by selling my ideas than by telling people what to do' (Sloan 1990: 131, 54).
81. Farber 2004: 86, 88. Farber describes Sloan as the first public representative of a new kind of corporate organization, which required the new kind of leadership provided by a professional corporate manager (2004: 90).

82. Farber 2004: 91–2.
83. Brooker 2010: 28.
84. Farber 2004: 87.
85. Sloan 1990: 100.
86. Farber 2004: 67.
87. Sloan 1990: 186, 188.
88. Sloan 1990: 188.
89. Sloan 1990: 187. Sloan later restructured and renamed the two governing committees—which became the Policy Committee and the Administration Committee—to embody his principle of distinguishing between policy and administration (1990: 185). The new structure was eventually abandoned, nearly ten years later, and the committees were renamed the Financial Policy Committee and the Operations Policy Committee—returning to their traditional titles of Finance Committee and Executive Committee some two years after Sloan's retirement (ibid.: 186). The Administration Committee continued to exist but was apparently demoted to the role of making recommendations to the CEO about manufacturing, selling or any other matters that he referred to it for consideration (ibid.: 435).
90. Chandler 1990: 155–6.
91. Chandler 1990: 156, 157.
92. Sloan 1990: 182–3. Pelfrey notes that this 'policy committee structure' survived until the 1990s (2006: 246).
93. Drucker 1993: 51–2.
94. Chandler 1990: 158, quoting Brown.
95. Farber 2004: 81.
96. Sloan 1990: 433, emphases added.
97. Pelfrey 2006: 272.
98. Whyte 1961: 8, 11.
99. Shapley 1993: 70. But McNamara also implies that the careerist pressures towards reticence could be neutralized by Machiavellian dexterity, as he notes that 'it also takes a certain dexterity to espouse an unpopular view and still keep your place in the pecking order certain' (Shapley 1993: 70).
100. Sloan 1990: xx.
101. Sloan 1990: xxii.
102. Sloan 1990: xxii, 4.
103. Sloan 1990: 3; Farber 2004: 104.
104. Curcio 2013: 69–72.
105. Curcio 2013: 72–3.
106. Curcio 2013: 123. His fixation on production hardware even included a tendency to gigantism. In the 1920s he built the gigantic Rouge River plant, which was so vertically integrated that it was 'capable of taking in iron ore and other raw materials at one end and putting out fully finished vehicles at the other end' (ibid.: 116).
107. Sloan 1990: 4; Tedlow 2003: 128.

108. Drucker 2006: 114. Other owner-managers had rarely been so concerned about extending and displaying personal control of their firm. For example, the most famous owner-manager of the previous century, John D. Rockefeller of Standard Oil, was a believer in 'management by consensus' and would tolerate long committee debates about a pet project instead of imposing his views upon the opposing minority (Chernow 2004: 285).

109. Curcio 2013: 93.

110. Curcio 2013: 205, 240. However, when Ford realized that his production prejudices were leading to serious financial losses in the making of his new Model A, he returned to his insistence 'on saving money, as he always had in the past, by using the best production methods available' (ibid.: 205).

111. Tedlow 2003: 145, 139.

112. Snow 2014: 288.

113. Curcio 2013: 240; Tedlow 2003: 172.

114. Curcio 2013: 241, 121. Again, there is a marked contrast with Rockefeller's owner-manager management style in the 1870s–80s. He had a 'special affinity for accounting' and used his era's number-crunching as 'an objective yardstick to compare his far-flung operations' and to extend 'rationality from the top of his organization down to the lowest rung' (Chernow 2004: 46, 179).

115. Tedlow 2003: 167; Farber 2004: 103.

116. Snow 2014: 300.

117. Snow 2014: 312. In the 1920s Ford actually concealed changes in the Model T, 'some of which were substantive,' even though General Motors 'was exploiting to the hilt the idea of change in the automobile' (Tedlow 2003: 166).

118. Curcio 2013: 197–8.

119. Pelfrey 2006: 253–4.

120. Sloan 1990: 163.

121. Sloan 1990: 163.

122. Sloan 1990: 163; Snow 2014: 315.

123. Womack et al. 1991: 41–2.

124. Farber 2004: 97.

125. Sloan 1990: 163, 164–5. In fact the car-making divisions had initially opposed the idea of an annual model change and, in contrast to Ford's management style, Sloan had allowed this new policy 'to evolve into a consensus' (Pelfrey 2006: 256).

126. Farber 2004: 104.

127. Farber 2004: 104; Curcio 2013: 197–8.

128. Curcio 2013: 200–1. The price was more than ten per cent lower than GM's comparable Chevrolet.

129. Snow 2014: 325. Tedlow believes the Model A brought Ford 'technological parity' with General Motors but it also revealed the gap or difference in their production flexibility (2003: 168). For nearly all of the 5,580 parts that were assembled to create a Model A were new parts and were made by specialized machine tools, unlike GM's use of standardized parts and flexible machine tools, and therefore Ford had to shut down his factories for six months in order to switch production from Model T to Model A: 'In business terms this was a disaster' (ibid.).

130. Curcio 2013: 205; Snow 2014: 324; Sloan 1990: 167.
131. Chandler 1990: 160, comparing 1921 with 1940.
132. Curcio 2013: 209, 240.
133. Chandler 1990: 373.
134. Shapley 1993: 68, 45, 48, 54. McNamara was a graduate of the Harvard Business School, where in the late 1930s he had been taught the financial and other quantitative controls that Sloan had established at General Motors (ibid.: 24).

Chapter 3

1. Cole 1979: 157–8.
2. Togo and Wartman 1993: 203–4; Fujimoto 1999: 43.
3. Womack et al. 1991: 13. The term 'lean production' was coined by John Krafcik.
4. Miller 2013: 154. But another exponent argues that most organizations seeking Ohno's ideal of continuous flow have found it 'elusive' and that this 'illustrates how challenging it is for leaders to adapt' (Emiliani 2013: 158).
5. Ohno 1988: 119.
6. Ohno 1988: 76; Togo and Wartman 1993: 115.
7. Ohno 1988: 75.
8. The Toyoda-family presidents have been Risaburo Toyoda and then his brother Kiichiro in 1937–50, their cousin Eiji Toyoda in 1967–82, Kiichiro's sons Shoichiro and then Tatsuro in 1982–95, and Shoichiro's son Akio from 2009 onwards. The post-war occupation authorities' policies led to Toyoda family-owned stock being 'released to the market' after 1945, and in 1950 the family 'held only a minor financial share' in the company (Togo and Wartman 1993: 90, 105). In 1984 its chairman Eiji Toyoda and its president Shoichiro Toyoda 'together held less than 1 percent of the corporation's shares; banks were the principal owners' (Cusumano 1985: 182).
9. Togo and Wartman 1993.
10. Togo and Wartman 1993: chs. 3–5 on diversification and 74–6 on spinning off. They note that initially 240,000 shares of stock were sold to 'twenty-six stockholders, primarily family members, company directors and the Mitsui Trading Company' but by 1939 the company's shares were also being bought by institutional investors (1993: 76, 81). According to Wada and Yui, the new company's shares were bought by 'firms in the Toyoda group and people with close ties with these firms' (2002: 275).
11. Togo and Wartman 1993: 73 on the public competition and why the name was changed. According to Cusumano, the new name of 'Toyota' rather than Toyoda was 'an alternate reading of the two ideographs that make up the family name [Toyoda]' and was chosen 'for its clarity in sound and potential advertising appeal' (1985: 59).
12. Togo and Wartman 1993: 102. The relationship was complicated by the fact that Risaburo was initially Kiichiro's brother-in-law but had been adopted by Kiichiro's father as his elder son and therefore successor as head of the family (ibid.: 28–9).
13. Ohno 1988: 123.

14. Ohno 1988: 91.
15. Fujimoto 1999: 67.
16. Togo and Wartman 1993: 79–80.
17. His biographers also relate how Kiichiro explained the just-in-time concept in the media—all parts were to be made and delivered to the assembly line 'just at the right time'—and they describe how retired employees still remember him trying 'to get the idea of "just in time" to permeate everything done on the production site' (Wada and Yui 2002: 279, and see also 289).
18. Wada and Yui 2002: 274, 294. Togo and Wartman point out that the war in China benefited Toyota by boosting the government's orders for trucks but it also led to more government control of the economy (1993: 77).
19. Wada and Yui 2002: 283–5, 294–6.
20. Togo and Wartman 1993: 83.
21. Risaburo retired to the position of chairman of the company (Togo and Wartman 1993: 82).
22. Togo and Wartman 1993: 83.
23. Wada and Yui 2002: 290, 291.
24. Wada and Yui 2002: 290–1, emphases added.
25. The post-war problems included not only reconstruction in a war-devastated country but also dealing with the occupation-authorities' policies and, as described in the next section, adjusting to unionization and the new labour-relations situation.
26. Wada and Yui 2002: 304–5; Togo and Wartman 1993: 101–6.
27. Togo and Wartman 1993: 104.
28. Ohno 1988: 79.
29. Fujimoto 1999: 61.
30. Cusumano 1985: 278.
31. Togo and Wartman 1993: 131.
32. Ohno 1988: 32.
33. Cusumano 1985: 278–9.
34. Cusumano 1985: 269.
35. Cusumano 1985: 269, 298; Ohno 1988: 32.
36. Cusumano 1985: 269; Shimokawa and Fujimoto 2009: 6; Ohno 1988: 135.
37. Ohno 1988: 31. Togo and Wartman note that Ohno's assembly-line innovations were being greeted with some scepticism and even passive resistance (1993: 131).
38. See, for example, Womack et al. 1991: 11, 49. According to Togo and Wartman, 'Eiji Toyoda, in particular, was supportive of Ohno's work' in the mid-1950s (1993: 131). Nonetheless, Eiji published an English-language autobiography in 1987 which claimed that Ohno merely 'revived and further refined' the just-in-time production system that was put into practice in the late 1930s (Toyoda 1987: 58). However, this view is not widely held and the modern tendency is to emphasize Ohno's role as 'the father of the Toyota Production System' (Shimokawa and Fujimoto 2009: 5).
39. Togo and Wartman refer to Ishida's 'rational business plans' and to him being a 'realist whose life was ruled by numbers and calculations' in the financial context of ensuring the firm would 'remain solvent so it could pay its employees and its bills' (1993: 112–13, 127).

40. Togo and Wartman 1993: 114, 128, 142, 146, 160.
41. Fujimoto 1999: 68.
42. Togo and Wartman 1993: 114.
43. Nemoto in Shimokawa and Fujimoto 2009: 177, 210–11; Togo and Wartman, 1993: 160. Fujimoto contrasts the 1961 introduction of Total Quality Control (TQC) with the diffusion of just-in-time production processes in the 1950s: 'TQC was diffused in a top-down manner and quickly' (1999: 71). However, TQC was a well-established programme that had already been introduced by other firms; just-in-time production had to be developed virtually from scratch before it could be introduced by Toyota and later by other firms.
44. Nemoto in Shimokawa and Fujimoto 2009: 210.
45. Toyota company history 1988: 155.
46. Toyota company history 1988: 461. By the early 1960s Toyota was producing 'close to twenty vehicles per employee' as compared to just 'two per employee in 1950' (Togo and Wartman 1993: 156).
47. Togo and Wartman 1993: 172. Eiji Toyoda's autobiography notes that 'Ishida had worked with two executive vice-presidents under him. Our duties were clearly divided, with Nakagawa in charge of business, and me handling the technical side of things' (1987: 128).
48. Cusumano 1985: 269; Shimokawa and Fujimoto 2009: 6.
49. For example, Togo and Wartman mention only how Nakagawa supported development of the Corolla but 'mindful of the company's finances' stipulated that the new design 'would have to use the existing 1,000-cc engine used in the second-generation Corona' (1993: 172).
50. Togo and Wartman 1993: 147 mentions a figure of 70 per cent for 1959, and the firm's production was skewed even more heavily towards trucks earlier in the 1950s. They point out that in 1965 'Toyota was close to being an automobile manufacturer that also made trucks' because cars now comprised 49 per cent of its production (1993: 170).
51. Togo and Wartman 1993: 148–9, 167, 180.
52. Toyota company history 1988: 461.
53. Togo and Wartman 1993: 175.
54. Toyota company history 1988: 461.
55. Togo and Wartman 1993: 190 says merely that he 'died suddenly in 1967'.
56. Toyota company history 1988: 461.
57. Cusumano 1985: 196. This figure had been adjusted for differences in the amount of vertical integration and therefore the extent to which parts-production had been out-sourced.
58. Cusumano 1985: 196.
59. Togo and Wartman 1993: 156.
60. Cusumano 1985: 379.
61. Fujimoto 1999: 50.
62. Cusumano 1985: 266. He also notes that 'the Japanese market was small and companies wanted to produce a variety of models but were unable to afford large supplies of parts or specialized assembly lines before the 1960s' (1985: 285).

63. Ohno 1988: 37–8.
64. Fujimoto 1999: 52.
65. Fujimoto 1999: 53.
66. Cole 1979: 98–9. The familial solidarity of the work group also increased productivity by strengthening motivation (ibid.: 209).
67. Ohno 1988: 3; Cole 1989: 96–7.
68. Cole 1989: 97.
69. Cole 1989: 57, 87, 97, 112. A workshop quality-control circle typically comprised five to eight workers of similar status who voluntarily met for about an hour each week to learn statistical and other problem-solving methods and to examine job-related quality and production problems (ibid.: 18–19). Although the circles were imitated in America, resistance at the office and factory-floor levels led to the Japanese origin of the circles being downplayed and to the development of new, local variations of what was generally known as a 'quality circle' (ibid.: 19, 112–13).
70. Ohno 1988: 23, 24.
71. Womack et al. 1991: 13, emphasis added.
72. Cole 1979: 99.
73. Cole 1979: 119.
74. Ohno 1988: 125, 128. Togo and Wartman 1993: 116–18 provides an in-depth description of how Ohno developed this continuous-flow innovation.
75. Ohno 1988: 125, 128.
76. Ohno 1988: 11. Fujimoto points out that here traditional craft jobs were being replaced not through 'American Taylor-Ford approaches that essentially created single-skilled workers' but instead through a shift to multiskilled jobs (1999: 64).
77. Ohno 1988: 14.
78. Cusumano 1985: 306. Togo and Wartman 1993: 118 has a different perspective on how this issue was handled by the union leaders and Ohno but agrees that his innovation aroused protests from 'some senior workmen in the machine shop' who had become 'highly skilled craftsmen on their individual machines'.
79. Cusumano 1985: 307.
80. Ohno 1988: 10, 13–14. In Germany, this function-oriented approach extended far beyond the labour unions and the factory environment; there was a social, educational, and even legal emphasis on workers having specialized and nationally standardized occupational skills (Streeck 1996: 145–7).
81. Cusumano 1985: 137.
82. Cusumano 1985: 272, 307.
83. Cusumano 1985: 171.
84. Ohno 1988: 14.
85. Brooker 1991: 274.
86. Brooker 1991: 275. Even when it reached its peak membership in 1936, the pre-war labour movement represented less than 10 per cent of the country's industrial work force.
87. Brooker 1991: 275–7.

88. Togo and Wartman 1993: 92, 99 describe the creation of Toyota's first union in 1946 and how in 1948 the union joined the new, American-style Japanese Automobile Manufacturers Labour Union. Cusumano notes that Toyota not only granted 'workers "lifetime" employment in exchange for their loyalty' in the contentious early 1950s but also treated these permanent workers in a privileged manner that 'tended to reduce opposition from union members' (1985: 182). According to Cole, the large firms' revival of familial paternalism succeeded in eliciting some feelings of obligation to management and to the company 'as a community' (1979: 243).
89. Cole 1979: 245. Some firms shifted in the 1960s from the *nenko* system to a job-related system of wage differentials but they implicitly retained much of the older system, and when many firms cut production in the mid-1970s, they improvised ways of avoiding lay-offs or redundancies (ibid.: 130, 176–7, 220, 256, 261).
90. Cusumano 1985: xix.
91. Cusumano 1985: 379.
92. Togo and Wartman 1993: 92.
93. Ohno 1988: 4, emphases added. Even Toyota has only been able to approach, not attain, 'zero' inventory (Fujimoto 1999: 63).
94. Ohno 1988: 5, emphasis added.
95. Ohno 1988: 26. In an interview with Cusumano, Ohno recalled how he had read in a Japanese newspaper about the 'supermarket method' adopted by American aircraft producers in the Second World War to deal with the component problems that arose when they rapidly and drastically increased production to meet wartime needs (1985: 277–8).
96. Cusumano 1985: 289.
97. Ohno 1988: 27–8.
98. Cusumano 1985: 292 Table 73.
99. Cusumano 1985: 298, 317–18.
100. Cusumano 1985: 298.
101. Ohno 1988: 35; Fujimoto 1999: 61.
102. Womack et al. 1991: 58.
103. Womack et al. 1991: 58. However, General Motors later changed the mixture to favour out-sourcing and by the early twenty-first century its 'payroll' of blue-collar and white-collar employees was 'about half the size it was in 1970' (Lichtenstein 2006: 10).
104. Womack et al. 1991: 60–1 describes the structure and workings of this two-tier alliance, such as the first-tier suppliers' cross-holdings of shares and the second-tier suppliers' information-sharing associations. Beneath these two tiers of suppliers there was a third and even fourth tier of less significant parts suppliers (Fujimoto 1999: 42).
105. Womack et al. 1991: 155.
106. Togo and Wartman 1993: 147; Ohno 1988: 32. See also Cusumano 1985: 291, 298 and Fujimoto 1999: 69 on extending the system to suppliers.
107. Ohno 1988: 32.

108. Ohno 1988: 34.
109. Cusumano 1985: 192. When Kiichiro began dealing with organized suppliers in 1939, there were only twenty firms in the Cooperation Association, but by 1958 there were already 160 members (ibid.: 252).
110. Toyota company history 1988: 461.
111. Ohno 1988: 36.
112. Ohno 1988: 37, emphases added.
113. Ohno 1988: 37, 126.
114. Ohno 1988: 38. See also Togo and Wartman 1993: 156.
115. Cusumano 1985: 287; Womack et al. 1991: 52–3; Togo and Wartman 1993: 155–6.
116. Ohno 1988: 39.
117. Cusumano 1985: 232.
118. Womack et al. 1991: 13.
119. Ohno 1988: 9, 54. Waste-reduction was nothing new in the sense that Henry Ford's 'abhorrence of waste' was actually 'one of the cornerstones of his business philosophy and his personality', but Ford's 'mania' for the adage 'waste not, want not' was focused on *by-products* of the production process rather than on reducing waste *within* the process itself (Curcio 2013: 80–1, 219).
120. Ohno 1988: 19–20.
121. Cusumano 1985: 305.
122. Ohno 1988: 67.
123. Ohno 1988: 69.
124. Ohno 1988: 46.
125. Ohno 1988: 45.
126. Ohno 1988: 74, 80.
127. Fujimoto 1999: 27, 50.
128. Ohno 1988: 100.
129. Curcio 2013: 74, 77; Snow 2014: 210 and ch. 13.
130. Curcio 2013: xii, 128.
131. Snow 2014: 209.
132. Curcio 2013: 160.
133. Curcio 2013: 128.
134. Beynon 1984: 25.
135. Cusumano 1985: 284.
136. Cole 1979: 160. He notes how this line-stopping policy contrasted with American car-producing firms' tendency to undertake line stoppages only 'with great reluctance' and to allow only plant managers and other 'select individuals' to stop the line (1979: 160). He also refers to the policy being adopted by Toyota from 1968 onwards, though Cusumano describes Ohno using line-stopping in parts of the main plant in the 1950s (1979: 160; 1985: 280).
137. Ohno 1988: 7, 122.
138. Ohno 1988: 104–5, and 95 on large Fordist versus small Toyotaist batch lots.
139. Ohno 1988: 97.

140. Ohno 1988: 97.
141. Curcio 2013: 248.
142. Ohno 1988: 103–4.
143. Ohno 1988: 104.
144. Cusumano 1985: 299, 301–2.
145. Fujimoto 1999: 43.
146. Togo and Wartman 1993: 204, 207.
147. Fujimoto 1999: 45.
148. Togo and Wartman 1993: 218–19.
149. Togo and Wartman 1993: 219. Creating a network of parts suppliers was a longer-term problem but Japanese parts suppliers, too, were setting up manufacturing operations in America—more than two hundred suppliers had done so by the mid-1980s (Fujimoto 1999: 45).
150. Ohno 1988: 109.
151. Womack et al. 1991: 241.
152. Womack et al. 1991: 86. This assessment was based on the authors' 1989 world survey of car-assembly-plant performance. Other imitators of Japanese production advantages had been less successful because these companies had lacked a less tangible feature of the Japanese approach: 'workers respond only when there exists some sense of reciprocal obligation' and therefore just 'changing the organization chart to show "teams" and introducing quality circles to find ways to improve production processes are unlikely to make much difference' (Womack et al. 1991: 99).

Chapter 4

1. Ritzer 1996: 33. He was describing a 'more extreme' version of formal rationalization than Weber's 1920s version (see Appendix) and Ritzer identified McDonaldization's four dimensions as emphases on (1) efficiency, (2) quantitative calculation, (3) predictability, and (4) 'control over people through the replacement of human with nonhuman technology' (1996: 19, 33). His initial, 1983 article on 'The McDonaldization of Society' had appeared in *Journal of American Culture* 6: 100–6.
2. Barber 2001: 12, 17. Barber's preceding article on 'Jihad Vs. McWorld' had appeared in *The Atlantic Monthly*, March 1992: 53–63. Ritzer noted that this article had expressed a viewpoint similar to but 'narrower' than his viewpoint on the impact of McDonald's (1996: 205 n. 1).
3. Napoli 2016.
4. However, this book will be using the posthumous 1987 edition with the Afterword by Robert Anderson, who had written the book 'with' Kroc. See Napoli 2016: 166–7 on the origins of Kroc's memoirs and Anderson's role in preparing them for publication.
5. Kroc 1987: 13.
6. Watson 2006: 25; Kroc 1987: 103. Watson acknowledged that 'McDonald's was certainly not the first enterprise to follow Fordist methods of food production': these

had been 'followed by various American enterprises that predated McDonald's, including railway dining cars and the Howard Johnson restaurant chain' (2006: 25).

7. Watson 2006: 20, 26.

8. Anderson in Kroc 1987: 208.

9. Kroc 1987: 70–1. The origins and development of the McDonald brothers' business is described in some detail in Napoli 2016: 15–26.

10. Kroc 1987: 71–2. See also Napoli on the contract and the McDonald brothers' pre-Kroc franchising of their business (2016: 24–6, 36–7).

11. Anderson in Kroc 1987: 208.

12. Kroc 1987: 202–3.

13. Kroc 1987: 150. The shift from drive-in to sit-down restaurant did not mean a shift away from drive-*thru* operations, in which customers bought their food in their cars but consumed it elsewhere. In the 1980s the average McDonald's restaurant was still earning half its revenue from drive-thru sales (Leidner 1993: 61).

14. Napoli 2016: 85.

15. Kroc 1987: 88.

16. Kroc 1987: 87, 108–9. The supplier aspect of the franchising system was also a case of adapting to a potential threat as well as exploiting an opportunity. 'Many franchise systems came along after us and tried to be suppliers, and they got into severe business and financial difficulty' (ibid.: 84). Instead McDonald's 'set the standards for quality' and also recommended methods through which a supplier could reduce costs and 'afford to sell to McDonald's for less' (ibid.: 100).

17. Napoli 2016: 55; Kroc 1987: 86, emphases added.

18. Love 1995: 144.

19. Love 1995: 145. McDonald's 'field service operation' has often been imitated by competitors but 'while they copied the chain's field service methods' they 'did not demonstrate the same zeal in enforcing their standards' (ibid.: 146).

20. Love 1995: 140.

21. Love 1995: 147.

22. Kroc 1987: 126, 167, 178.

23. Love 1995: 140.

24. Leidner 1993: 49, 50.

25. Leidner 1993: 29.

26. Love 1995: 150, emphasis added.

27. Sloan allowed his divisional managers some control over the advertising of their division's cars but it was his central headquarters' staff that came up with the styling changes for each car's annual model change (Sloan 1990: 104–5, 241–2; Farber 2004: 103).

28. Kroc 1987: 172.

29. Love 1995: 225, and see also 225 and 318 on the Quarter Pounder and Chicken McNuggets.

30. Love 1995: 220–2. Napoli provides a different perspective on these Washington origins of Ronald McDonald and his eventual adoption by the corporation (2016: 102–3, 112).

31. Love 1995: 213.
32. Kroc 1987: 109.
33. Kroc notes that 'it would be unwieldy and counterproductive for the corporation to own [rather than franchise] more than about thirty percent of all stores' (1987: 109). In 1967–76 Kroc and Turner greatly increased the number of company-operated restaurants by buying out hundreds of franchisees but the expansion was reined in when the advantages of franchising became clear: 'Lacking the incentive and drive of entrepreneurial owner/operators, company-run stores rarely equaled the profit margins of franchised units' and in difficult markets 'it was becoming clear that the above-average dedication of an owner/operator was critical to profitability' (Love 1995: 290).
34. Kroc 1987: 172, 173.
35. Love 1995: 218–21. See also Napoli 2016: 102–3.
36. Napoli 2016: 101.
37. Kroc 1987: 84; Love 1995: 142.
38. Kroc 1987: 84; Love 1995: 142.
39. Kroc 1987: 138–9, 150, 160; Love 1995: 222, 303. Eventually, 96 per cent of American children would be familiar with Ronald McDonald (Watson 2006: vi).
40. Watson 2006: 33.
41. Love 1995: 145.
42. Love 1995: 145.
43. Kroc 1987: 139. 'My way of fighting the competition is to emphasize *quality, service, cleanliness, and value*, and the competition will wear itself out trying to keep up'—it can be defeated 'simply by giving the public the old McDonald's QSC and V' (Kroc 1987: 115, 116).
44. Leidner 1993: 53.
45. Love 1995: 308.
46. Love 1995: 148.
47. Leidner 1993: 50.
48. Yan 2006: 44.
49. Yan 2006: 71.
50. Love 1995: 143; Napoli 2016: 75. Love noted that even McDonald's competitors conceded that its 'uncommon dedication to running a clean restaurant set a standard in the industry that others aimed for but seldom hit' (1995: 142).
51. Watson 2006: 31, 36.
52. Kroc 1987: 102, 145.
53. Kroc 1987: 159.
54. Napoli 2016: 99. See Love 1995: 274 on the 1970s.
55. Kroc 1987: 72, 87–8; Love 1995: 154, 157; Napoli 2016: 86.
56. Kroc 1987: 88, and another advantage of the income from leasing rentals was that, unlike income from franchisee royalties, it did not have to be split with the McDonald brothers (ibid.: 72).
57. Love argues that without Sonneborn's new financing formula, 'McDonald's would never have become a viable competitor in fast food' and that Sonneborn 'must be

credited for converting the flawless Kroc–Turner operating system into a highly profitable corporation' (1995: 152, 153).

58. Farber 2004: 56–8.
59. Farber 2004: 56.
60. Kroc 1987: 147, 191–2.
61. Love 1995: 6, 7.
62. Kroc 1987: 124–5, 151.
63. Kroc 1987: 172.
64. Kroc 1987: 96, 98. In effect, Kroc was the 'people' person, Sonneborn the 'numbers' person and Turner the 'rules' person.
65. Kroc 1987: 108–9, 121–2. See also Napoli 2016: 93 on buying-out the McDonald brothers.
66. Kroc 1987: 132; Napoli 2016: 87–8.
67. As Chapter 1's note 58 pointed out, Drucker argued that two-person teams rarely worked but if they did, they made an ideal team (2006: 177).
68. Brandt 2011a: 8.
69. Kroc 1987: 132, 133. Love describes the geographical division of labour as 'McDonald's East, McDonald's West' (1995: 252).
70. Napoli 2016: 111; Love 1995: 264.
71. Love 1995: 254. 'Ray favored an aggressive growth strategy, while Harry pushed for more measured, deliberate expansion' (Napoli 2016: 113).
72. Napoli 2016: 181. Kroc 1987: 155, 160 and 166 describes the 1967–8 origins and 1977 retirement-ending of their dual leadership.
73. Kroc 1987: 147, 166.
74. Kroc 1987: 143.
75. Chapter 2 contains a detailed survey and analysis of Sloan's committee-based system of deliberation.
76. Love 1995: 7.
77. Sloan 1990: xviii, 433.
78. Kroc 1987: 191.
79. Love 1995: 7.
80. Kroc 1987: 170.
81. Napoli 2016: 103, 107.
82. Kroc 1987: 138.
83. Love 1995: 8.
84. Kroc 1987: 202–3.
85. Watson 2006: 185.
86. Kroc 1987: 203.
87. Leidner 1993: 47.
88. Watson 2006: 38.
89. Kroc 1987: 206, referring to the situation in 1976. By then McDonald's global expansion included Germany, Britain, France, and Sweden in Europe; Japan and Hong Kong in Asia; and both Australia and New Zealand in Australasia (Watson 2006: 15 Table 2).

90. Love 1995: 428. Love acknowledged that 'no two foreign partners have similar backgrounds or even similar arrangements with McDonald's' but it had 'entered most countries by forming a joint venture which involves 50 percent ownership by McDonald's and 50 percent by a local entrepreneur', who in some cases owns and operates the stores through his/her joint-venture company and in other cases licenses them to local franchisees in typical McDonald's fashion (1995: 428).
91. Love 1995: 428, emphases added.
92. Watson 2006: 12, ix. Watson also noted that McDonald's preferred to describe itself as multilocal rather than multinational (ibid.: 12).
93. Watson 2006: 13, 14, 204 n. 28.
94. Watson 2006: 13–14.
95. Love 1995: 434. His exception-that-proves-the-rule is the German experience with adapting the menu and restaurant décor to local conditions. The German operation was a commercial failure until it switched to the standard, American-style menu and design and confined its innovations to marketing changes, especially in its advertising—which was unusually humorous and also emphasised that it was 'not a typical American multinational operation but rather the product of German franchisees, German workers, and homegrown food' (ibid.: 433–6).
96. Watson 2006: 23.
97. Watson 2006: 24.
98. Love 1995: 437–8. An innovative television advertising campaign also emphasized McDonald's quality and its menu's 'crisp fries' and 'thick shakes', which differed in form or quality from anything its fast-food competitors could offer (ibid.: 438).
99. Ohnuki-Tierney 2006: 162–3.
100. Ohnuki-Tierney 2006: 162, 170, 172–3.
101. Ohnuki-Tierney 2006: 164–5, 173. The experiments with adding rice-based items to the menu were partly due to the fact that the absence of rice is the 'deciding factor that makes hamburgers a snack in Japanese eyes' and therefore limits their appeal as an alternative to traditional restaurant options (ibid.: 168).
102. Watson 2006: 7.
103. Ohnuki-Tierney 2006: 170–1.
104. Yan 2006: 47, 50, 55–6, 58. School students appear to have been less attracted to McDonald's restaurants, perhaps because they had not yet been built in favourable locations, and it was not only young people who liked to use McDonald's as a place for socializing (ibid.: 56).
105. Yan 2006: 45, 74.
106. Yan 2006: 50–1.
107. Yan 2006: 62, 65. The children's families therefore go to McDonald's not only for birthday parties and other celebrations but also to give the children 'a special treat', even though the parents and grandparents in many cases 'dislike or cannot afford the foreign food' (ibid.: 52, 65).
108. Yan 2006: 60–1.
109. Kroc 1987: 205.

Chapter 5

1. Walton's autobiography was written with John Huey in the early 1990s (Walton 1993: 329–30, 333–4).
2. The book begins by describing how his life was disrupted after *Forbes* magazine named him the 'richest man in America' in 1985 (Walton 1993: 1–3). In 1989 he dropped from number one to number twenty on the *Forbes* list, having transferred more than $7 billion of assets to his children (Moreton 2006: 75). If he had lived another decade and had not transferred any of his fortune, 'his net worth of $100 billion would have made him twice as rich as Bill Gates, with his measly $50 billion' (Hoopes 2006: 96).
3. Tedlow 2003: 355.
4. Soderquist 2005: 29. In 1992, the year Walton died, there were only five Wal-Mart stores outside the US, specifically a joint-venture in Mexico, and Walmart International was not established until 1993 (Berg and Roberts 2012: 196–7, 217).
5. Soderquist 2005: 29.
6. Berg and Roberts 2012: 2–3.
7. Tedlow 2003: 340, quoting Walton 1993: 53. See Tedlow 2003: 341 on Walton having fifteen variety stores by 1960.
8. Walton 1993: 63.
9. Walton 1993: 27.
10. Walton 1993: 53; Vance and Scott 1994: 14.
11. Vance and Scott 1994: 15.
12. Vance and Scott 1994: 26.
13. Vance and Scott 1994: 38, emphasis added.
14. Walton 1993: 55, 57.
15. Moreton 2009: 38.
16. Walton 1993: 64.
17. Walton 1993: 59.
18. Vance and Scott 1994: 47.
19. Vance and Scott 1994: 54; Ortega 1999: 68–71; Walton 1993: 121–5, 153, 154. 'Wal-Mart blew right through the stagflation "malaise" of the 1970s that was so hard on so many other retailers' (Tedlow 2003: 313).
20. Walton 1993: 112, 116. The firm ordered merchandise from manufacturers on behalf of its stores, the merchandise was delivered by manufacturers to the firm's warehouse distribution centres, and there the merchandise was assembled into store-by-store orders that were delivered to each store by the firm's fleet of trucks. Wal-Mart's reliance on its own fleet of trucks was an unusual and lasting feature that was in marked contrast to its competitors' preference for contracting-out the delivery of merchandise from their distribution centres (ibid.: 266–7).
21. Vance and Scott 1994: 158–9.
22. Walton 1993: 113–14, 264; Vance and Scott 1994: 70–1.
23. Ortega 1999: 110, 111.
24. Ortega 1999: 75.
25. Berg and Roberts 2012: 122 on the 'hub and spoke model'.
26. Walton 1993: 140.

27. Walton 1993: 140–1. The saturation strategy also deterred competition from other discounting retailers. For example, there were eventually forty Wal-Mart stores within a hundred miles of Springfield, Missouri, and so any competing firm entering the territory would have 'a rough time going up against our kind of strength' (ibid.: 142).
28. Walton 1993: 264–5.
29. See Vance and Scott 1994: 82–3, 85, and 156–8.
30. Vance and Scott 1994: 85, 86.
31. It became the number-one retailer after a year of more than twenty per cent growth in net sales and net income (Vance and Scott 1994: 158).
32. Walton 1993: 141.
33. Ortega 1999: 75.
34. Vance and Scott 1994: 84.
35. Vance and Scott 1994: 84.
36. Walton 1993: 142. The firm's expansion in the 1980s had also been aided by acquisitions, notably the 1981 takeover of Kuhn's Big K Stores through which Wal-Mart acquired more than a hundred discount department stores located in nine different states in the southeast of the country (Walton 1993: 251–3; Vance and Scott 1994: 82; Ortega 1999: 103–5).
37. Vance and Scott 1994: 113, 115; Ortega 1999: 140–4; Walton 1993: 255–6.
38. Trimble 1990: 209; Ortega 1999: 148; Vance and Scott 1994: 118–19; Walton 1993: 256–7. Originally, they had been called Sam's Wholesale Clubs but in 1990 the name was changed to Sam's Clubs: Members Only, after a legal challenge to the use of the word 'wholesale' to describe a store selling goods to customers for their own use rather than for on-selling (Vance and Scott 1994: 118).
39. Walton 1993: 260.
40. Walton 1993: 254. The first Wal-Mart hypermarket opened in December 1987 and the final, fourth example in 1990; the first Supercenter opened as early as 1988 and only eleven had been added by 1992 (Vance and Scott 1994: 129–32, 166).
41. Ortega 1999: 164; Vance and Scott 1994: 133. The addition of groceries also meant that Wal-Mart was becoming more of a convenient one-stop shop for its customers (Strasser 2006: 55).
42. Berg and Roberts 2012: 161, 164 Fig. 10.1. More than half of the new Supercenters had been created through a modernization programme that converted many ageing discount stores into the new hybrid discount/grocery Supercenter (Vance and Scott 1994: 134; Berg and Roberts 2012: 162).
43. See the Appendix on Barnard's distinction between technical, rational leadership and the *moral* leadership involved in creating and maintaining a corporate culture.
44. Walton 1993: 216. Years earlier he had told an interviewer that one of his assets 'is my willingness to try something new, to change. I think that is a concept we carry throughout the company. We have a low resistance to change' (quoted by Trimble 1990: 142).
45. See how innovative adaptation is defined in Chapter 1 in terms of Schumpeter's concept of creative response.
46. Fishman 2011: 24.

47. Walton 1993: 147.
48. Walton 1993: 147.
49. Walton 1993: 148.
50. Soderquist 2005: 148.
51. See Walton 1993: 193 on mismanagement, 151 on concepts getting out of control, and 318 on the next trouble spot.
52. Walton 1993: 271, 272.
53. Slater 2003: 54.
54. Lichtenstein 2010: 34–5.
55. Walton 1993: 64.
56. Vance and Scott 1994: 69–70. See also Trimble 1990: 151.
57. Vance and Scott 1994: 69; Trimble 1990: 118; Walton 1993: 64.
58. Even in the 2010s global Wal-Mart was pursuing an 'Everyday Low Cost' (EDLC) grand strategy: 'saving money (or pursuing an EDLC strategy) is at the heart of most Walmart strategies' (Berg and Roberts 2012: 56, 132).
59. Walton 1993: 295. However, he then remarks that 'I think we came to work earlier and stayed later', which is *not* the waste-eliminating way in which Ohno reduced the number of workers and 'operated with fewer people'!
60. Walton 1993: 295.
61. Walton1993: 317. For example, when describing his innovative distribution network, he noted that 'cost savings alone would make the investment worthwhile' and that it was costing Wal-Mart markedly less than its competitors to distribute goods to stores (ibid.: 265). Vance and Scott point out that the 'expansion of Wal-Mart's sophisticated distribution system during the 1980s was central to its cost-cutting strategy' and in fact by the end of the 1980s its distribution costs were down to 1.3 per cent of sales, compared to the 3.5 per cent and 5 per cent of its two main competitors (1994: 92).
62. Walton 1993: 317.
63. Vance and Scott 1994: 90. In the 1990s, too, Wal-Mart's percentage of sales revenue spent on selling and general expenses was markedly lower than that of its competitors (Hoopes 2006: 93).
64. Walton 1993: 294. See Trimble 1990: 152 on being 'far below industry norms' for office expenses.
65. Ortega 1999: xv, xxv. See also Vance and Scott 1994: 108 on political criticism of Wal-Mart's employment policies. However, even one of the critics of Wal-Mart's labour policies acknowledges that the firm was 'lowering prices and raising the standard of living of the working-class and middle-class customers who are its main clientele' (Hoopes 2006: 88).
66. Walton 1993: 164, 162.
67. Walton 1993: 165, 169. The share-buying and bonus programmes gave employees the chance to buy Wal-Mart shares at a discount and to earn bonuses for boosting their store's sales and for reducing its 'shrinkage' of merchandise due to theft or damage (Ortega 1999: 90–1; Trimble 1990: 234, 274). The profit-sharing plan used a formula based on profit growth to calculate the percentage of every eligible worker's wages that the firm would contribute to his or her personal account

within the firm's overall profit-sharing plan (Walton 1993: 169). In 1976 workers' eligibility for participating in the profit-sharing plan was reduced from two years to one year's employment (Ortega 1999: 93).

68. Ortega 1999: 90.
69. Walton 1993: 168, 173, 181, 200 on new features and 166–7 on opposition to unionization; Ortega 1999: 91 on the 1973 re-naming employees as 'associates' and 93, 105, and 230–3 on the continuing fight against unionization; Vance and Scott 1994: 107 on informal use of first names—and also the apparent 'sense of family' in the firm, if only because many employees felt they were part of Walton's extended family. See also Trimble's chapter 'Labor Unions Not Wanted' (1990: ch. 22).
70. Moreton 2009: 185.
71. Moreton 2009: 185.
72. Tedlow 2003: 343.
73. Fishman 2011: 62, 227. Walton was also not monopolistic. He was not one of those merchants whom Adam Smith described in *The Wealth of Nations* as exploiting their monopolistic power 'to levy, for their own benefit, an absurd tax upon the rest of their fellow-citizens' (1992: 231–2).
74. Ortega 1999: 126.
75. He acknowledged that if he had not recruited these technocrats, 'we would have come apart somewhere there in the seventies, or we certainly wouldn't have been able to pull off our really incredible expansion in the eighties' (Walton 1993: 157–8).
76. Walton 1993: 263.
77. Walton 1993: 270. See also Ortega 1999: 78 and 99 on how they and the earlier generation of technocratic executives pushed for technological investment during the pivotal 1970s phase in Wal-Mart's development.
78. Ortega 1999: 131. It is not clear whether Walton was in fact told that the technology 'wasn't there yet' and a 'million different things could go wrong with something so untested' (ibid.).
79. Ortega 1999: 131–2, 133. Wal-Mart signed the contract for a satellite system in 1984 but the installation of the system was not completed until 1987 (Berg and Roberts 2012: 141–3).
80. Ortega 1999: 104. Similarly, retired-COO Arend said, 'I always knew when it was time to stop arguing a point when Walton thundered, "By golly, I still own most of the stock in this company, and this is the way we are going to do it"' (quoted by Trimble 1990: 143).
81. Ortega 1999: 211, 135.
82. Hillary Clinton was also the wife of Arkansas Governor Bill Clinton. She lobbied Walton and the board about involving Wal-Mart in environmental affairs, sold Walton the proposal to establish an environmental advisory board, and eventually saw her efforts rewarded when the corporation launched 'its green effort' in 1989 (Ortega 1999: 215, 216). See Vance and Scott 1994: 111–12 on this environmentally friendly 'green' campaign, such as Wal-Mart stores switching to shopping bags made of recycled paper rather than non-biodegradable plastic.
83. Walton 1993: 278. Ortega confirms that Walton 'encouraged those lower down to debate and challenge ideas' (1999: 122). Vance and Scott confirm that his efforts

had some success, as a 'tendency to encourage independent thinking permeated every level of the organization, from top managers down to hourly associates' (1994: 100).

84. Vance and Scott 1994: 99.
85. Vance and Scott 1994; Ortega 1999: 136; Walton 1993: 198.
86. Walton 1993: 259, 216.
87. Vance and Scott 1994: 99.
88. Walton 1993: 259 and Ortega 1999: 136 on Glass as the preferred successor, even though after the job-swapping these two executives were officially equal in status. Shewmaker resigned soon after his rival became CEO in 1988, 'leaving Glass, along with Walton, to lead the company' (Vance and Scott 1994: 99).
89. Walton 1993: 263.
90. Berg and Roberts 2012: 138. Walton's attitude to technology has also been described as embracing the new technology 'but always with a heathy dose of skepticism. He knew how to put technology in its place. It was a means to an end' (Tedlow 2003: 312).
91. Walton 1993: 117.
92. The introduction of barcode scanning in the 1980s required 'testing the system for a couple of years to get the bugs out' (Ortega 1999: 130). In the late 1970s, the mechanization of the Searcy distribution centre became 'such a nightmare that Sam began to question the whole idea of mechanized distribution' (Glass quoted in Walton 1993: 264). Earlier in the decade, the introduction of electric cash registers ran into unforeseen problems that one of the victims later blamed on a technocrat's choice of equipment: 'right idea but the wrong register' (quoted in Walton 1993: 159).
93. Ortega 1999: 125.
94. Walton 1993: 252; Ortega 1999: 103. Ortega describes how debates about the acquisition had dominated board meetings for more than a year beforehand, and he argues that Walton would not have 'quietly acceded to the majority' if the vote in the Executive Committee had been four-to-two against the acquisition (1999: 103).
95. Vance and Scott 1994: 98; Ortega 1999: 104, 73, 166 and see 214 on membership of the dual leadership Executive Committee.
96. Trimble mentioned not only a finance committee but also a real-estate committee and personnel committees (1990: 138–9).
97. Walton 1993: 97, 199. See also Vance and Scott 1994: 68, 101 on the size of meetings and who attended them. The regional managers spent several days each week in their regions, commuting weekly by small plane from an airport near Bentonville (Walton 1993: 286–7; Trimble 1990: 278).
98. In Walton's book, Soderquist said that the meetings did not really have an agenda but 'the chairman always has his yellow legal pad with notes scribbled on it of things he wants to discuss' (quoted in Walton 1993: 211–12).
99. Walton 1993: 209. According to Walton, the Saturday-morning meeting was also 'where we discuss and debate much of our philosophy and our management strategy' but it is unlikely that the meeting was deliberating about the actual content, not just the implementation, of the firm's philosophy and management strategy (1993: 209).

100. Vance and Scott 1994: 101.
101. Vance and Scott 1994: 68, 101.
102. Learning about a problem may lead to an adaptive response that solves the problem, as learning about a change, threat, or opportunity is usually the first part of an adaptive process that produces a rapid or innovative adaptation.
103. Walton 1993: 209, 291.
104. Ortega 1999: xxiv and it was only one of several occasions that he refers to Walton learning something (ibid.: 80, 85, 117, 140).
105. Tedlow 2003: 312, 332.
106. Learning and adaptation should be viewed as separate business processes and methods even though learning is usually included in the first part of an adaptive process. The distinction between learning and adaptation is also found in military analysis, such as Cohen and Gooch's chapter on 'Failure to Learn: American Antisubmarine Warfare in 1942'. It analyses the failure of the US Navy to learn organizational lessons from how the British fought Germany's U-boat submarines in 1939–41. This failure to *learn* proved costly in 1942, when America was targeted by the U-boats, but the Navy eventually *adapted* organizationally to the problems and environment of antisubmarine warfare in the Atlantic (Cohen and Gooch 2006: 94).
107. In addition to Dassault, Grove and Whitman will be described in Chapters 6 and 7 as emphasizing learning.
108. Walton 1993: 29, 289.
109. Walton 1993: 57, 102, 104–5.
110. Walton 1993: 191, 192.
111. Walton 1993: 254.
112. Kroc 1987: 191.
113. Tedlow 2003: 340, 341.
114. Tedlow 2003: 340.
115. Tedlow 2003: 344.
116. Walton 1993: 53–4.
117. Walton 1993: 59.
118. Walton 1993: 59.
119. Walton 1993: 200–2.
120. Vance and Scott 1994: 78.
121. Walton 1993: 47. One of the lessons he learnt from his training by JC Penny 'was not to be so smug you ignored your competitors, especially their successful policies and practices' (Trimble 1990: 91).
122. Walton 1993: 102, 255.
123. Walton 1993: 243. Kmart's stores were so superior 'back then that sometimes I felt we couldn't compete' (ibid.: 104). But, as he told Trimble, 'we were protected by our small-town market. It would have been unthinkable for them to have tried to put a competing store in a small town. They gave us a ten-year period to grow, and finally we were able to hold our own' (quoted by Trimble 1990: 93).
124. Trimble 1990: 148.

125. Walton 1993: 293.
126. Ortega 1999: 193. See also Trimble 1990: 146–7.
127. Walton 1993: 293 and see also 316.
128. Walton 1993: 285 and see also 267 on a similar learning-monitoring by talking to Wal-Mart's truck drivers.
129. Soderquist 2005: 118.
130. He changed his name from Marcel Bloch to Marcel Dassault after the Second World War, as 'Dassault' had been the pseudonym used by his brother when fighting with the Resistance insurgency against France's occupation by Nazi Germany.
131. He was estimated to have the 'largest fortune in France in 1985' (Villette and Vuillermot 2009: 121).
132. The talisman mentioned by his book's title was a four-leaf clover that he had discovered in 1939 and kept in his wallet ever since (Dassault 1971: 126–7).
133. Dassault 1971: 32–3.
134. Dassault 1971: 32–3.
135. Dassault 1971: 32–3. His firm's official history describes it as a 'two-seat combat aircraft' (Carlier and Berger 1996: 11–12).
136. Dassault 1971: 34–5.
137. Dassault 1971: 38.
138. Dassault 1971: 41–2.
139. Dassault 1971: 43 and 43–4 on the later government order for planes to be used in the colonies.
140. See Dassault 1971: 44–7 on this period. Villette and Vuillermot 2009: 124–7 provides a different perspective on this period.
141. Dassault 1971: 47, 106; Carlier and Berger 1996: 22–4.
142. Villette and Vuillermot 2009: 127, emphases added.
143. Bergerud 2000: 179–81.
144. Carlier and Berger 1996: 25.
145. Carlier and Berger 1996: 28. However, this method of technological development involved the risk of being leapfrogged by a less derivative, more innovative aircraft. A very relevant case is the American F-16 fighter that defeated Dassault's F 1E in the mid-1970s 'contract of the century' to sell a new fighter to the air forces of Belgium, Denmark, the Netherlands, and Norway. The innovative F-16 not only had a more powerful engine but also was constructed of composite materials as well as metal and was pioneering fly-by-wire, computerized flight controls (Carlier and Berger 1996: 119).
146. Dassault 1971: 113.
147. Dassault 1971: 113.
148. Dassault 1971: 105.
149. Waterton 2012: 197, 165.
150. Carlier and Berger 1996: 37.
151. Waterton 2012: 167. A British test pilot from a later era confirms that the flight characteristics of prototypes were less predictable in Waterton's era, which lacked sophisticated computer-assisted design techniques, and that there was indeed

'always a tendency then, without the multitude of recorders now fitted to test aircraft, for the firm to prefer not to believe their own test pilot and take no action until the certification pilot or the customer criticised the product' (Blackman in Waterton 2012: x–xi).

152. Waterton 2012: 166.
153. On the importance of exports see Carlier and Berger 1996: 64, 68, 71, 84–5, 132–3; exports in fact averaged 58 per cent of sales in the period from 1952 to 1977 (ibid.: 133).
154. Dassault 1971: 108–9. The Falcons had been sold in more than twenty countries on five continents.
155. Dassault 1971: 109.
156. Carlier and Berger 1996: 29, 161.
157. Carlier and Berger 1996: 85, 148.

Chapter 6

1. Tedlow 2007: 121.
2. Tedlow 2007: xiv–xv.
3. Tedlow 2007: 385, 278.
4. Grove's concern with adaptive crises was part of his wider concern with business survival and guardianship. He argued that 'when it comes to business, I believe in the value of paranoia. I believe that the prime responsibility of a manager is to guard constantly against other people's attacks' (1999: 3). Bill Gates experienced a similar anxiety about the future of his corporation Microsoft. His 'concern that Microsoft could always be surpassed and made irrelevant is a constant theme for Gates' (Becraft 2014: 117).
5. Grove's facility with concepts and conceptualization is one of the reasons why he might be considered a business equivalent of Plato's philosopher-king rulers, in the sense of kings who 'genuinely and adequately philosophize' (Strauss 1972: 29).
6. Grove 1999: 32, and he explains that the term 'inflection point' was used in mathematics to describe a change in sign from negative to positive or vice versa and to describe where a curve changes from convex to concave or vice versa.
7. Grove 1999: 4, 5, 20.
8. Grove 1999: 5, 6, 7.
9. Grove 1999: 95.
10. Grove 1999: 88.
11. Jackson 1998: 253.
12. Jackson 1998: 253–4, citing Grove's own assessment, which acknowledges that the adaptive response 'took us a total of three years': the firm's 'performance started to slump when the entire industry weakened in mid-1984', but the decision to get out of memories was not made until mid-1985, took 'until mid-1986 to implement', and then 'took another year before we returned to profitability' (Grove 1999: 95).
13. Jackson 1998: 358.
14. Grove 1999: 22.

15. Grove 1999: 66–7. Tedlow notes that 'the Intel Inside program had succeeded to a remarkable degree' in creating a consumer-recognized brand *but* 'no one at Intel had any experience at brand management' (2007: 332–3).

16. Grove 1999: 90. Two intellectual prejudices 'that were as strong as religious dogmas' were that 'our salesmen needed a full product line [including memory-chip products] to do a good job in front of our customers' and that memory chips were 'technology drivers' because 'we always developed and refined our technologies on our memory products first because they were easier to test' (ibid.: 90, 91).

17. Grove 1999: 92–3.

18. It might be argued that Intel was indirectly benefiting from an innovative adaptation because in 1985 it was able to fall back on a microprocessor business created largely by IBM's innovative adaptation to disruptive technology, namely the IBM personal computer's exploitation of new markets for desktop personal computers (Christensen 2000: 109–10, 217).

19. Grove 1999: 143.

20. Grove 1999: 94; Berlin 2005: 64.

21. Thackray et al. 2015: 441, 439.

22. Tedlow 2007: 224.

23. Malone 2014: 364. Grove's account of second-sourcing notes that once a second source is in production, 'multiple companies now compete for the same business. This may please the customer but [it] certainly hurts the wallet of the prime source' (1999: 70). Yet when he then describes the 'enormous' impact on the PC industry of Intel's shift from second-sourcing to sole-sourcing, he mentions that 'our influence on customers increased' but fails to note that this increased influence included being a monopolistic supplier and price-setter (ibid.).

24. Thackray et al. 2015: 437, and 436 on Windows being designed for Intel's microprocessors. But the first, 1985 version of Windows was actually a 'flop' and not until the third, 1990 version would it meet the great expectations (Wallace and Erickson 1993: 314, 362–3). Nonetheless, 'Wintel' was an effective 'bilateral monopoly' when compared to the highly competitive market of IBM/clone PC manufacturers (Tedlow 2007: 305). 'What really mattered from Intel's point of view was the birth of the IBM "clones." A clone worked just like an IBM PC' and so when 'IBM wanted to hold off on its purchase of the 386' microprocessor, Intel found ready customers among the clone-makers, who were able to gain a competitive advantage over IBM by manufacturing 386-equipped PCs which were more capable and popular than IBM's non-386 version (ibid.: 227, 228).

25. Thackray et al. 2015: 439.

26. Thackray et al. 2015: 439.

27. Tedlow 2007: 395, and 230 on how the sole-sourcing strategy had put Intel 'in a position to print money'.

28. Grove 1999: 4.

29. Tedlow 2007: 369, and 282 on being described by *Fortune* as the world's most profitable firm.

30. Moore's Law was first formulated by Gordon Moore in a 1965 magazine article, where he had predicted that the number of transistors being chemically imprinted

on a microchip would double every year and therefore in ten years' time would total 65,000 transistors per chip (Thackray et al. 2015: xix–xx).

31. Thackray et al. 2015: 375. Furthermore, he phrased Moore's Law in economic as well as technological terms by phrasing in terms of a doubling of the capability that it would be *economical* to produce in a microchip (ibid.: 507, 381, 460). In other words, there would have to be a market for these continually updated, exponentially more capable microchips: there would need to be sufficient customers willing to pay for the research, development, and manufacturing costs involved in maintaining Moore's Law.

32. Thackray et al. 2015: 377, and see 277, 310, 329, 348 on the treadmill strategy and 325–6, 462–4 on Moore's strategic role. Similarly, Malone's history of Intel's triple leadership describes how Moore devised 'an incredibly powerful business strategy' based on Moore's Law (2014: 375).

33. Malone 2014: 435.

34. Malone 2014: 436. Malone prefers the analogy with a spiral rather than a treadmill but his analysis is applicable to both conceptions of Intel's strategy: because Intel had set the rate of the spiral/treadmill 'at the pace of Moore's Law, its competitors had to maintain that breakneck pace always or risk falling back' and 'it was almost impossible for competitors to gain ground on Intel as long as it hewed to the law': that is, to Moore's Law (ibid.). Cringely simply suggested that Grove's strategy was to outspend Intel's competitors in order to speed up its product development and 'result in Intel's building the very profitable leading-edge chips, leaving its competitors to slug it out in the market for commodity processors' (1996: 354).

35. Grove 1999: 28. Substitution would include what Christensen termed 'disruptive' new technologies, which pose a threat to the leading firms in an industry (see Chapter 1 and the Appendix).

36. Grove 1999: 30.

37. Grove 1999: 56–7, 66. These two examples were mentioned in Chapters 2, 5, and 6.

38. Grove 1999: 181–2.

39. Grove 1999: 182, 183.

40. Malone 2014: 430.

41. Malone 2014: 431.

42. Grove 1999: 7. See ibid.: 153 and 164 for two different descriptions of the three stages.

43. Grove 1999: 108. Grove's term 'Cassandras' comes from the Trojan priestess in *The Iliad* who prophesied the destruction of Troy. Most strategic inflection points are hard to identify: 'instead of coming in with a bang, [they] approach on little cat feet. They are often not clear until you can look at the events in retrospect' (ibid.: 107).

44. Grove 1999: 109–10.

45. Grove 1999: 110, 119.

46. Grove 1999: 117.

47. Grove 1999: 35.

48. Tedlow 2007: 190; Thackray et al. 2015: 387.

49. Grove 1999: 146–7, 149–50.

50. He even co-taught a course on strategic management at Stanford University's Graduate School of Business in the 1990s (Grove 1999: xi).

51. Grove 1999: 114, 162. Moore's biographers note that debates among Intel's management could be very vigorous: 'macho and combative posturing often preceded "rational judgment." Andy Grove set the tone, frequently shouting and hurling insults at opponents' (Thackray et al. 2015: 387). This was likely an example of what Intel's corporate culture called 'constructive confrontation', which was described by Grove as 'a style of ferociously arguing with one another while remaining friends' (1999: 84).
52. Grove 1999: 157.
53. Grove 1999: 155.
54. Grove 1999: 153, 154.
55. Grove 1999: 155, 156.
56. Tedlow 2007: 335. General Electric's CEO, Jack Welch, acknowledges that he was 'late' in adopting email in 1999 (2003: 341–2).
57. Tedlow 2007: 334.
58. Welch 2003: 341–2.
59. Grove 1999: 156, and 157 on world-wide firms.
60. Packard 2005: 155.
61. Grove 1999: 153, and 130 on experimenting with new products or other new things.
62. Grove 1999: 130.
63. Berlin 2005: 217, 203.
64. Berlin 2005: 183.
65. Berlin 2005: 227.
66. Berlin 2005: 227; Tedlow 2007: 241.
67. Tedlow 2007: 407.
68. Malone 2014: 482.
69. Malone 2014: 482, where he also describes how Intel 'had developed a new, very-low-power processor family called Atom but had designed it for laptops and net-books, not tablets and smartphones. Intel had blown it.'
70. Berlin 2005: 185–6.
71. Berlin 2005: 193. Berlin notes that another feature of Noyce's deliberative style was that he 'spoke of "hierarchy power" and "knowledge power" and firmly believed that when it came to technical decisions, the word of the person with the most knowledge ought to trump the opinion of the one with the higher title' (2005: 191).
72. Packard 2005: 96.
73. Packard 2005: 97. Another factor involved in the selection of new ideas for further development was of course the likelihood of high profits or rate of return: 'we often used to select projects on the basis of a six-to-one engineering return. That is, the profit we expected to derive over the lifetime of a product should be at least six times the cost of developing the product' (ibid.: 97–8). Furthermore, Packard later referred to HP selecting new ideas for products that 'will meet *latent* needs of *future* importance to our customers' (ibid.: 110, emphases added).
74. Packard 2005: 100.
75. Packard 2005: 100.

76. Packard 2005: 100.
77. Packard 2005: 100–1.The deliberative process's informal rules gave inventors and Hewlett reciprocal rights and duties, such as the right/duty of initial encouragement and then 'inquisitorial' questioning.
78. Malone 2007: 139.
79. Packard 2005: 141–2.
80. Packard 2005: 140.
81. Packard 2005: 140–1. However, HP soon discovered that operating divisions' focus on their divisional profit-and-loss statements led them to focus on their existing markets rather than seeking opportunities to diversify into new markets; in contrast, its eventual companywide experimentation system encouraged cooperative cross-divisional efforts at innovation and diversification (House and Price 2009: 99).
82. Malone 2007: 144–5.
83. Malone believes that the primary reason was the leaders' desire to strengthen their firm's corporate culture: 'the primary reason was cultural' and, specifically, 'retaining the company's innovative, and already well-established, "[HP] Way" of doing business' (2007: 145).
84. Packard 2005: 146. An organizational structure containing many small-sized divisions had already been pioneered by Cordiner at General Electric in the 1950s (Chandler 1990: 368).
85. House and Price 2009: 4–5, 142.
86. A relatively recent example of these treadmill-like strategies is the printer-upgrading treadmill of the 1980s–90s. HP 'upgraded its printer generations so quickly that [its] competitors barely had time to react before its superior replacement arrived' (Malone 2007: 332–3).
87. House and Price 2009: 86.
88. Packard 2005: 140–1; Malone 2007: 211.
89. Packard 2005: 147.
90. House and Price 2009: 264; Malone 2007: 212.
91. Malone 2007: 212. The need for inter-divisional coordination was highlighted by the failure of HP's entry into the 1980s personal-computer market, its HP150, which 'opened everyone's eyes at HP to problems of cooperation across divisions' (Bowen et al. 1994: 418).
92. House and Price 2009: 90.
93. House and Price 2009: 90.
94. Packard 2005: 142.
95. House and Price 2009: 113.
96. House and Price 2009: 308–11; Bowen et al. 1994: 418–25.
97. House and Price 2009: 5, 33.
98. House and Price 2009: 150–1.
99. House and Price 2009: 151. The desktop calculator was the HP9100A, introduced in 1968, the handheld calculator was the pioneering HP-35, introduced in 1972, and the small computer was the HP3000, especially the highly successful Series II introduced in 1975 (Malone 2007: 291).

100. House and Price 2009: 518 Fig. A.4.
101. House and Price 2009: 518 Fig. A.5.
102. Burgelman et al. 2017: 124, 126.
103. Burgelman et al. 2017: 138–9.
104. Burgelman et al. 2017: 139.
105. Burgelman et al. 2017: 154–5. Young's efforts took HP from number seventeen to number three in the field of business computing (ibid.: 149).
106. Burgelman et al. 2017: 154. HP became the number-four provider of personal computers and was actually number one in the home personal-computer market (ibid.).
107. Burgelman et al. 2017: 158, 170.
108. Burgelman et al. 2017: 152, 158–9.
109. House and Price 2009: 518 Fig. A.6.
110. In addition, the experimentation system was affected by such new moves as the reduction in divisional R&D budgets and the reduced funding of HP Labs (Burgelman et al. 2017: 174–5).
111. Burgelman et al. 2017: 170–1, 176.
112. Burgelman et al. 2017: 175. Malone pointed out that inkjet printing 'was the last great technical breakthrough at Hewlett-Packard in the twentieth century' (2007: 330).
113. Burgelman et al. 2017: 175.
114. Isaacson 2013: xxi.
115. Speech at Stanford University, 2005, quoted by Lee 2011: 7.
116. Isaacson 2013: 375.
117. Isaacson 2013: 424.
118. Young and Simon 2005: 276.
119. Young and Simon 2005: 277.
120. Young and Simon 2005: 278–9.
121. Young and Simon 2005: 280.
122. Stone 2014: 232–4 on top-down experimentation and 236, 238–9, 248 on hands-on approach.
123. Young and Simon 2005: 285. A key factor in the iPod's success was Jobs's negotiation of agreements with music firms that allowed Apple to sell their music through the on-line iTunes Music Store (ibid.: 290).
124. Isaacson 2013: 429. His anxiety may have been fuelled by his knowledge of Grove's book, as was described at the beginning of this chapter, and also by his knowledge of Christensen's concept of disruptive technology, as 'Jobs was deeply influenced by his book *The Innovator's Dilemma*' (ibid.: 376).
125. Isaacson 2013: 430.
126. Isaacson 2013: 433.
127. Isaacson 2013: 433, 434, 436.
128. Isaacson 2013: 438. Another diversification was that the iPhone earned huge, continuing revenues from the non-phoning activities, the applications, which could be performed with this portable IT platform. Apple's on-line App Store

opened in July 2008 and, less than two years later, was offering 185,000 different applications for sale—thanks in part to an innovative policy of allowing independent apps-designers to sell their products through Apple (ibid.: 463).

129. Isaacson 2013: 431–2, 452–3.
130. Isaacson 2013: 453. However, it was apparently not Jobs but one of his key team members who wanted to change from an Intel to an ARM-based microprocessor—and persuaded Jobs to make the change (ibid.: 454).
131. Isaacson 2013: 455, 459.
132. Sloan 1990: 433–4.
133. Brandt 2011a: 177.
134. Brandt 2011a: 177.
135. Brandt 2011a: 178.
136. Brandt 2011a: 178.
137. Malone 2014: 338. Grove made these remarks in a 2004 interview. The management book was Drucker's 1954 classic *The Practice of Management* (Drucker 2006).
138. Malone 2014: 448.
139. Jackson 1998: 377.

Chapter 7

1. Cohen 2003: 9, 314.
2. Cohen 2003: 8–9.
3. Whitman 2010: 9–10.
4. Van Dijck 2013: 62.
5. Whitman 2010: 3–4.
6. Whitman 2010: 9. Details of her pre-eBay career can be found in her book and in Horvitz 2006: 11–17.
7. Whitman 2010: 248.
8. Viegas 2007: 11. These statistics include only individuals over sixteen years old but, on the other hand, include Canadians as well as residents of the US.
9. Viegas 2007: 65.
10. Bunnell 2000: 46. He also describes the advantages of online auctions for small-business dealers in used goods (ibid.: 42–3). But later he points out that the high-volume sellers on eBay 'face daunting back-office chores that effectively limit their potential revenues and profits' and indeed 'many volume sellers of low-priced items must find themselves working for very low hourly wages' (ibid.: 52).
11. Horvitz 2006: 360. By the time Whitman retired, there were more than a million (Whitman 2010: 9).
12. Bunnell 2000: 10, 36.
13. Cohen 2003: 117.
14. Cohen 2003: 25, 58. But many auctions did not result in a final-sale fee. For sellers could also include a reserve price, known to eBay but not the bidders, and Bunnell pointed out that many auctions were not 'consummated' because the bidding failed to reach the secret reserve price (Bunnell 2000: 49).

15. Bunnell 2000: 120; Viegas 2007: 48, 56.
16. Whitman 2010: 8. On the other hand, once eBay became a public company, Whitman had to deal with the tension between the user-community's needs and the revenue needs of stockholders. 'We really lived in la-la land with our community for two wonderful years', Whitman said in an interview, but then went on to acknowledge that 'once you go public the pressures are completely different. You've got investors and analysts looking at you, you've got the media looking at you, you've got to worry about shares and stockholders and revenue' (Horvitz 2006: 60).
17. Cohen 2003: 28–9. According to Cohen, too, Omidyar had tried to register 'AuctionWeb.com' but it had already been registered by another online-auction pioneer, so the site continued to have the online address of 'eBay.com', which Omidyar had chosen when he found that his first-preference 'EchoBay.com' had already been registered by another company (ibid.: 79 footnote).
18. Cohen 2003: 28; Viegas 2007: 46.
19. Cohen 2003: 50.
20. Bunnell 2000: 64–5. 'The users who posted and lurked in the eBay Café were for the most part middle-aged, middle-class, and lived in Middle America, and they chatted as if they had known each other all their lives' (Cohen 2003: 50). Amazon, too, had moved in this direction in 1996 by not only inviting readers to post reviews of books but also enabling browsers to communicate with one another: 'it became an early social network site for book fans' (Brandt 2011b: 86).
21. Kirkpatrick 2011: 67. In fact Usenet's social messaging began in 1979 (ibid.: 66).
22. Kirkpatrick 2011: 67, 69.
23. Van Dijck 2013: 57; Kirkpatrick 2011: 71–5, 145, 151–2.
24. Bilton 2013: 62, 67, 174. Twitter might well be categorized as a 'microblogging' information network rather than some form of e-socializing, especially as most tweeting is not reciprocal or interactive but merely providing information to a prominent tweeter's following of fans, admirers, supporters, and so forth (Van Dijck 2013: 74, 78–9).
25. Bunnell 2000: 105; Cohen 2003: 59, 93.
26. Cohen 2003: 56, 59.
27. Cohen 2003: 30–2.
28. Viegas 2007: 76; Cohen 2003: 79–80.
29. Cohen 2003: 126. Omidyar and Skoll began to disengage from the firm in 1999 (ibid.: 303–4).
30. Cohen 2003: 186, 189.
31. Cohen 2003: 147–8. Even in 1997 Whitman had never come across 'a young enterprise' with such impressive numbers as, for example, eBay's profit margin: 'their costs were so low that their profits were 85 percent of revenues' (Whitman 2010: 19).
32. Whitman 2010: 4.
33. Whitman 2010: 46.
34. Whitman 2010: 68–9, emphases added. She also seems to share Grove's preference for an early-mover strategy. There is something Grove-like about her maxim that 'the price of inaction is far greater than the cost of making a mistake' and her warning that

no matter how 'confusing or hard or even paralyzing your circumstances might feel, the price you'll pay for treading water, dithering, not moving forward, is far higher than the cost of making a mistake' (ibid.: 46, 72). There is a very similar warning in Grove's analytical framework for dealing with inflection points (Grove 1999: 152).

35. 'When you operate in a technology-driven space, everything can change overnight and you have to change with it' (Whitman 2010: 260).
36. Cohen 2003: 183.
37. Cohen 2003: 181; Whitman 2010: 206–7. Her longer-term response included hiring the best technical expert that 'money could buy', and in her book she noted that hiring and retaining him, with the highest salary paid to any of the firm's managers, was 'the best money we ever spent' (ibid.: 121).
38. Whitman 2010: 211; Cohen 2003: 184. A week after the outage ended, listings on the eBay site were almost back to the pre-outage level (Horvitz 2006: 58).
39. Global expansion was the other source or area of innovative adaptations, as in the case of the joint-venture relationship that was pioneered in China in 2003 (Whitman 2010: 70–1).
40. Horvitz 2006: 40.
41. Whitman 2010: 167.
42. Whitman 2010: 251.
43. Whitman 2010: 88.
44. Cohen 2003: 131–2. Another example of her use of diverse deliberation was the recruitment of outside directors who had developed new firms in other industries, such as the chairman/CEO of Starbucks and the chairman of Intuit software (Bunnell 2000: 32).
45. Horvitz 2006: 34.
46. Whitman 2010: 169.
47. Cohen 2003: 209.
48. Bunnell 2000: 100.
49. The board was also helped to perform its auditing (rather than deliberative) role by her informal rule that all senior executives were to attend board meetings so that directors 'could ask them questions' (Whitman 2010: 97).
50. Whitman 2010: 91.
51. Whitman 2010: 90.
52. Whitman 2010: 90, emphasis added.
53. Burgelman et al.: 287–8, 296.
54. Burgelman et al.: 297, 326–7.
55. Whitman 2010: 137, emphasis added.
56. Cohen 2003: 126.
57. Whitman 2010: 138; Horvitz 2006: 46.
58. Horvitz 2006: 45, 48.
59. Whitman 2010: 140.
60. Whitman 2010: 187–8.
61. Whitman 2010: 188. The collectibles-focused strategy might well be viewed as a niche-market strategy but Bunnell preferred to describe it in terms of market

segmentation and concentrating the firm's marketing resources on the 20 per cent of registered users who accounted for 80 per cent of its revenues (Bunnell 2000: 124).

62. Cohen 2003: 132.
63. Cohen 2003: 132, 138.
64. Viegas 2007: 70.
65. Bunnell 2000: vii, 5. He noted that the figure for registered users is nothing like the number of *active* users, which may be only half or a third of the official count (ibid.: 120).
66. Cohen 2003: 132. Bunnell noted that in 1998 trading in Beanie Babies accounted for some 6 per cent of eBay's revenue (2000: 25).
67. Horvitz 2006: 63.
68. Cohen 2003: 208, and 279 quoting Whitman.
69. Cohen 2003: 279.
70. Cohen 2003: 200.
71. Bunnell 2000: 121 and 188 n. 1 on the 1999 move towards globalization.
72. Bunnell 2000: 75–6. Later he describes this as a land-grab approach and mentions the 'positive network effect' that eBay enjoyed as a 'first mover' (ibid.: 134).
73. Whitman 2010: 226–8.
74. Horvitz 2006: 2. The figures for users and countries are for 2004.
75. Horvitz 2006: 48; Whitman 2010: 228.
76. Stone 2014: 264, 265.
77. Stone 2014: 263, 264.
78. Bunnell 2000: 15. In 2000 most analysts were predicting that eBay would keep on growing at its current rapid rate 'for two or three more years, and then experience the usual tapering off that comes with market maturation' in the mid-2000s (ibid.: 181).
79. Stone 2014: 263–4.
80. Whitman 2010: 44.
81. Cohen 2003: 235. 'We were about to start experimenting with our own "buy it now" [fixed-price] format' (Whitman 2010: 44).
82. Whitman 2010: 258.
83. Whitman 2010: 69.
84. Cohen 2003: 155.
85. See Whitman 2010: 60–2 and 218–19 on the learning part of iteration; 212, 216 on validating; and 168–9 on feedback. Unlike Walton, she has little to say about copying others' ideas but she does mention 'borrowing' good ideas and following 'best practice' (ibid.: 219, 221).
86. Whitman 2010: 156.
87. Whitman 2010: 72.
88. Burgelman et al. 2007: 296.
89. Bunnell 2000: 22, 101.
90. Cohen 2003: 188.
91. Whitman 2010: 258.
92. Born in 1964, he was a Princeton graduate in computer science and electrical engineering who had worked in three Wall Street financial-computing firms,

where he had managed computer programmers, an engineering department, and then a large team exploring new opportunities, such as those offered by the burgeoning Internet (Brandt 2011b: 31, 35–9).

93. Bezos's use of three of these rational methods is mentioned in this section: his learning on the job, his Kindle rapid adaptive response, and his Web Services innovative adaptation. There is also plenty of evidence of him using the other four methods. In the case of strategic calculation there is, for example, his 1999 strategy of not 'working toward a profit' until the Internet's 'cone of opportunity' had narrowed enough 'to make it difficult for newcomers to squeeze through ahead of him' in the markets he desired for Amazon (Brandt 2011b: 128–9). In the case of quantitative calculation there is, for example, his 'vision of an Amazon with data at its heart', which meant in practice that it 'relies on metrics to make almost every important decision' (Stone 2014: 204, 327). In the case of the deliberative methods there is, for example, his belief that 'truth springs forth when ideas and perspectives are banged together', which in practice meant policy-making arguments 'backed by numbers and passion' (Stone 2014: 326, 328), and his formal rule that policy-making discussions were to be based on written 'narratives' similar to an essay or to a press release—if a new feature or product was being proposed (Stone 2014: 175–6).

94. Whitman 2010: 268.

95. Stone 2014: 24–6; Brandt 2011b: 5.

96. Whitman 2010: 247.

97. Cohen 2003: 136.

98. Brandt 2011b: 107 on new high-tech warehouses as well as quadrupled computer capacity; 121, 124 on heavy losses; 129–30 on efficiency campaign; 122–3 on making a profit; Stone 2014: 101, 120, 168 on efficiency campaign and lay-offs.

99. Stone 2014: 340.

100. Whitman 2010: 247.

101. Making the customer happy included both ensuring 'that people left the site happy' and ensuring that they were happy with their post-site experiences: even the packaging was redesigned to make it easier for people to open (Brandt 2011b: 10). Furthermore, Amazon's customer obsession included the notion that the customers might not be aware of what would make them happy until the company showed it to them (Brandt 2011b: 185).

102. Stone 2014: 107.

103. Bunnell 2000: 159 and 158–9 on how they operated. Stone, however, presents the zShops as a failure (2014: 80, 107, 114).

104. Stone 2014: 107–11.

105. Stone 2014: 115. Marketplace earned 'a flat 6 to 15 percent commission on each sale' (ibid.: 303).

106. Stone 2014: 116. In fact Marketplace would be used by Amazon as a way of learning about a category of goods before it began selling items in that category. 'If you don't know anything about a business, launch it through Marketplace, bring retailers in, watch what they do and what they sell, understand it, and then get into it' (ibid.: 182, quoting an Amazon retail manager). However, this did not

prevent Marketplace becoming an increasingly important part of Amazon's business. In late 2001 'sales from third-party sellers on the vaunted Amazon platform made up 15 percent of company's orders' but ten years later some 36 per cent of the goods sold on Amazon 'were brokered over its third-party marketplace' (ibid.: 134, 301).

107. Stone 2014: 194.
108. Brandt 2011b: 119.
109. Brandt 2011b: 109, 113, 118, 130.
110. Stone 2014: 67, 123.
111. Bunnell 2000: 115.
112. Stone 2014: 277.
113. Whitman 2010: 44, 63.
114. Whitman 2010: 63.
115. Van Dijck 2013: 68, 186 n. 2.
116. In 1998 Amazon claimed that the majority of its customers came to its site 'because of positive word-of-mouth' rather than advertising, but by the end of the year it was spending nearly a quarter of its revenues on advertising (Brandt 2011b: 10, 100). In 2000, however, it completely abandoned television advertising and by 2003 was relying on word of mouth and lower prices to attract customers to Amazon.com (Stone 2014: 128–9, 368 n. 12). But of course even this involved a costly emphasis on customer happiness and continuing to be 'obsessed with the customer experience' and 'to cater obsessively for its customers' (Stone 2014: 111, 355).
117. Cohen 2003: 101.
118. Cohen 2003: 101.
119. Cohen 2003: 100, 101.
120. Van Dijck 2013: 57.
121. Bunnell 2000: 161. In fact 'some 800 auction sites popped up between 1995 and 2000, many inspired by eBay's success' (ibid.: 161–2).
122. Cohen 2003: 101, emphasis added.
123. Bunnell 2000: 156–7.
124. Bunnell 2000: 157. Stone, too, ascribes the failure of Amazon Auctions to 'the dynamics of network effects' and notes that 'eBay already had an insurmountable advantage' (2010: 79–80).
125. Stone 2014: 262, 263.
126. Brandt 2011b: 140–1, 145.
127. Stone 2014: 231. Bezos believed that 'if Amazon didn't lead the world into the age of digital reading, then Apple or Google would' (ibid.: 234).
128. Stone 2014: 211; Brandt 2011b: 180.
129. Stone 2014: 211. Some two years after its July 2002 launch there were said to be 65,000 such 'developers' using Amazon Web Services (Brandt 2011b: 179).
130. Brandt 2011b: 182. Web Services enjoyed 'up to 23 percent operating margins compared to 5 percent in the rest of the business' (ibid.: 180–1). Its growth was so rapid that only two years later, in 2012, it was earning an estimated $2.2 billion in annual revenue (Stone 2014: 211). And by 2016 it was earning some $12 billion in annual revenue (see note 134).

131. Stone 2014: 293.
132. Whitman 2010: 260.
133. Stone 2014: 265.
134. Stone 2014: 354. By 2015, too, it would employ more than 120,000 people and would have more than 200 million customers (ibid.). A 2017 *Economist* article on 'Amazon's empire' noted that the firm's 'e-commerce site accounts for about 5% of retail spending in America, roughly half the share of Walmart, the biggest firm in the sector' (25–31 March 2017: 17). Presumably this figure of 5% included the third-party sellers who used Amazon as a platform and in 2016 paid it $23 billion in fees, as compared to the $12 billion Amazon was earning from its Web Services (ibid.: 18).
135. Stone 2014: 285, 286. Amazon was mentioned alongside Wal-Mart and Exxon as well as Apple and Google in a 2016 *Economist* article, 'The Rise of the Superstars', about the domination of the global economy by a small group of giant companies (17–23 September 2016: 3–16). Amazon had the group's sixth largest market capitalization, approaching $400 billion, and Apple was top of the group with a market capitalization of nearly $600 billion.
136. Brandt 2011a: 81–6.
137. Brandt 2011a: 86–7.
138. Brandt 2011a: 229–30.
139. An *Economist* article of 11 August 2015 about this new corporate structure was titled 'What's in a name?' and gave Page's explanation that the name Alphabet referred to 'one of humanity's most important innovations' and to buying stock that would be an 'alpha-bet' in the sense of outperforming the market.

Chapter 8

1. Armani 2015: 272d.
2. Armani 2015: 272d.
3. Armani 2015: 28k.
4. Roddick 2000: 14.
5. Agins 2000: 8–14. The fourth 'megatrend' was that 'top designers stopped gambling on fashion' as public companies, in particular, 'can't afford to gamble on fashion whims' (ibid.: 13–14). But fashion had become a 'gamble' only because of the megatrend changes in fashion preferences, which meant that customers could no longer be relied upon to follow the directions of designers and their publicists. Agins subtitled her book *How Marketing Changed the Clothing Business Forever* but the marketing changes were responding to earlier changes in preferences created by socioeconomic and cultural factors, such as the growing number of career women.
6. Agins 2000: 6, 7, 9.
7. Agins 2000: 8, emphases added.
8. Armani 2015: 28k–l.
9. Molho 2007: 53. She suggests that Armani began designing for the Hitman line in 1962 or 1963 but he mentions 1965 in his book (Molho 2007: 33, 39; Armani 2015: 28h).
10. Molho 2007: 60–1.

11. White 2000: 17, 19.
12. White 2000: 17, 19; Molho 2007: 63.
13. Armani 2015: 28m, 96a. He also refers to his designs being known for 'a certain sartorial androgyny' and notes that 'I invented the unstructured jacket for both men and women' (ibid.: 133a, 96c).
14. Armani 2015: 28k; Molho 2007: 69–71. Some idea of the difference in costs between the traditional haute couture production methods and Armani's manufactured ready-to-wear is that by the 2000s a haute couture suit started at $25,000 but a top-line Armani suit at only about $2,000 (Thomas 2008: 29; White 2000: 13).
15. Agins 2000: 131.
16. Fraser 1981: 91.
17. White 2000: 17, 24. She acknowledges that he had also 'recognized the shift in the socioeconomic position of women' as another opportunity (ibid.: 24).
18. Armani 2015: 28k, 400d.
19. Molho 2007: 65, 69; Thomas 2008: 115.
20. Molho 2007: 97. This was referring to his menswear as well as womenswear designs and indeed the previous year he had won two international menswear design awards (ibid.: 92–3).
21. Molho 2007: 65, 124–5.
22. Grove 1999: 65, 66.
23. Kapferer and Bastien 2012: 176–7, 305–8, and 309 discusses vertical and horizontal stretching, compares examples of the 'pyramid business model', and analyses the distinctive Armani pyramid.
24. Thomas 2008: 33.
25. Thomas 2008: 33.
26. The 'Armani power suit' had as dramatic an effect on menswear as on womenswear: its success 'would transfer the locus of tailored fashion southward from London to Milan' (Ball 2010: 87).
27. White 2000: 10.
28. White 2000: 13; Molho 2007: 81.
29. Armani 2015: 68d.
30. White 2000: 13.
31. Kapferer and Bastien 2012: 309.
32. Kapferer and Bastien 2012: 178. However, the glasses, cosmetics, and perfumes were licensed to other firms (ibid.: 191).
33. Kapferer and Bastien 2012: 178.
34. Armani 2015: 352a.
35. Ball 2010: 75.
36. Molho 2007: 93.
37. Kapferer and Bastien 2012: 178, 191.
38. Agins 2000: 136; White 2000: 22.
39. Molho 2007: 163, 264.
40. Molho 2007: 232. From 1994 to 2000 Brusone had been Armani's managing director and had supervised the 'gradual process of industrial acquisitions' (ibid.: 125, 215).

41. Molho 2007: 128, 214–15. In contrast to his out-sourcing in the 1970s–80s, 'all formal apparel was produced directly by Armani himself' by 2001 (ibid.: 215). This reversal was similar to what happened in the luxury company Louis Vuitton, where Arnault and Carcelle reversed the previous policy of out-sourcing. 'Carcelle pulled it all back in-house and increased the number of factories from five to fourteen' and Arnault explained that 'If you control your factories, you control your quality' (Thomas 2008: 51–2).
42. Molho 2007: 232.
43. White 1999: 10. She published a similar book on Armani in 2000.
44. White 1999: 15.
45. White 1999: 22. Turner simply declares that Versace 'sold sex and glamour' (1997: 35).
46. Molho 2007: 158–9.
47. Ball 2010: 118.
48. Ball 2010: 77.
49. Ball 2010: 190; Gastel 2008: 168.
50. Gastel 2008: 73–4.
51. White 1999: 17.
52. By 1995 'about 18 per cent of Versace's sales' were in North America (Gastel 2008: 204). Ball describes Versace's problems in the early 1980s with department-store retailers who 'felt that American women, just entering the workplace in force, wanted to be taken seriously; they wouldn't want to sport black leather biker jackets, peekaboo black lace gowns with beading applied like clusters of caviar, and skirts so short they were little more than belts' (Ball 2010: 85).
53. Ball 2010: 121.
54. Ball 2010: 121.
55. Ball 2010: 175.
56. Ball 2010: 175.
57. Versace depicted the exclusive Couture line as focused on 'daytime wear, on clothes dedicated to the active, successful working woman' (quoted by Gastel 2008: 117).
58. Gastel 2008: 122, 140. The Versus line was introduced in 1989, by when Donatella had become her brother's 'muse, sounding board and first assistant' (Ball 2010: 99). Furthermore, she performed the crucial role of keeping him on the novelty tread-mill: 'she wouldn't let him repeat himself or rest on the laurels of previously successful design ideas' (ibid.: 100).
59. Agins 2000: 14.
60. Ball 2010: 121, 176; Gastel 2008: 175–6, quoting a boutique-owner in Palermo.
61. Turner 1997: 53–4. She listed the diffusion lines as 'Versus, Istante, Versace Jeans Couture, Signature, Versace Sport, Versatile and Versace Classic V2' (ibid.: 54).
62. Turner 1997: 55–6.
63. Turner 1997: 54. There were also Versace watches (Gastel 2008: 47).
64. Turner 1997: 54. The homeware category encompassed 'everything from china, glass, quilts and cushions, vases, picture frames, lamps and tiles to furnishing

fabrics, beds, tables, and bath linen: a Versacian can furnish an entire home with Versace items' (ibid.).

65. His massive advertising in fashion and other magazines is described by White 1999: 20; Gastel 2008: 217–18; and Ball 2010: 143–4. His dramatic modernizing of fashion shows is described by Gastel 2008: 135–8. His creation and use of the 'supermodel' is extensively described by Turner, 1997: ch. 4 and Ball 2010: ch. 9. Versace's and Armani's use of celebrities is extensively described by Turner 1997: ch. 5; Ball 2010: ch. 8; Agins 2000: ch. 4; and Thomas 2008: ch. 4.

66. There seems to be some doubt or dispute about when the haute couture line was launched. According to Turner, the Atelier haute couture line was launched in 1989; Gastel mentions Atelier Versace haute couture debuting in Paris in January 1990; Ball, too, mentions a January 1990 haute couture show in Paris; and White refers to the 'atelier' line haute couture collection being introduced in 1993 (Turner 1997: 51; Gastel 2008: 142; Ball 2010: 116; White 1999: 21).

67. For example, menswear accounted for nearly half of Armani's clothing sales in 1997–8 (White 2000: 23). Versace presented separate menswear collections and clothing lines, as well as including menswear in a few of his diffusion lines, but his menswear designs were characterized by Turner as 'if not an acquired taste, aimed a niche market' (1997: 53).

68. Gastel 2008: 46; Ball 2010: 75.

69. Ball 2010: 76.

70. Gastel 2008: 108, 227; Turner 1997: 43. Ball, too, notes that by 1997 'Versace products sold in three hundred boutiques around the world, as well as four thousand department stores' (Ball 2010: 190).

71. Santo's business difficulties included (1) relying too much on licensing for sales growth in the 1990s, (2) problems with diffusion lines that were not clearly identified as Versace and were cannibalizing one another's sales, and (3) the cost of the firm's new strategy of owning rather than franchising its retail network, which meant opening its own stores and buying back franchises (Ball 2010: 176–7). Santo believed that going public would provide the funds to deal with such problems and he had won Gianni's approval for a planned IPO that would 'sell as much as 40 percent of the company to stock market investors' (ibid.: 190).

72. Agins 2000: 7.

73. Gastel 2008: 237, quoting Versace.

74. Ball 2010: 314.

75. Turner 1997: 47.

76. Agins 2000: 135–6.

77. Agins 2000: 136.

78. Molho 2007: 213.

79. White 2000: 18–19. The mid-1990s Versacian change led to sequinned hot-pants by 2000 but Armani 'explained this [change] as a reflection of socio-economic change, expressing the belief that women no longer need to "dress like a man to be taken seriously"' (ibid.: 18).

80. White 2000: 18.

81. Armani 2015: 400d.
82. Gastel 2008: 64, 119.
83. Gastel 2008: 174–5, 183, 216 and 221 quoting Versace.
84. Gastel 2008: 117, 247. There seems to be no comprehensive analysis of Versace's stylistic variations but there is enough descriptive material in Gastel's *The Versace Legend* to make a partial analysis of the 1987–97 collections. At least thirteen changes in style can be identified: (1) from Optical to mini-skirted Armanian jackets, (2) to targeted prints, (3) neo-Baroque, (4) sadomasochist, (5) country-style, (6) punk, (7) grunge, (8) space-galactic, (9) demure women, (10) Armanian, (11) white-out, (12) modern art, and (13) Ravenna mosaics.
85. Ball 2010: 245.
86. Thomas 2008: 50–4, 59–60, 66–7, 192; Agins 2000: 19–20, 41, 278.
87. One of the firm's business problems was Santo's continuing pursuit of his pre-1997 strategy of increasing the number of owned rather than franchised stores. 'He had tripled the number of Versace-controlled stores since Gianni's death, but the strategy . . . was a costly mistake, perhaps born from a refusal to accept that his sister's work would never sell well enough to support such a grand store network' (Ball 2010: 269).
88. Ball 2010: 219.
89. Ball 2010: 265.
90. Ball 2010: 292–5.
91. Davis 2011: 75, 79, 88.
92. Davis 2011: 75, 81–2, 90.
93. Ball points out that going public 'not only brought in a wave of fresh money, but [also] a company's stock options were juicy bait in recruiting talented executives,' as when Gucci went public in the mid-1990s and 'succeeded in attracting some of the best managers in the business' (Ball 2010: 240).
94. The Roddick biographies published by Alcraft in 1999 and by Paprocki in 2010 are brief accounts and were apparently aimed at what the libraries categorized as 'juvenile' readers. Jones's 2010 magisterial history of the beauty industry contains some material on Roddick but it is based largely on her *Body and Soul*.
95. Roddick 2000: 36.
96. Roddick 2000: 247.
97. Jones's history of the beauty industry defines it as 'including fragrances; hair and skin care products; sun care; color cosmetics, including make-up and other products for the face, eyes, lips, and nails; men's grooming products, including shaving creams; bath and shower products, including toilet soap; deodorants; oral care; and baby care' (2011: 9 n. 2).
98. Roddick 1991: 71.
99. Roddick 1991: 73. Roddick also lacked business training and experience. She had been trained as a teacher and her business experience was largely confined to having run a small hotel with her husband. In contrast, the famous American cosmetics entrepreneur, Mary Kay Ash, started her direct-sales cosmetics business after years of experience in the 1960s as national sales director for a large direct-sales company (Brands 1999: 249–50).

100. Roddick 1991: 73.
101. Roddick 1991: 73.
102. Roddick 2000: 37, emphasis added.
103. Roddick 1991: 82.
104. Jones 2011: 283, 285.
105. Roddick 1991: 92.
106. Jones 2011: 282.
107. Roddick 1991: 90, 230, 235–6.
108. Roddick 1991: 132.
109. Roddick 1991: 111–13. These green 'political' campaigns had begun in 1985 with a Greenpeace-linked Body Shop campaign against acid rain (ibid.: 111). A rather different approach was adopted by the 'green' clothing company Patagonia in California. In the mid-1980s it was making 'regular donations to smaller groups working to save or restore habitat' (Chouinard 2006: 61). It later adopted the idea of an environmental 'tax' that took the form of donating to these small groups an 'annual one percent of sales, or 10 percent of profits, whichever is greater' (Chouinard and Stanley 2012: 45).
110. Alcraft 1999: 50.
111. Roddick 2000: 14, emphasis added.
112. Roddick 1991: 131.
113. Jones 2011: 285.
114. Paprocki 2010: 62, 64.
115. Roddick 2000: 141.
116. Roddick 2000: 141. Roddick refers to the first B&BW being opened in 1990, not 1988, and being opened by 'retail mogul Leslie Wexner' rather than being founded by Limited Brands. Furthermore, Paprocki notes that when The Body Shop came to America, 'cosmetics company Estee Lauder *had* opened an environmentally conscious division called Origins, and The Limited, a clothing company, was *about to* open a line of stores called Bath & Body Works' (Paprocki 2010: 60–2, emphases added).
117. Roddick 2000: 141, 143–4, 154, 156 on marketing details, discounting, politics, humour, advertising, pricing promotions, and shopping malls.
118. Roddick 2000: 139, 141. In her earlier book she noted 'we managed to get twenty-three franchises open that first year [1990]. Another fifty-plus are scheduled to open in 1991, and probably double that number in 1992' (Roddick 1991: 139).
119. Roddick 2000: 151, 154. 'For every 100 customers, we were losing five' (ibid.: 154).
120. Roddick 2000: 154; Alcraft 1999: 38.
121. Roddick 2000: 157.
122. Roddick 2000: 67–70. This social audit included an environmental audit and an 'ethical' audit that assessed the social impact and behaviour of the firm in relation to its stakeholders, which included the communities in which it operated. Boyle cited Roddick and The Body Shop as an example of social auditing in *The Tyranny of Numbers* (Roddick 2001: 145). And indeed the social audit was another example of her moving away from rational business leadership, in this case from the method of quantitative calculation. In 2004 she and Boyle co-authored the brief

Numbers, which included criticism of management being 'done by numbers' and of modern life being 'reduced to numbers' (Boyle and Roddick 2004: 80, 82).

123. Roddick 2000: 244.
124. Roddick 2000: 253; Paprocki 2010: 76. An *Economist* article of 14 May 1998 described the co-chair positions as Roddick serving alongside Gordon as 'executive co-chairman' and it also declared that 'Ms Roddick deserves much of the blame for the decline' in the fortunes of the corporation, whose share price had fallen 'from a peak of 370 pence ($6.50) in 1992 to 111 pence in March' 1998.
125. Roddick 2000: 254, 259, 260 and 261.
126. Paprocki 2010: 76, 86.
127. Paprocki 2010: 89; Jones 2011: 330.

Appendix

1. See, for example, the extensive survey of theories and varieties of leadership presented by Bass and Bass 2008 or Northouse 2016.
2. Weber 1978: 108. Political rationalization, too, needed free competition as well as calculation, rules, and numbers (Brooker 2014: ch. 8). The rules included constitutions, electoral laws, legislative procedures, and the internal rules of political parties; the numbers included the voting figures and majorities in elections, parliaments, congresses, committees, and political parties. When combined with free competition, they produced the highest level of rationality in politics—modern democracy.
3. Weber 1978: 245.
4. Weber 1970: 138–9. Intellectualization was described by Weber in a speech titled 'Science as a Vocation' which he gave in 1918 and was published the following year.
5. Weber 1978: 1156. Although he described it here as the 'American' system of 'scientific management,' Weber referred to it as 'the Taylor system' in other rationalizing contexts in *Economy and Society*, such as the rational specialization and selection of workers on the basis of their personal aptitudes (ibid.: 150).
6. Kanigel 2005: 530.
7. Taylor's fundamental thesis was that the productivity of any system of production could be maximized by selecting and training workers so that 'at the fastest pace and with the maximum of efficiency' they could do the highest class of work for which their 'natural abilities' suited them (Taylor 1998: 2–3).
8. Taylor 1998: 16.
9. Weber 1978: 1150.
10. Burns 1978: 446, 446–7.
11. Howard 1984: 254–5.
12. Howard 1984: 254–5. A similar approach was shown by the commander of a British army in Burma in 1943 when he analysed the 'intellectual' foundations of morale. The soldier must be convinced that the objective is attainable, must be convinced that the organization is efficient and must have confidence in his leader—must be convinced that 'whatever dangers and hardships he is called upon to suffer, his life will not be lightly thrown away' (Slim 2009: 208).

13. Barnard stayed in that post until his retirement in 1947 but he also had a distinguished post-1938 career of public service as head of the wartime United Services Organizations, the Rockefeller Foundation charity, and the National Science Foundation (Scott 1992: ch. 4).

14. Scott 1992: ch. 5.

15. Williamson 1995: 172.

16. Scott 1992: 112–13 and 116–17. See also ibid.: 113, 117 on how the famous business book *In Search of Excellence* (Peters and Waterman 1982) pointed out that Barnard had discussed corporate culture and value-shaping more than forty years earlier.

17. Barnard 1968: 283.

18. Barnard 1968: 261, 279, 283 and see also 259 on 'creating faith'.

19. However, charismatic leadership may well be secular rather than religious, as in the case of military charismatic leadership. 'In primitive circumstances this peculiar kind of quality [charisma] is thought of as resting on magical powers, whether of prophets, persons with a reputation for therapeutic or legal wisdom, leaders in the hunt, or heroes in war' (Weber 1978: 241).

20. Weber 1978: 215.

21. Barnard 1968: 260. Presumably the superiority in skill and perception includes superiority in what Barnard had characterized earlier as 'executive' processes, namely the 'logical processes of analysis and the discrimination of the strategic factors' (ibid.: 233).

22. Barnard 1968: 236, emphasis added.

23. Barnard 1968: 173, 174.

24. Barnard 1968: 236, emphases added. The rational type of leadership that he is describing has similarities with what Northouse's recent leadership textbook refers to as the 'skills' approach, which is 'a leader-centered perspective that emphasizes the competencies of leaders' and has developed a 'capability' model of leadership (Northouse 2016: 47, 69). It also has similarities with what Northouse describes as the typical twenty-first-century perspective on defining leadership, 'whereby an individual influences a group of individuals to achieve a common goal' (ibid.: 4).

25. However, the purpose of this technical-rational leadership was not to inspire confidence but to perform the executive's adaptive function, which Barnard compared to that of 'the nervous system, including the brain, in relation to the rest of the body. It exists to maintain the bodily system by directing those actions which are necessary more effectively to adjust to the environment' (Barnard 1968: 217). For the survival of a formal organization depends upon its relationship with a 'continuously fluctuating environment' and upon the accompanying 'readjustment of processes internal to the organization' (ibid.: 6 and see also 35, 61).

26. Burns 1978: 20.

27. Burns 1978: 254.

28. Burns 1978: 20.

29. Burns 1978: 19, emphases added.

30. Burns 1978: 258. The reference to sellers and buyers is one reason why transactional leadership seems similar to the deliberative form of leadership discussed in Chapter 1. However, deliberative leadership's selling and buying of leads is not 'an

exchange of valued things' but instead the seller convincing the buyer that the lead *is* a valuable thing that is worth accepting and also is more valuable than any other lead being offered.

31. Burns 1978: 20.
32. Burns 1978: 258. There are also similarities between transactional leadership and Neustadt's 1960 theory of presidential power, which has been described as presenting 'an early example of an exchange theory of politics' (Brooker 2010: 141). The obvious similarity is with Neustadt's famous pair of maxims that presidential leaders' power 'is the power to persuade' and 'the power to persuade is the power to bargain' (Neustadt 1990: 11, 32).
33. Harris 2004: 13–14, quoting Berne's definition.
34. Harris 2004: 262–5.
35. Christensen 2000: ix.
36. This term is reminiscent of Schumpeter's famous concept of Creative Destruction, which described the revolutionary restructuring of industries that is caused by the introduction of new commodities, markets, methods of production, forms of organization, or sources of supply (Schumpeter 1974: 83, 68). However, Christensen's conception of disruptive technology is solely concerned with technologically new commodities and the new markets which they open up.
37. Christensen 2000: xv.
38. Christensen 2000: xv.
39. Christensen 2000: xv, 227.
40. Christensen 2000: x, xi and especially 108–9 on new entrants.
41. For 'the logical, competent decisions of management that are critical to the success of their companies are also the reasons why they lose their positions of leadership' when they face the challenge of disruptive technologies (Christensen 2000: xiii). In this situation, management decisions logically derived from listening to customers and tracking competitors' activities will not bring success if these customers and competitors prefer sustaining, not disruptive, technological innovations (ibid.: 98). In this situation, too, decisions logically aimed at designing and building higher-performance products that offer greater profit will not bring success if disruptive technologies underperform existing technologies, offer lower profit, and can be sold only in what *appear* to be insignificant markets, whose growth and profit opportunities have not yet been identified (ibid.).
42. Christensen 2000: xii, emphasis added. Steve Jobs apparently 'was deeply influenced' by Christensen's book and in a 2010 interview referred to 'what Clayton Christensen calls "the innovator's dilemma"' (Isaacson 2013: 376, 490).
43. Christensen 2000: xii–xiii.
44. Modern students of leadership have created a 'Mach' scale that measures 'the extent to which respondents subscribe to Machiavelli's dictums' and 'a high score on the Mach scale was seen as an indication of a predisposition to maximize self-interest using *deceit and manipulation* at the expense of others' (Bass and Bass 2008: 161, emphasis added).
45. Pocock 2003: 154, 167 and see ch. 6 on *The Prince*. Machiavelli's 'great originality is that of a student of delegitimized politics' in an era where legitimacy is still based

on tradition rather than rational-legal sources and where charismatic legitimacy is problematic: 'the new prince can outshine the hereditary and evoke more loyalty; his *virtu*—functioning where rational and traditional authority are both absent—is a kind of charisma' (ibid.: 163, 179). The great originality of Machiavelli's thinking is also pointed out in Isaiah Berlin's landmark essay 'The Originality of Machiavelli', which highlights Machiavelli's distinction between Christian-private morality and classical-public morality (Berlin 2013: 299–324).

46. Pocock 2003: 178–9.
47. Machiavelli 2012: 85–6.
48. Machiavelli 2012: 86.
49. Machiavelli 2012: 61. Machiavelli's famous analogy with the fox and the lion was borrowed from the Roman writer Cicero, who had written that the use of force and fraud reduces men to the level of beasts, respectively the lion and the fox (Skinner 2012: xix–xx).
50. This similarity in form is very different from the 'similarity' of actually applying Machiavelli to modern times, which many theorists have attempted. During the First World War, Pareto published a theory of political elites with an updated version of Machiavelli's contrast of fox-like cunning and lion-like forcefulness (Parry 1971: 47, 60–1). Nearly thirty years later, Burnham's famous *The Machiavellians* described Pareto as well as Mosca, Sorel and Michels as 'modern Machiavellians' (Burnham 1987). In the twenty-first century, too, Ledeen presented Machiavelli's ideas as still relevant for leaders in politics and other fields, Morris updated *The Prince* for twenty-first-century politics and, more recently, Lisch applied Machiavelli's ideas to modern business management (Ledeen 2000; Morris 2000; Lisch 2012).
51. Machiavelli 2012: 87.
52. Brooker 2009.
53. The three methods were (1) a threatened-coup or actual-coup form of military intervention, (2) a local or central form of threatened/actual coup, and (3) a factional or corporate form of threatened/actual coup (Brooker 2009: 92–3).
54. Weber 2001: 103.
55. Weber 2001: 103. Franklin was a former apprentice-printer who had acquired a printing business, a publishing house and a newspaper before he retired from business at the age of forty-two in order to pursue his political, scientific and other interests (Isaacson 2004: 126–8).
56. Weber 2001: 14–16, 138 n. 2. Franklin also wrote an autobiography and one of its stated aims was 'to provide some useful hints about how he succeeded' in the hope 'that others might find them suitable to be imitated' (Isaacson 2004: 255). It is surprising that Weber did not use the autobiography as evidence but this was only one of several ways in which his application of the methodology could have been improved: he did not provide a wide range of representative writings; he did not provide an in-depth description of them, apart from the Franklin writings; and he did not offer much in the way of comparison.

References

Agins, T. (2000) *The End of Fashion: How Marketing Changed the Clothing Business Forever* (New York: HarperCollins).

Alcraft, R. (1999) *Anita Roddick* (Oxford: Heinemann).

Allison, G. (1971) *Essence of Decision: Explaining the Cuban Missile Crisis* (Boston, MA: Little, Brown).

Allison, G. (2007) 'Institution Builder' in M. J. Dickinson and E. A. Neustadt (eds.) *Guardian of the Presidency: The Legacy of Richard E. Neustadt* (Washington DC: Brookings Institute).

Armani, G. (2015) *Giorgio Armani* (New York: Rizzoli International Publications).

Ball, D. (2010) *House of Versace: The Untold Story of Genius, Murder and Survival* (New York: Three Rivers Press).

Barber, B. R. (2001 [1995]) *Jihad vs. McWorld* (New York: Ballantine Books).

Barnard, C. I. (1968 [1938]) *The Functions of the Executive* (Cambridge, MA: Harvard University Press).

Bass, B. M. and Bass, R. (2008) *The Bass Handbook of Leadership: Theory, Research and Managerial Applications* (New York: Free Press).

Beahm, G. (2012) *The Boy Billionaire: Mark Zuckerberg in his Own Words* (Chicago: Agate).

Becraft, M. B. (2014) *Bill Gates: A Biography* (Santa Barbara, CA: Greenwood).

Berg, N. and Roberts, B. (2012) *Walmart* (London: Kogan Page).

Bergerud, E. M. (2000) *Fire in the Sky: The Air War in the South Pacific* (Boulder, CO: Westview).

Berlin, I. (2013 [1972]) 'The Originality of Machiavelli' in I. Berlin, *The Proper Study of Mankind: An Anthology of Essays* (London: Vintage).

Berlin, L. (2005) *The Man Behind the Microchip: Robert Noyce and the Invention of Silicon Valley* (New York: Oxford University Press).

Beynon, H. (1984) *Working for Ford* (Harmondsworth, UK: Penguin).

Bilton, N. (2013) *Hatching Twitter* (New York: Portfolio).

Bowen, H. K., Clark, K. B., Holloway, C. A. and Wheelwright, S. C. (eds.) (1994) *The Perpetual Enterprise Machine* (New York: Oxford University Press).

Boyle, D. (2001) *The Tyranny of Numbers: Why Counting Can't Make Us Happy* (London: Flamingo).

Boyle, D. and Roddick, A. (2004) *Numbers* (Chichester, UK: Anita Roddick Publications).

Brands, H. W. (1999) *Masters of Enterprise: Giants of American Business* (New York: The Free Press).

References

Brandt, R. L. (2011a) *The Google Guys* (London: Portfolio Penguin).

Brandt, R. L. (2011b) *One Click: Jeff Bezos and the Rise of Amazon.com* (London: Portfolio Penguin).

Brooker, P. (1991) *The Faces of Fraternalism: Nazi Germany, Fascist Italy, and Imperial Japan* (Oxford: Oxford University Press).

Brooker, P. (2009) *Non-Democratic Regimes* (Basingstoke, UK: Palgrave).

Brooker, P. (2010) *Leadership in Democracy* (Basingstoke, UK: Palgrave).

Brooker, P. (2014) *Non-Democratic Regimes* (Basingstoke, UK: Palgrave).

Bunnell D. with Luecke, R. A. (2000) *The eBay Phenomenon* (New York: John Wiley and Sons).

Burgelman, R. A., McKinney, W. and Meza, P. E. (2017) *Becoming Hewlett Packard: Why Strategic Leadership Matters* (New York: Oxford University Press).

Burnham, J. (1987 [1943]) *The Machiavellians: Defenders of Freedom* (Washington DC: Gateway).

Burns, J. M. (1978) *Leadership* (New York: Harper and Row).

Carlier, C. and Berger, L. (1996) *Dassault: The Corporation* (Paris: Editions du Chene).

Chandler, A. D. (1990 [1962]) *Strategy and Structure: Chapters in the History of the American Industrial Enterprise* (Cambridge, MA: MIT Press).

Chang, S.-J. (2008) *Sony vs. Samsung* (Singapore: Wiley).

Chernow, R. (1998) *Titan: The Life of John D. Rockefeller, Sr* (New York: Vintage Books).

Chouinard, Y. (2004) *Let My People Go Surfing: The Education of a Reluctant Businessman* (New York: Penguin).

Chouinard, Y. and Stanley, V. (2012) *The Responsible Company: What We Have Learned from Patagonia's First 40 Years* (Ventura, CA: Patagonia).

Christensen, C. M. (2000) *The Innovator's Dilemma* (Boston, MA: Harvard Business Review Press).

Clausewitz von, C. (1984 [1832]) *On War* (Princeton, NJ: Princeton University Press).

Cohen, A. (2003) *The Perfect Store: Inside eBay* (New York: Back Bay).

Cohen, E. A. and Gooch, J. (2006) *Military Misfortunes: The Anatomy of Failure in War* (New York: Free Press).

Cole, R. E. (1979) *Work, Mobility, and Participation* (Berkeley, CA: University of California Press).

Cole, R. E. (1989) *Strategies for Learning: Small-Group Activities in American, Japanese and Swedish Industry* (Berkeley, CA: University of California Press).

Cringely, R. X. (1996) *Accidental Empires* (New York: HarperCollins).

Curcio, V. (2013) *Henry Ford* (New York: Oxford University Press).

Cusumano, M. A. (1985) *The Japanese Automobile Industry* (Cambridge, MA: Harvard University Press).

Dassault, M. (1971) *The Talisman: The Autobiography of Marcel Dassault* (New Rochelle, NY: Arlington House).

Davis, D. K. (2011) *Versace* (New York: Chelsea House).

Dickinson, M. J. (2007) 'Practicum on the Presidency, 1946 to 1953' in M. J. Dickinson and E. A. Neustadt (eds.) *Guardian of the Presidency: The Legacy of Richard E. Neustadt* (Washington DC: Brookings Institute).

Drucker, P. F. (1993 [1946]) *Concept of the Corporation* (New Brunswick, NJ: Transaction).

Drucker, P. F. (2006 [1954]) *The Practice of Management* (New York: Harper).

Drucker, P. F. (2007 [1985]) *Innovation and Entrepreneurship: Practice and Principles* (Oxford: Elsevier).

Emiliani, B. (2013) 'Ohno's Insights on Human Nature' in *Taiichi Ohno's Workplace Management* (New York: McGraw-Hill).

Farber, D. (2004) *Sloan Rules: Alfred P. Sloan and the Triumph of General Motors* (Chicago: University of Chicago Press).

Fishman, C. (2011) *The Wal-Mart Effect* (London: Penguin).

Fraser, K. (1981) *The Fashionable Mind: Reflections on Fashion 1970–1981* (New York: Alfred A. Knopf).

Fujimoto, T. (1999) *The Evolution of a Manufacturing System at Toyota* (New York: Oxford University Press).

Gastel, M. (2008) *The Versace Legend* (Milan: Baldini Castoldi Dalai).

George, A. I. (1972) 'The Case for Multiple Advocacy in Making Foreign Policy', *American Political Science Review*, 66/3, 751–85.

Gould, S. J. (2002) *The Structure of Evolutionary Theory* (Cambridge, MA: Harvard University Press).

Grove, A. S. (1999) *Only the Paranoid Survive* (New York: Crown).

Harris, T. A. (2004 [1967]) *I'm OK—You're OK* (New York: HarperCollins).

Hoopes, J. (2006) 'Growth Through Knowledge: Wal-Mart, High Technology, and the Ever Less Visible Hand of the Manager' in N. Lichtenstein (ed.) *Wal-Mart: The Face of Twenty-First Century Capitalism* (New York: The New Press).

Horvitz, L. A. (2006) *Meg Whitman: President and CEO of eBay* (New York: Ferguson).

House, C. H. and Price, R. L. (2009) *The HP Phenomenon: Innovation and Business Transformation* (Stanford, CA: Stanford University Press).

Howard, M. (1984) *The Causes of Wars* (London: Unwin).

Huff, D. (1954) *How to Lie with Statistics* (London: Gollancz).

Isaacson, W. (2004) *Benjamin Franklin: An American Life* (New York: Simon & Schuster).

Isaacson, W. (2013) *Steve Jobs* (London: Little, Brown).

Jackson, T. (1998) *Inside Intel: Andy Grove and the Rise of the World's Most Powerful Chip Company* (New York: Plume).

Jones, G. (2011) *Beauty Imagined: A History of the Global Beauty Industry* (New York: Oxford University Press).

Kanigel, R. (2005) *The One Best Way: Frederick Winslow Taylor and the Enigma of Efficiency* (Cambridge, MA: MIT Press).

Kapferer, J. N. and Bastien, V. (2012) *The Luxury Strategy: Break the Rules of Marketing to Build Luxury Brands* (London: Kogan Page).

Khurana, R. (2002) *Searching for a Corporate Savior: The Irrational Quest for Charismatic CEOs* (Princeton, NJ: Princeton University Press).

Kirkpatrick, D. (2011) *The Facebook Effect* (New York: Simon & Schuster).

Knight, F. H. (2014 [1921]) *Risk, Uncertainty and Profit* (Mansfield Centre, CT: Martino).

Kroc, R. with Anderson, R. (1987) *Grinding It Out: The Making of McDonald's* (New York: St Martin's).

Ledeen, M. A. (2000) *Machiavelli on Modern Leadership* (New York: St Martin's Griffin).

Lee, S. W. (2011) *The Legacy of Steve Jobs: 92 Inspirational Quotes of Steve Jobs* (Seattle, Washington: Create Space Independent Publishing Platform).

Leidner, R. (1993) *Fast Food, Fast Talk: Service Work and the Routinization of Everyday Life* (Berkeley, CA: University of California Press).

Lichtenstein, N. (2006) 'Wal-Mart: A Template for Twenty-First Century Capitalism' in N. Lichtenstein (ed.) *Wal-Mart: The Face of Twenty-First-Century Capitalism* (New York: The New Press).

Lichtenstein, N. (2010) *The Retail Revolution: How Wal-Mart Created a Brave New World of Business* (New York: Picador).

Lisch, R. (2012) *Ancient Wisdom for Modern Management: Machiavelli at 500* (Farnham, UK: Gower).

Love, J. F. (1995) *McDonald's: Behind the Arches* (New York: Bantam).

Machiavelli, N. (2012 [1532]) *The Prince* (Cambridge: Cambridge University Press).

Malone, M. S. (2007) *Bill & Dave: How Hewlett and Packard Built the World's Greatest Company* (New York: Portfolio).

Malone, M. S. (2014) *The Intel Trinity: How Robert Noyce, Gordon Moore, and Andy Grove Built the World's Most Important Company* (New York: HarperCollins).

Marder, A. J. (2015 [1974]) *From the Dardanelles to Oran: Studies of the Royal Navy in War and Peace* (Barnsley, UK: Seaforth).

McCraw, T. K. (2007) *Prophet of Innovation: Joseph Schumpeter and Creative Destruction* (Cambridge, MA: Harvard University Press).

McDonald, J. (2003) *A Ghost's Memoir: The Making of Alfred P. Sloan's 'My Years with General Motors'* (Cambridge, MA: MIT Press).

Michell, T. (2010) *Samsung Electronics and the Struggle for Leadership of the Electronics Industry* (Singapore: Wiley).

Miller, J. (2013) 'Seeking What Taiichi Ohno Sought' in *Taiichi Ohno's Workplace Management* (New York: McGraw Hill).

Molho, R. (2007) *Being Armani* (Milan: Baldini Castoldi Dalai).

Moreton, B. E. (2006) 'It Came from Bentonville: The Agrarian Origins of Wal-Mart Culture' in N. Lichtenstein (ed.) *Wal-Mart: The Face of Twenty-First Century Capitalism* (New York: The New Press).

Moreton, B. (2009) *To Serve God and Wal-Mart: The Making of Christian Free Enterprise* (Cambridge, MA: Harvard University Press).

Morris, D. (2000) *The New Prince: Machiavelli Updated for the Twenty-First Century* (New York: Renaissance Books).

Napoli, L. (2016) *Ray & Joan: The Man Who Made the McDonald's Fortune and the Woman Who Gave It All Away* (New York: Dutton).

Neustadt, R. E. (1990 [1960]) *Presidential Power and the Modern Presidents* (New York: The Free Press).

Northouse, P. G. (2016) *Leadership: Theory and Practice* (Los Angeles: Sage).

O'Boyle, T. F. (1999) *At Any Cost: Jack Welch, General Electric, and the Pursuit of Profit* (New York: Vintage).

Ohno, T. (1988) *Toyota Production System: Beyond Large-Scale Production* (Boca Raton, FL: CRC Press).

Ohnuki-Tierney, E. (2006) 'McDonald's in Japan: Changing Manners and Etiquette' in J. L. Watson (ed.) *Golden Arches East: McDonald's in East Asia* (Stanford, CA: Stanford University Press).

Ortega, B. (1999) *In Sam We Trust: The Untold Story of Sam Walton and How Wal-Mart is Devouring the World* (London: Kogan Page).

Packard, D. (2005 [1995]) *The HP Way: How Bill Hewlett and I Built Our Company* (New York: HarperCollins).

Paprocki, S. B. (2010) *Anita Roddick: Entrepreneur* (New York: Chelsea House).

Parry, G. (1971) *Political Elites* (London: George Allen & Unwin).

Pelfrey, W. (2006) *Billy, Alfred, and General Motors* (New York: AMACOM).

Peters, T. J. and Waterman, R. H. (1982) *In Search of Excellence* (New York: Harper and Row).

Pocock, J. G. A. (2003 [1975]) *The Machiavellian Moment: Florentine Political Thought and the Atlantic Republican Tradition* (Princeton, NJ: Princeton University Press).

Ritzer, G. (1996 [1993]) *The McDonaldization of Society* (Thousand Oaks, CA: Pine Forge Press).

Roddick, A. (1991) *Body and Soul: Profits with Principles—The Amazing Success Story of Anita Roddick & The Body Shop* (New York: Crown Publishers).

Roddick, A. (2000) *Business as Unusual* (London: Thorsons).

Sandberg, S. with Scovell, N. (2013) *Lean In: Women, Work, and the Will to Lead* (New York: Alfred A. Knopf).

Schumpeter, J. A. (1961 [1934]) *The Theory of Economic Development* (New York: Oxford University Press).

Schumpeter, J. A. (1974 [1947]) *Capitalism, Socialism and Democracy* (London: Allen and Unwin).

Schumpeter, J. A. (1989 [1947]) 'The Creative Response in Economic History', in J. A. Schumpeter, *Essays on Entrepreneurs, Innovations, Business Cycles and the Evolution of Capitalism* (New Brunswick NJ: Transaction Publishers).

Scott, W. G. (1992) *Chester I. Barnard and the Guardians of the Managerial State* (Kansas: University Press of Kansas).

Shapley, D. (1993) *Promise and Power: The Life and Times of Robert McNamara* (Boston: Little, Brown).

Shimokawa, K. and Fujimoto, T. (2009) *The Birth of Lean* (Cambridge, MA: Lean Enterprise Institute).

Skinner, Q. (2012) 'Introduction' in *The Prince* (Cambridge: Cambridge University Press).

Slater, R. (2003) *The Wal-Mart Decade: How a New Generation of Leaders Turned Sam Walton's Legacy into the World's #1 Company* (New York: Portfolio).

Sloan, A. P. (1990 [1964]) *My Years with General Motors* (New York: Doubleday).

Slim, W. J. (2009 [1956]) *Defeat into Victory* (London: Pan Macmillan).

Snow, R. (2014) *I Invented the Modern Age: The Rise of Henry Ford* (New York: Scribner).

Soderquist, D. (2005) *The Wal-Mart Way* (Nashville: Nelson).

Stone, B. (2014) *The Everything Store: Jeff Bezos and the Age of Amazon* (New York: Back Bay Books).

Strasser, S. (2006) 'Woolworth to Wal-Mart: Mass Merchandising and the Changing Culture of Consumption' in N. Lichtenstein (ed.) *Wal-Mart: The Face of Twenty-First Century Capitalism* (New York: The New Press).

Strauss, L. (1972) 'Plato' in L. Strauss and J. Cropsey (eds.) *History of Political Philosophy* (Chicago: Rand McNally).

References

Strayer, J. R. (2005 [1970]) *On the Medieval Origins of the Modern State* (Princeton NJ: Princeton University Press).

Streeck, W. (1996) 'Lean Production in the German Automobile Industry: A Test Case for Convergence Theory' in S. Berger and R. Dore (eds.) *National Diversity and Global Capitalism* (Ithaca, NJ: Cornell University Press).

Taylor, F. W. (1998 [1911]) *The Principles of Scientific Management* (Mineola, NY: Dover).

Tedlow, R. S. (2003) *Giants of Enterprise: Seven Business Innovators and the Empires They Built* (New York: HarperCollins).

Tedlow, R. S. (2007) *Andy Grove: The Life and Times of an American Business Icon* (New York: Portfolio).

Thackray, A., Brock, D. C. and Jones, R. (2015) *Moore's Law: The Life of Gordon Moore, Silicon Valley's Quiet Revolutionary* (New York: Basic Books).

Thomas, D. (2008) *Deluxe: How Luxury Lost its Luster* (New York: Penguin).

Thorndike, W. N. (2012) *The Outsiders: Eight Unconventional CEOs and Their Radically Rational Blueprint for Success* (Boston, MA: Harvard Business Review Press).

Togo, Y. and Wartman, W. (1993) *Against All Odds: The Story of the Toyota Corporation and the Family That Created It* (New York: St. Martin's Press).

Toyoda, E. (1987) *Toyota: Fifty Years in Motion* (Tokyo and New York: Kodansha International).

Toyota company history (1988) *Toyota: A History of the First 50 Years* (Toyota City, Japan: Toyota Motor Corporation).

Trimble, V. H. (1990) *Sam Walton: The Inside Story of America's Richest Man* (New York: Dutton).

Turner, L. (1997) *Gianni Versace: Fashion's Last Emperor* (London: Essential).

Van Dijck, J. (2013) *The Culture of Connectivity: A Critical History of Social Media* (New York: Oxford University Press).

Vance, S. S. and Scott, R. V. (1994) *Wal-Mart: A History of Sam Walton's Retail Phenomenon* (New York: Twayne).

Viegas, J. (2007) *Pierre Omidyar: The Founder of eBay* (New York: Rosen).

Villette, M. and Vuillermot, C. (2009) *From Predators to Icons: Exposing the Myth of the Business Hero* (Ithaca, NJ: Cornell University Press).

Wada, K. and Yui, T. (2002) *Courage and Change: The Life of Kiichiro Toyoda* (Toyota City, Japan: Toyota Motor Corporation).

Wallace, J. and Erickson, J. (1993) *Hard Drive: Bill Gates and the Making of the Microsoft Empire* (Chichester, UK: John Wiley & Sons).

Walton, S. with Huey, J. (1993) *Sam Walton: Made in America, My Story* (New York: Bantam).

Waterton, W. A. (2012 [1956]) *The Quick and the Dead: The Perils of Post-War Test Flying* (London: Grub Street).

Watson, J. L. (2006) 'Introduction' in J. L. Watson (ed.) *Golden Arches East: McDonald's in East Asia* (Stanford, CA: Stanford University Press).

Weber, M. (1970 [1919]) 'Science as a Vocation' in H. H. Gerth and C. Wright Mills (eds.) *From Max Weber: Essays in Sociology* (London: Routledge & Kegan Paul).

Weber, M. (1978 [1922]) *Economy and Society* (Berkeley, CA: University of California Press).

Weber, M. (2001 [1904–5]) *The Protestant Ethic and the Spirit of Capitalism* (London: Routledge).

Welch, J. with Byrne, J. A. (2003) *Straight From the Gut* (London: Headline).

White, N. (1999) *Versace* (London: Carlton).

White, N. (2000) *Giorgio Armani* (London: Carlton).

Whitman, M. with Hamilton, J. (2010) *The Power of Many: Values for Success in Business and in Life* (New York: Three Rivers Press).

Whyte, W. H. (1961 [1956]) *The Organization Man* (Harmondsworth, UK: Penguin).

Williamson, O. E. (1995) 'Chester Barnard and the Incipient Science of Organization', in O. E. Williamson (ed.) *Organization Theory: From Chester Barnard to the Present and Beyond* (New York: Oxford University Press).

Womack, J. P., Jones, D. T. and Roos, D. (1991) *The Machine that Changed the World: The Story of Lean Production* (New York: Harper Collins).

Yan, Y. (2006) 'McDonald's in Beijing' in J. L. Watson (ed.) *Golden Arches East: McDonald's in East Asia* (Stanford, CA: Stanford University Press).

Young, J. S. and Simon, W. L. (2005) *iCon: Steve Jobs, the Greatest Second Act in the History of Business* (Hoboken, NJ: Wiley).

Index

accounting 4, 23, 34, 36, 177
  see also quantitative calculation
acquisitions
  eBay 137, 138
  Hewlett-Packard 120
  Intel 115
  Wal-Mart 13, 94
activism 150, 167–8
adaptation
  business definition of 6–8
  combining rapid and innovative
    adaptation 63–4, 81, 149, 151, 154
  globalized adaptability 6–8
  Grove's three-stage adaptive framework
    111–16
  resistance to 7, 106–7, 108
  see also innovative adaptation; rapid
    adaptation
adaptive crises
  Grove 104–5, 106–9, 110, 111, 112–14, 171
  Hewlett-Packard 121
  Whitman 133
advertising
  Amazon 144
  eBay 136
  Facebook 10–11
  Ford 34, 36
  General Motors 27
  McDonald's 67, 68, 69, 74
  quantitative assessment of 4
  Versace 160
  see also marketing
African Americans 57–8
Agins, T. 150, 152, 159, 162
Alphabet Inc. 147
  see also Google
Amazon 122, 126, 128
  Amazon Auctions 142, 145
  competition with eBay 138, 140
  eBayism versus Amazonism 141–7
  Kindle 123, 145–6
  Marketplace 143, 145
  Web Services 146
  zShops 142
  see also Bezos

Anderson, R. 62
Apple 105, 110, 115, 122–4, 145–6, 147
  see also Jobs
'appropriate rational means' 1–3, 12, 141, 148,
    170, 173
  Barnard 176, 180
  Christensen 182, 183
appropriate rational methods
  appropriate for developing corporations 2–3
  basis of corporation-developing version of
    rational leadership 1–3
  set of six appropriate rational methods 2–3
  seventh appropriate rational method:
    learning 79, 95, 171–2
  three pairs of appropriate rational
    methods 2–3
    (a) adaptive: rapid and innovative 6–8
    (b) calculative: quantitative and
      strategic 4–6
    (c) deliberative: diverse and
      institutionalized 8–10
  see also emphasizing particular methods;
    non-rational methods; selecting
    appropriate method
ARM 115
Armani, Giorgio 15, 148–61, 172
  adaptation in artistic industries 148
  adapting stylistically to new times 150–2
  androgynous style? 151–2
  combining rapid and innovative
    adaptation 149, 151, 154
  establishes own firm 152
  fashion's 1970s–90s new times 150–1
  organizationally adapting 153–4,
    155–6
  photographical autobiography 148
  private company 154, 156
  product pyramid 154–5
  see also Versace, Gianni
Arnault, Bernard 164
assessment 4
  Ford 36
  Sloan 19, 23–4, 25
Auction Web 129–31
  see also eBay

Index

Australia 137, 161
authoritative leadership 9–10
authority 29–30, 180
autobiographical material, use of 3, 14, 185
  see also leader's-eye view
automation 62, 83

Ball, D. 158–9, 163, 164
Barnard, Chester 1, 176, 178, 179–81, 183
Bath & Body Works (B&BW) 168
beauty industry 165–9
Berg, N. 93
Berne, Eric 182
Beynon, H. 58
Bezos, Jeff 2, 122, 123, 128, 140, 146–7
  comparison with Whitman 128, 140–1, 146–7
  establishes Amazon 140
  opportunity 141, 145–6, 147
  rational methods 140, 143, 145–6
  scaling-up and diversifying 142–7
  see also Amazon; eBayism versus Amazonism
'bias for action' 132
boards of directors 9
  eBay 134
  General Motors 30–1
  Hewlett-Packard 134–5
  Toyota 44
  Wal-Mart 91, 94
The Body Shop 15, 149–50, 165–9, 172
Brandt, R. L. 125
brand value 4
Brin, Sergey 72, 122, 125, 147
Britain 76, 137, 149, 165, 167, 168
Brooker, P. 182
Brown, Donaldson 23, 68, 70, 80
Bunnell, D. 129, 143, 145
bureaucratic politics 8
Burgelman, R. A. 120, 121–2
Burns, J. M. 175, 178, 181–2

calculation *see* quantitative calculation;
    strategic calculation
capability 149
capitalism 177, 185
career women 150–2, 158
celebrities 160
centralization
  Apple 122
  Ford 33–4
  General Motors 19–20, 21–2, 23, 31
  McDonald's 65, 66, 67
Chandler, Alfred 4, 18, 19, 21, 23, 28
change
  car industry 35
  economic 6, 24
  innovative response to 7
  Sloan 18

'10×' change 104, 111, 153
  Walton 92
charisma 12, 155, 163
charismatic leadership 12, 167–8, 175, 176, 179
child-based marketing 77–8
China 76, 77–8, 137
Christensen, C. M. 4–5, 7, 13, 175, 182–3
Chrysler 46
Clairol 167
Clausewitz, Carl von 5–6, 13
cleanliness 69–70
Clinton, Hillary 91
Cohen, A. 126, 130, 132, 134, 136–7, 144–5
Cole, R. E. 48, 58
collectibles 136–7, 138
collegiality 28, 30
committees 10
  General Motors 9, 19, 21, 28–32, 74
  McDonald's 74
  Wal-Mart 90, 94
communication with employees 113–14
company cheer 89, 97
competition
  adaptation to local 78
  Amazon 143–4
  American versus Japanese cars 59–60
  The Body Shop 168
  copying from competitors 97
  eBay 140, 145
  fashion industry 164
  General Motors 26
  Intel 110
  McDonald's 67
  six forces 110–11
  'treadmill' strategy 110
  Wal-Mart 88, 90, 97
competitive advantage
  Armani 150
  Auction Web 129
  The Body Shop 166, 167
  General Motors 27
  network effects 145
  Toyota 48, 60
  Wal-Mart 86, 87
computers 3
  disruptive technologies 182
  Hewlett-Packard 119, 120, 121, 135
  Intel 106, 108–9, 111, 115, 116
confidence *see* rational leadership
conformity 32, 33
consensus 30
consumer democracy 89
consumerism 159
continuous-flow innovations 43, 47, 49, 50, 52
controls
  Ford 36
  General Motors 24, 25, 56–7, 67, 70–1

Walton 88
see also quality control
cooperation 52
corporate culture *see* organizational culture
corporation-developing version of rational
 leadership 1–3
 capably using appropriate rational
  methods 1, 3, 15, 170
 employee-followers inspired with rational
  confidence 1, 12, 14
 Grove 104
 Kroc 63
 Ohno 39
 Roddick 'an exception that proves the rule'
  149, 165
 Sloan 17
 special case of Armani 148
 Walton 79
 Whitman 126
 see also appropriate rational methods;
  employee-followers
corporation development *see* enhancing;
 establishing
cosmetics 165–9
cost controls 88
cost reduction
 Toyota 56
 Walton 80, 86, 87–8, 90, 93
creativity
 Hewlett-Packard 117, 118
 McDonald's 67
 Sloan 32
 Versace 163, 164
crisis management 104, 108, 109, 133
culture
 Barnard 179
 eBay 139
 Facebook 11
 Japan 51
 McDonald's 69
 Wal-Mart 85
 see also organizational culture
customers
 Amazon 142, 144
 Armani 162
 changes in preferences 27, 35, 111,
  151–2, 155
 eBay's Voice of the Customer
  programme 133
 green preferences 166
customer service 70
Cusumano, M. A. 46, 47, 50–2, 55, 56, 58, 59

Dassault Aviation 15, 81, 98–102
Dassault, Marcel 2, 15, 81, 98–102, 104
 autobiography *The Talisman* 98
 dual leadership 102

establishes Dassault Aviation 98, 99
learning 98–101
see also Dassault Aviation
decentralization
 General Motors 3, 18, 19–20, 23, 33
 Google 124–5
 Hewlett-Packard 105, 118, 120–1, 124
 McDonald's 66, 67, 73
decision making
 eBay 133, 134
 General Motors 28–9, 30
 McDonald's 73, 74
deliberation *see* diverse deliberation;
 institutionalized deliberation; policy
 deliberation; product deliberation
deliberative leadership 9–10, 13, 182
demand
 forecasting 24
 General Motors 35
 Toyotaism versus Fordism 58
 Wal-Mart 82
Deming, W. E. 48–9
'diffusion' fashion lines 159–60, 161,
 163, 164
discount retailing 80, 81–2, 84–5, 87–8, 90,
 91, 96
disruptive technologies 4–5, 7–8, 153, 182–3
distribution 81, 82–3, 87
diverse deliberation 1, 2–3, 4, 8, 13, 185
 conformist pressures 32
 Grove 113, 171
 Ishida 44–5
 Kroc 61–2, 63, 71–2, 75, 171
 reticence factor 8, 11, 32, 71, 91, 134
 Sandberg 10–12
 Sloan 28, 31
 Toyota 38
 Walton 80–1, 90–2, 93
 Whitman 133–4
diversification
 Amazon 143
 Apple 122–3
 Armani 154
 eBay 137, 139, 143, 146
 Hewlett-Packard 118–19, 120, 121–2, 124
 Intel 105, 115–16
diversity 71, 72, 91
division of labour 15–16, 72–3, 92, 125
divisions, operating
 General Motors 3, 18, 19, 21–3, 25–6, 31
 Hewlett-Packard 118–19, 120–1, 122
 see also organizational structure
downsizing 108
Drucker, Peter 2, 6–7, 13, 18, 23, 34, 125
dual-leadership teams 15–16, 172
 Armani 154
 The Body Shop 167

dual-leadership teams (*cont.*)
  Dassault Aviation 102
  Facebook 10
  General Motors 21
  Hewlett-Packard 117, 120
  innovation-introducing 16, 21, 37, 38–9, 40,
    44, 46, 72, 172
  Intel 103, 106
  McDonald's 71, 72–3
  Ohno 37
  Toyota 38–9, 40, 44, 45, 46
  two-generation 16, 92, 172
  two-role 15–16, 72–3, 103, 154, 161
  Versace 161
  Wal-Mart 92
  see also triple leadership teams
Du Pont, Pierre 21, 24–5, 44
Durant, William 20–1, 22, 28–9

'early-mover' strategy 112–13
eBay 15, 122, 126–47
  adaptation 132–3
  Café 130
  calculation 135–9
  deliberation 133–4
  early development 129–32
  eBayism versus Amazonism 141–7
  eBay Motors 134, 137
  globalization 137
  learning 139–40
  user-community 127, 128, 130, 133, 141,
    142, 144
  see also Whitman
e-commerce 3
  Amazon 138, 140, 144–5
  big retailers 143–4
  eBay 126–8, 129–31, 133, 139, 145
  Half.com 137
  opportunities 126–7, 140, 147
  start-ups 122
economic change 6
economic rationality 7
efficiency 33, 58, 177
email 113–14
emphasizing particular methods 3, 13, 171
  due to circumstances 13, 171
  due to personal preferences 13, 171
  Grove 104, 106
  Kroc 63, 72
  Ohno 38, 47
  Sloan 19, 27–8, 29
  Walton 80, 86, 95
  Whitman 126, 135, 136, 139
employee-followers 1, 3, 12, 39, 79,
    148, 165
  rational and discerning 12, 178, 180
  their jobs and career prospects 1, 150, 164

employees
  Armani 156
  The Body Shop 150, 165, 169
  communication of new direction to 113–14
  eBay 127–8
  Facebook 11
  General Motors 17
  Grove's three-stage adaptive framework 112
  Intel 104
  Japanese unions 48, 50–1
  McDonald's 69
  multi-skilled workers 48, 49–50, 56, 58
  scientific management 177–8
  Toyotaist teams 49, 60
  Versace 164
  Wal-Mart 88–9, 94, 97–8
  see also employee-followers
enhancing (developing) a corporation
  definition 2
  Grove 103–4
  Ohno 37
  Sloan 17
  Whitman 126
  see also establishing a corporation
enterprise-family culture 51
entrepreneurship 6–7, 122
environmental issues 166, 167–8
e-socializing 127, 128, 130–1
establishing (developing) a corporation
  definition 2
  Dassault 98
  Hewlett and Packard 116
  Kroc 61
  Roddick 165
  Walton 79–80
  see also enhancing a corporation
exchange 181–2
expansion
  Amazon 142
  The Body Shop 167
  eBay 140
  General Motors 20
  Hewlett-Packard 120
  Kroc 63
  McDonald's 61, 75
  Toyota 54–5
  Wal-Mart 80, 81–5, 88, 93
  Whitman 127–8
  see also growth
expenses 88
experimentation
  Amazon 123
  Apple 123–4
  Google 125
  Hewlett-Packard 105, 116–22
  Intel 104–5, 114–15
export-oriented strategy 101–2

Facebook 10–12, 127, 131, 132, 144, 145
factory environment in Japan 48–52, 57
    familial paternalism 51–2
    family image 68
    labour unions 50–1
    multi-skilled workers 49
    permanent employment 51–2
    work groups 48
Farber, D. *see* Sloan's biographer
fashion industry 3, 148–64
femininity 148, 151, 157, 159
finance
    General Motors 23–4
    McDonald's 65, 68, 70–1, 72
Fishman, C. 86
flexibility
    General Motors 35
    Machiavelli 184
    Toyota 46, 48
    Walton 87
fluctuations in production 55
Ford, Henry 2, 17, 19, 39, 57, 58
Fordism
    assembly-line production 33, 57, 58
    mass-production efficiency 33
    Sloanism versus Fordism 19, 33–6, 59
    Toyotaism versus Fordism 39, 57–60
Ford Motor Company 28, 37, 111, 177
    dominance initially 38
    low-price range 26
    Model T 26, 33, 34–5, 36
    overtaken later by General Motors 35–6
    Sloanism versus Fordism 19, 33–6, 59
    Toyotaism versus Fordism 39, 46, 57–60
Ford, Tom 164
forecasting 24
formal rules 29, 94
founder-CEOs 2
France 98, 99, 101, 154, 157, 158
franchising
    The Body Shop 167, 169
    McDonald's 3, 62–7, 70, 75–6, 78, 81
    Versace 161
'friction' 5
frugality 87–8
Fujimoto, T. 41, 43, 47, 48, 57, 59–60

Galeotti, Sergio 154
Gastel, M. 158, 163
Gates, Bill 18
gender diversity 91
General Electric (GE) 5, 114
General Motors (GM) 14, 16, 17–36, 111
    adaptive capacity 67
    Brown's role 23, 70–1
    customer preferences 111
    dominance of 17, 38

in-house and out-sourced production 53
    institutionalized deliberation 9, 28–33, 74
    marketing strategy 25–8
    joint venture with Toyota 60
    organizational structure 3, 18, 19–25,
        34, 118
    Sloanism versus Fordism 19, 33–6, 59
    Toyota compared with 43, 46, 56–7
    see also Sloan
genius 124
Germany 99, 137
Glass, David 90–1, 92, 172
globalization
    Amazon 142
    Armani 155–6, 161
    eBay 137, 139, 143
    McDonald's 75–8
    Versace 160, 161
    Wal-Mart 79, 85
Google 72, 122, 124–5, 140, 147
    decentralized experimentation 124
    dual and triple leadership 72, 125, 147
    product deliberation 125
'grand' strategy 6
    Ohno 56
    Walton 80, 86, 87–8, 90
Great Depression 17, 24, 36, 58–9
green market preferences 166–7, 168
group vice-presidents 22–3, 119
Grove, Andy 7, 13, 14–15, 103–16, 121, 171–2
    autobiographical *Only the Paranoid
        Survive* 103–4, 105
    adaptive crisis 104, 105–6
    dual leadership with Moore then CEO of
        Intel 103, 109
    diverse deliberation 113
    experimentation (and
        diversification) 114–16
    innovative adaptation 108–9
    institutionalized deliberation 113–14
    learning 104, 105, 112, 171–2
    quantitative calculation 112
    rapid adaptation 104, 106, 111–12
    strategic calculation 112–13
    strategic inflection point *see* inflection points
    'strong' leadership 12
    '10X' change 104, 111, 153
    three-stage adaptive framework 111–16
    triple-leadership team with Moore and
        Noyce 103, 125
    Whitman compared with 128, 133
    see also Intel
growth
    Amazon 141, 142, 145
    The Body Shop 169
    eBay 131, 136, 137–8, 141
    Hewlett-Packard 118

growth (*cont.*)
  Intel 109
  social media 144
  Versace 158
  Wal-Mart 81, 83, 84
Gucci 164
gut instinct 13–14, 79–80
  see also vision

Half.com 137, 138
Harris, Thomas A. 182
haute couture 150, 154, 157, 158
Hewlett-Packard (HP) 6, 15–16, 105, 124
  diversification problems (1950s) 118
  diversification problems (1990s) 121–2
  dual-leadership team of Hewlett and
    Packard 116, 117, 120, 172
  experimentation and diversification 116–22
  HP Laboratories 119
  managing by walking around 114
  two-role leadership team 72
  see also Hewlett; Packard
Hewlett, William 117, 118, 120
high-tech consumer products 3
Hoff, Ted 116
Honda 59
'how to' leadership 178

IBM 106, 108–9, 110, 122
IBM PCs and 'clones' 106, 109
imitation 97
impartiality 31–2
'impetuosity' 184
inertia 32
inflection points *see* strategic inflection points
informal rules 8–9
  eBay 134
  General Motors 29
  Hewlett-Packard 117, 119
  McDonald's 74–5
  Wal-Mart 93
informally institutionalized deliberation 74,
    93–4, 134
innovation
  Apple 122, 124
  Armani 162
  Dassault 100–1
  experimentation 105
  freedom to innovate 67
  Google 124–5
  Grove 115–16
  Hewlett-Packard 121–2, 124
  Machiavelli 183–4
  Schumpeter's theories 6
  Sloan 20, 21–2, 32, 35
  systematic 6–7
  Toyota 37–8, 39, 40–7, 57

innovation-introducing leadership teams 16,
    21, 37, 38–9, 40, 44, 46, 72, 172
innovative adaptation 1, 2–3, 4, 6–7, 8,
    12–13, 185
  Armani 148, 149, 151, 153, 154, 157
  combining innovative and rapid
    adaptation 63–4, 81, 149, 151, 154
  Grove 108, 109, 115
  Hewlett-Packard 117, 118, 119
  Kroc 61, 63–7, 75, 78, 171
  Ohno 38, 42–3, 47–52, 60, 171
  Roddick 165, 166, 169
  Sloan 18, 19, 21–2, 25, 171
  Toyoda family 40
  Versace 149, 157, 160
  Walton 80, 81–5
  Whitman 133
'innovator's dilemma' 7, 182
inspectors 65
inspirational leadership 1–2, 13–14, 172–3,
    175, 176, 178, 179–81
instinct 13–14, 79–80, 112
institutionalized deliberation 1, 2–3, 4, 8–10,
    13, 185
  Grove 113, 171
  Hewlett-Packard 117
  Ishida 44–5
  Jobs 122–3
  Kroc 63, 71, 73–5
  Sandberg 11
  Sloan 19, 28–33, 73, 74, 171
  Toyota 38
  Walton 80–1, 92–4
  Whitman 133–4
  see also informally institutionalized
    deliberation
Intel 14–15, 103–16, 171
  diversification problems 115
  dual-leadership team 172
  learning to adapt 105–11
  memory microchips 106
  microprocessors 103, 106–10, 114–15, 116
  Moore's Law 110
  'Pentium Bug' 107, 110
  treadmill strategy 110
  triple leadership 103, 125
  see also Grove; Moore; and Noyce
intellectualization 177, 179
intermediate management levels 121
Internet 3, 111
  Amazon 146
  eBay 126–7, 129–31
  network effects 144–5
  'second stage' of Internet revolution 143–4
  see also e-commerce; social media
intuition 32
  see also instinct

investment
General Motors 23
quantitative calculation 5
Toyota 44–5, 55
Wal-Mart 91
iPad 105, 115, 124, 146
iPhone 105, 115, 123–4
iPod 105, 115, 123, 145–6
Isaacson, W. 123
Ishida, Taizo 39, 42, 44–5, 46, 171, 172
Isuzu 59
Italy 151, 152, 155, 156, 157

Jackson, T. 106, 107
Japan
eBay 137, 139
factory environment 48–52, 57
McDonald's 75–7
semiconductor industry 106, 108
Toyota 38, 39, 40–1, 47–52, 57
Walton's visit to 97
see also Ohno
job diffuseness 49
Jobs, Steve 105, 122–4
CEO of Apple during 2000s
diversifications 122
diversification centralized 122
hands-on experimentation 123–4
top-down experimentation 123–4
see also Apple; iPad; iPhone; iPod
job-swapping 92
joint ventures
McDonald's 3, 63, 75–6, 78
Toyota 60
Jones, D. T. 38
Jones, G. 167, 168
just-in-time production 3, 37, 39, 40–4, 47, 52–7, 59

Kanban information system 39, 47, 53, 54–5, 56
Khurana, R. 12
Kindle 123, 145–6
Kirkpatrick, D. 10
Kmart 97
Knight, F. H. 4
knowledge 65
see also learning
Knudsen, William 35
Kroc, Ray 14, 61–78, 171, 172
autobiographical Grinding It Out 61–2
combining rapid and innovative adaptation 63–4
compared with Ohno 64
diverse deliberation 8, 71–2
dreamer 63, 75
establishes McDonald's 62

globalization 75
globalized adaptability 75–8
informally institutionalized deliberation 71, 74–5
innovative adaptation, franchising 62–3, 64–7
institutionalized deliberation 71, 73–5
licensing agreement with McDonald's 62
Quality, Service, Cleanliness and Value (QSC&V) 68–70
quantitative calculation 70–1
rapid adaptation 63–4
Sonneborn's role 68, 70–1, 72–3
strategic calculation of marketing 68–70
two-generation leadership team 92, 172
two-role leadership team 172
Walton compared with 80, 81, 90, 93
Whitman compared with 134, 139
see also McDonald's; Sonneborn

labour costs 56, 58–9, 88
labour relations
Toyota 42, 51
Walton 80, 86, 88–9
labour unions 48, 50–1, 89
lay-offs
The Body Shop 150, 165, 169
Intel 108
Toyota 42
Versace 164
Lazarus, Charles 91
leader-follower relations 177, 178, 180, 182
leader's-eye view (autobiographical) 3
Armani 148
Dassault 98
Grove 104
Kroc 61
Ohno 38
Packard 116
Roddick 165
Sandberg 11
Sloan 19
Walton 79
Whitman 126
see also autobiographical material, use of
leadership 9–10
authoritative 9–10
charismatic 12, 167–8, 175, 176, 179
deliberative 9–10, 13, 182
inspirational 1–2, 13–14, 172–3, 175, 176, 178, 179–81
military 2, 3–4, 5, 21–2, 172–3, 178, 184
moral 179
'natural' versus calculated 178
political 3–4, 173, 176, 182, 184
rational 1, 170, 175
rational leadership theory 1, 172, 175–85

leadership (*cont.*)
  'strong' 12
  technical 176, 179–81
  transactional 175, 181–2
  transformational 175, 181
  see also appropriate rational methods;
    corporation-developing version of
    rational leadership
leadership paradigm 172
leadership teams *see* dual leadership teams;
    triple leadership teams
'lean' production 38, 39, 49, 52–7, 60
  see also just-in-time production
learning
  Dassault 98–9, 101–2
  Grove 104, 111, 112, 125, 171
  Walton 79, 80, 81, 95–8, 171–2
  Whitman 135, 139–40, 171–2
leasing arrangements 65, 70–1
Leidner, R. 66, 69
Lichtenstein, N. 87
localization 76–7, 118
L'Oréal 169
Louis Vuitton 164
Love, J. F. 65, 67, 69, 71, 74, 76
loyalty 183–4
luxury leatherwear companies 164
luxury products 3, 164
LVMH 164

Machiavelli, N. 8–9, 13, 17, 32, 183–5
Malone, M. S. 111, 115, 118
managers
  eBay 134
  Ford 34, 36
  General Motors 21, 22, 23, 31
  Hewlett-Packard 119
  McDonald's 66, 69, 71
  middle management 112
  rationalization 179
  scientific management 177–8
  Wal-Mart 89, 92, 93, 94
managing by walking around (MBWA) 114
marketing
  Amazon 144
  Armani 154–5
  Dassault 101–2
  eBay 136–7
  Ford 36
  General Motors 19, 21, 25–8
  Intel 107–8, 110
  McDonald's 63, 65, 67–70, 77–8
  Versace 160, 163
market share 36
mass production
  American system of 47, 60
  Ford 33, 37, 177

General Motors 35
just-in-time production compared with
  41, 52
'lean' production compared with 55–6
McDonald's 62
Toyota 41, 46
'mavericks' 10, 90, 91–2
Mayer, Ron 90–1
McDonaldization 61
McDonald, John 18
McDonald, Maurice and Richard 62–3, 70, 72
McDonald's 3, 14, 61–78
  adaptive innovation in franchising 63–7
  deliberation 71–5
  diversity 8, 71
  dual-leadership teams 172
  globalization 75
  globalized adaptability 75–8
  joint ventures 75–6, 78, 169
  leasing arrangements 70
  local adaptation 66–7, 118
  marketing strategy 68–70
  Quality, Service, Cleanliness and Value
    (QSC&V) 68–70
  Sonneborn's role 68, 70–1, 72–3
  standardization 115
  see also Kroc; Sonneborn
McKinney, W. 120, 121–2
McNamara, Robert 32, 33, 36
media 162
meetings
  Apple 122–3
  Dassault 101
  eBay 134
  Intel 116
  Wal-Mart 92–3, 94, 95
  see also committees; institutionalized
    deliberation
megatrends in fashion 150
memory microchips 106
Metcalfe's Law 144
metrics 135–6
Meza, P. E. 120, 121–2
microprocessors 103, 106–10, 114–15, 116
Microsoft 109
military leadership 2, 3–4, 5, 21–2, 172–3,
  178, 184
mistakes
  fixing 132
  learning from 96, 97, 139
mobile technology 3, 115
monitoring 86, 97
Moore, Gordon 103, 106, 108–10, 115,
  125, 172
Moore's Law 110
'moral creativeness' 179
morale 179

motivation
Hewlett-Packard 118
Schumpeter on entrepreneur's 6
scientific management 177
transformational leadership 181
Motorola 110
multi-skilled workers 48, 49–50, 56, 58
Myspace 131

Nakagawa, Fukio 39, 45–6, 171, 172
Napoli, L. 64, 65, 68, 70, 74
network effects 143, 144–5
Neustadt, R. E. 8
niche markets 158, 167
Nissan 46, 50, 59
non-rational methods
Kroc 63, 75
Walton 13–14, 79–80, 85
novelty 161–2, 163, 164
Noyce, Robert 103, 115, 116, 122, 125, 172

objectives 1–2, 183
Ohno, Taiichi 2, 14, 37–60, 171–2
adapting to Japanese conditions 47–52
autobiographical *Toyota Production System* 38
continuous flow 43, 47, 49, 50, 52
dual-leadership teams but never CEO 37, 172
exports to the United States 38, 45, 59
just-in-time production 37, 39, 43–4, 47, 52–5
innovative adaptation 38–9, 47–8
Japanese car-market environment 47–8
Japanese factory environment 48–52
Kanban information system 53
Kroc compared with 64
'lean' production 38, 55–6
production innovations 40–7
quantitative calculation 56
rapid adaptation discussed 56–7
strategic calculation of cost/waste reduction 56
supplier relationships 53–5
Toyotaism versus Fordism 57–60
Walton compared with 88
see also Toyota
oil crisis 59
Omidyar, Pierre 122, 129–30, 131–2
online communities 127, 130, 144
operating controls 24, 67
opportunities
Armani and Versace 157
eBayism versus Amazonism 140, 141
e-commerce 147
Grove 109, 110–11, 115
Ohno 39, 47, 48
Whitman and Bezos 140–1, 146–7

organizational culture
Barnard 179
eBay 139
Facebook 11
McDonald's 69
Wal-Mart 85
organizational structure
Ford 34
General Motors 3, 18, 19–25, 34, 118
Hewlett-Packard 105, 118–19, 120–1
McDonald's 73–4
see also centralization; decentralization
organization theory 179
Ortega, B. 83, 84, 89, 91, 93–4, 95, 97
out-sourcing 53–4, 152

Packard, David 105, 114, 116–19, 121, 122
autobiographical *The HP Way* 116
dual leadership with Hewlett 116, 117, 120, 172
experimentation/diversification decentralized 118–22
innovative adaptation 118
product deliberation institutionalized by Hewlett 117
see also Hewlett-Packard
Page, Larry 72, 122, 125, 147
'paranoia' 7, 123–4
performance assessment 4, 23–4, 65
see also assessment; quantitative calculation
personal rule 33–4
planned obsolescence 150, 162
Platt, Lew 121, 122
policy deliberation
Ford 34
General Motors 28–33, 74
McDonald's 74
Wal-Mart 90
see also deliberation; policy proposals
policy proposals 9–10
eBay 134
General Motors 28, 74
Toyota 44–5
Wal-Mart 93
political leadership 3–4, 173, 176, 182, 184
politics
bureaucratic 8
Roddick's political activism 150, 167–8
Walton's lobbying and strategy 89
power 8, 92
'Power of Many' 127, 128, 130, 142, 144
Prada, Miucci 164
pricing
Armani 154–5
Ford 36
General Motors 25–6
McDonald's 70

pricing (*cont.*)
  Toyota 46
  Versace 160
  Wal-Mart 87, 90
Procter & Gamble 128
product deliberation 116–17, 122–3, 125
product development
  Apple 123–4
  Dassault Aviation 100–1
  experimentation 114, 118–22, 123–4
  Ford 34
  Hewlett-Packard 117, 119–20, 121
  McDonald's 66–7
production
  Armani 162
  Ford 33, 36, 37, 57–9
  General Motors 35, 37, 53, 59
  Intel 115
  McDonald's 66
  Toyota 37–8, 39, 40–7, 48–9, 52–7, 58, 60
production and inventory controls 24
productivity
  Ford 33, 58
  scientific management 177
  Toyota 45, 46, 48, 51, 60
product pyramids 3
  Armani 154, 155, 160–1
  Versace 158, 159–61, 163, 164
professionalization 132
profit
  Amazon 142
  Auction Web 130
  eBay 127, 132, 143
  Ford 58
  General Motors 24–5
  Intel 103, 106, 109–10
profit-sharing plans 88–9
'Protestant ethic' 185
public relations (PR) 27

quality control
  McDonald's 65, 68–70
  quality control 'circles' 48–9
  Total Quality Control (TQC) 45
  Toyota 41, 45, 48–9, 58
Quality, Service, Cleanliness, and Value
  (QSC&V) 68–70
quantitative calculation 1, 2–3, 4–5,
    13, 185
  Grove 112
  Ishida 44
  Kroc 63, 68, 70–1
  Ohno 38, 39, 44, 56, 171
  Sloan 19, 23, 25, 70–1
  Walton 13, 80, 86–7, 90, 171
  Weber 177
  Whitman 135–6, 171

rapid adaptation 1, 2–3, 4, 7–8, 12–13, 185
  Armani 148–9, 151, 152–4, 157
  combining rapid and innovative
    adaptation 63–4, 81, 149, 151, 154
  General Motors 24–5
  Grove 104, 106, 108, 109, 111–12, 171
  Kindle 145–6
  Kroc 63–4, 67
  Ohno 56–7
  Roddick 165, 166–7, 169
  strategic calculation used in conjunction
    with 5–6
  Versace 149, 157, 160
  Walton 81, 84–5
  Whitman 132–3
rationality 12, 175–6
  economic 7
  Ford 34
  General Motors 17, 19, 25, 27–8
  military leadership 178
  Roddick 150
  Sloan 17, 18
  Weber 177
rationalization
  Barnard 179
  Ford 33, 36
  scientific management 177–8
  Sloan 17, 21, 25, 26, 28, 33
  societal institutions and processes 176
  Weber 175, 177, 181
rational leadership 1, 170, 175
  inspiring rational confidence 1, 170,
    175, 180
  see also appropriate rational methods;
    corporation-developing version;
    rational leadership theory
rational leadership theory 1, 172, 175–85
  Barnard 179–81
  Burns 181–2
  Christensen 182–3
  Machiavelli 183–5
  Weber 177–8, 181
  see also appropriate rational means
reputation 104, 130, 161–2
responsibility 134–5, 179
restructuring
  Ford 36
  General Motors 19–25
  Hewlett-Packard 118
  see also centralization; decentralization;
    organizational structure
retail networks 155–6, 160, 161
reticence 8, 11, 32
return on investment 23
revenues
  Amazon 146
  Armani 152–3

eBay 131, 132, 137–8, 143
Facebook 10–11, 131
Hewlett-Packard 121
Intel 109, 111
McDonald's 65, 68, 70–1, 72
Twitter 131
Versace 158, 159–60
rigidity 7, 18, 106–7, 109, 132
risk 4
risk-taking 32, 74, 78, 132
Roberts, B. 93
Roddick, Anita 15, 149–50, 165–9, 172
    autobiographical writings 165
    dual leadership with husband
        Gordon 167
    establishes The Body Shop 166–7
    innovative and then rapid
        adaptation 165–6
    political activism 167–8
    shifts away from adaptive methods 167, 169
    see also The Body Shop
Roddick, Gordon 167, 169, 172
Roos, D. 38
Rubin, Robert 12
rules
    formal 29, 94
    informal 8–9, 29, 74–5, 93, 117, 119, 134

Salvaneschi, Luigi 71, 74
Sam's Club stores 85
Samsung 4
Sandberg, Sheryl 10–12, 131, 132
    autobiographical Lean In 11
    comparison with Whitman 132
    diverse deliberation 10, 11–12
    dual leadership with Zuckerberg 10
    enhances Facebook 11, 131
    institutionalized deliberation 11
    see also Facebook
'saturation strategy' 81, 83
scaling up
    Amazon 140
    eBay 128, 135, 136–7, 139, 141, 142, 146–7
Schmidt, Eric 125, 147
Schumpeter, Joseph 6–7, 13
scientific management 177–8
Scott, R. V. 84
selecting appropriate methods
    appropriate for developing
        corporations 12–13
    appropriate rational methods 13
    non-rational methods, if appropriate 13–14,
        63, 79–80
    selecting/choosing methods to
        emphasize 13
    see also appropriate rational methods;
        emphasizing particular methods

Shewmaker, Jack 90–1, 92, 93
Simon, W. L. 123
Skoll, Jeff 131–2
Sloan, Alfred P. 2, 14, 17–36, 37, 111, 171
    autobiographical My Years With General
        Motors 18–19, 28
    Brown's role 23, 70–1
    customer preferences 111
    decentralized multi-divisional
        organisation 19–20
    diverse deliberation 28, 31–3
    dual leadership then CEO of General
        Motors 21
    group managers 119
    innovative adaptation 21–3
    institutionalized deliberation 9, 28–33,
        73, 74
    Kroc compared with 62, 64, 66, 68, 73, 74
    Ohno compared with 43, 44, 56–7
    on genius 124
    production flexibility 35
    quantitative calculation 23–4
    rapid adaptation 21, 24–5
    rectifying by administrative
        rationalization 17, 20, 23, 24, 25, 28, 33
    Sloanism 33, 35, 36, 59
    Sloanism versus Fordism 33–6, 59
    strategic calculation of marketing 25–8
    Walton compared with 79, 80, 85, 90, 93
    Whitman compared with 128, 139
    see also General Motors
Sloanism see Sloan
Sloan's biographer (Farber) 18–19
small-town strategy 81–2, 96–7
social auditing 169
social media 127, 131, 144
    see also Facebook; Twitter
Soderquist, D. 86, 97–8
Sonneborn, Harry 63, 68, 70–1, 72–3, 74, 80, 172
Sony 4
standardization
    General Motors 35
    Intel 115
    McDonald's 66, 115
standards, operating 68–9
start-up strategy 100
Stone, B. 138
store visits by central management 97–8
strategic calculation 1, 2–3, 4–5, 6, 13, 185
    Grove 112–13
    Ishida 44
    Kroc 61, 63, 68–70, 75, 171
    Ohno 38, 39, 44, 56, 171
    Roddick 169
    Sloan 19, 25–8, 171
    Walton 80, 83, 86–90, 171
    Whitman 136–9, 171

strategic inflection points 7, 103–6, 109,
    110–11, 112–13, 171
strategy
    definition of 5
    'early-mover' 112–13
    eBay 136
    General Motors 21–2, 25–8
    Hewlett-Packard 135
    Intel 110
    McDonald's 68–70
    product-development 100–1
    'saturation' 81–3
    start-up strategy 100
    'treadmill' 110, 118, 162, 163, 164
    Wal-Mart 81–2, 83, 84
    see also 'grand', strategy
style
    car styling 27, 35, 36, 37
    Versace versus Armani 157, 159, 162–3
sub-discounting 85
Supercenters 85
supermodels 160
suppliers
    Intel 111
    McDonald's 64
    Toyota 42, 45, 46, 52, 53–5

tactics 21–2
Taylor, Frederick 177
Taylorism 33, 177–8
teams
    Japanese work groups 48–9, 58
    Sloan 30
    Toyotaism 60
    see also dual-leadership teams;
        triple-leadership teams
technocrats 90–1
technology
    aircraft 99–100
    Amazon 123, 145–6
    Apple 123–4
    disruptive 4–5, 7–8, 153, 182–3
    eBay 127, 133
    HP 118–19, 120–1
    Intel 106–7, 110, 115
    McDonald's 62
    memory microchips 106
    microprocessors 103, 106–10, 114–15, 116
    mobile 3, 115
    satellite-based communications 91, 93
    Wal-Mart 3, 90–1, 93–4
    see also computers; email; Internet
Tedlow, R. S. 15, 18, 25, 34, 79, 80, 89,
    95, 96
'10×' change 104, 111, 153
Togo, Y. 40–6, 60
top-down experimentation 123, 124

Total Quality Control (TQC) 45
    see also quality control
Toyoda, Eiji 44–5, 46
Toyoda, Kiichiro 37, 39, 40–2, 45, 47,
    52, 57
    pioneering just-in-time production 37, 39,
        40–1
    pioneering supplier network 42
Toyoda, Risaburo 40
Toyota 3, 14, 37–60, 171
    continuous flow 49–50
    dual-leadership teams 172
    exports to United States 38, 45, 59
    factory environment 48–52
    growth 45–6
    just-in-time production 37, 39, 40–1, 43–4,
        52–5, 59
    Kanban information system 53
    market environment 47–8
    production innovations 40–7
    supplier relationships 53–5
    Toyotaism versus Fordism 57–60
    see also Ohno; Toyoda, Kiichiro
Toys 'R' Us 91, 143
training 65–6, 69
transactional leadership 175, 181–2
transformational leadership 175, 181
'treadmill' strategy 110, 118, 162, 163, 164
trends 150, 157, 158
trial and error 43, 74
Trimble, V. H. 87, 97
triple-leadership teams
    Google 125, 147
    Intel 103, 125
    Toyota 44
    see also dual-leaderhip teams
trust 52
Turner, Fred 72, 73, 92
Turner, L. 159, 162
Twitter 127, 131, 144
two-generation leadership teams 16, 92, 172
two-role leadership teams 15–16, 72–3, 103,
    154, 161, 172

uncertainty 4, 13
unions see labour unions
United States
    Armani expansion into 155, 156
    Japanese car imports 38, 45, 59–60
    online market for e-commerce 138
    Tedlow on success of US business leaders 15
    The Body Shop failed expansion 167,
        168, 169
    Versace expansion into 158–9
unpredictability 5
user-community for eBay 127, 128, 130, 133,
    141, 142, 144

Vallières, Benno-Claude 102
values
  fashion industry 150, 152
  McDonald's 69
  Roddick's political activism 167–8
Vance, S. S. 84
Van Dijck, J. 127
variety of products 26–7
Versace, Donatella 159, 161, 163, 164
Versace, Gianni 15–16, 149, 156–64, 167, 172
  adapting to fashion's new times 157–8, 160
  contrast with Armani's adaptations 149,
    156–61, 162–3, 164
  creativity treadmill 162
  dual leadership with brother Santo 161
  establishes own firm 157
  firm's post-Versace problems 161, 163–4
  product pyramid 159–60
  see also Armani; Donatella Versace
Versace, Santo 161
vision 13–14, 79–80
  see also gut instinct

wages
  Ford 57
  Toyota 51, 56
  Wal-Mart 88
Wal-Mart 3, 14, 79–102
  adaptive expansion 81–5
  cost-reduction strategy 87–8
  deliberation and technology 90–4
  global expansion 79
  green campaign 91, 167, 168
  Internet operation 144
  labour-relations strategy 88–9
  Sam's Club stores 85
  Supercenters 85
  regional to nation-wide empire 80, 84
  see also Walton
Walton, Bud 94
Walton, Rob 94
Walton, Sam 13–14, 79–102, 171, 172
  autobiographical Made in America 79
  combining rapid and innovative
    adaptation 81
  Dassault compared with 98, 101
  discount retailing 81–2
  diverse deliberation 90–1
  dual-leadership team with his successor
    92, 172
  establishes Wal-Mart 80, 82
  expansion system 81–4
  frugal cost-reduction strategy 87–8
  Grove compared with 104
  innovative adaptation 81–4
  institutionalized deliberation 92–4
  labour-relations strategy 88–9

learning 95–8, 171–2
  'mavericks' 10, 90, 91–2
  quantitative calculation 13, 86
  rapid adaptation 84–5
  Saturday-morning management
    meetings 94
  store visits 97–8
  strategic calculation 87–90
  technocrats 90–1
  technology 90–1, 93–4
  vision and gut-instinct 13, 79–80
  Whitman compared with 126, 134
  see also Wal-Mart
Wartman, W. 40–6, 60
waste elimination 56
Waterton, W. A. 101
Watson, J. L. 62, 68, 70, 76
Weber, Max 1, 4, 6, 13, 175–6, 177–8, 179,
    181, 185
Welch, Jack 5–6, 114
White, N. 151, 162–3
Whitman, Meg 2, 15, 126–47, 171
  autobiographical The Power of Many 126
  becomes eBay CEO 128, 132
  eBay pre-Whitman 129–32
  eBayism versus Amazonism 141–7
  diverse deliberation 134
  globalisation 137
  innovative adaptation 133
  institutionalized deliberation 134
  later leadership of Hewlett-Packard 134–5,
    139, 147
  learning 135, 139–40, 171–2
  network effects 144–5
  opportunities compared with Bezos 140–1,
    146–7
  'Power of Many' 127, 128, 130, 142, 144
  quantitative calculation 135–6
  rapid adaptation 132–3
  scaling-up eBay 128, 141
  strategic calculation 136–9
  user-community 127, 128, 130, 133, 141,
    142, 144
  see also eBay
Windows 109
'Wintel' 109
Whyte, W. H. 32, 71
Womack, J. P. 38, 55–6, 60
women 15, 91, 150–2, 157, 158–9, 163
work groups 48–9, 58

Yahoo 140
Young, John 120, 121
Young, J. S. 123
Yves Saint Laurent 154

Zuckerberg, Mark 10, 11, 131, 132